Dedication

To my husband Ed, with love. Thanks for hiking with me, giving me shuttle rides, reading my manuscripts, and providing honest criticism.

And to my sister Christina, with love and gratitude. She accompanied me on my latest trip to Maui, having made all the arrangements, and did an incredible job of shuttling me to and from Maui's most remote corners.

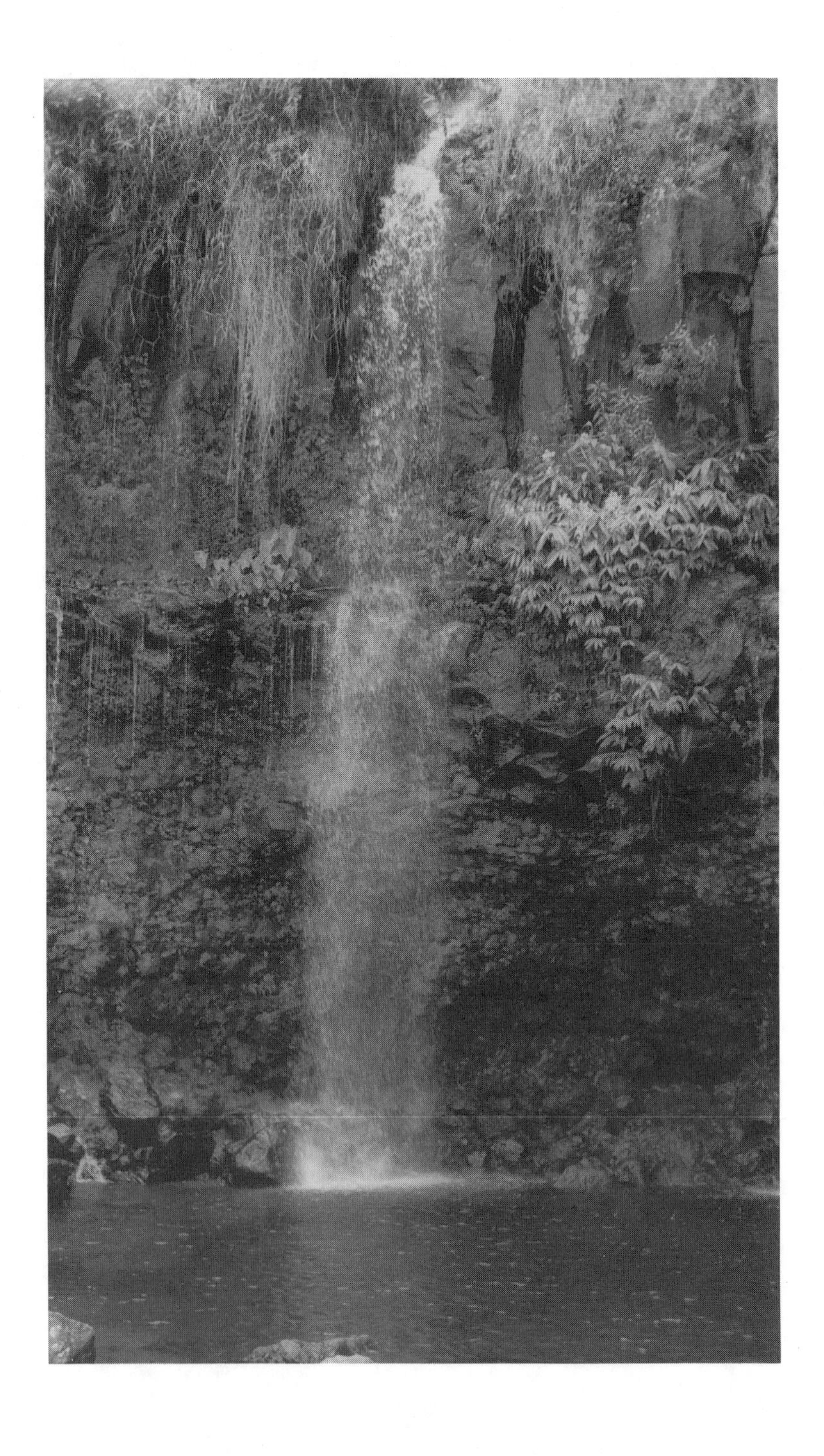

MAUI TRAILS

Walks, Strolls and Treks on the Valley Isle

Kathy Morey

WILDERNESS PRESS
BERKELEY

FIRST EDITION August 1991
Second printing August 1993
Third printing June 1995
SECOND EDITION March 1996
Second printing July 1997
Third printing February 1999
Fourth printing May 2000

Photos and maps by the author, except as noted
Cover photos © 1991 by David Muench
Book design by Kathy Morey and Thomas Winnett
Cover design by Larry B. Van Dyke

Library of Congress Card Catalog Number 96-6853
ISBN 0-89997-196-2

Manufactured in the United States of America

Published by **Wilderness Press**
1200 5th Street
Berkeley, CA 94710
(800) 443-7227; FAX (510) 558-1696
mail@wildernesspress.com
www.wildernesspress.com

Contact us for a free catalog

 Printed on recycled paper, 20% post-consumer waste

Library of Congress Cataloging-in-Publication Data

Morey, Kathy.
Maui trails: walks, strolls, and treks on the valley isle / Kathy Morey. — 2nd ed.
p. cm.
Includes bibliographical references and index.
ISBN 0-89997-196-2
1. Maui (Hawaii) — Guidebooks. 2. Hiking — Hawaii — Maui.
I. Title.
DU628.M3M67 1996
919.69'21 — dc20

96-6853
CIP

Contents

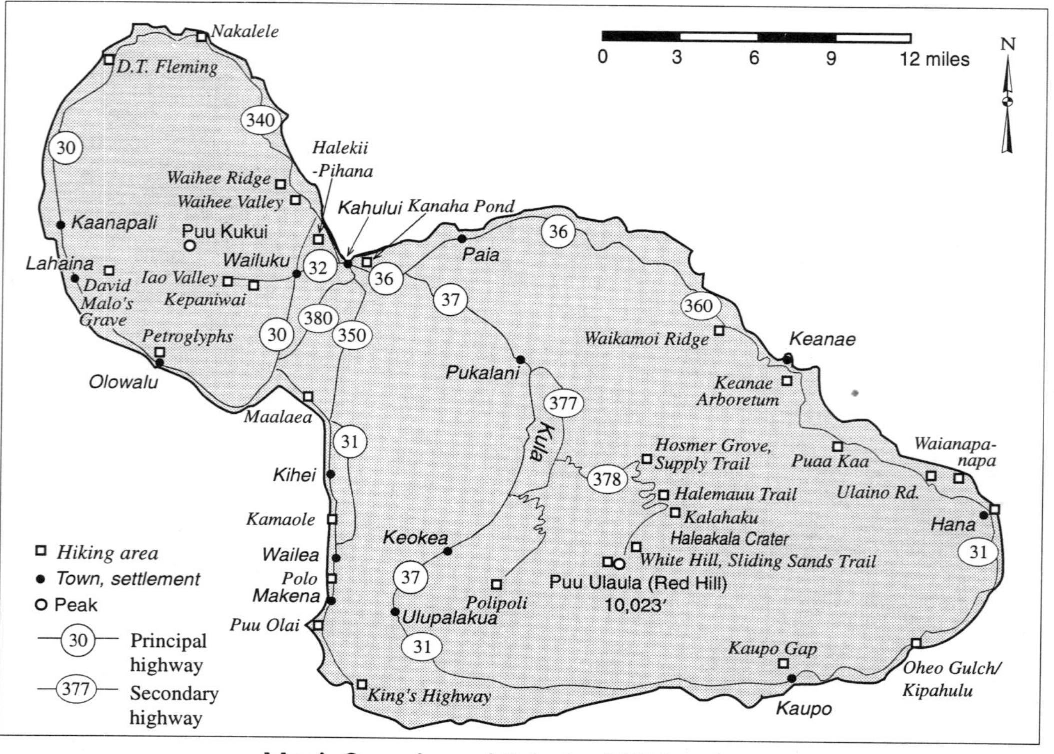

Maui: Overview of Principal Hiking Areas

Introduction

"Maui? What do I know about Maui? Nothing! I just own a condo there."

What a shame! Maui is an island of overwhelming beauty and of great contrasts; it defies the mind's attempts to take it all in. It's a large island whose shape, rugged terrain, and road conditions defy the driver's attempts to see it by car. A drive around it or a flight over it may satisfy the eyes, but it denies the other senses their experiences: the fragrance of yellow ginger, the sound of rainforest bamboo rattling in the breeze, the feeling of warm sand underfoot, the sharp taste of wild guavas.

You can't experience Maui fully from a condo or even from a vehicle. The best of the island is outside, along the trails, where there's nothing to separate you from the immediate sensory experience, even sensory overload, of Maui. You don't have to walk far: a worthwhile hike on Maui can be as short as a quarter-mile stroll suitable for anyone who's ambulatory, or it can be as long as a three-day backpack in Haleakala's crater. How do I know? I walked every trail that's used as a trip in this book at least once in the summer and fall of 1990 for the first edition of this book and most of them again in 1995 for this second edition.

The shape of things. Maui consists of a west lobe and an east lobe connected by an isthmus. Maui's older, smaller, west lobe, West Maui, is a single volcano whose flanks have eroded into deep valleys and knife-thin ridges. Its upper slopes and cloud-covered peak harbor a nearly impenetrable swamp. Maui's younger, much larger east lobe, East Maui, is also a single volcano, Haleakala. On Haleakala's vast flanks are rainforests, huge cattle ranches, parched deserts of jagged lava, and native dryland forests. Erosion has carved immense stream valleys into Haleakala. Two of the largest of those valleys meet atop Haleakala to form what's commonly referred to as Haleakala's "crater."[1] Recently, it's been discovered that glaciation also played a role in shaping Haleakala's "crater" when Haleakala itself was younger and higher—an estimated 15,000 feet rather than its present 10,023 feet—during the most

---

[1] "Crater" implies a volcanic origin to most people. A geologist suggested I refer to Haleakala's most famous feature as its "stream- and glacier-carved valley," but I found that very clumsy and have chosen to stick to "crater."

recent ice age. No matter how it got there, it *is* a crater in the very loose sense of being a big pit at the top of a big mountain.) Long white beaches backed by thorny *kiawe* trees face bays of turquoise water on the drier west and south shores of West and East Maui. The north and east slopes are covered by rainforests and corrugated by steep cliffs and deep gullies. Between West and East Maui lies a low, sandy isthmus where business and industry are concentrated. Broad fields of pineapple and sugarcane carpet the isthmus and the drier slopes of both volcanoes.

Take time for Maui. It takes time to see Maui, partly because there's so much to see and partly because most of the tourist accommodations are far from the major scenic areas (including the best hiking areas). The resorts are concentrated almost exclusively on the west shore of West Maui (Lahaina, Kaanapali, and Kapalua) and on the southwest shore of East Maui (Kihei, Wailea, and Makena). There are some very good hikes scattered near the resorts. However, the only major scenic and hiking area that's "convenient" to the resorts is Iao Valley State Park. The resorts are a *long* way from scenic areas like Haleakala National Park, Hana town and the road to it, and the Oheo Gulch/Kipahulu District of Haleakala National Park.[2]

If you have only a day or two on Maui, stay put and enjoy what's nearby. There's probably a short hike or two in this book that will be very near you. Come back for a longer visit when you can!

If possible, stay a week or two on Maui. Allow at least half a day to visit Iao Valley State Park. Allow a full day to visit Haleakala's summit area; realize that you'll spend about half of it driving. If you want to drive to Hana, plan to stay at least one night in or near Hana, at least two nights if you also wish to visit Kipahulu.[3] Backpackers will probably want to spend three nights—the maximum allowed in any 30-day period—in Haleakala's crater, though three nights (or, rather, the four days around them) are barely enough to see the entire crater.

Be a good visitor. Traffic and crowding near resort and urban areas can be as bad as on the mainland. Developers in resort areas

---

[2] Oheo Gulch/Kipahulu was for a time referred to as "Seven Sacred Pools," a name that seems to have been a travel promoter's thoughtless invention. There are more than seven pools, and none was ever sacred. The Park Service refers to the area as the Kipahulu District; when I say "Kipahulu," I mean the Kipahulu District of Haleakala National Park. (There's also a tiny Kipahulu village beyond the Kipahulu District of Haleakala National Park.)

[3] A few tourist accommodations, including budget accommodations in Hana, exist outside the resort areas. See J.D. Bisignani's *Hawaii Handbook* (in the Bibliography) for more information—though the prices may be out of date. Bed-and-breakfast accommodations exist, too. See also Appendix A, Camping on Maui, in this book.

are bulldozing the wild, natural Maui into a tame, plastic Maui almost faster than Maui natives can get out of the way. Local people may (understandably) worry that if they stand still too long, they'll be 'dozed, too. In these areas, even in once-remote Hana, the *aloha* spirit seems tattered. Hawaii is not Paradise. Paradise is infinite and self-renewing. Hawaii is a real place of finite space and resources, where real people live real lives with jobs, families, budgets, and bills. Hawaii needs loving care from its visitors as well as from its natives. As the number of tourists increases, I think it becomes important that we visitors actively contribute to the *aloha* spirit instead of just passively expecting to receive it. Bring your best manners and your patience with you to Maui. Be the first to smile and wave. Be the first to pull your car over (safely) so that someone else can pass. Be scrupulous in observing the rules of the trail in order to help preserve what's left of Maui's vanishing wild places. NO TRESPASSING, KEEP OUT, or KAPU ("forbidden") signs mean, "You stay out." Please respect those signs.

Pool beside Ulaino Road

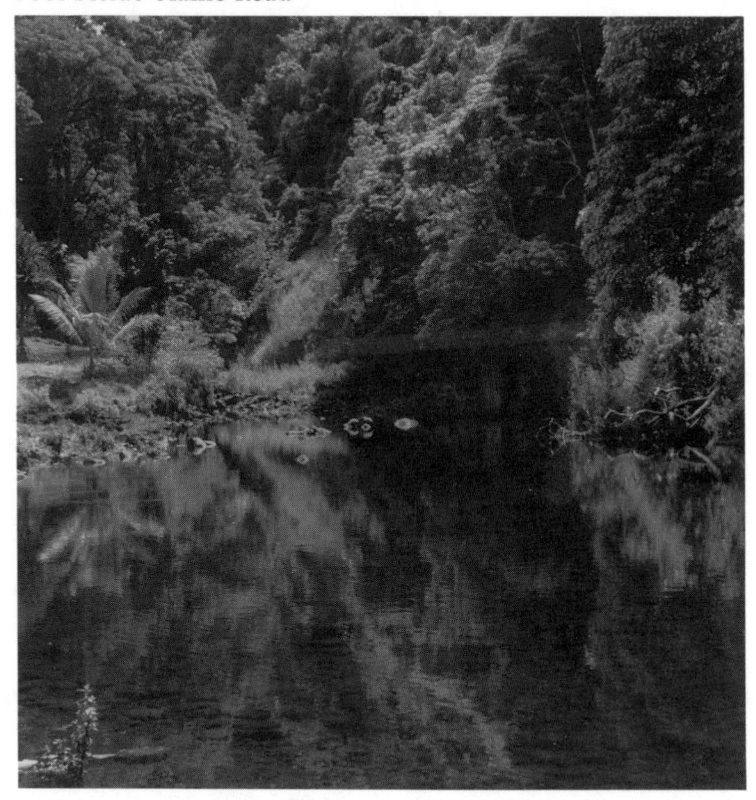

Getting Information About Maui

The search for the perfect trail guide. I wish I could be certain this was a flawless book. However, some things limit an author's ability to produce a perfect, error-free, always up-to-date book. Here are some of the factors, and what you can do to help yourself (and me).

Nature makes constant revisions; so do agencies. Nature constantly reshapes the landscape across which we plan to trek. That's usually a gradual process, but once in a while she makes drastic changes overnight. A landslide can erase a trail in seconds. Erosion can undercut a cliff edge and make last year's safe hike an extremely dangerous one, so that the local authorities close a trail you'd hoped to ramble on. And Maui's fragile volcanic terrain erodes quite rapidly.

Agencies in charge of hiking areas may close an area because they've realized it's environmentally too sensitive to withstand more human visits. An area once open to overnight camping may become a day-use-only area. Trails become impassable from lack of maintenance. Happily, agencies may open new areas because they've been able to acquire new acreage or complete a trail-building project.

Change is the only thing that's constant in this world, so that guidebook authors and publishers always play "catch up" with Nature and with agencies. We want to keep guidebooks up to date, but we are always at least one step behind the latest changes. The day when you'll have constantly revised books on-line at your wristwatch/computer terminal isn't here yet. So it's possible that a few trail descriptions are becoming obsolete even as this book goes to press.

Write for the latest information. It's a good idea to use this book in conjunction with the latest information from the agency in charge of the areas you plan to hike in. However, this book gives you a far more complete and detailed picture of Maui's principal hiking and backcountry camping opportunities than the current recreation map does. And it describes those opportunities from a hiker's perspective.

Still, it's a good idea to write to these agencies as soon as you've read this book and decided where you want to hike and camp on Maui. Ask them for their latest trail and camping maps, regulations, and permit-issuing procedures. Except for Haleakala National Park, enclose a stamped, self-addressed envelope for your convenience in getting the information you need as soon as possible. (National parks almost always use the franking privilege of Federal agencies, so you'd be wasting a stamp.) Their addresses and telephone numbers are in "Getting Permits or Permission."

Prepare yourself with general information, too. A generous source of a wide variety of useful information about Hawaii is the Hawaii Visitors Bureau. Here are the 800 numbers as well as the addresses and the phone and FAX numbers of their offices and affiliates on the mainland:

800 numbers:

For a vacation planner for **all the islands** ("Isles of Aloha" package), call 1 (800) GO-HAWAI (1 (800) 464-2924)

For a vacation planner for the **Big Island of Hawaii** only, call 1 (800) 648-2441

For a vacation planner for **Kauai** only, call 1 (800) AH-KAUAI (1 (800) 245-2824)

For a vacation planner for **Maui** only, call 1 (800) 525-MAUI (1 (800) 525-6284)

There's no separate vacation planner for **Oahu**; get the all-islands "Isles of Aloha" package, above, for Oahu information

To write, call, or FAX their offices and affiliates:

Canada: affiliates Nick Hughes and Barbara Newton, 1260 Hornby St., #104, Vancouver, BC V6Z 1W2, (604) 669-6691, FAX (604) 683-9114

New York: in the Empire State Building at 350 Fifth Avenue, Suite 1827, New York, NY 10118, (212) 947-0717, FAX (212) 947-0725

Washington, D.C.: 3975 University Drive, Suite 335, Fairfax, VA 22080, (703) 691-1800, FAX (703) 691-4820

Check out the following Web sites and their links, too:

Hawaii Visitors Bureau sites: www.visit.hawaii.org, www.gohawaii.com
Hawaii State Government offices: www.hawaii.gov
Division of Land and Natural Resources (DLNR): www.hawaii.gov/dlnr/
DLNR, Division of Forestry: www.hawaii.gov/dlnr/dfw/dfw.html

DLNR, Division of State Parks: www.hawaii.gov/dlnr/dsp/dsp.html
State Tourism office: www.hawaii.gov/tourism/index.html
Haleakala National Park: www.nps.gov/hale/
Great Outdoors Recreation Pages (GORP): www.gorp.com—lots of info as well as an on-line bookstore

To see some of your hikes in advance as well as to read about them here, get the video trail guide *Pathways in Paradise: Maui.* If your outdoor or travel store doesn't carry the video, you can find it on the Web via the on-line bookstore at the Great Outdoors Recreation Pages (www.gorp.com). It includes coverage of a new trail, the Lahaina Pali Trail. Call the Hawaiian trail organization, Na Ala Hele, at (808) 871-2521 for more information.

Let me know what you think and what you find. I hope this book helps make your visit to Maui even more enjoyable than it would have been. I plan to update it regularly, and you can help me. Letters from readers, which I enjoy reading and answering, have been a great help to me in keeping this book up to date and in planning my repeat visits to Maui. Let me know what you think of this book. Did you find it helpful when you visited Maui? Was it accurate and complete enough that you enjoyed the walks and hikes you took based on the book? Did you notice any significant discrepancies between this book and what you found when you visited Maui, discrepancies that you judge are not just the result of two different perceptions of the same thing? What were they? The publisher and I are very concerned about accuracy. We'd appreciate your comments. I'd also like to know about it if you think there are ways in which the book can be improved. Write to me in care of Wilderness Press, 2440 Bancroft Way, Berkeley, CA 94704.

Spoken Hawaiian: An Incomplete and Unauthoritative Guide

What, only 12 letters?! Nineteenth-century American missionaries used only 12 letters to create a written version of the spoken Hawaiian language. Superficially, that might make Hawaiian seem simple. But Hawaiian is a much more complex and subtle language than 12 letters can do justice to. However, we're stuck with those 12 letters—the five English vowels (a, e, i, o, u) and seven of the consonants (h, k, l, m, n, p, w).

Consonants. The consonants have the same sound in Hawaiian as they do in your everyday English except for "w." "W" is sometimes pronounced as "v" when it follows "a," always pronounced as "v" when it follows "e" or "i."

Vowels. The vowels are generally pronounced as they are in Italian, with each vowel sounded separately. Authentic Hawaiian makes further distinctions, but those are of more interest to scholars than to hikers.[1] The following is a simplified system. Vowel sounds in general are:

a	like "ah" in "Ah!"
e	like "ay" in "day."
i	like "ee" as in "whee!"
o	like "o" in "go."
u	like "oo" in "food" (or "u" in "rude").

Notice that that means that when you see two or more of the same letter in a row, you pronounce each of them separately:

Kaanapali is Ka-a-na-pa-li (but everyone pronounces it "Ka-na-pa-li").
Waihee is Wai-he-e.
Piilani is Pi-i-la-ni.
Hookipa is Ho-o-ki-pa.
Puu is Pu-u.

---

[1] Remember that Hawaiian evolved as a spoken, not a written, language. Authentic written Hawaiian uses two special marks to indicate other variations on pronouncing vowels in spoken Hawaiian. Those variations change the meaning of a word. One is the glottal stop, indicated by a single quotation mark ('). It indicates that you should make a complete break in your voice before sounding the vowel that follows it. There really isn't an English equivalent, though the break in "uh-oh!" is close. Another is the macron mark, which is a straight line over a vowel. It indicates that you should pronounce a vowel as a long sound instead of a short sound. For example, the Hawaiian long-a sound is "ah," and the Hawaiian short-a sound is "uh." We have the same sounds in English but don't use special marks to distinguish between them except in dictionaries. Road signs, topographic maps, and this book don't use glottal stops or macron marks.

That seems too simple, and it is. If you tried to pronounce every vowel, speaking Hawaiian would turn into a nightmare. You wouldn't live long enough to pronounce some words. Fortunately, several pairs of vowels often—but not always—form merged sounds.

Vowel Pairs Whose Sounds Merge. Like every other language, Hawaiian has vowel pairs whose sounds naturally "smooth" into each other. They're similar to Italian or English diphthongs. The degree to which the two sounds are merged in Hawaiian is officially less than occurs in English, but most Hawaiian people I've talked with merge them fully. Vowel-pair pronunciation is approximately:

- ae often smoothed to "eye" as in "eyeful" or "i" in "ice." It's the English long-i sound.
- ai often smoothed as for "ae," above.
- ao often smoothed to sound like "ow" in "cow."
- au often smoothed to "ow" in "cow", too.
- ei sometimes smoothed to "ay" as in "day." It's the English long-a sound.
- eu smooth the sounds together a little, like "ayoo."
- oi usually like "oi" in "oil"—in other words, just what you're used to.

Syllables. Every Hawaiian syllable ends in a vowel sound. A Hawaiian syllable never contains more than one consonant. That means every consonant goes with the vowel that follows it. Every vowel not preceded by a consonant stands alone when you break a written word into syllables (you may smooth some of them together when you speak). For example:

Aa consists of the two syllables a-a (it's a kind of lava flow).

Kihei consists of the three syllables Ki-he-i (but everyone pronounces it "KEE-hay").

Kipahulu consists of the four syllables Ki-pa-hu-lu (an area famed for its cascades, falls, and natural swimming pools, now part of Haleakala National Park)

Haleakala consists of the five syllables Ha-le-a-ka-la (the dormant volcano that makes up East Maui; the national park that encompasses its upper slopes and a strip of its southeast flank).

Ulupalakua consists of the six syllables U-lu-pa-la-ku-a (a huge ranch on the southwest slopes of Haleakala; home of Maui's Tedeschi Winery).

Liliuokalani consists of the seven syllables Li-li-u-o-ka-la-ni (Hawaii's last monarch and writer of the beloved song "Aloha Oe").

Accent. In general, the accent falls on the next-to-last syllable for words with three or more syllables and on the first syllable for words of two syllables. For words of more than three syllables, you put a little stress on every other syllable preceding the accented one. Don't worry about this; it seems to come naturally.

There are common-usage exceptions, such as makai (ma-KAI, with the accent on the last syllable). When you see exceptions such as those, chances are that what has happened is that European usage has fully merged two sounds into one. Proper Hawaiian pronunciation of makai would be closer to "ma-KA-i," a three-syllable word with the last two syllables almost merging.

Hint for Longer Words: Repetition and Rhythm. Have you noticed the tendency in long Hawaiian words for groups of letters to repeat? That kind of repetition is fairly common. When you see a long Hawaiian word, don't panic. Identify its repeating letter groups, figure out how to pronounce them individually, then put the whole word together. Chances are you'll come pretty close to getting it correct.

For example, *Waianapanapa* throws a lot of people. But look at the repeating letter group *napa* (*na-pa*). See the word as *Waia/napa/napa*. So, two *na-pa*s prefixed with a *wai-a* (the *ai* in *wai* merges here)—that makes *wai-a/na-pa/na-pa*. Once you've identified the repeating groups, the rhythm of the word comes naturally. Try this approach for longer words, including the state fish: *humuhumunukunukuapuaa*: two *hu-mu*s, two *nu-ku*s, and an *a-pu-a-a*. Now try it: *hu-mu/hu-mu/nu-ku/nu-ku/a-pu-a-a*. . . .Very good!

***Makai* and *mauka*.** In Hawaii, local people often give directions or describe the location of a place as *makai* (merge the *ai*), which means "toward the sea," or *mauka* (merge the *au*), which means "toward the mountains; inland." I had a terrible time remembering which was which until I came up with this mnemonic:

> Go *makai*
> Where sea meets sky,

and Tom Winnett came up with:

> *Mauka* is toward the MAUntains.

However, I still think in terms of left, right, north, south, east, and west. I don't often use *mauka* and *makai* in this book.

Do your best, with respect. Approach the language with respect, and give it your best shot. Then be prepared to hear local people pronounce it differently. Learn from them. Maybe it's part of our jobs as visitors to inadvertently provide a little comic relief for those living and working here as opposed to just vacationing here.

Instant Hawaiian (see Bibliography) is a useful booklet that's a lot less frivolous than its title implies. It begins, "So you'd like to learn to speak Hawaiian—you should live so long!" I felt I'd come to the right place. Look for it when you get to Maui.

Geology and History, Natural and Human

First, the earth

According to the theory of *plate tectonics*, the earth consists of:

A rigid, rocky outer shell, the *lithosphere* ("rocky zone").

Beneath the lithosphere, a hot, semifluid layer, the *asthenosphere* ("weak zone").

A *core* that doesn't play a part in this oversimplified discussion.

The lithosphere is broken into *plates* that move with respect to one another. Hot, fluid material, possibly from the asthenosphere or melted by contact with the asthenosphere, penetrates up through the lithosphere at three kinds of places:

Mid-oceanic ridges, where plates spread apart.

Subduction zones, where plates collide and one dives under the other (subducts).

Hot spots, where a plume of molten material appears in the middle of a plate.

Next, the land

It's believed that the Hawaiian Islands exist where the Pacific Plate, on which they ride, is moving northwest across a hot spot. An undersea volcano is built at the place where the plate is over the hot spot. If the volcano gets big enough, it breaks the ocean's surface to become an island. Eventually, the plate's movement carries the island far enough away from the hot spot that volcanism ceases on that island. Erosion, which begins the moment the new island appears above the sea, tears the land down.

The Hawaiian Islands are successively older toward the northwest and younger toward the southeast. Northwestern islands, like Necker, are hardly more than bits of volcanic rock now. Southeastern islands, including the major Hawaiian Islands, are still significant chunks of land. The big island of Hawaii is the youngest and the farthest southeast of the major islands; Maui is the next youngest; and Kauai and Niihau are the oldest and the farthest northwest of the major islands.

The molten material—lava—characteristic of Hawaiian volcanoes is relatively fluid. The fluidity of the lava allows it to spread widely, and repeated eruptions produce broad-based, rounded volcanoes called shield volcanoes. The volcano expels not only flowing lava but volcanic fragments such as cinder and ash. Alternating layers of these materials build up during periods of volcanic activity.

Erosion has sculpted the exotic landscapes we associate with volcanic tropical islands. Waves pound the volcano's edges, undercutting them and, where the volcano slopes more steeply, forming cliffs. Streams take material from higher on the volcano, cutting valleys into its flanks and depositing the material they carry as alluvium, like the broad alluvial apron formed on the isthmus side of West Maui by the deposits of four of its streams: Waihee, Waiehu, Iao, and Waikapu. New episodes of volcanism wholly or partly fill in those landscapes, and erosional forces immediately begin sculpting the new surface as well as the remaining older surface.

Maui is geologically an infant on an Earth more than four billion years old. Potassium-argon dating of rocks suggests that lava welled forth to build West Maui beginning a little less than two million years ago. Volcanism ended on West Maui just over a million years ago. Haleakala literally burst upon the scene less than a million years ago. Outpourings from Haleakala built the isthmus that now connects West and East Maui. West Maui's volcano, Puu Kukui, may be extinct now; East Maui—Haleakala—is only dormant. The last lava flow on Maui occurred along Haleakala's southwest rift zone in about 1790, forming Cape Kinau and dividing what had been one huge bay into Ahihi and La Pérouse bays. Haleakala may erupt again; no one knows whether it will or when or where. On West Maui, and on East Maui while Haleakala sleeps, erosion reigns, changing the landscape constantly.

Life arrives

Living organisms colonize new land rapidly. In Hawai, plants established themselves once there was a little soil for them. Seeds arrived on the air currents, or floated in on the sea, or hitched a ride on the feathers or in the guts of birds. Insects and spiders also took advantage of the air currents. Birds were certainly among the first visitors. Living things found little competition and quickly adapted to their new home, evolving into an astonishing variety of species many of which occur naturally only on the Hawaiian islands ("endemic to Hawaii"). The only mammals to arrive were the bat and the seal. Some birds became flightless—a fairly common adaptation on isolated islands with no ground predators.

People arrive

It's unlikely that the site of the very first human colony in the Hawaiian Islands will ever be found. Too much time has passed; too many destructive forces have been at work. However, recent archaeological work has established that people had settled in Hawaii by 300–400 A.D, earlier than had previously been thought. Linguistic studies and cultural artifacts recovered from sites of early colonization point to the Marquesas Islands as the colonizers' home; the Marquesas themselves seem to have been colonized as early as 200 B.C.

The colonizers of Hawaii had to adapt the Marquesan technology to their new home. For example, the Marquesans made distinctive large, one-piece fishhooks from the large, strong pearl shells that abounded in Marquesan waters. There are no such large shells in Hawaiian waters, so the colonists developed two-piece fishhooks made of the weaker materials that were available in Hawaii (such as bone and wood). Over time, a uniquely Hawaiian material culture developed.

At one time, scholars believed that, as related in Hawaii's oral traditions and genealogies, a later wave of colonizers from Tahiti swept in and conquered the earlier Hawaiians. Research does not support that theory. Instead, research has revealed that before European contact, Hawaiian material culture evolved steadily in patterns that suggest gradual and local, not abrupt and external, influences. The archaeological record hints that there may have been some Hawaiian-Tahitian contact in the twelfth century, but its influence was slight.

The Hawaiians profoundly altered the environment of the islands. They had brought with them the plants they had found most useful in the Marquesas Islands: taro (in Hawaiian, *kalo*), ti (*ki*), the trees from which they made a bark cloth (tapa (*kapa*)), sugar cane, ginger, gourd plants, yams, bamboo, turmeric, arrowroot, and the breadfruit tree. They also brought the small pigs of Polynesia, dogs, jungle fowl, and, probably as stowaways, rats. They used slash-and-burn techniques to clear the native lowland forests for the crops they had brought. Habitat loss together with competition for food with and predation by the newly introduced animals wrought havoc with the native animals, particularly birds. Many species of birds had already become extinct long before Europeans arrived.

On the eve of the Europeans' accidental stumbling across Hawaii, the major Hawaiian islands held substantial numbers of people of Polynesian descent. They had no written language, but their oral and musical traditions were ancient and rich. Their social system was highly stratified and very rigid. Commoners, or *makaainana*, lived in self-sufficient family groups and villages, farming and fishing for most necessities and trading for necessities they could not otherwise obtain. The land was divided among hereditary chiefs of the noble class (*alii*). Commoners paid part of their crops or catches as taxes to the chief who ruled the land-division they lived on; commoners served their chief as soldiers. Higher chiefs ruled over lower chiefs, receiving from them taxes and also commoners to serve as soldiers. People especially gifted in healing, divination, or important crafts served the populace in those capacities (for example, as priests). There was also a class of untouchables, the *kauwa*. Most people were at death what they had been at birth.

Strict laws defined what was forbidden, or *kapu*, and governed the conduct of kauwa toward everyone else, of commoners toward *alii*, of *alii* of a lower rank toward *alii* of higher rank, and of men and women toward each other. Some of the laws seem irrationally harsh. For example, a commoner could be put to death if his or her shadow fell on an *alii*.

Chiefs frequently made war on one another. If the chiefs of one island were united under a high chief or a king, often that island would make war on the other islands. In the late 1700s, war raged between Maui and the big island of Hawaii for many years. Hawaii's king was able to hold Maui's Hana district for much of the time, and periodically he tried to conquer the rest of Maui. The young warrior and future king Kamehameha served Hawaii's king and first saw combat in these wars against Maui.

The Hawaiians worshipped many gods and goddesses. The principal ones were Ku, Kane, Kanaloa, and Lono. Ku represented the male aspect of the natural world. Ku was also the god of war, and he demanded human sacrifice. Kane was the god of life, a benevolent god who was regarded as the Creator and the ancestor of all Hawaiians. Kanaloa ruled the dead and the dark aspects of life, and he was often linked with Kane in worship.

Lono was another benevolent god; he ruled clouds, rain, and harvests. The annual winter festival in Lono's honor, Makahiki, ran from October to February. Makahiki was a time of harvest, celebration, fewer *kapu*, and sporting events. Images of Lono were carried around each island atop tall poles with crosspieces from which banners of white tapa flew. (Legend said Lono had sailed away from Hawaii long ago and would return in a floating *heiau* (temple) decked with poles flying long white banners from their crosspieces.) Chiefs and chiefesses met the image of Lono with ceremonies and gifts, and commoners came forward to pay their taxes.

Systems like that can last for hundreds and even thousands of years in the absence of compelling internal problems or changes and of external forces, as the Hawaiian system did. But change eventually comes.

The Europeans arrive by accident

Christopher Columbus had sailed from Spain to what he thought was the Orient, hoping to find a sea route to replace the long, hazardous land route. But in fact he discovered an obstacle called North America. With a direct sea route between Europe and the Orient blocked, people sought other sea routes. The southern routes around the Cape of Good Hope at the tip of Africa and Cape Horn at the tip of South America proved to be very long and very treacherous. Still, the trade was lucrative. The European demand for Oriental goods such as spices, Chinese porcelain, and silk was insatiable. By trading their way around the world, a captain, his crew, and the government or the tradesmen that financed them might become very wealthy in just one voyage.

All over Europe, people came to believe that a good, navigable route *must* exist in northern waters that would allow them to sail west from Europe around the northern end of North America to the Orient. (It doesn't exist.) Captain James Cook sailed from England on July 12, 1776, to try to find the Northwest Passage from the Pacific side.

In December of 1777, Cook left Tahiti sailing northeast, not expecting to see land again until he reached North America. Instead, he sighted land on January 18, 1778, and reached the southeast shore of Kauai on January 19th. In Hawaii, it was the time of Makahiki, the festival honoring the god Lono. The Hawaiians mistook the masts and sails of Cook's ships for the poles and tapa banners of the floating *heiau* on which Lono was to return and received Cook as if he were Lono.

Cook was an intelligent and compassionate man who respected the native societies he found and who tried to deal with their people fairly and decently. He tried to keep crewmen who he knew had venereal diseases from infecting the natives, but he failed. Cook did not stay long in Hawaii. He spent most of 1778 searching for the Northwest Passage; unsuccessful, he returned to Hawaii in early 1779 to make repairs and resupply. It was Makahiki again. All went well at first, but the Hawaiians stole an auxiliary boat from one of his ships. When he tried to retrieve it, there was a brief skirmish, in which Cook and four of his crew were killed.

Cook's ships survived a second futile search for the Northwest Passage, after which the crew sailed westward for England, stopping in China. There the crew learned the astonishing value of another of the expedition's great discoveries: the furs of the sea otters and seals of the Pacific Northwest. Trade with the Orient suddenly became even more profitable, and Hawaii was to become not an isolated curiosity but an important point on a major world trade route.

In Hawaii, the young chief Kamehameha began his conquest of the islands in 1790. Kamehameha actively sought Western allies, weapons, and advice. He subdued Maui for the first time after a bloody battle in Iao Valley. Maui's defiant king recaptured the island; years passed before Kamehameha reconquered Maui. He conquered all the islands but Kauai and Niihau.

Kamehameha's wars, Western diseases, and the sandalwood trade decimated the native Hawaiians. Chiefs indebted themselves to foreign merchants for weapons and other goods. New England merchants discovered that Hawaii had abundant sandalwood, for which the Chinese would pay huge prices. Merchants demanded payment from the chiefs in sandalwood; the chiefs ordered the commoners into the mountains to get the precious wood. The heartwood nearest the roots was the best part; the whole tree had to be destroyed to get it. The mountains were stripped of their sandalwood trees. Many of those ordered into the mountains died of exposure and starvation. Communities that had depended on their labor for food also starved.

Kamehameha I died in 1819, leaving the monarchy to his son Liholiho and a regency in Liholiho's behalf to his favorite wife, Kaahumanu. Liholiho was an amiable, weak-willed alcoholic. Kaahumanu was strong-willed, intelligent, capable, and ambitious. She believed that the old Hawaiian *kapu* system was obsolete: no gods struck down the Westerners, who daily did things that were *kapu* for Hawaiians. Six months after Kamehameha I's death, she persuaded Liholiho to join her in breaking several ancient *kapu*. The *kapu* system, having been discredited, crumbled; the old order was dead.

The missionaries arrive

Congregationalist missionaries from New England reached Hawaii in 1820; Liholiho grudgingly gave them a year's trial. The end of the *kapu* system had left a religious vacuum into which the missionaries moved remarkably easily. To their credit, they came with a sincere desire to commit their lives to bettering those of the people of Hawaii. Liholiho's mother converted to Christianity and made it acceptable for other *alii* to follow her example. Kaahumanu became a convert, too, and set about remodeling Hawaii socially and politically, based on the Ten Commandments.

Plaque at Kaahumanu's birthplace

An ecosystem passes

Cook and those who came after him gave cattle, goats, and large European pigs as gifts to the Hawaiian chiefs, and the animals overran the islands. They ate everything. Rainwater sluiced off the now-bare hillsides without replenishing the aquifers. Areas that had been blessed with an abundance of water suffered drought now. Native plants could not reestablish themselves because the unrestrained animals ate them as soon as they sent up a shoot. People wrongly concluded that native plants were inherently unable to reestablish themselves, and they imported non-native trees like the eucalyptuses and ironwoods that you see so often today.

The native habitat area and diversity shrank still more before the new sugar plantations. Planters drained wetlands for the commercially valuable crop and erected dams, ditches, and sluices to divert the natural water supply into a controllable water supply. What they did was not so very different from what the Polynesians had done when they had cleared the native lowland forests in order to plant their taro, but the scale was far vaster. In one particularly terrible mistake, growers imported the mongoose to prey on the rats that damaged their crops. But the rat forages at night, while the mongoose hunts by day: they seldom met. What the mongooses preyed on instead were the eggs of native ground-nesting birds.

Few of Hawaii's native plants put forth showy flowers or set palatable fruit, so the new settlers imported ornamental and fruiting plants to brighten their gardens and tables. Many shrubs and trees did so well in Hawaii's favorable climate that they escaped into the wild to become pest plants, crowding out native species and interrupting the food chain.

Birds brought over as pets escaped to compete with native species. More species of native birds have become extinct in Hawaii than anywhere else in the world, and most of the birds you see will be introduced species like the zebra dove and the myna.

It is tragic but true that when you visit Hawaii, you will probably see very few of its native plants and animals. The dryland forest on Haleakala's upper, western slopes and the alpine plants in Haleakala's crater, now fenced to keep out goats and pigs, offer you chances to see remnants of native Hawaiian plant communities.

A culture passes

Literacy replaced the rich Hawaiian oral tradition, and many legends and stories were forgotten before someone thought to write them down. The significance of many place names, apart from their literal meaning, has been lost forever. Zealous missionaries and converts believed that the native traditions were evil, and they nearly succeeded in eradicating all traces of the native culture.

A nation passes

Hawaiians saw that their only hope of surviving as an independent nation in the modern world was to secure the protection and guarantees of freedom of one of the major powers. The Hawaiian monarchs would have preferred the British, but British influence was ultimately inadequate to withstand American influence. American missionaries doled out God's grace. American entrepreneurs established plantations and businesses. American ships filled the harbors. Economic and cultural domination of Hawaii eventually passed into American hands, particularly after the new land laws of 1850 made it possible for foreigners to own land in Hawaii. The Hawaiian monarchy lasted until 1893, but most of its economic and therefore its political power was gone. Hawaii as an independent nation disappeared soon after.

A race passes

The native Hawaiian people lost much of their importance in the changing, Westernized economy early in the nineteenth century. The burgeoning sugar and pineapple plantations needed laborers, and the Hawaiians were diligent, capable hired hands when they wanted to be. But they did not comprehend the idea of hiring themselves out as day laborers for wages. Planters began to import laborers from other parts of the world: China, Japan, the Philippines, Portugal. Many imported laborers stayed, married, raised families, and went on to establish their own successful businesses. The Hawaiians were soon a minority in their own land.

The numbers of full-blooded Hawaiians declined precipitously throughout the nineteenth century. Beginning with the tragic introduction of venereal disease by Cook's men, venereal diseases swept through the native population who, particularly at Makahiki, exchanged partners freely. Venereal disease often leaves its victims sterile, and many who had survived Western diseases, wars, and the sandalwood trade were unable to reproduce. Others married foreigners, so their children were only part Hawaiian. Today most authorities believe that there are no full-blooded Hawaiians left, not even on Niihau, the only island where Hawaiian is still the language of everyday life.

Hawaii becomes American

In the late nineteenth century, the Hawaiian monarchy seemed to some powerful businessmen and civic leaders of American descent to get in the way of the smooth conduct of business. They thought Hawaii would be better off as an American territory. Queen Liliuokalani did not agree. She wanted to assert Hawaii's independence and the authority of its monarchs. The business community plotted a coup, deposed Liliuokalani in 1893, formed a new government, and petitioned the United States for territorial status. The United States formally annexed Hawaii in 1898.

Military projects and mass travel brought mainland Americans flooding into Hawaii. Many stayed, and so the majority of people in Hawaii came to see themselves as Americans, though a minority disagreed (some still do). After many years as a territory, Hawaii became the fiftieth state in 1959.

Things to come

The huge tourist industry is both a blessing and a curse. Massive development pushes the Hawaii-born off the land to make way for hotels. Displaced Hawaiians, whatever their ethnic background, find themselves having to survive as waiters, chambermaids, clerks—in essence, as the servants of those who have displaced them. Many also fear that tourism will result in the Hawaiian paradise being paved over and lost forever; others feel that it already has been. The story of Hawaii's evolution is far from over.

Maui Historical Society Museum

The Maui Historical Society Museum is well worth a visit. It's in Hale Hoikeike, formerly known as Bailey House, at 2375-A Main Street, Wailuku, Maui, HI 96793, telephone (808) 244-3326. Call to check on its hours. You can easily include a visit to the museum as part of your day of seeing Kepaniwai County Park and Iao Valley State Park (see Trips W5 through W8). The house itself dates from the missionary era and is home to a good bookstore/gift shop and to exhibits of Hawaiian craftsmanship and missionary life. Missionary Edward Bailey, who lived here with his family for 45 years beginning in 1840, was also an artist whose works, on display here, record many scenes of nineteenth-century Maui life. A preserved *oo* in one of the exhibit cases offers the only chance you and I are likely to get to see that probably-now-extinct native bird. The museum asks for a modest donation.

Getting Around on Maui and Finding Maps to Help You

Driving

Maui has no public transportation. That leaves most of us dependent on a car, which you should arrange for well in advance of your visit. Ask for a modest vehicle in a drab color so it's inconspicuous when parked at trailheads. Get a road map of Maui in advance, perhaps from one of the national automobile clubs if you belong to one. Even better, get the excellent "Map of Maui" published by the University of Hawaii Press. It's good to be able to study the map in advance and have some notion of the island's roads before you tackle them. Some of the maps provided by tourist bureaus are so cute they're useless.

Driving conditions on Maui vary widely, and driving time can make serious inroads on your hiking time. Major roads between Wailuku and Kahului and Pukalani, Lahaina, and Kihei have stretches where the legal limit is 55 mph. However, look out for traffic jams around Lahaina, Wailuku, Kahului (particularly near the airport), and Kihei. Road construction and the periodic burning of canefields can slow traffic and even close roads. And some roads, described below, are in a class of their own.

Hana and Kipahulu. The road to Hana (Hana Highway—Highway 36, then Highway 360) has been improved to the point where everyone can take surviving the road to Hana for granted. The entire road is paved to and through Hana. The first 16 miles from Kahului and through Paia are rather easy. After it becomes Highway 360, however, it's extremely slow (10 mph recommended), winding, and narrow (often just one lane wide, where drivers going one way may have to stop for traffic going the other way). The Hana Highway is not a seacoast drive, despite its coastal location. It's a rainforest drive; one writer aptly described it as "burrowing through a tunnel of green." It may also be jammed with sightseers. The road becomes Highway 31 after Hana.

Kipahulu to Kaupo. Highway 31 gets worse beyond the Kipahulu District of Haleakala National Park, though it is currently paved at least as far as Alelele Stream except for one 3-mile stretch. However, it is so narrow and winding that signs are posted warning you to sound your horn before going around a curve. It eventually degenerates into a twisting, unpaved 4WD road with oil-pan-eating rocks (we did not make it to Kaupo from the Hana side). This stretch is subject to storm damage. To get to Kaupo, it's better to drive there from the west, through Keokea and Ulupalakua.

Kaupo to Ulupalakua. The road is less winding near Kaupo, but some stretches are covered with smooth beach pebbles offering poor traction. The pavement resumes for good several miles west of Kaupo, but the road remains narrow and slow until Ulupalakua (15 mph recommended). Have a full gas tank if you drive to Kaupo, as there's no gas east of Keokea and west of Hana. The Kaupo Store is open and keeping regular hours, so you can get drinks and snacks there (see Trip E14 for details).

Around the north end of West Maui. The road around the north end of West Maui (Highway 30 north of Kapalua; Highway 340 north of Wailuku) is slow, narrow, winding, and not particularly scenic. I can't recommend it between the turnoff to Waihee Ridge (Trip W1) and Nakalele Blowhole (Trip W13).

Polipoli. The 10-mile road from Highway 377 to Polipoli is narrow, steep, winding, and very slow. Its last 4 miles are unpaved and vary from deep dust to protruding rocks to lumpy clay. Allow at least an hour each way just for this road.

What to leave in the car. Nothing. Never leave valuables in your car, even in a locked trunk. "Valuables" include not only jewelry, money, checks, and credit cards but things you can't readily replace: glasses, prescription medication, identification, keys, snapshots of loved ones, etc.

Hiking

Road maps are useless for hiking trails. For trail maps, I recommend the maps in this book and the United States Geological Survey (USGS) 7 1/2′ series of topographic ("topo") maps for Maui. Topos show elevation details as well as roads and trails. However, topos are not updated as often as you'd like. That's why you should use them in conjunction with the maps in this book and information from the agencies in charge of the island's hiking areas—the Division of State Parks, Maui District, and the Division of Forestry and Wildlife, Maui District. If you do not write for these in advance, you will need to go into Wailuku to get them. See their addresses in "Getting Permits or Permission" in this book.

Those visiting Haleakala National Park will appreciate Earthwalk Press's *Haleakala National Park Recreation Map*. The map includes topographic data, trail descriptions, and a wealth of other information. If you can't find their maps in your travel store, call them at 1 (800) 828-MAPS.

Maui is covered by 17 topos, as shown in the illustration below. It's also nice to have the USGS *Maui County* topo map. As of this writing, no one on Maui sells topos. If your mainland backpacking store does not carry the Maui topos, you can get them in person or by mail from:

Western Distribution Branch
U.S. Geological Survey
Box 25286, Federal Center
Denver, CO 80225

or

Western Mapping Center
U.S. Geological Survey
345 Middlefield Road
Menlo Park, CA 94025

Write first for catalogs and prices. When you order the maps, enclose your check for the required amount, made out to the U.S. Geological Survey.

Or there may be a store near you that specializes in maps. Look in your telephone directory under "Maps." For example, the store where I used to get my topos isn't a backpacking store, it's a mining-supplies store, Allied Services, 966 N. Main St., Orange, CA 92667, (714) 637-8824. Its stock of maps, including topos, puts any backpacking store in my area to shame ten times over. Another store I get my topos from is a travel store, California Map and Travel Center, 3211 Pico Boulevard, Santa Monica, CA 90405, (310) 829-6277 or FAX (310) 829-2316. Both of these stores will take map orders over the phone when you pay with a valid, major credit card.

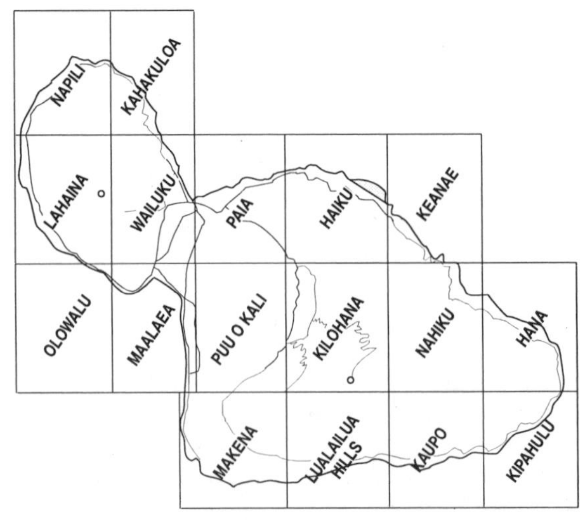

USGS 7½′ Topographic Maps of Maui

Getting Permits or Permission

The trip descriptions in this book include information about what permits you need (if any) and to whom you should apply for them. A few interesting dayhikes are on private property. This section gives the addresses and telephone numbers of private parties you must apply to for permission to hike in those areas. As of this writing, the government agencies—federal, state, and county—don't require you to have permits in order to *dayhike* on Maui in areas under their jurisdiction (Haleakala National Park does require permits for backpacking; see Appendix A). For completeness, this section also includes the addresses and telephone numbers of the government agencies, as you may want to write or call them for more information. Appendix A in this book gives you detailed information about camping—car camping, tent camping, and cabins—including permit requirements, fees, etc.

Waihee Valley hike (Wailuku Agribusiness)

You must get a permit *in person* for this hike (Trip W2) from Wailuku Agribusiness ((808) 244-9570). Call ahead to find out their current hours. They're in Waikapu, a community 2 miles south of Wailuku on Highway 30. As you approach Waikapu, look for Waiko Road (it's just north of the bridge over Waikapu Stream; it may be marked by a blue-and-white sign that points along it to the Waikapu Community Center). Turn east onto Waiko Road and follow it a short distance to the gates of Wailuku Agribusiness, on your left. Turn in here, park, and go into the office to apply for your permit.

Hikes to David Malo's grave and to Olowalu petroglyphs (Pioneer Mill Company)

You must get a permit *in person* from the Pioneer Mill Company ((808) 661-3106) in Lahaina to hike to David Malo's grave (Trip W11). The office is in an old cream-colored building on Lahainaluna Road in Lahaina. Lahainaluna Road is easy to find because of the big sugar mill and its prominent stacks on the corner of Highway 30 and Lahainaluna Road. Turn inland on Lahainaluna Road. As you drive inland toward the famous high school, the mill is on your left and the office building is on your right about 1 block farther inland. It's a good idea to call in advance to find out their current hours and in order to be sure someone will be there to type up the form and sign it. Or ask them if they can make up your permit in advance so that you can just pick it up. The permit comes with regulations that you must follow while on their land.

The cane road you must walk up to get to the petroglyphs at Olowalu (Trip W10) is posted NO TRESPASSING by the Pioneer Mill Company. The latest information I have from the person who issues the permits for the hike to David Malo's grave is that in spite of the posting, you don't need a permit to walk to the petroglyphs, but you must not go any farther. I suggest you call the company and make sure that's still true.

Haleakala National Park

No permits are required to dayhike or car camp in Haleakala National Park. Backpacking in the crater, including camping or use of the cabins in the crater, requires permits; see Appendix A in this book. For more information, write or call:

> Haleakala National Park
> Box 369
> Makawao, Maui, HI 96768
> (808) 572-7749 (recording of general information); (808) 572-9177 (recording of camping and cabin information); (808) 572-9306 (park headquarters; 7:30 A.M. to 4:00 P.M. Hawaii Standard Time)

See also the park's Web site (page 6).

Division of State Parks

No permits are required to hike in Maui's state parks, and none is big enough for or equipped for backpacking. Car camping and use of the cabins do require permits; see Appendix A in this book. For more information, write or call:

> Department of Land and Natural Resources
> Division of State Parks, Maui District
> P.O. Box 1049
> Wailuku, Maui, HI 96793
> (808) 244-4324 (or (808) 243-5354 for camping and cabin reservations)

If you need to see them in person, they are currently in Wailuku in the State Office Building at 54 High Street, on the southeast corner of Highway 30 (Honoapiilani Highway/High Street) and Main Street, just across the street from Kaahumanu Church. Their offices are on the bottom floor, and they share them with the

Division of Forestry and Wildlife. However, you should address inquiries to each separately. See also their Web site (page 6).

Division of Forestry and Wildlife

At present there are no trails, campgrounds, or cabins under the control of the Division of Forestry and Wildlife for which you are required to have permits for hiking or camping. Surprisingly few of the many areas under this agency's control offer hiking opportunities suitable for the tourist from the mainland. Camping opportunities are almost nil (but see the notes at the ends of Trips E16 and E18). Many areas seem to be managed for hunting but not for hiking. For more information, write or call:

Department of Land and Natural Resources
Division of Forestry and Wildlife, Maui District
P.O. Box 1015
Wailuku, Maui, HI 96793
(808) 243-5352

See also the note on actually going into Wailuku to see them in person in the paragraph above. Also see their Web site (page 5).

A handsome old church in the Kihei-Makena area

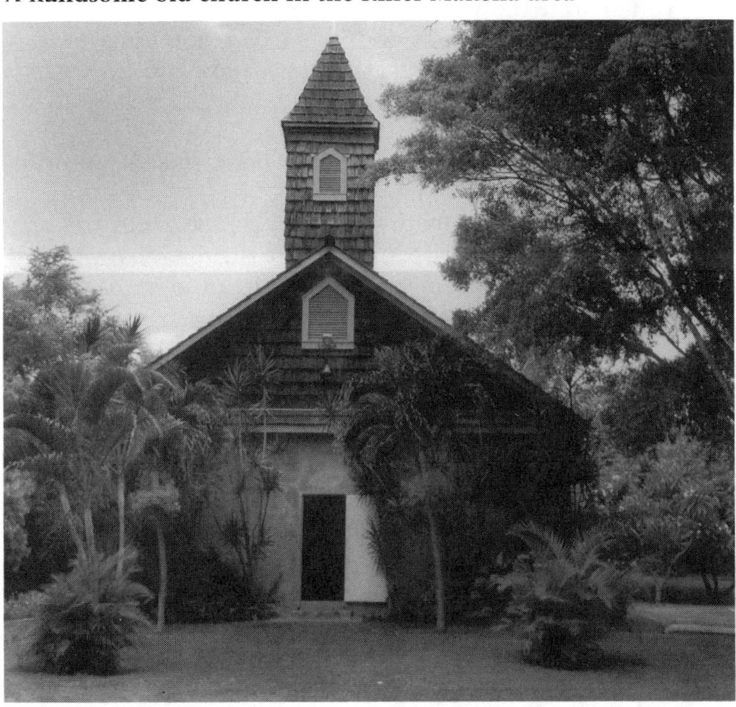

Weather

The short of it. Maui's eastern and western lobes are almost like two separate islands. Each is:

- Rainier on its north side, which boasts rainforests. Waihee Valley on West Maui is a rainforest. The Hana Highway on East Maui tunnels through a rainforest.
- Less rainy on its east side, but still rainy enough to support lush tropical growth. Iao Valley State Park on West Maui is filled with dense tropical vegetation. Hana on the east end of East Maui is famous for its frequent rain, hothouse climate, and colorful gardens.
- Driest and hottest on the south and west. These areas lie in the rain shadow of the volcano that dominates the lobe. Lahaina on the west side of West Maui averages only 17 inches of rain annually and can be fiery hot. Kihei, Wailea, and Makena lie in Haleakala's rain shadow and are not only hot and dry but frequently very windy, especially in the afternoon.
- Rainy in the mountains, especially between 5000 and 7000 feet.

The isthmus is generally dry and windy. The south and west coasts attract the most visitors, are where the resorts are located, and have the most popular beaches. The figure at the top of the next page summarizes the situation.

The long of it. Hawaii's weather is temperate to a degree that puts the so-called "temperate" zones of the world to shame. The humidity is moderate, too: 50 to 60%, not the sweltering horror of some other tropical lands. It is warmer in the summer and cooler in the winter, but the extremes are nothing like on the mainland.

Hawaii's mild climate is determined largely by its tropical location and also by the northeast trade winds that sweep across it. The northeast trade winds—so-called because sea captains took advantage of them on their trade routes—are dependable, steady winds that blow from the northeast across the thousands of miles of open sea that separate the Hawaiian Islands from the continents. They are responsible for keeping the temperature and the

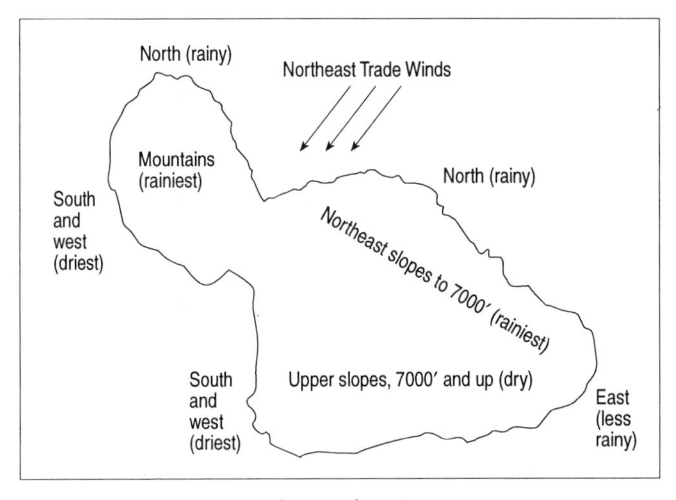

Maui Weather Map

humidity moderate. Since they are the prevailing winds in this area, the side of the island that faces them is called the "windward" side. The opposite side of the island is the opposite of windward; in nautical terms, "leeward."

Sometimes the trade winds fail and are replaced by "kona" winds coming from the south. "Kona" means "leeward," because it's the leeward side of the island that more or less faces these occasional winds. Kona winds bring hot, sticky air. Fortunately, they are rare in summer, when they would be really unpleasant, and occur mostly in winter, when the lower overall temperatures moderate their effect. Kona storms are subtropical low-pressure systems that occur in winter, move in from the south, and can cause serious damage. There is apparently no pattern to them; in some years, they do not occur at all, but in others they occur every few weeks.

On Maui, average temperatures along the coast range from highs of 79–87° F to lows of 62–70° F. The "cooler" ones are winter temperatures, the warmer ones summer. It's rainier from November through March than it is the rest of the year. Expect cooler temperatures, more wind, and considerably more rain if you are in a mountainous region (my thermometer read 40° F one clear morning in Haleakala crater).

Equipment Suggestions and Miscellaneous Hints

TAKE CARE OF THE LAND...SOMEDAY YOULL BE PART OF IT
——Sign, Big Santa Anita Canyon,
Angeles National Forest, California

This book isn't intended to teach you how to hike or backpack. If you can walk, you can hike, especially the "very easy" hikes. You can learn about backpacking in *Backpacking Basics* by Thomas Winnett and Melanie Findling (see Bibliography). Just be sure the trip you pick is within your hiking limits.

This book is intended specifically to let you know *where* you can hike on Maui, *what* to expect when you hike there, and *how* to get to the trailhead for each hike. And that, I hope, will help you decide *which* hikes to take.

This section contains suggestions which I hope will make your hikes even more pleasant, and perhaps better protect you and the environment. Of course, you're the only person who lives in your body, so you'll have to judge what's really appropriate for you. But there are a few things you might want to know before you go—things that may be very different from the hiking you've done at home on the mainland. (Maybe you already know them, but it's hard to shut me up when I think I have some good advice.)

It's up to you. No book can substitute for, or give you, five things only you can supply: physical fitness, preparedness, experience, caution, and common sense. Don't leave the trailhead without them.

Don't spread pest plants. As I mentioned in the chapter on geology and history, Hawaii has been overrun by introduced plants. It's important to try to control the spread of these plants. One thing you can do to help is to wash the soil, and with it the seeds of any pest plants, you hope, off of your shoes or boots *before you leave* a hiking area. Note also that you, like any other animal, can carry pest-plant seeds in your digestive tract and deposit them, ready to sprout, in your solid wastes. Either hold it till you get to a toilet or dig your hole deep enough to make it impossible for the seeds to sprout (one foot deep, according to a pamphlet on the subject. I have no idea how to dig a hole one foot deep with a shovel that a hiker can reasonable carry; I'm just telling you what I've read). Pest plants include all the guavas. For more information, call the Hawaii State Department of Agriculture, (808) 548-7119, Weed Control Section.

Equipment for strolls and easy hikes. You don't need to make extensive preparations for a stroll along a beach or a half-mile nature trail as long as there's food, water, and shelter nearby—perhaps in your car. The things you must not go without are:

Sunglasses
Appropriate footwear
Mosquito repellent ("jungle juice")
Strong sunblock applied *before* you set out

Your mosquito repellent should be "jungle juice"—that is, have a high percentage of DEET (diethyltoluamide). DEET is pretty vile stuff, but it works.

Equipment for moderate and strenuous hikes. Carry at least the Ten Essentials Plus One as I've adapted them from the Sierra Club. Besides sturdy boots, they are:

Pack (to put these good things in; could be a large fanny pack)
Food and water (assume that all open water sources are unsafe to drink)
Extra clothing (always take rain gear, as it can rain any time on Maui)
Map (and compass if you can use it)
Flashlight with extra bulbs and batteries
Sunglasses and strong sunblock applied *before* you set out
Means to dig a hole 6–8 inches deep and at least 200 feet from water, in order to bury solid body wastes; tissue that you will also bury (or pack out)
Pocket knife
First-aid kit
Waterproof matches and something you can keep a flame going with (such as a candle) *only when necessary to start a fire in order to save a life*
Mosquito repellent ("jungle juice")

Equipment for backpacks. The following is a minimal checklist for backpacking equipment.

Minimal Backpacking Equipment List

Backpack	Tent	Sleeping pad
Sleeping bag	Permit	Ten Essentials Plus One (above)
Boots	Socks	Shirts
Shorts or long pants	Hat	Rain gear
Underwear	Toiletries	Personal medication
Stove and fuel*	Eating utensils	Cookware and clean-up stuff

* You cannot take stove fuel on a plane. You must buy it at your destination. Be sure your stove's fuel tank and any fuel bottles you take are empty before you pack them.

Tennis shoes? I've noted in the hike descriptions whether tennis shoes are okay to wear or whether I think you should wear boots. I base that recommendation on the length of the hike and the difficulty of the terrain. What tennis shoes may lack that boots can provide are ankle support and soles that grip. Only you can really decide how important those are to you.

Boot care. If you're going to hike a lot, be sure your boot seams are freshly sealed and you've freshly waterproofed the entire boot, including the cloth part, if any. Use a heavy-duty waterproofing compound like a wax, and bring some of it along in order to renew the coating if necessary. Chances are your boots will get wet, especially in the winter. And they'll stay wet, because things dry slowly in the tropical humidity. It's pretty tough on the boots and, together with the abrasion of mud particles, could cause boot seams to fail.

Hiking stick. Take your hiking stick if you usually hike with one. The flight attendants can put it in the closet where they hang the carry-on suits and dresses or in the overhead compartments. Maui's terrain can be very slippery when wet, and a hiking stick can be a big help in maintaining your footing. And it can double as a spider stick (see below).

Spider stick. There are a very few overgrown trails (for example, the Tableland Trail in Iao Valley State Park) where you and some orb spiders may meet unexpectedly, head-on. You probably don't like collecting spiders with your face, but these critters make it hard not to do so. Here's one way to avoid them without killing them. Pick up and use a "spider stick"—a long, strong stick that you carefully wave up and down in front of you as you hike through brushy country. You can feel the tug when the stick connects with a web. Detach the anchor strands that hold the web in your way, and lay them aside on the adjacent shrubbery. An orb spider normally rebuilds most or all of its web daily, so you've caused it only minor inconvenience. Your hiking stick can probably double as a spider stick.

Sleeping bag. It should be able to tolerate wet conditions. For example, it could have a Gore-Tex shell or it could have a synthetic fill. You are almost certain to get rained on a bit while camping.

Tent. You'll need one for protection from the rain.

Clothes while backpacking. On the one hand, it's best to go as light as possible; on the other hand, almost nothing—not even synthetics—dries overnight in Maui's damp climate under backpacking conditions. Consider which things you can stand to wear damp and which you can't stand unless they're dry. Pack just one or two of the "okay if damp" things. Pack a set of the "gotta be dry!"

things for each day plus one or more extras, just in case. (For me, it's socks.)

At the end of a soggy day of camping out. On those occasional rainy days, you may wonder how you're going to get reasonably clean without getting any wetter than you already are. The socks you've worn all day are "goners" for the time being, wet and muddy on the outside but relatively clean on the inside. While you're changing into dry clothes, turn your "used" socks inside out and mop yourself off with them.

Hypothermia? On Maui? It's possible if you go into the mountains. Remember that going higher is equivalent to going north into colder climates, and mountains are often very windy. Please be prepared as you would be for going into any mountainous region.

Biodegradable? Ha, ha, ha! The following things are popularly supposed to be biodegradable if you bury them: toilet tissue; facial tissue; sanitary napkins; tampons; disposable diapers. That must be a joke. They often last long enough for either running water to exhume them or animals to dig them up. It's actually pretty easy to carry them out if you put them in a heavy-duty self-sealing bag. I use a quart-size Ziploc bag. If I'm feeling squeamish about handling an item, I'll coax it into the bag with the help of a small stick.

Getting hiking and backpacking food. If you are planning to backpack on Maui, consider shopping for your hiking and backpacking chow on Maui. Food prices are higher in Hawaii, but you have enough stuff to put in your luggage without bringing your food, too. There are several well-stocked supermarkets on the island, particularly around Kahului, Kihei, and Lahaina. I couldn't find freeze-dried chow, but there was an adequate selection of long-lasting, lightweight, quick-cooking foods.

Companions. The standard advice is: never hike alone; never camp alone.

Water. Take your own drinking water for the day. Plan on treating water while backpacking. No open source of water anywhere in the U.S. is safe to drink untreated. Treat water chemically (iodine or chlorine preparations designed for the purpose) or by boiling (1–5 minutes at a rolling boil). It now seems that filtering may be ineffective against the bacterium that causes leptospirosis (below). Backpacking opportunities on Maui are, in my opinion, limited to Haleakala crater where the drinking water supply is rain collected from the roofs of the cabins and stored in closed tanks, so that it is presumed to be safe to drink. Tap water at these campgrounds is reported to be safe to drink: Hosmer Grove

Campground; Polipoli State Park; and Waianapanapa State Park. There is no safe drinking water at Kipahulu; you must treat stream water there (or, better yet, fill your jugs with clean water at Hana).

Avoiding leptospirosis. Fresh water on Maui may be contaminated with the bacterium that causes leptospirosis. A pamphlet about leptospirosis is available from the Epidemiology Branch of the Hawaii State Department of Health (on Maui, call (808) 244-4288). The following summarizes some of its contents: Muddy and clear water are both suspect. The bacterium invades through broken skin or the nose, mouth, or eyes. It enters the bloodstream and infects different organs, particularly the kidneys. Precautions that would especially apply to you here are not to go into streams if you have open cuts or abrasions and not to drink (untreated) stream water. Treat water chemically or by boiling it.

If you do swim in fresh water on Maui, you should know that the incubation period of leptospirosis is 2–20 days. The onset is sudden, and the symptoms may resemble those of flu: fever, chills, sweating, severe headache, conjunctivitis (red eyes), muscle pains, weakness, vomiting, and diarrhea. You should see a physician immediately if you suspect leptospirosis. It's believed that administering certain antibiotics early in the course of the disease will shorten the disease and make symptoms less severe. The pamphlet says that most cases are mild and that people (with mild cases) recover in a week or two without treatment. However, severe leptospirosis infections may damage kidneys, liver, or heart or even cause death.

Using This Book

How this book organizes the trips: the "clocks"

Imagine the hour hand of a clock pinned to a point near the center of a rounded island. Think of it sweeping around clockwise from a 12-o'clock position that's due north. It's easy to envision the hour hand pointing to 3 o'clock (due east), 6 o'clock (due south), and 9 o'clock (due west) as it moves around.

You can think of Maui, with its two rounded lobes, as two clocks, one for the west lobe and another for the east lobe. I've added a third clock just for Haleakala.

The West Maui "clock" has its hour hand pivoted on Puu Kukui, its highest point, and its hour hand sweeps clockwise around West Maui. For convenience's sake, I'll consider the isthmus to be part of the West Maui clock. Trips on West Maui and the isthmus start at the 2-o'clock point with Waihee Ridge (Trip W1). Here's the West Maui clock at right:

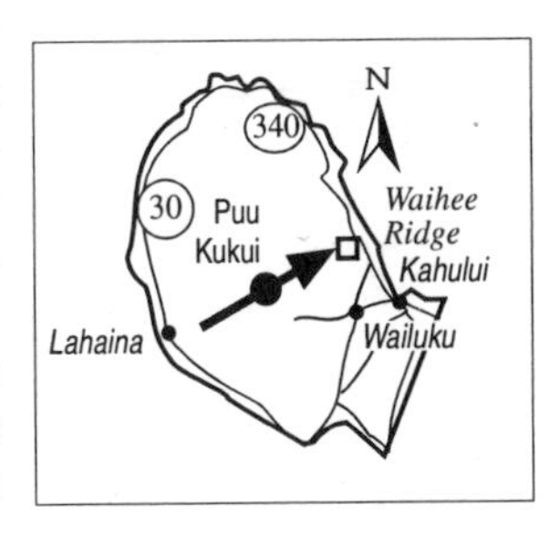

The East Maui "clock" has its hour hand pivoted on a point that's about halfway up the highway to Haleakala. Trips on East Maui start near 1 o'clock at Waikamoi Ridge (Trip E1). Distances are much more compressed on the East Maui clock than they are on the West Maui clock: East Maui is much larger than West Maui, but both "clocks" need to fit into the same space for this book. Here's the East Maui clock at right:

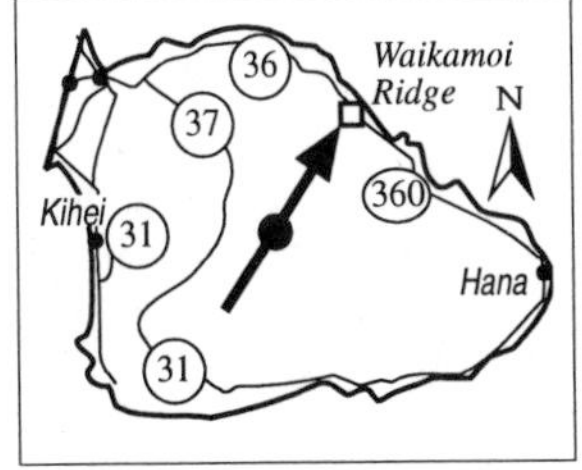

The Haleakala "clock." Distances are so compressed on the East Maui clock that it would be very hard to use it to show the hikes that start in and around Haleakala's crater. Yet that's the most important single hiking area on Maui! Hikes in that area are all together at the end of the book and have their own "clock" that's an enlargement of the East Maui clock area around Haleakala's crater. They are numbered H1, H2, etc., beginning with the Hosmer Grove Nature Loop (Trip H1) a little past 3 o'clock. Here's the Haleakala clock at right:

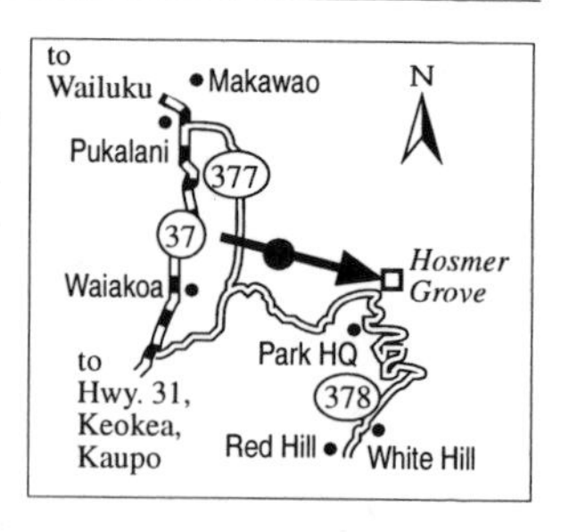

How to Read the Trip Descriptions

The trip descriptions are in the following format, and here is what the information in each description means. Items marked "(icon)" are shown in the trips by icons (small pictures) arranged in a box at the beginning of each trip and defined below.

Title (pretty self-explanatory).

Type (icon): There are four types of trips described:

Loop trips: You follow trails that form a closed loop; you don't retrace your steps, or you retrace them for only a proportionally short distance.

Semiloop trips: The trip consists of a loop part and an out-and-back part.

Out-and-back trips: This is by far the most common type of trip in this book. You follow trails to a destination and then retrace your steps to your starting point.

Shuttle trips: You start at one trailhead and finish at another, "destination" trailhead. They are far enough apart (or walking between them is sufficiently impractical) that you need to have a car waiting for you at your "destination" trailhead or to have someone pick you up there.

Difficulty (icon): A trip's difficulty is based first on total distance and second on cumulative elevation gain and rate of gain. Let's say that the elevation gain is negligible to moderate (it's never steeper than about 500 feet/mile for any significant distance). In that case:

V A very easy trip is 1 mile or less.
E An easy trip is 1–2 miles.
M A moderate trip is 2–5 miles.
S A strenuous trip is more than 5 miles.

If the trip has a section of, say, a half-mile or more where it's steeper than 500 feet/mile, or if the trail is hard to follow, I've given it the next higher difficulty rating.

Shoes (icon): Some trips just aren't safe if you're not wearing boots which have soles that grip and which will give you some ankle support. However, only you live in your body, so you will have to be the final judge of what you can safely wear.

Tennis shoes are okay.

Boots recommended.

Boots necessary, as terrain is rough.

Coastal or inland (icon): General type of area this hike is in. This is a judgement call for those hikes that include both coastal and inland segments.

Hike is along the coast, possibly on a beach or on cliffs above the ocean. Includes hikes like E4, where you are technically on the coast but can't see it for the forest until the very end. (The icon suggests waves.)

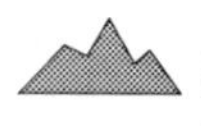
Hike is inland, possibly in the hills or mountains. Includes valley hikes like W2 and E2, too. (Suggests mountains.)

Distance: The distance is the total distance you have to walk.

Elevation gain: This figure is the approximate cumulative elevation gain, and counts all the significant "ups" you have to walk, not just the simple elevation difference between the trailhead and the destination. It's the cumulative gain that your muscles will complain about. Some trips are upside-down: you go downhill on your way out to the destination, uphill on your return.

Average hiking time: This is based on my normal hiking speed, which is a blazing 2 miles/hour.

Location (icon defined in previous section): The West Maui clock, East Maui clock, or Haleakala clock illustrates the trip's general location relative to the rest of Maui.

Topos: The topo or topos listed here are the ones that cover the area you'll be hiking in on this particular trip. Topos are strictly optional for the very easy and easy trips but are strongly recommended for the other trips.

Trail map: This tells you where this book's trail map for this trip is (usually at the end of the trip or of another trip in the same area). As explained in Appendix C, the trail maps are based on the topos wherever possible. However, quite a number of trails on Maui do not appear on any official agency map or on the topos. I have approximated their routes based on field notes and sketches and labeled them "(route approximated)." Some maps are too big for one page and are continued on another page, sometimes at the end of another trip, as noted on the edges of those maps. I've allowed a little overlap between those maps to help you follow them from one page to another.

The following figure shows the trail map legend:

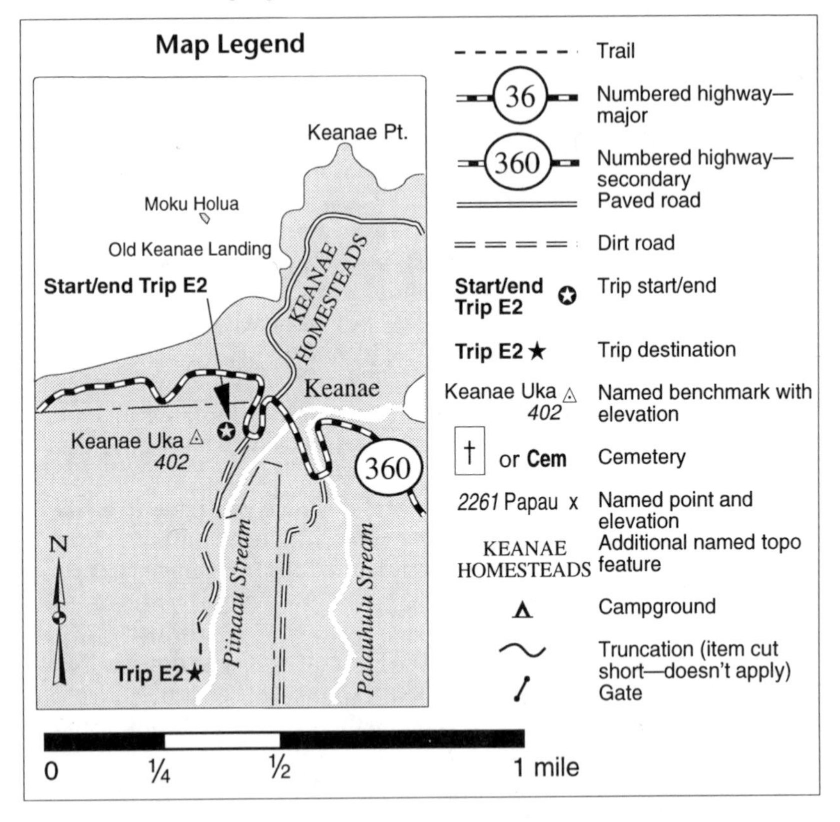

Highlights: This gives you an idea of what I think the best features of the trip are. Usually, it's the scenery—that's one of the principal things you came to Maui for!

Driving instructions: This gives you instructions for driving to the trailhead, usually in terms of driving from Wailuku, the county seat. You may be staying anywhere on Maui, but Wailuku is a convenient reference point. The starting point in Wailuku is the intersection of Highways 30 and 32 (High Street and Main Street, respectively). Kaahumanu Church and the State Office Building are on the south corners of that intersection, and you must go through that intersection on your way to what's likely to be your first sightseeing destination, Iao Valley State Park.

Some trips simply aren't feasible unless you're staying much nearer to them than Wailuku. Trips like that include those in the Hana area (I recommend you stay in Hana), the Kipahulu District (again, stay in Hana), Polipoli (stay in Polipoli), and Haleakala crater (backpack into the crater). Those trips are treated as side trips from the nearest place where it's practical for you to stay.

Be sure you have a good road map of Maui to supplement these instructions.

Permit/permission required: A few trips require you to have someone's permission to cross private land or to camp. This section will tell you what you need permission for, if anything, and whom to apply to. See "Getting Permits or Permission" in this book for addresses.

Description. This is the detailed description of the trip as I perceived it. I've tried to give you an idea of the more obvious plants and other features you'll find, where the rough spots are, when you'll be ascending or descending, where viewpoints are, and what you'll see from those viewpoints. On some trips, the trail is faint to nonexistent, and the agency in charge has attempted to mark the route by tying tags of colored plastic ribbon to plants along the route. You navigate by moving from tag to tag. I found route-tagging on Maui to be largely unreliable, I'm sorry to say; don't count on tags to get you in and out of an area. Always keep track of where you've been by map and compass or by landmarks, as the tags can be misleading.

Supplemental information.... At the bottom of most of the trips, there's some extra information about the historical significance of places you'll see along the route. Or maybe there's a story—a myth, for example—related to the trip which I hope will add to your enjoyment of the trip. Perhaps there'll be a bit more information about the plants or the geology in the area. I put most of the supplemental information at the end so that it wouldn't interfere too much with the description of the trip itself. I think safety dictates that you give your attention first to the trip and only secondarily to the supplemental information. That is not a problem with easy and very easy hikes, so the supplemental information is often part of the main description in those hikes.

Hiking table

The following table summarizes the trips and also indicates

whether the trips are backpacks or dayhikes. Some trips are suitable for dayhikes *or* backpacks. Dayhikes listed as "Side trips" are treated as side trips from a point that you must drive to or backpack to and that you stay overnight at. Backpacks show the number of hiking days for the least strenuous trip. A dash under "Miles" means the total distance is negligible.

Hiking Table*

Trip Number and Name	Best As...	Type	Difficulty	Miles
West Maui Hikes				
W1, Waihee Ridge	Dayhike	O&B	Moderate	4 1/2
W2, Waihee Valley	Dayhike	O&B	Moderate	4 1/4
W3, Halekii-Pihana	Dayhike	O&B	Very easy	2/5
W4, Kahana Pond	Dayhike	O&B	Very easy	—
W5, Kepaniwai Park	Dayhike	Loop	Very easy	2/3
W6, Iao Nature Trail	Dayhike	Semiloop	Very easy	1/4
W7, Needle Overlook	Dayhike	O&B	Very easy	1/3
W8, Streamside	Dayhike	O&B	Easy	1 1/5
W9, Maalaea Beach	Dayhike	O&B	Moderate	4
W10, Olowalu	Dayhike	O&B	Easy	1
W11, Malo's Grave	Dayhike	O&B	Strenuous	4 1/2
W12, D.T. Fleming	Dayhike	Semiloop	Easy	1 3/4
W13, Nakalele	Dayhike	O&B	Easy	1
East Maui Hikes				
E1, Waikamoi Ridge	Dayhike	Loop	Easy	1/3–1 1/8
E2, Arboretum	Dayhike	O&B	Easy	1
E3, Puaa Kaa	Dayhike	O&B	Very easy	—
E4, Ulaino Road	Dayhike	O&B	Moderate	4
E5, Caves	Dayhike	O&B	Very easy	1/5
E6, Black Sand Beach	Dayhike	O&B	Very easy	1/10
E7, King's Hwy-North	Dayhike	O&B	Moderate	2 2/3
E8, King's Hwy-*Heiau*	Dayhike	O&B	Easy	1 1/2
E9, King's Hwy-Bay	Dayhike	O&B	Strenuous	5
E10, Hana Bay	Dayhike	O&B	Very easy	2/3
E11, Oheo Gulch/Pools	Dayhike	Loop	Very easy	2/3

* Abbreviations: b'pk = backpack; da = day; O&B = out-and-back

Hiking Table (continued)*

Trip Number and Name	Best As...	Type	Difficulty	Miles
E12, Makahiku Falls	Dayhike	O&B	Easy	2/3
E13, Waimoku Falls	Dayhike	O&B	Moderate	4
E14, Kaupo to Bndy	Dayhike	O&B	Strenuous	6 1/2
E15, Fuchsia Wall	Dayhike	O&B	Moderate	3
E16, Kahua Road	Dayhike	O&B	Strenuous	9
E17, Skyline Road	Dayhike	O&B	Strenuous	13
E18, King's Hwy-Kanaio	Dayhike	O&B	Moderate	4
E19, Puu Olai	Dayhike	Semiloop	Moderate	1 1/2
E20, Polo Beach	Dayhike	O&B	Very easy	2/3
E21, Kamaole Beach	Dayhike	O&B	Very easy	1
Haleakala Hikes				
H1, Hosmer Grove	Dayhike	Loop	Very easy	2/3
H2, Supply Trail	Dayhike	O&B	Strenuous	5 1/3
H3, Halemauu-View	Dayhike	O&B	Easy	1 1/2
H4, Halemauu-Holua	Dayhike 2-da b'pk	O&B O&B	Strenuous Moderate	8 8
H5, Holua-Kapalaoa	Side trip	Semiloop	Strenuous	6
H6, Halemauu-Paliku	3-da b'pk	O&B	Strenuous	20 2/3
H7, Paliku-Bndy	Side trip	O&B	Strenuous	8
H8, Kalahaku	Dayhike	Loop	Very easy	1/5
H9, White Hill	Dayhike	O&B	Easy	1/2
H10, Rock Garden	Dayhike	O&B	Moderate	2
H11, Ka Lua o Ka Oo	Dayhike	O&B	Strenuous	4 3/4
H12, Sliding Sands-Kapalaoa	Dayhike 2-da b'pk	O&B O&B	Strenuous Moderate	12 1/2+ 12 1/2+
H13, Kapalaoa-Holua	Side trip	Semiloop	Strenuous	8 2/3
H14, Slidling Sands-	2-da b'pk	O&B	Strenuous	19 1/2
H15, Sliding Sands-Halemauu	Dayhike	Shuttle	Strenuous	13
H16, Grand Crater Tour	3-da b'pk	Shuttle	Strenuous	20
H17, Red Hill	Dayhike	Loop	Very easy	—

* Abbreviations: b'pk = backpack; da = day; O&B = out-and-back

Kiawe tree and beach morning-glory, Maalaea Beach

Trip W1. Waihee Ridge

M

Distance: 4½ miles	
Elevation gain: 1500′	
Hiking time: 2¼ hours	

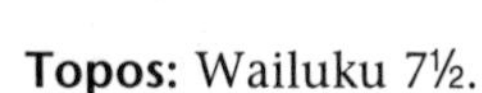

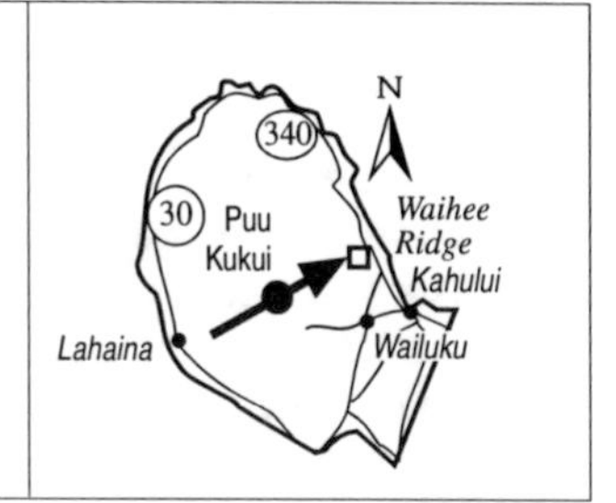

Topos: Wailuku 7½.

Trail map (route approximated): At the end of this trip.

Highlights: On this route, you ascend from pasturelands to a ridge that reaches into the rainforest of the West Maui Mountains. Weather permitting, several points offer sweeping views over Waihee Valley and the isthmus, even to the western slopes of Haleakala. An early-morning start may put you at the top here before the clouds roll in.

Driving instructions: From Wailuku (intersection of High Street (Highway 30) and Main Street (Highway 32) drive 2 short blocks east on Main Street to Market Street, where you turn left (north). Market Street is a one-way street (for northbound traffic) for the next few blocks. Follow Market Street down through Old Wailuku and uphill as it becomes Highway 330 to a **Y**-junction with Highway 340. Bear left (northwest) on Highway 340 through Waihee town; look for the school on your left. At 6¾ miles from Wailuku and 2 miles beyond the school, you turn inland (left) through a gate onto a potholed 1-lane road to Camp Mahulia (a Boy Scout camp). Follow this road as it winds uphill for about ⅘ mile. Where the road bears right to Camp Mahulia, you should bear slightly left, off the road and up a small rise to a fence. Park near the fence, but don't block the gate. The trailhead is a few yards to the right of the gate.

Description: Don't let the mileage signs on this trail confuse you. For example, when I was there in June 1995, the trailhead sign said the trail was 3 miles long one way (it's much less, 2¼ miles as I measured it). The elapsed-mileage signs along the way were arranged so that the 1½-mile sign came before the 1¼-mile sign, and the 1¼-mile sign was the more accurate of the two!

Squeeze through the hiker's pass-through; you may have to take your pack off to do so. Near the fence you may notice some bush-sized plants with globular yellow fruit. This is the deadly poisonous apple of Sodom, not the edible guava! Ahead of you, up the slope and southwest, the trail is marked by a few small, faded red signs saying RIGHT OF WAY (or, sometimes, R/W). The pasture is private property; the trail is a public right-of-way through it. Please stick to the right-of-way.

Follow the signs southwest up a faint, eroded track just to the right of a very steep, paved road. Keep a sharp eye out for cow pies, as this is a pasture. In ⅕ mile, veer left across the road, as indicated by a small sign, and pick up an obvious, wide, grassy track—an old road—that continues southwest up the slope toward a small wood of swamp mahogany, while the paved road levels out and curves right. Where the old road veers slightly to the left and forks, you take the right (lower) fork, contouring around a low, Christmas-berry-clad hill. Just as you start uphill again, look to your right (west-northwest) across Christmas berry and *kukui* trees for waterfalls plunging from the next major ridge.

At the ¼-mile marker, you enter a dense forest of guava and *kukui*. Soon you reach a locked gate, which you circumvent by scrambling down some slippery, muddy rocks to another narrow hiker's pass-through. Now you get to scramble back up to the road on some more slippery, muddy rocks on the other side. A few Norfolk pines grace the left side of the road here. Stay on the road and ignore a track that leaves the road going uphill on your left.

At a saddle the trail bears right (north-northwest) through guava and strawberry guava, emerging amid eucalyptuses just before the ½-mile marker. It's a single-track trail now, and you soon make a long switchback leg as you climb a hill. At the switchback turn, the waterfalls you saw earlier are even more visible. Ahead, there's a wonderful viewpoint overlooking the isthmus. Just past the ¾-mile marker, you have your first good view into the deep slash of Waihee Valley and into the steep gullies in its southern rim, their dark-green forest canopies slashed by the brash light green of *kukui*. (To hike in Waihee Valley, see Trip W2.)

Now you dip across a long saddle to another hiker's pass-through—the last one, thank goodness. Beyond here, a pattern emerges: you make a few switchbacks, contour across a slope for a while, then switchback again. You're soon climbing, and you may need a spider stick here. Huge land snails swim slowly across the damp trail, which is framed by ferns and by the handsome, native *ohia* tree. Look for the red *apapane* bird in this shrubbery. The trail becomes narrow, steep, and slippery here, but there's a fine panorama over West Maui's northwest coast and the isthmus.

You cross a narrow saddle just beyond the 1½-mile marker, climb a razorback ridge, switchback up a knob, and then traverse the knob's west side through some paperbark eucalyptuses and Norfolk pines. Soon you descend slightly through tall, purple-flowered weeds and squish across a muddy track through a meadow to the next hill west. Here, you contour, climb, and switchback again, passing some mountain *naupaka* shrubs as you go. Tall sedges and branched ferns appear. *Ieie*, a vine whose leaf clusters make it look like a series of miniature palm trees, twines up dwarfed *ohia* trees, and the going is very muddy.

At the top of the hill, "Lanilili 2563" on the topo, you reach a small, grassy area with a picnic table and an END OF TRAIL sign. Weather permitting, there are far-ranging views from this little summit; look for high waterfalls deep in the misty canyons of West Maui's mountains. But it's more likely that the clouds will have closed in around you, leaving you alone in this silent, rain forest world. Wait a few minutes; maybe the clouds will part. In either case, you'll enjoy taking a rest and having a snack here.

When you're ready, return the way you came.

Bad guys in the brush.... Non-native, invading plants you'll pass as you cross the pasture include the little "bashful plant" with its small, pink powderpuff blossoms and tiny, ferny leaves that fold shut when you stroke them. A real hiker's pest is a clover with tiny, innocent, cherry-pink blossoms and strings of tiny, not-so-innocent, sticky seeds which you will find in abundance on your boots and socks at the end of this trip. Try to pick them all off and leave them here before you drive away. Spikes of blue-flowered cayenne vervain wave amidst the grasses, too. Copses of the Christmas berry tree dot the slopes; look for its seasonal clusters of tiny red, inedible berries. Finally, you can't help but notice clumps of that aggressive invader lantana, with its brilliant pink, orange, and yellow blossoms, rough, dark green leaves, and thorny limbs. Bashing through lantana—not yet necessary on this trip—is a hiker's nightmare. Even if you succeed in making your way through it, lantana will leave bare arms and legs so scratched that they look like street maps and will leave clothing and skin covered with its strong, herbal fragrance.

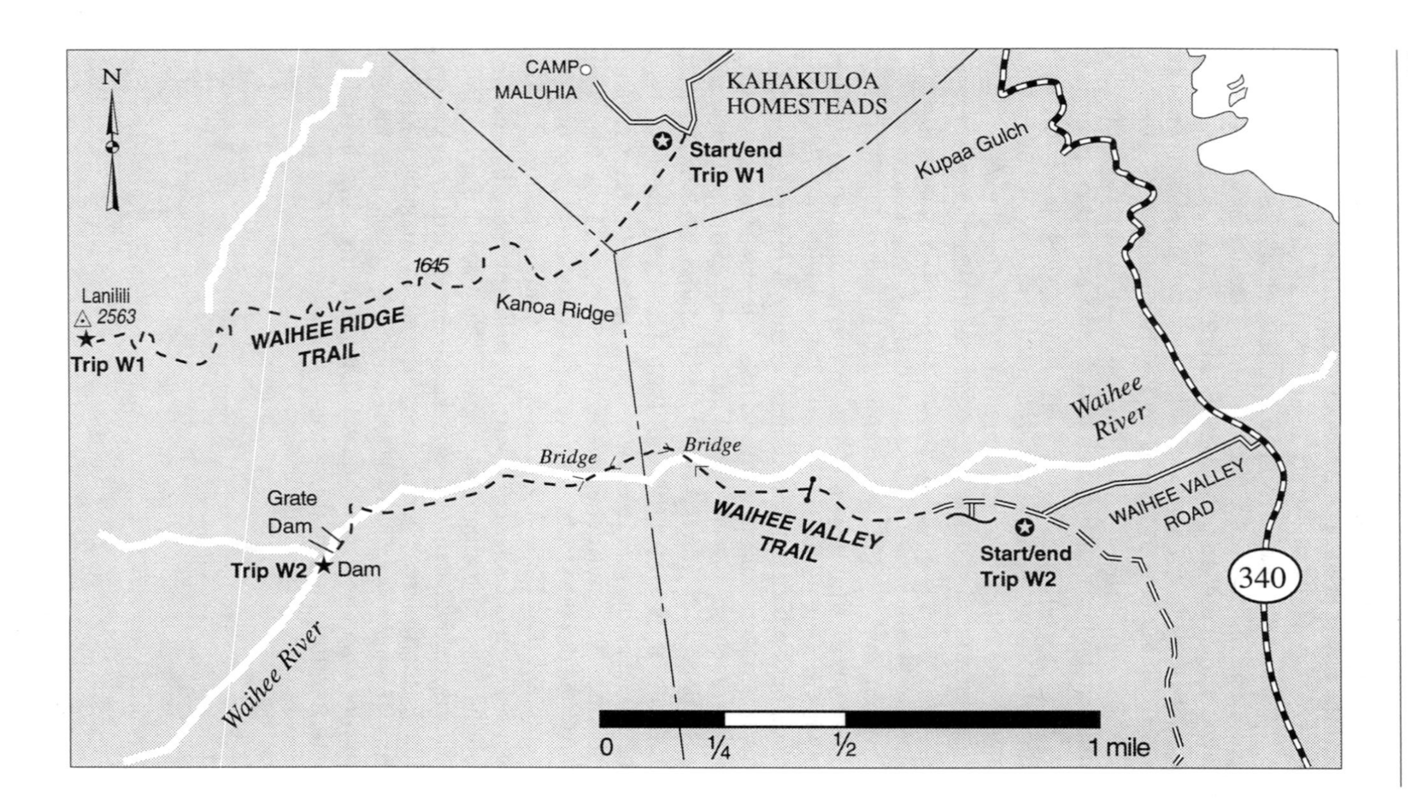
N
CAMP
MALUHIA
KAHAKULOA HOMESTEADS
Start/end Trip W1
Kupaa Gulch
1645
Lanilili
2563
Trip W1
WAIHEE RIDGE TRAIL
Kanoa Ridge
Waihee River
Bridge
Bridge
Grate
Dam
Trip W2
Dam
WAIHEE VALLEY TRAIL
Start/end Trip W2
WAIHEE VALLEY ROAD
340
Waihee River
0
1/4
1/2
1 mile

Trip W2. Waihee Valley

Distance: 4¼ miles

Elevation gain: 370′

Hiking time: 2+ hours

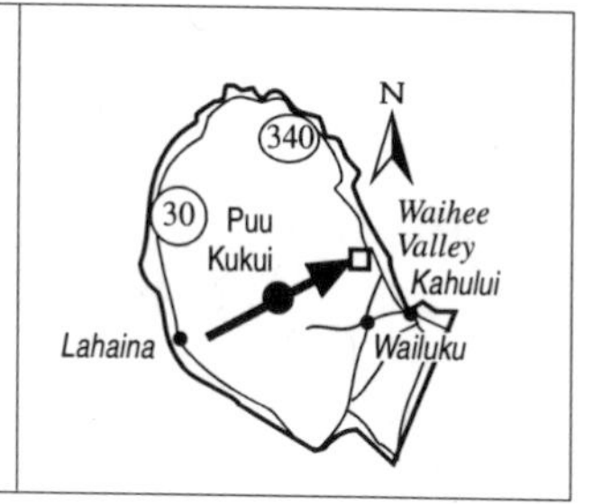

Topos: Wailuku 7½.

Trail map (route approximated): At the end of Trip W1.

Highlights: This may be the best of the rainforest stream-valley walks on Maui. The luxuriant, exotic forest and tricky footbridge crossings treat you to a fine combination of beauty, novelty, and excitement. Don't forget your jungle juice and rain gear: Waihee Valley is Mosquito Central and very rainy.

Driving instructions: Follow the driving instructions of Trip W1 to Waihee town; look for the school on your left as you pass through town. Turn left (inland) onto Waihee Valley Road just over ½ mile past the school. Follow Waihee Valley Road for another ½ mile or less, but no farther than the **T**-junction where the pavement ends at a cane road, just over 4½ miles from Wailuku. Look for a place to park off the road; please don't block anyone's driveway. (The dirt road becomes impassable to passenger vehicles well before there's another place to park off the road safely.)

Permit/permission required: From Wailuku Agribusiness; see "Getting Permits and Permission."

Description. Walk up to the **T**-junction, where this trip starts. Turn right (west) and follow the road past *mao*, reeds, guavas, and Koster's curse. An irrigation ditch, mostly hidden by the shrubbery, bubbles along downhill on your right, bringing water to some taro patches. *Lilikoi* vines festoon some trees, morning-glory vines others. Ignore the side road a little beyond ⅒ mile. Your road soon becomes very rocky and potholed; if it's rained recently, there may be huge puddles to get around. This road continues up the valley, though the topo shows it swinging south.

You cross a dry streambed and bear west-northwest uphill under *kukui* and swamp mahogany trees to a rain gauge. Here the road bears west again, and near ⅓ mile you pass a couple of defunct cable gates. Ferns abound here, sword fern on your left, sweet fern downhill on your right.

Nearing ½ mile, you level out at an open spot; ahead, there's a steep gully filled with *kukui* trees. On your left, the irrigation ditch flows through a tunnel under Java plum and Christmas berry trees. Soon the road reaches a locked gate. Duck under the gate or swing around the posts and then follow the road northwest along the ditch. In the next ½ mile, you pass mango trees, ginger plants, and some banyan trees with spectacular roots. The road twists west and northwest, sometimes along the ditch, and always above the river, which is mostly hidden by the rainforest vegetation.

At last, near 1 mile, the rocky riverbed comes into view about 30 feet below. "Cathedral columns" of banyan roots rise on the uphill (left) side of the road. You hop across the ditch where it flows across the road and presently reach the first of Waihee Valley's swinging footbridges. Because of the way the irrigation system diverts water, the riverbed may be dry at this point. Still, who can pass up a chance to cross a bridge that's straight out of an Indiana Jones epic? Carefully climb the stairs to gain the wire-cable-and-plank bridge. You'll want to hold on tightly as you cross, because not only does the narrow tread bounce as you go, but it's noticeably tilted to one side. Watch out for frayed wire ends protruding from the cables you hold onto; they can inflict nasty cuts. Descend carefully on the other side, where there are no steps down from the bare bridge support. But there are lots of stones wrapped in leaves—offerings from travelers grateful for a safe crossing.

Bear left (southwest) into the forest on a narrow track that winds along the bank of a tributary. The next swinging bridge is just a few minutes down the trail. Over the bridge and on the other side now, you bear northwest into the forest on the path from the end of the bridge. Bamboo thickets often line one side or the other of the river along this stretch. At a **T**-junction at 1⅓ miles (not shown on the map), you turn left (west; uphill); the right branch is a spur trail to the river. It's worth your while to pause at open spots to look for cascades high on the lush green walls across the river.

You reach a spot where you have to ford the river—not dry here—on some extremely slippery boulders. Beyond the ford, you bear southwest into the forest under arches of hau and past riverbank bamboo thickets. You soon ford the river again near 1¾ miles, where banyans shade pools upstream and downstream. Across the river, you briefly follow a dry, very rocky streambed to a footpath that goes steeply up on your left a short way, past some elaborate tree roots, and levels out as a muddy track. The track soon climbs again to meet the dry channel of an out-of-use ditch. Under a canopy of *kukui*, the track briefly follows the ditch, crosses a streambed, and, almost abreast of a ruined shed, passes some old flow-control machinery for the ditch system. A spur trail leads right to an overlook of a low dam topped by a grate on which fallen guavas may be trapped.

As the vegetation thins, you see the Waihee River foaming along on your right. Just beyond the 2-mile point, one short, steep, downhill pitch and a few level yards bring you to the foot of a dam and to the end of the trail. There are a few spots to plop down for lunch here, and a deep pool below the dam makes a fine swimming hole. The steep concrete wall that descends from the trail to the pool has iron brackets set into it to form a ladder to help you get in and out of the pool.

When you're through with your lunch and swim, return the way you came. Ideally, you'd have views down the valley to the ocean on your way back, but the vegetation is too dense for that.

But this is the rainy side.... Rainwater coursing down the sides of a has volcano created streams that have cut the many canyons you see as you drive around Maui. Logic tells you that the greater volume of water falling on the rainy side of a volcano ought cut more and bigger canyons than on the dry side. Yet here on the rainy side of West Maui, there are fewer deep stream canyons than there are on the dry, leeward side of West Maui. What could account for the difference?

According to *Maui: How It Came To Be*, it's the relative hardness or softness of the lavas, not the volume of the streams, that makes the difference on West Maui. The lavas of West Maui's second period of volcanism are harder than those of its initial period of volcanism. The rainy side is covered with a veneer of those harder lavas; the dry side is not. The veneer on the rainy side resists erosion better than the softer material from the initial period, which is exposed on the dry side. That's why the rainy side of West Maui is visibly less eroded than the dry side. On the dry side, the smaller streams have eroded the softer material to create an exotic landscape of deep tropical valleys separated by narrow ridges, of broad alluvial plains, and of one magnificent beach after another—a breathtaking sight!

Swinging bridge in Waihee Valley

Trip W3. Halekii-Pihana *Heiau* State Monument

V

Distance: ⅖ mile

Elevation gain: Negligible

Hiking time: 13 minutes

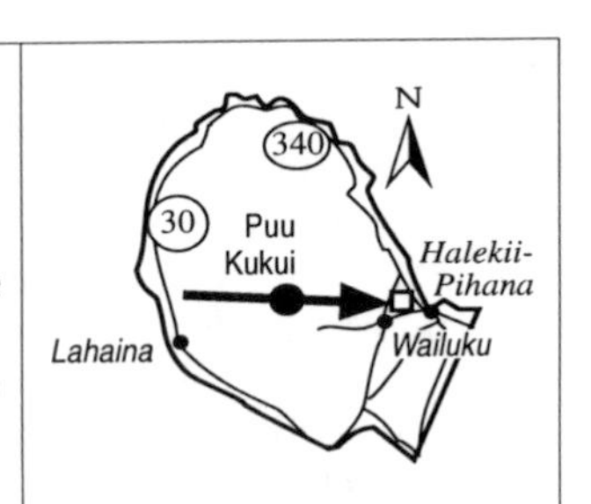

Topos: Optional: Wailuku 7½.

Trail map (route approximated): At the end of this trip.

Highlights: Halekii-Pihana *Heiau* (temple) State Monument has been overlooked by visitors, judging by its state of neglect, but it has features of geological and historical interest, as you'll see. It offers some fine views over the isthmus, too; just ignore the light-industrial areas surrounding the monument. Early in the morning on a clear day, you can see Haleakala from top to bottom from here, backlit against the eastern sky.

Driving instructions: This one's hard to find, which may be one reason it's so neglected. You can't get there directly from Wailuku, no matter what it looks like on the road map. Instead, you need to take a rather circuitous route. Follow the driving instructions of Trip W1 as far as the junction with Highway 340. Here, turn right onto Highway 340, back toward Wailuku and Kahului. Just as the road begins to climb a little, turn right on Kuhio Place. Go a couple of blocks to Hea Place (there's a very faded Hawaii Visitors Bureau sign on the corner), turn left onto Hea Place, and wind up the short, steep road through the gate to the parking area, 3½ miles from Wailuku. The monument is open from 7 A.M. to 7 P.M., but it's best to come early in the morning. Local people enjoy having lunch up here and socializing here later on. The parking lot can be jam-packed then!

Permit/permission required: None.

Description. An asphalt-paved trail leads south away from the parking lot, but the first feature you'll want to see is at the south end of the lot to the right of the trailhead. Look at the delicate layering pattern exposed in the low, sandy cliff face here. How fragile these thin layers are, almost crumbling into loose sand under the pressure of your gaze. What you're seeing is a cross-section of a lithified sand dune—that's right, a sand dune turned to stone! Much of the isthmus is covered with similar sand dunes, which generally consist of a stony crust and an unconsolidated interior (see below for more on how they formed). Many years ago, your view from here would have swept across sand dunes covered with *kiawe* trees instead of homes and factories. The dunes yield readily to the bulldozer's blade, as you can see in nearby construction sites.

Climb steeply but briefly on the paved path to the top of Halekii *Heiau,* where there's a bare cement circle for a now-missing water tank. Halekii *Heiau* was restored under the direction of anthropologists from the Bishop Museum in 1958. The path becomes a dirt trail now, and a few milo and hala trees dot the barren plateau. Stray to your left to look down the slope, where elaborate, chambered stone terraces descend to Iao Stream some 160 feet below. According to *Maui: How It Came To Be,* a meander of Iao Stream is gradually undercutting the hill on which these massive structures stand, and eventually they will collapse into its gully. Across an intervening gully to the southeast, you'll see a huge, triangular, stonework wall of Pihana *Heiau* exposed. The great boulders it's made of weigh about 3 times as much as a full-grown adult, yet they are fitted snugly together here without mortar—a work of great skill and dedication.

Follow the path south across a ridge, descending very slightly. The path, as wide as a road here, turns left (east) as you reach a ridge that connects it with the ridge Pihana *Heiau* is on. Look for more evidence of lithified sand dunes along here. *Koa haole* forms thickets from which your approach may flush game birds; *kiawe* trees spread their feathery leaves over the ruins of Pihana and fill the gully below it. In the grass around you, you'll find *mao* (a wild, native relative of cotton), Chinese violets, and a passionflower vine called love-in-a-mist. (Lacy bracts covering buds and fruits distinguish this passionflower from its larger relatives like the edible *lilikoi* and the pesky banana passionflower.)

Now the path bears left (east) and a little uphill to Pihana's simple marker. From here, you can turn left again and walk north a few more steps to the top of the triangular wall you admired from Halekii for a different view of it and for fine views of the landscape.

Return the way you came. Driving back, you'll probably notice other lithified sand dunes exposed by the road cuts. (Also when driving back, you'll need to dodge left or right to avoid the one-way segment of Market Street.)

Lithified *whats?...* Of all the things that might turn to stone, a sand dune seems one of the least likely. What are sand dunes of this size and extent doing here between two volcanoes, anyway? The dunes rest on lava flows from Haleakala which have piled up against West Maui. And, according to *Maui: How It Came To Be*, the dunes are in a way the work of the great, far-away glaciers of the Ice Ages. Each Ice Age lowered the level of the oceans by locking water up in glaciers. The lower ocean level exposed wide, sandy beaches at the isthmus. Trade winds piled the sand over the isthmus "into long ridges, sorting it into coarse and fine layers." Plants took root on the dunes, anchoring them. Carbonic acid from the roots dissolved a constituent of the sand, calcium carbonate, which is insoluble in water. The dissolved calcium percolated through the layers, changing as it went back to calcium carbonate, which is a natural cement and which bound the sand grains together. It was this cementing process that produced the stony layers. Beneath them, as you can see, less-cemented sand now exposed to weathering has fallen away from the stony part to form pockets where new plants can grow.

The shield volcanoes of Maui, Molokai, Lanai, and Kahoolawe meet at relatively shallow depths in the sea now. It's believed that when the ocean level was lower during the Ice Ages, the four islands were joined above sea level to form an island, called Maui-nui, which would have been about half the size of the present Big Island of Hawaii. On all the islands, erosional features attributed to wave action now lie below as well as above present sea level. They're interpreted as testifying to higher as well as lower sea levels than at present—and to the power of glaciers far to the north to reshape these tropical islands.

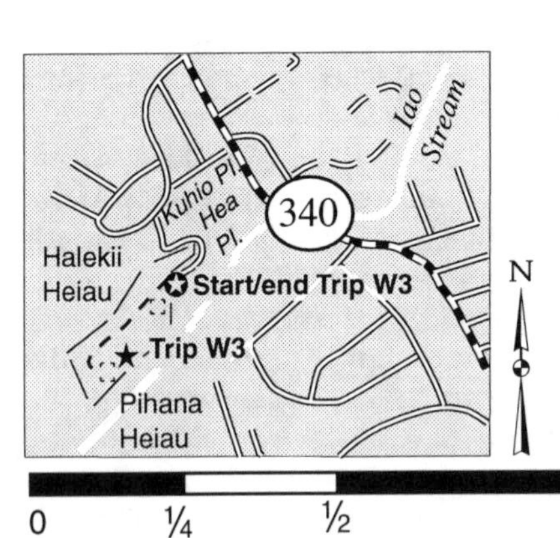

Trip W4. Kanaha Pond

 	**Distance:** Negligible* **Elevation gain:** Negligible **Hiking time:** Less than 5 minutes	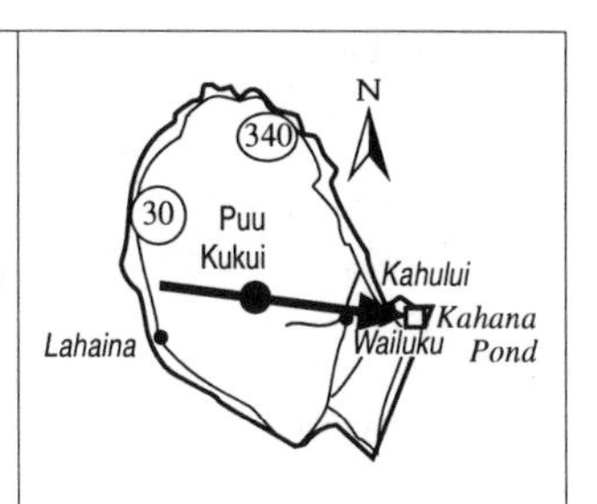

Topos: Optional: Wailuku, Paia 7½.
Trail map: At the end of this trip.
Highlights: Waterfowl, especially in the winter, when Kanaha Pond is home to many migratory birds. Birders will want to bring their binoculars and guides along.
Driving instructions: From Wailuku, drive east on Highway 32 past Maui Community College to the point where the main highway bears southeast (right) to become Highway 36 (the Hana Highway). Stay in the left lane here, because in a few blocks you'll bear left (east) onto Haleakala Road where a sign says this is the way to Kahului Airport. You'll be on Haleakala Road for barely a block. As you head toward the airport, you'll notice a large, fenced, undeveloped area on your left. Look for a barely visible turnoff to the left into the undeveloped area. It's hard to spot in time; if you reach the junction with Highway 380, you've gone too far, so turn around and go back. There's a small parking lot here for Kanaha Pond's observation shelter, 3⅓ miles from Wailuku.
Permit/permission required: None.
Description. Walk through the gate (be sure to close it) and out to the observation shelter, about 100 yards. The concrete benches here are not particularly comfortable, but the shelter does help conceal your presence. Ignore the occasional roar of airplane engines and the smell of jet fuel as you concentrate on watching the birds. Year-round residents include noisy, black-necked stilts (*aeo*) with red legs and in black and white plumage so formal-looking as to rival that of the "tuxedo-clad" penguin; plump, white-beaked coots (*alae ke okeo*, close relatives of the "mudhens" from whom, according to Hawaiian legend, the demigod Maui stole the secret of fire); and black-crowned night-herons (*aukuu*), the juveniles of which are brown with white streaks.

Birds are more numerous in the winter, when many migratory species winter over here. Still, a visit at any time is rewarding and

*Other trips possible; see text.

educational. I watched a young night-heron stand so still for so long, not even blinking, that I decided it was a decoy stuck into the mud to attract other birds. A black-necked stilt came poke-poke-poking along through the mud almost to the motionless heron's feet—yes, that heron was a decoy—and *fwoom!* the heron snapped back to life and flapped away.

Retrace your steps to your car.

***Other Kanaha Pond trips....** There are other, longer trails into Kanaha Pond Wildlife Sanctuary, particularly on the airport side. However, construction activity can block public access from time to time. Call the Division of Forestry and Wildlife in Wailuku to find out which of the other trails, if any, are open. See "Getting Permits or Permission" in this book for their telephone number.

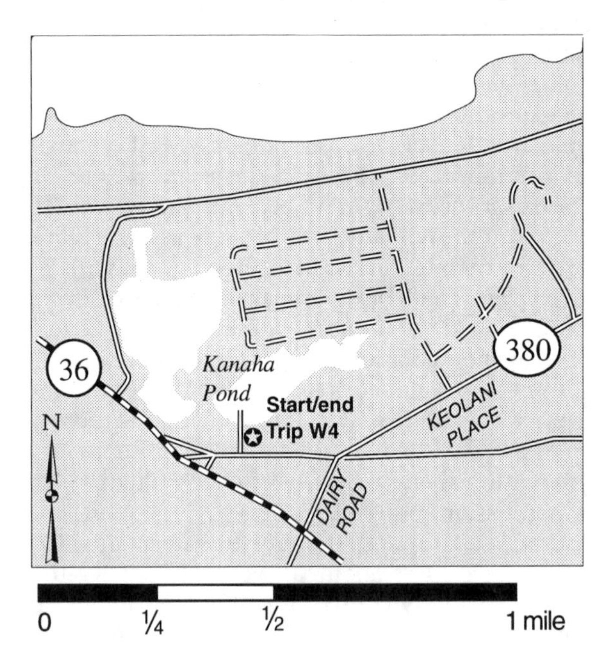

Trip W5. Kepaniwai County Park

V

Distance: ⅔ mile

Elevation gain: Negligible

Hiking time: 20 minutes

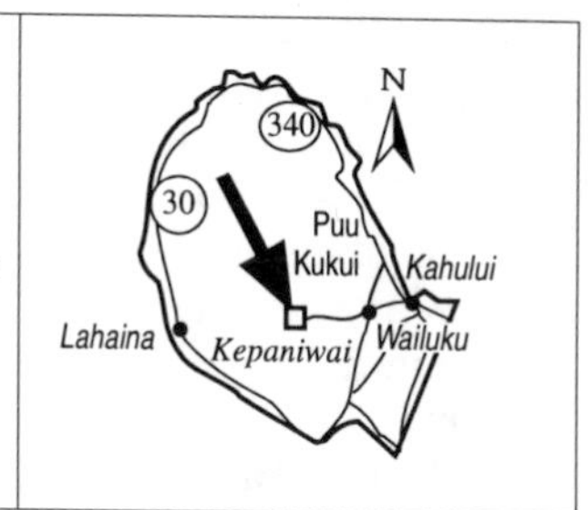

Topos: Optional: Wailuku 7½.

Trail map (no particular route shown, as so many are possible): At the end of this trip.

Highlights: Kepaniwai County Park, in beautiful Iao Valley, offers a unique opportunity to remember the people who immigrated to Hawaii long ago. The park also offers plenty of pavilions where you can picnic.

Don't miss the Hawaii Nature Center in Iao Valley near Kepaniwai County Park. Hawaii Nature Center personnel lead daily hikes (fee) in Iao Valley. Write or call in advance for more information; include a SASE. They're at 875 Iao Valley Road, Wailuku, Maui, HI 96793, (808) 244-6500.

Driving instructions: From the intersection of Main Street (Highway 32) and High Street (Highway 30) in downtown Wailuku, drive west (toward the mountains) on Main Street, past the Maui Historical Society Museum ("Bailey House"). At a fork in the road, take the right fork slightly downhill to the turn-in (on your left) for Kepaniwai Park, just over 2 miles from downtown Wailuku.

Permit/permission required: None.

Description. The principal feature of Kepaniwai County Park is a series of "pavilions"—gardens, paths, streams, miniature homes, and monuments—in honor of the major ethnic groups that settled in Hawaii over the past 1300 years: Polynesians, people of Northern European descent (New England missionaries), Chinese, Japanese, Portuguese, and Filipinos. You can wander along the pleasant maze of walkways and waterways, across miniature bridges, and past simple replicas of typical houses as long as you wish. If you belong to a group represented here, you may wish to go to that "pavilion" first in honor of your ethnic kin; see the map following this trip.

Or you may want to try this exercise in historical imagination. Walk to each "pavilion" in turn and imagine yourself in the place of someone emigrating from that land to distant Hawaii over a hundred or more years ago. Stand near the door of the miniature house. Imagine that it's your home, which you are leaving forever, as far as you know. At least 2000 miles of open, wild ocean lie between you and a strange land called Hawaii. What draws you to Hawaii? Are you pulled toward Hawaii by hope for a better life, by a love of adventure, or by a commitment to saving souls? Or are you pushed toward Hawaii by hopeless conditions at home, by banishment, or by a vow to follow someone else? Friends and relatives whom you will never see or hear again call farewell to you; you try in these last few minutes to fix their faces in your memory. But the ship is ready to sail; you can wait no longer. You pick up your few belongings, take a deep breath, and walk away toward your new life....

Or you may prefer simply to stroll along, appreciating this pretty little park and its monuments. You'll certainly want to spend more time here than the distance given above would suggest. When you're ready to leave, you'll probably just make a beeline for your car, as the parking lot is more or less central to the park.

Battle of Kepaniwai.... Life in old Hawaii was far from peaceful. In 1790, Kahekili, king of Maui, was trying to conquer Oahu as part of his plan to conquer all the islands. He had left his son Kalanikupule to rule Maui in his absence. Kahekili was well on his way to achieving his objective, but he wasn't the only ambitious chief. The chief who would ultimately succeed in ruling all the islands, Kamehameha, attacked Maui in Kahekili's absence. With the help of European guns, Kamehameha defeated Kalanikupule here at Kepaniwai. So fierce and bloody was the battle of Kepaniwai that the corpses dammed Iao Stream. Kalanikupule escaped from Kamehameha this time, fleeing up Iao Valley, over the ridge, and down to Olowalu. They would meet again.

Kahekili wrested Maui away from Kamehameha and was king of all the islands but Hawaii—for a while. He soon lost control of Kauai and Niihau. After old Kahekili died, the islands were divided between Kalanikupule and Kahekili's younger brother, Kaeo. Kalanikupule and Kaeo coveted each other's share of Kahekili's islands, and soon they were at war. Needing modern weapons, Kalanikupule enlisted the help of Americans and Europeans, including the services of two British ships. With their aid, he defeated Kaeo's forces on Oahu, killing Kaeo in the battle. Now Kalanikupule became ambitious to oust Kamehameha from the Big Island and to rule all the islands. He thought he could do so if he controlled those fine British ships and their weapons, so he murdered the ships' captains and took the crews as prisoners. Kamehameha learned of Kalanikupule's plans when the ships' crews rebelled and fled to the Big Island, and, before sailing for China, presented Kamehameha with the ships' armaments and apprised him of Kalanikupule's plots. Kamehameha pursued his rival, conquering first Maui and then Molokai. He caught up with Kalanikupule on Oahu and defeated him at the terrible battle of Nuuanu Pali in 1795. Kalanikupule escaped once more and wandered in the mountains of Oahu for some months before he was captured and sacrified to Kamehameha's war god.

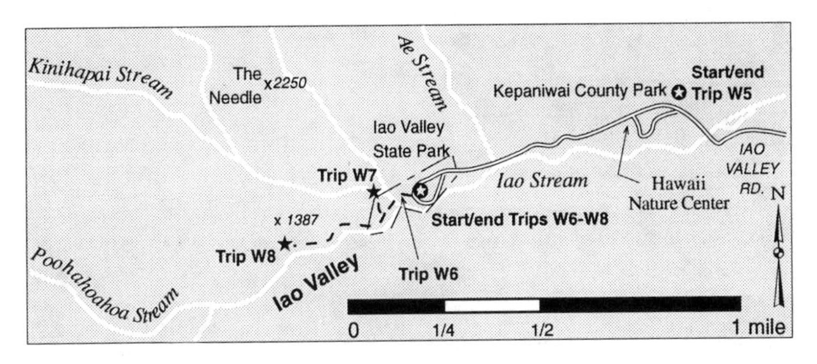

Overview: Kepaniwai County Park and Iao Valley State Park

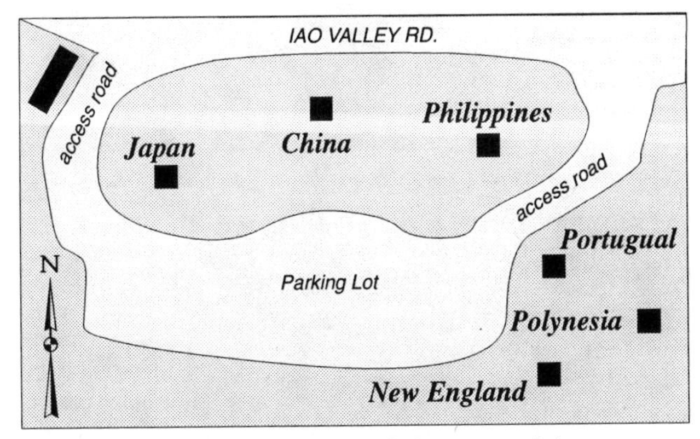

Closeup: Kepaniwai County Park (not to scale)

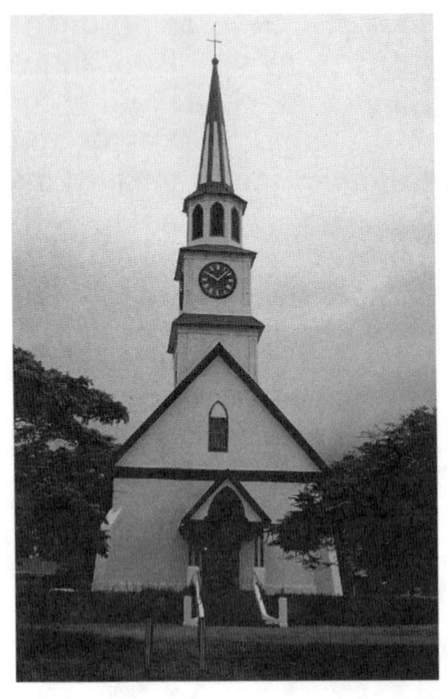

The steeple of Kaahumanu Church, built in 1837, is a prominent landmark at High and Main streets in Wailuku, on the way to Kepaniwai County Park and Iao Valley State Park. Bailey House (Maui Historical Society Museum) on Main Street is just out of sight behind the church

In Kepaniwai County Park: Japanese pavilion at left, Chinese pavilion in background at right

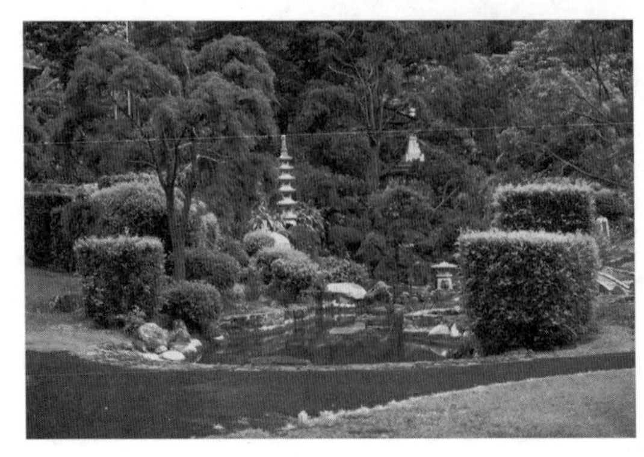

Lush greenery, shrines, pools, and streams line Kepaniwai's garden paths

Trip W6. Iao Valley State Park: Nature Trail

V

Distance: ¼ mile

Elevation gain: 60′ (upside-down trip)

Hiking time: Less than 10 minutes

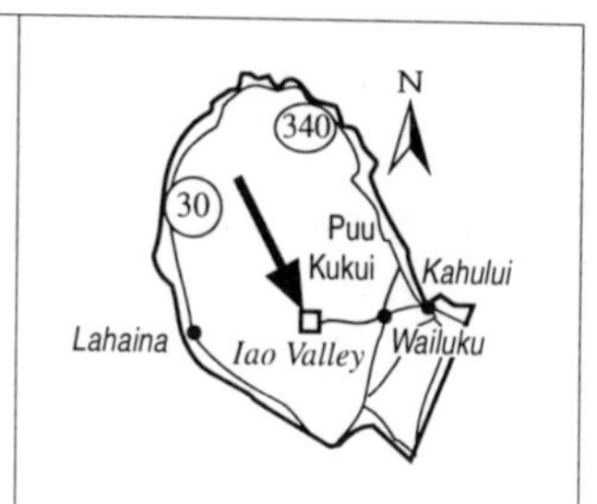

Topos: Optional: Wailuku 7½

Trail map (route approximated): At the end of Trip W5; close-up at the end of this trip.

Highlights: This pleasant trail takes you down through handsome tropical plants to Iao Stream. As of this writing, many of the plants are identified by signs at their bases, giving you a chance to learn the names of some of the non-native landscaping plants and a few of the native plants you'll see around Maui.

Iao Valley State Park is justly famous for its great beauty and draws many visitors. Often, its parking lot overflows by midday. The park's gates are open from 7 A.M. to 7 P.M. Be there around 7 A.M. to avoid the crowds (trust me: it's worth the trouble). Whatever else you do on Maui, I hope you'll make time for Iao Valley State Park!

Driving instructions: Follow the driving instructions of Trip W5 past Kepaniwai Park (on your left) to Iao Valley State Park, 2⅘ miles, at the end of the road.

Permit/permission required: None.

Description. From the end of the parking lot, walk west on the asphalt trail past the restrooms and drinking fountain. Trees and shrubs bordering the path include *kukui*, octopus tree, strawberry guava, and yellow ginger. Look for red and orange heliconia "blossoms" downslope on your left; the "blossoms" are actually the colorful bracts of the inconspicuous flowers. Just before you'd cross a footbridge, an asphalt path branches left (southwest), descending. Follow that path downhill past royal poinciana trees, angel's-trumpet trees, torch ginger, yellow heliconia, and many more splendid tropical plants. Some of them are sure to be in bloom while you're there, no matter when you visit! Soon you're at the loop portion of the trail (see the close-up at the end of this trip), where you wander around and through the loop as you wish.

Where the loop touches the streambank, there are wonderful views along Iao Stream, especially upstream to some cascasdes.

Close the loop when you've seen enough, and retrace your steps to your car if you're "hiked out." It's certainly feasible for most people to continue to the Needle overlook (Trip W7). Experienced hikers will have no trouble taking all the Iao Valley State Park hikes in this book (Trips W6 through W8) in half a day or less.

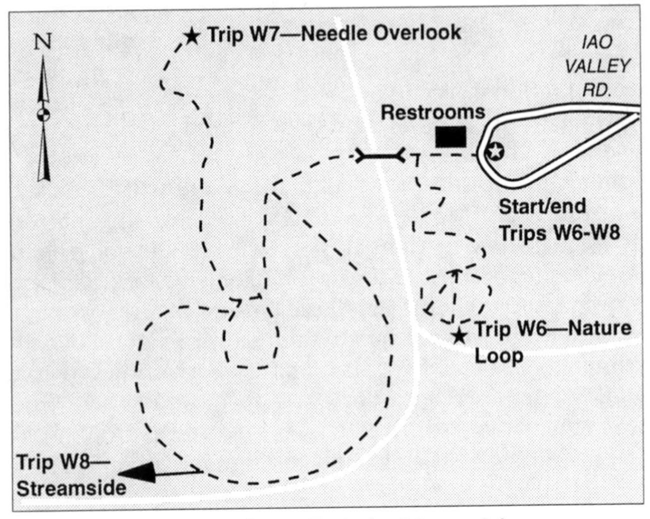

Close-up: Iao Valley State Park *(not to scale)*

Trip W7. Iao Valley State Park: Needle Overlook

V

Distance: 1/3 mile

Elevation gain: 110′

Hiking time: 10 minutes

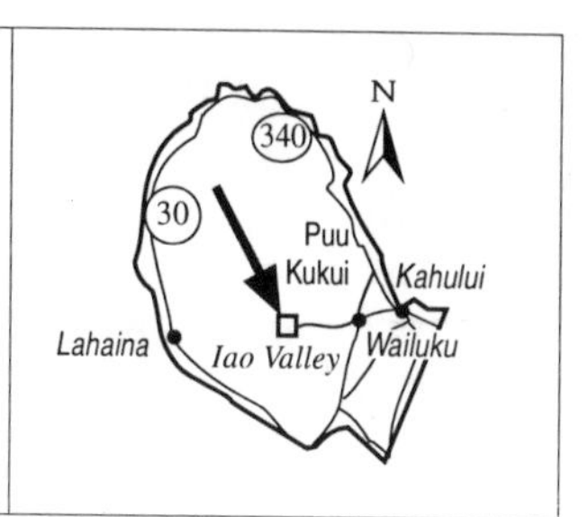

Topos: Optional: Wailuku 7½

Trail map (route approximated): At the end of Trips W5 and W6.

Highlights: A close-up view of West Maui's most famous scenic attraction, Iao Needle.

Driving instructions: Follow the driving instructions of Trip W6.

Permit/permission required: None.

Description. If you're a card-carrying couch potato, you can get a pretty decent view of Iao Needle from the end of the parking lot and let it go at that. But you'll probably want to see more of it, so follow Trip W6 to the trail junction just before the footbridge. The footbridge takes you safely across a tributary of Iao Stream. The bridge offers a wonderful view of the Needle. On the other side of the stream, curve left on the paved path. (The sign you may notice pointing to the right here does not point out a trail; it's pointing out the Needle to you, as if you hadn't already figured out that that big green thing *is* Iao Needle.)

The path climbs slightly past *ti*, giant philodendron, guava, and plumeria, quickly reaching another junction. You bear right at this fork, pass two more forks (bear sharply right at each), and continue climbing, now on stairs, toward the overlook. The going gets steeper, and there's an opportunity partway up the stairs to stop, rest, and enjoy the view. Climbing again, you soon reach the overlook with its shelter, benches, and pavilion. What wonderful views you have from here, just over 1/10 mile from the parking lot! You can see northwest toward Iao Needle, east down Iao Valley, and south toward the steep valley walls.

Retrace your steps to your car, or head off on another Iao hike, when you're ready.

What is Iao Needle?... The rocky material a volcano produces isn't uniform. Its mineral composition varies from one eruption to the next, so that cooled lava from one eruption may be harder than that from another eruption of the same volcano. Sometimes the lava is deposited as a flow, becoming dense and hard when it cools. Other times, it's spewed out as ash or clinker, small particles which may consolidate with time and with pressure from overlying material into a layer that is relatively soft and easily eroded. Older volcanic material cracks as it's stressed by later geological events. Newer, fluid lavas can invade these cracks, forming "dikes" of tough rock that can actually strengthen the older material.

Iao Needle is a lump of older material from the first phase of volcanic activity of West Maui. Later eruptions strengthened what would become Iao Needle by filling its cracks with numerous, newer dikes. When streams flowing down Puu Kukui's slopes scoured out Iao Valley from the old volcano's softer material, Iao Needle and its ridge withstood the streams' cutting forces. At 2250 feet high, Iao Needle now stands over 1200 feet above the valley floor. The streams long ago deposited the softer material as alluvium at the mouth of Iao Valley or carried it out to sea. Iao Needle appears to be a spire because from the park, you see its narrow southeast edge. From most other directions, it's the last big hump on a small, steep ridge which has several other humps.

Who's (or what's) that on the trail?....Besides the true wildlife, company you may have on most trails can include other hikers, hunters and their dogs, feral animals (goats and pigs), and lost hunting dogs. Be alert for vehicles when your trail is actually a road. Many trails on Maui pass through areas where hunting is legal. (The occasional terrible stench from some unidentifiable source may be a carcass rotting in the forest.)

You'll have to use your own judgment about how to handle what you meet. Here are some things that worked for me: You should *always* stay on established routes, trails, or roads in order to avoid being mistaken for a game animal. If you meet lost hunting dogs, try what one hunter advised me: tell them firmly, "Go home." Wild goats are very alert and shy; you can't get close to them. It's possible you'll surprise wild pigs rooting along the trail. Slow your pace to give them time to get away. Give vehicles the right-of-way.

Visitors enjoy excellent views of Iao Needle from the footbridge over a tributary of Iao Stream

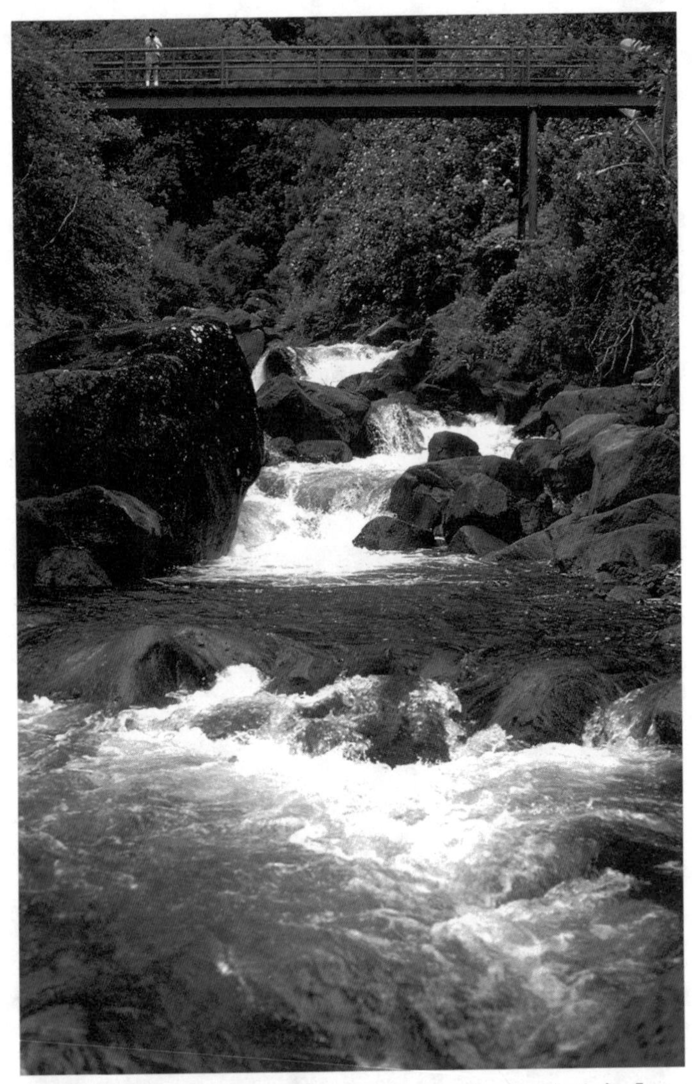

Rain-swollen and swift, a tributary on its way to join Iao Stream churns through dark basaltic rocks, dwarfing a visitor on the footbridge above

Trip W8. Iao Valley State Park: Streamside Walk

E

Distance: 1 1/5 miles

Elevation gain: 200′

Hiking time: 1/2+ hour

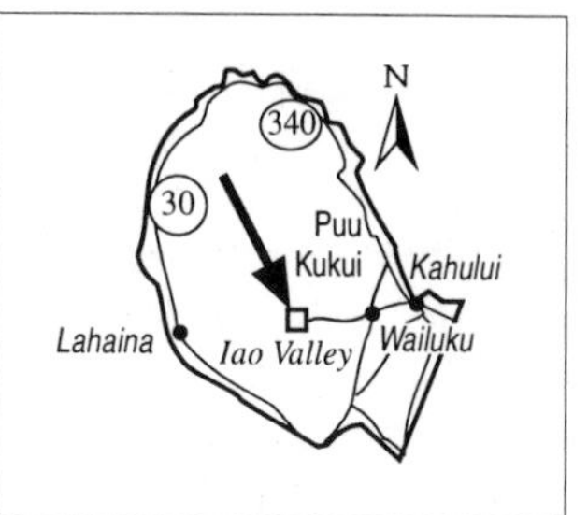

Topos: Optional: Wailuku 7 1/2

Trail map (route approximated): At the end of Trip W5.

Highlights: After enjoying the overlook of Iao Needle, you descend to one of the park's streams and enjoy a pretty streamside walk through a lush tropical landscape.

Driving instructions: Follow the driving instructions of Trip W6.

Permit/permission required: None.

Description. Follow Trip W7 to the Needle overlook and then retrace your steps to the last junction you passed as you came up. Turn right at this fork and almost immediately turn right again onto a trail that leads down to the stream. Descend on this trail under Christmas berry and guava, past fragrant yellow ginger, to a lovely overlook of the stream. An unpaved path branches west (right) away from this point; turn right onto it and pass under a big mango tree. Stay on the path as it veers right into the forest where a side track (not on the book's map) branches left down to the stream. Soon you climb a little to circumvent a hedge of ginger, descend, and climb again into a forest of guava, *ti*, and papaya.

At the next fork, you go left toward the stream, descending a little, to yet another fork (not on the book's map). You stay on the path by going right. (The left fork leads to a stream view under a huge guava tree.) The path dips past an exposed dirt-and-rock face and ends at a stony "beach" in a little over 1/3 mile from the paved path. There's an idyllic view upstream here, where the water bubbles merrily down a little cascade. A needle-like formation on the canyon wall opposite you proves that while Iao Needle may be the showiest of the needle formations here, it isn't the only such feature in the park. It's a pleasant spot to relax in and enjoy your lunch or eat those guavas you picked as you walked along this path.

When you're ready, retrace your steps to the junction with the paved trail. At that junction, continue ahead (right), descending, on the paved trail past mango and *kukui* to the confluence of two of the Park's streams. Curve around to the left on the paved trail, pausing to enjoy the scenery. There are some especially photo-worthy views upstream to Iao Needle and the footbridge. However, if you are tempted to scramble out onto one of the midstream boulders for a photo of the Needle, be aware that getting out there and back can be difficult, especially if your shoes don't have soles that grip when wet. You, your camera, and that great shot may go for an unscheduled swim.

Now the trail climbs steadily up toward the footbridge and the junction with the main trail. At that junction, turn right and retrace your steps to the parking lot.

Walking upstream.... It's tempting to continue working your way upstream when the trail ends, but that's not a good idea. Streambanks may be unstable or nonexistent, offering no safe foot passage, so you're forced to detour into the stream itself. But streambeds and their boulders are often very slippery, so you're risking injury if you try to hike up them. You may also find the water surprisingly deep and swift. Rain can quickly swell these streams (and all Hawaiian streams) to flood proportions. If the stream begins to rise, get away from it before you're caught in a flash flood! Finally, Iao Valley State Park is quite small. You are probably trespassing if you continue upstream beyond the end of a trail in Iao Valley State Park.

Poohahoahoa Stream

Trip W9. Maalaea Beach

M

Distance: 4 miles

Elevation gain: Negligible

Hiking time: 2 hours

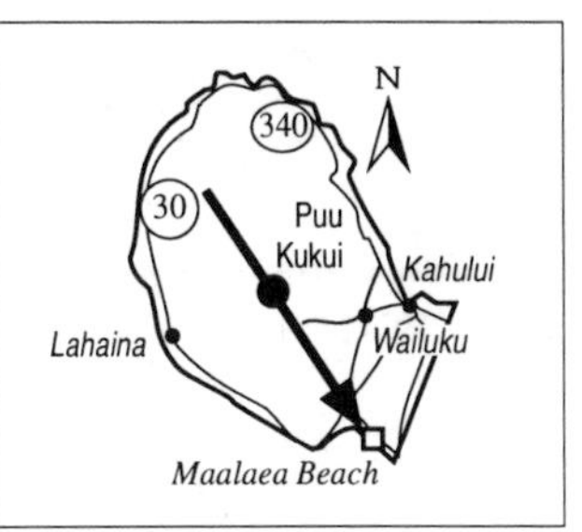

Topos: Optional: Maalaea $7\frac{1}{2}$.

Trail map (there's no trail as such; you just follow the shoreline): At the end of this trip.

Highlights: Maalaea (locally pronounced "mah-LY-ah") Bay, sometimes called "the nursery of the humpback whales," is a prime whale-watching spot during the winter months. Its long, narrow beach is presently unbroken by buildings for 2 miles and offers great views of Kahoolawe and of West or East Maui (Haleakala), depending on the direction you're walking. Wear tennis shoes or sandals you don't mind getting wet, so you can splash in the water if the surf's calm. This is best as a morning walk. By midday, the normal strong breezes will drive sand against you with stinging force, which is why you rarely see sunbathers on Maalaea Beach. (If it's not as windy as usual, consider making this a sunset hike. Sunset over West Maui from here can be a glorious spectacle!)

Driving instructions: From Wailuku, drive south on Highway 30 for 5 miles to the junction with Highway 31, which goes southeast to Kihei. Turn left onto Highway 31 and drive about $3\frac{1}{3}$ miles. On the left, you pass a power plant and Kealia Pond; on the right, you pass mud flats and then a narrow beach backed by *kiawe* trees. This hike starts at the southeast end of that beach, near the northernmost condominium building in Kihei. As you near that building, look on the beach side of the road for a spot where you can safely park. A sailing club uses the very last spot, right next to the condo building, so pick one a little earlier.

Permit/permission required: None.

Description. You're probably parked just a few steps from the beach. Thread your way along any of the many paths worn through the dunes and *kiawe* trees to the beach. Once you're at the water's edge, pause to enjoy the magnificent views and to snap a few photos. East and West Maui are so huge as seen from here, and the isthmus so low and inconspicuous, that it's easy to imagine for a moment that East and West Maui are separate islands.

Now turn right toward West Maui (northwest) and begin your walk along this strand. There may be some abandoned junk back in the dunes, perhaps even some illegal campsites, but you can ignore them and concentrate on the beauty of this bay. Depending on the tide conditions, the beach may become so narrow at places that you'll need to walk on the stony shelves of beach rock or in the water. (If the surf is rough, stay out of the water!) The beach rock forms some lovely, clear, pale-blue tide pools, and you'll probably see people fishing here. However, the beach rock can be slippery and sharp, so keep your shoes on and watch your step.

Just beyond the 1-mile point, two parallel lines of black boulders and some old remnants of a wharf extend toward the sea from an arm of Kealia Pond. Birders may want to detour inland here, especially in winter, when many migratory birds stop at Kealia Pond. The main body of the pond lies across the highway, but you may be able to spot some feathered visitors along this small arm. The mud flats on this side of the highway may have some birds, too, if they are flooded. But people use the flats as a motocross course on the weekends, so they're more likely to be uninteresting, possibly even hazardous. Back on the beach, you get over the boulders and continue your stroll until, at 2 miles, a spit of black boulders and more rusty equipment block your way. The buildings of Maalaea village rise a little beyond these boulders, so it's time to retrace your steps to your car.

Birding at the ponds.... Two large ponds on the isthmus provide places for migratory waterfowl to winter over and for non-migratory waterfowl to live: larger Kealia Pond here on the south side of the isthmus and smaller Kanaha Pond on the north side. Kanaha Pond (Trip W4) is open to the public and developed for birding. Kealia Pond has now been purchased and become a sanctuary open to the public, too, but remains undeveloped. There are plans to construct parking areas, boardwalks, and interpretive aids at Kealia Pond. But for now you must park on the highway's shoulder and follow any of the many use trails that bash their way through the dense weeds surrounding the pond in order to view the birds. Depending on the bird activity at Kealia Pond, a visit can be well worth your trouble.

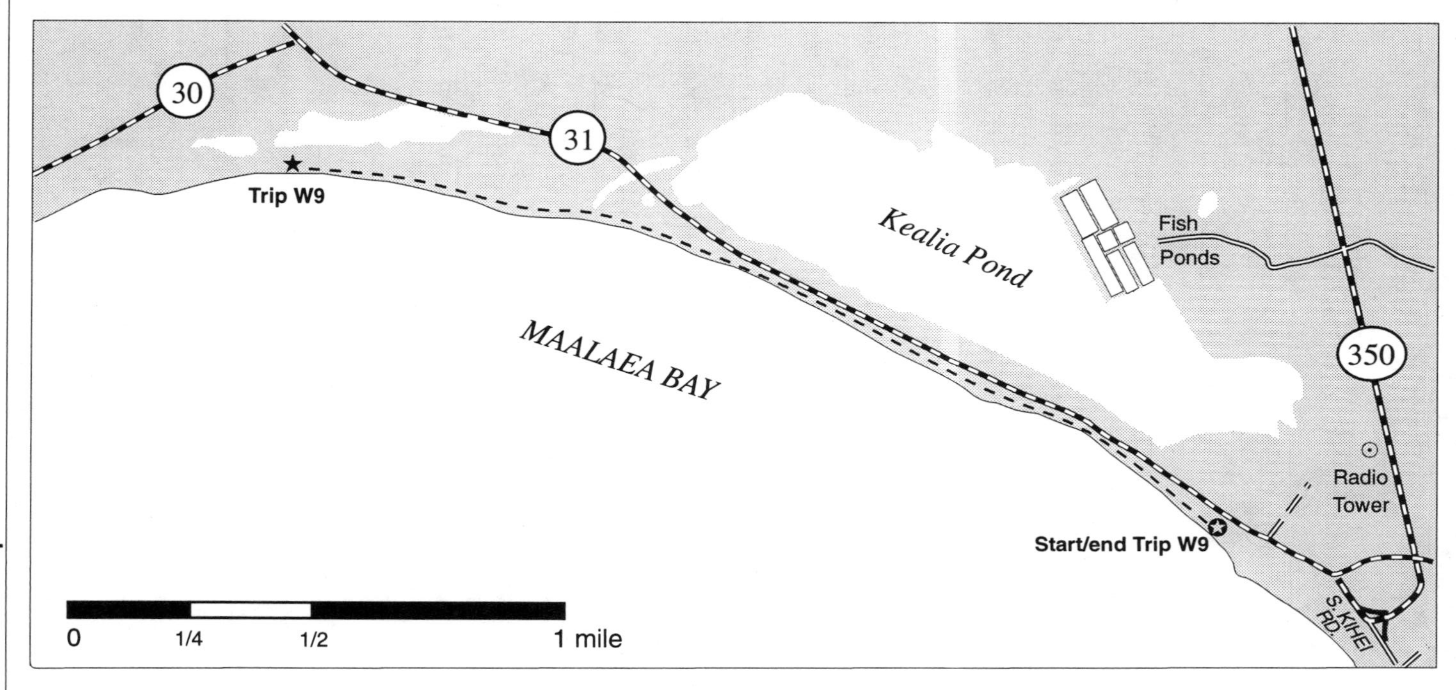
30
31
350
Trip W9
MAALAEA BAY
Kealia Pond
Fish
Ponds
Radio
Tower
S. KIHEI
RD.
Start/end Trip W9
0
1/4
1/2
1 mile

Trip W10. Olowalu: Kilea Cone Petroglyphs

E

Distance: 1 mile

Elevation gain: 80′

Hiking time: 1/2 hour

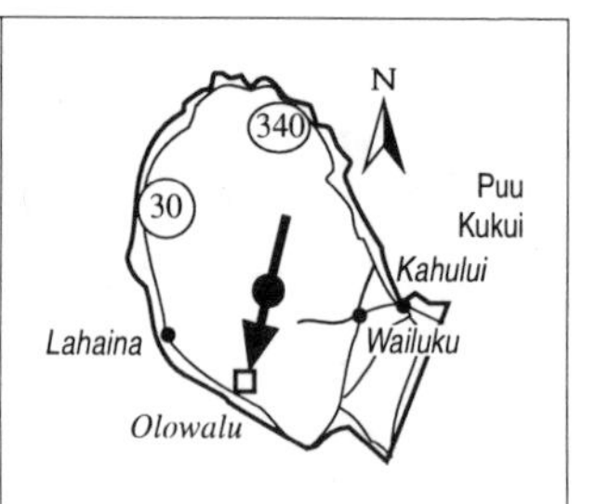

Topos: Optional: Olowalu 7 1/2.

Trail map: At the end of this trip.

Highlights: Centuries ago, Hawaiians carved drawings of people, animals, and everyday objects into exposed stone faces. Drawings in stone such as these, called petroglyphs, are typical of stone-age societies. Many petroglyph sites exist on Maui, but often they're hard to find or hard to get to. The petroglyphs on an exposed rock face of Kilea cone near Olowalu are in good condition, and you can easily see them on this little hike.

Driving instructions: From Wailuku, drive south on Highway 30. Follow it around McGregor Point to Olowalu village, 15 miles. Olowalu Store is on the inland side of the highway. Turn in here; find a place to park where you won't block any of the dirt roads and aren't taking up room in the store's and restaurant's parking lot.

Allow plenty of time for this drive—and for any other drive around to the west side of West Maui. The scenery is spectacular, and you'll want to stop often to enjoy it safely. There are also a number of beautiful public beaches where you'll find it hard to resist the temptation to picnic and swim.

Permit/permission required: None. Pioneer Mill Company owns the land behind the store, and there is a NO TRESPASSING sign. However, the person at Pioneer Mill Company who issues the permits for the hike to David Malo's grave (Trip W11) told me that it is all right for hikers to walk as far as the petroglyphs, but they must not walk any farther. You may want to reconfirm this; see Pioneer Mill Company's phone number in "Getting Permits and Permission" in this book.

Description: A good dirt road leads inland (north-northeast) away from the highway and past a house. Follow that road as it rises almost imperceptibly past an old water tower and through canefields. The reservoir you see on the topo is invisible from the road. The irrigation ditch is usually out of sight, too, though you may hear it. The walk can be very hot on a still afternoon, so it would be better to visit the petroglyphs in the morning.

Soon you approach the west face of an old volcanic cone called Kilea 264 on the topo. Smooth, reddish rock is exposed on this face, and here the Hawaiians of long ago have chiseled drawings. Drawings of stylized human figures are particularly prominent. Unfortunately, some of the petroglyphs have been vandalized with spray paint. It appears that at one time there were stairs, railings, and possibly walkways to let you get closer to the petroglyphs; now, they've decayed into uselessness. It's not a problem, though, as you can see the petroglyphs fairly well from the road. Or, if you feel like bashing over boulders and through weeds, you can pick your way about 20 feet up toward them for a closer look. Be careful of the debris left from the stairs, railings, and walkways.

When you've had a good look at the petroglyphs and a chance to photograph them, return the way you came. (Please remember not to go any farther than the petroglyphs.)

The Olowalu massacre.... One of the many tragic episodes of late-eighteenth-century Hawaii took place here at quiet Olowalu village. Coincidentally, that tragedy gave Kamehameha his two most trusted European advisors, the Englishmen Isaac Davis and John Young. An American, Captain Simon Metcalfe of Boston, was the villain.

In his ship the *Eleanora*, Metcalfe sailed first to the Big Island of Hawaii. His son Thomas followed him in a smaller ship, the *Fair American*, and did not reach Hawaii until some weeks after his father. While trading on the Big Island, Simon Metcalfe caught a high chief stealing and, never one for diplomacy, struck the chief with the end of a rope. The chief vowed revenge for the insult, but Simon Metcalfe sailed off to Maui. Someone else would have to suffer the chief's vengeance.

Simon Metcalfe was trading off the coast of Maui at Honuaula in 1790 when some natives stole one of the *Eleanora*'s auxiliary boats, killing the crewman in it. Another native tried to pry the copper plating off the bottom of the ship. Metcalfe refused to trade any more. The next day, he fired on Honuaula to drive the natives away and then sent a party ashore to burn the village.

Metcalfe then heard that the boat thieves had come from Olowalu, so he sailed to Olowalu for revenge. He invited the natives there to come out to trade, and scores of natives flocked to the *Eleanora*. The treacherous Metcalfe told the natives that one side of the *Eleanora* was *kapu*. That meant the natives would have to bring all their canoes up to the other side of the ship. And on that side, Metcalfe had placed all his cannons and guns, loaded not with their usual ammunition but with musket balls, nails, and scraps of metal. He waited until the canoes were within range and then fired a broadside that killed at least a hundred natives outright and wounded an estimated two hundred more—the Olowalu massacre.

In the meantime, his son Thomas had reached the Big Island in the Fair American. The high chief whom Simon Metcalfe had struck now took his revenge, not knowing that one of his victims was the son of the man who had insulted him. The chief and his men boarded the *Fair American*, seized its crew, and threw them overboard to drown. Only the mate, Isaac Davis, survived after having struggled for so long that the chief finally took pity on him. Kamehameha heard of the attack, chastised the chief, appropriated the *Fair American*, and put Davis under his protection.

Simon Metcalfe sailed back to the Big Island, leaving Olowalu to mourn its dead and heal its wounded. He sent the *Eleanora*'s boatswain, John Young, ashore to inquire after the *Fair American* and her crew. Kamehameha, fearing an ugly confrontation, took Young prisoner so he could not report back and put a *kapu* on the *Eleanora* so that Hawaiians could not go out to it and tell Simon Metcalfe what had happened. After days of fruitless waiting, Simon Metcalfe sailed away from Hawaii, still ignorant of his son's fate.

Kamehameha needed Europeans to help him deal with other Europeans and manage the modern weapons he'd acquired. Isaac Davis and John Young had little formal education, but each possessed a great deal of common sense and integrity. They tried to escape Kamehameha but failed; eventually, they agreed to serve him. They served him loyally and well. Their excellence accounted for much of the Hawaiian monarchy's preference for Great Britain over the United States. Both married Hawaiian women, raised families, and never returned to England. Isaac Davis died of poisoning in 1810; he had helped to foil a plot, and his death was the plotters' revenge. "Old John Young" outlived Kamehameha I by many years; his granddaughter Emma became Kamehameha IV's queen.

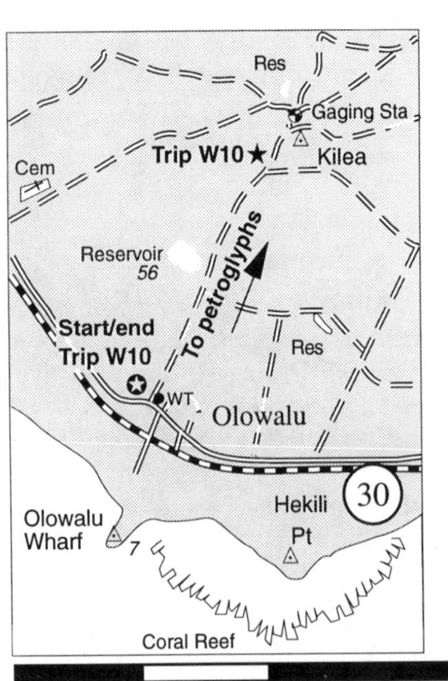

Trip W11. David Malo's Grave

Distance: 4 1/2 miles

Elevation gain: 2070′

Hiking time: 2 1/4 hours

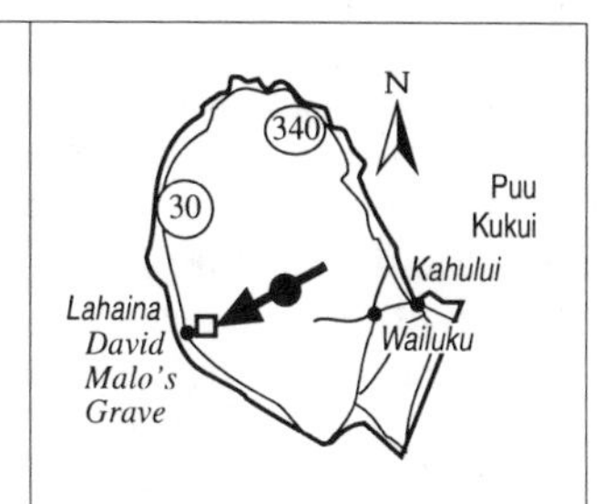

Topos: Lahaina 7 1/2.

Trail map (route approximated): At the end of this trip. Choose your own route up through the maze of steep cane roads to the old cattle pen, where the "trail" part of this trip begins.

Highlights: Currently, this is the only trip that allows you to ascend the west side of West Maui. The views over Lahaina to Lanai and Molokai are stunning throughout this trip; still higher up, you can see Kahoolawe, too. It also gives you a chance to pay your respects to Hawaii's first great scholar (by European standards), David Malo. (If you don't feel up to the entire hike, consider doing part of it in order to enjoy the views.) Note that the trailhead is at Lahainaluna High School and that Lahaina can be extremely hot. To avoid the heavy school traffic and Lahaina's fierce midday heat, take this hike early on a weekend morning. Carry plenty of water and bring that insect repellent.

Driving instructions: From Wailuku, drive south on Highway 30 around McGregor Point and then northwest past Olowalu. Continue northwest on Highway 30 to Lahaina. Turn right onto Lahainaluna Road (the sugar mill, easily spotted on account of its big smokestacks, is almost on the corner of Highway 30 and Lahainaluna Road). Drive up Lahainaluna Road, passing Lahainaluna Intermediate School, and climbing as you near Lahainaluna High School. Near the top of the road, just before you'd turn into the school proper, turn right into a small parking lot for a building and a practice field, 22 1/3 miles from Wailuku. Park here to begin your hike.

Permit/permission required: From Pioneer Mill Company; see "Getting Permits and Permission" in this book.

Description. You'll notice a short stairway next to the building (at the end of the parking lot). Walk up that stairway and turn right onto the road just uphill of the building. Follow this road south for a short distance to a cane road, which you now take southward.

You walk at first under mango trees and along a flume; soon you're in the canefields. David Malo's grave lies near the point marked "Paupau VABM 2261" on the topo, above the big red "L" you see on the face of Paupau hill (locally called Mt. Ball). However, to get to the grave, you need to work your way southeast and uphill through the canefields to an abandoned cattle pen, as shown on the map at the end of this trip. Numerous cane roads crisscross these fields, so you can alternately walk uphill on one of them until you're good and tired *(how can they possibly get a vehicle up anything this steep!)*, then turn right onto one that contours along the face of this hill to catch your breath, then go uphill again....Stop often to turn seaward and enjoy the superb views. Kahoolawe lies to the south. The rounded island almost due west is Lanai, and the long island to the northwest is Molokai. Biting flies may snack on you when you stop, so have your jungle juice handy.

Most of the roads are bordered on both sides by sugar cane. However, the uphill side of the uppermost road (the one just below Paupau Ditch) is sparsely shaded by eucalyptuses and silk oaks. As you near the old cattle pen on the uppermost road, you pass below a couple of small tanks.

Just under 1/8 mile beyond the tanks, look to your left (uphill) for a board laid over a grate to allow you to cross Paupau Ditch to the ruined cattle pen in a grove of eucalyptuses.* Walk through the cattle pen and pick up a steep track in the dry, red hillside. There are actually multiple tracks; the most trodden is generally the better choice. Tags of plastic ribbon help you find your way up the hill northeastward through *pukiawe, ulei, aalii*, tall *ilima*, silk oak, guava, and grasses.

The track presently bears north, contours across a bare patch, and rises to a point somewhat above the "Paupau VABM". The path then turns west and descends a little to a carefully cleared space where you'll find David Malo's stone-covered grave. Students from Lahainaluna High School come up here each year to leave a tribute to David Malo, as dozens of plaques attest. It's interesting to walk around and compare the plaque designs and sentiments from different years as you think about David Malo and his fears for Hawaii (see below).

The students also come up here to tend the giant red "L," which lies downslope of the grave via an unbelievably steep, eroded set of tracks. Your knees will thank you if you give this little detour a miss. The "L" looks much better from down below, near the beginning of this hike. Up here, the curve of the hill is so precipitous that you can't see the "L" until you're on top of it. The "L" is made by outlining the red soil with white material.

* You may run into the remains of a movie set at this point. A reader has reported "an old cabin front" here, obscuring the route. Pioneer Mill was unclear on whether the set was still there (one person said she'd heard of it; another said she hadn't).

When you've had your fill of the tremendous views from David Malo's grave, return the way you came.

"They will eat us up"....David Malo wrote in 1837 to the queen regent, Kinau, describing to her his fear that the large, technologically superior nations would soon overwhelm the little kingdom of Hawaii:

> ...the Ships of the whitemen have come, and smart people have arrived from the Great Countries which you have never seen before, they know our people are few in number and living in a small country; they will eat us up, such has always been the case with large countries, the small ones have been gobbled up.

Malo was an exceptionally bright, sensitive, and intense young man. He was born on the big island of Hawaii in about 1793. Though he was a commoner, his ability to remember the complicated genealogies of the chiefs won him royal favor. He moved to Lahaina in the 1820s, where he attended school and quickly learned to read and write Hawaiian, even to become fairly proficient in English. He was among those chosen to be in the first class at Lahainaluna School in 1831. He became a devout Christian and a good friend of the missionaries, helping them translate the Bible into Hawaiian. He was a successful businessman, served in the Hawaiian government, and was ordained a minister.

David Malo eloquently warned that Hawaii would lose its sovereignty to foreigners. In the absence of enough Western-educated native Hawaiians, foreigners from Western nations—*haoles*—served in Hawaii's government in many capacities. The government didn't appreciate his criticism, but Malo was too popular and too well-respected to be silenced. When dying in 1853, he asked to be buried on a hill high above Lahaina instead of in the Lahaina cemetery, for he believed that one day the *haoles* would covet the cemetery lands and would disturb his bones. Look down from his quiet hillside grave to the sprawling development around Lahaina. Was David Malo right?

David Malo's grave above Lahaina

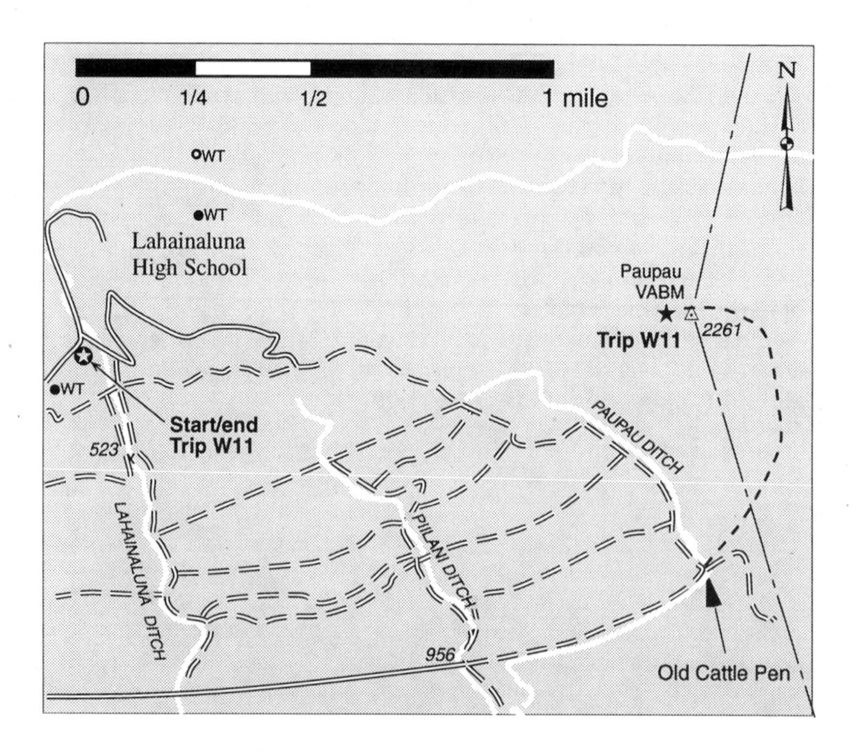

Trip W12. D.T. Fleming Beach Park to "Dragon's Teeth"

E

Distance: $1^{3}/_{4}$ miles

Elevation gain: Negligible

Hiking time: 1 hour

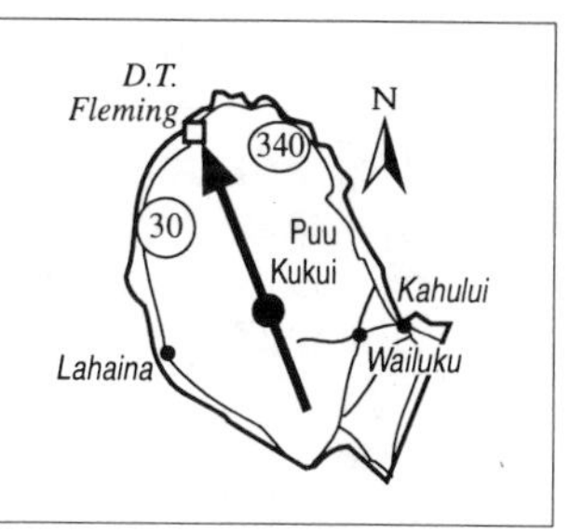

Topos: Napili $7^{1}/_{2}$.

Trail map (route approximated): At the end of this trip.

Highlights: D.T. Fleming Beach Park is a beautiful tropical beach where you're sure to enjoy sunning and picnicking (the surf's a bit rough for swimming, and it's day use only). But the real highlight here is your walk out onto Makaluapuna Point through its unusual trachyte formations that *Maui: How It Came To Be* calls "dragon's teeth."

Driving instructions: From Wailuku, follow Highway 30 through Lahaina, Kaanapali, and Kapalua. D.T. Fleming Beach Park is adjacent to the huge Kapalua resort development. At the north end of Kapalua, an old coast road joins Highway 30 from the southwest, coming in from the left side (as you're driving north on Highway 30); that's the road you turn onto to get to D.T. Fleming. However, the turnoff to D.T. Fleming is not marked on the highway as of this writing and can be hard to spot. Kapalua has several golf courses; one set brackets the highway south of D.T. Fleming Beach Park; another, north of D.T. Fleming, is on the inland side of the highway. If you are driving north and have passed one set of Kapalua golf courses bracketing the highway and then get to a right turn inland into another golf course—and residential development—on the inland side of the highway, you have overshot the old coast road that leads to D.T. Fleming. Turn around and then, as you head back (south), take the next right (seaward) turnoff. Or, if you're northbound and haven't overshot the turnoff, turn left onto the old coast road and go southwest a very short distance to the park entrance. D.T. Fleming Beach Park is on your right (seaward) as you pass a lovely old building on your left that looks like a church but is currently serving as a preschool. The park entrance isn't well-marked either, as of this writing, so don't be surprised if you pass it and have to backtrack. There's a parking lot here with restrooms at its north end, 9 miles past Lahaina and 31 miles from Wailuku.

Permit/permission required: None.

Description. From the parking lot, walk past the restrooms toward the northeast end of the beach, where pretty Honokahua Stream empties into Honokahua Bay under ironwood, *kiawe*, and sisal. Now turn around to enjoy the sweeping view of Honokahua Bay and Makaluapuna Point, which is your destination. Drift back southwest along the shoreline toward the point, dabbling your feet in the water if the surf is calm. In ⅓ mile, the beach ends at the lava rocks of the point.

Carefully pick your way up onto the point, keeping outside the fence of a golf course (not shown on the map). If the tide is high, crashing surf may make this unsafe. Atop the point, you'll find a use trail that leads through a wall of black boulders and through beach *naupaka*. The use trail soon peters out, leaving you to pick your way across the mostly gray-white lavas of Makaluapuna Point. These light-colored lavas are characteristic of the second period of volcanism on West Maui and are poorer in iron than the basalts that originally formed West Maui's shield volcano. They're also sharp; this is no place for bare feet or sandals. Look for a low, white-flowered variety of the succulent plant *akulikuli* trailing across the rocks here.

As you continue out on the east side of the point, you'll notice that salt spray has eroded these rocks into sweeping, sharp "dragon's tooth" shapes—or are they the dragon's backbone? They're almost as tall as a person! Take some time to explore this world of gray, black, and reddish lavas, unexpected grassy flats, and small tide pools. There's a miniature natural arch, far too fragile to step on, over a tiny, deep cove whose wave-battered black lava rocks are stained pink by algae. Near the very end of the point, you'll find rusty pipes set in concrete bases. Pause to look inland. Somewhere up on that slope above Kapalua lies the vent from which these lavas poured, dividing what was once a single long bay into the two bays you see now, Honokahua (from which you just came) on the east and Oneloa on the west.

You can trace your way back on the west side of the point as far as the golf course. The sands of Oneloa Bay are inviting, but you'd have to trespass on the golf course to get there from here. So, when you're through exploring Makaluapuna Point, return to D.T. Fleming Beach Park and to your car.

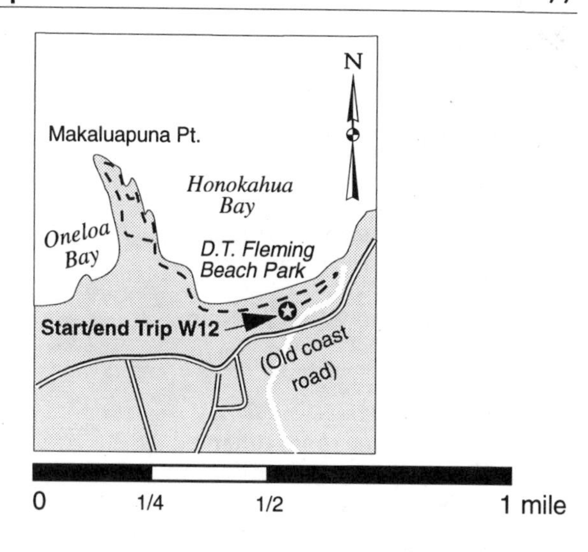

Dragon's teeth at Makaluapuna Point (note person at upper left)

Trip W13. Nakalele Blowhole

 E 	**Distance:** Just under 1 mile **Elevation gain:** 150′ (upside-down trip) **Hiking time:** 1/2 hour	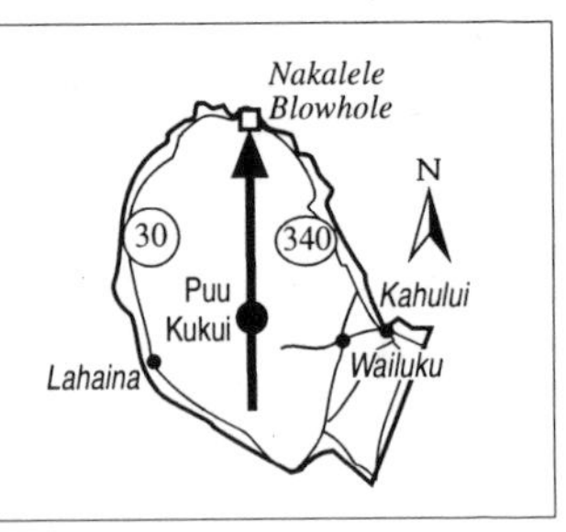

Topos: Optional: Napili 7 1/2.

Trail map (route approximated): At the end of this trip.

Highlights: The blowhole is located in a small, extremely rugged cove, surrounded by fantastically sculpted formations. It's far too rough and dangerous for swimming, but it certainly is picturesque.

Driving instructions: Don't waste your time driving around the north end of West Maui to get to Nakalele Blowhole (see page 21). You'll see better scenery and have an opportunity to visit many more attractions if you take the highway through Lahaina. From Wailuku, follow Highway 30 through Lahaina, Kaanapali, and Kapalua. Beyond Kapalua, the road narrows and becomes more winding.You'll find the trailhead on the seaward side of the highway some 37 1/3 miles from Wailuku. Nakelele is currently signed; turn into the big, bare area on the seaward side of the highway, and park here to start your hike.

Permit/permission required: None.

Description. There are two conflicting signs at the parking area, a NO TRESPASSING sign and a Maui County Parks and Recreation sign. Here's the situation: The public access route, to which the Maui County sign refers, is an old road which you may hike on. The land on either side of the road, to which the NO TRESPASSING sign refers, is private property where you may not go. Stick to the old road as described below.

An old jeep road, far too rough for driving but fine for hiking, bears east away from the parking area, descending a little as it goes. It becomes indistinct at a grassy area, but look to your right (east) for a gully with a stand of ironwood trees. Follow the road toward the gully, which has cut its way across the old road, cross the gully—don't hike up or down it—and then bear left toward the old Nakalele beacon ("Light" on the topo), 1/3 mile.

There's no trail beyond the beacon, so you pick your way down and to your right as you face the sea, to the cove below the beacon. Small piles of rocks indicate routes others have taken, but you should use your own judgement. Be careful to avoid cutting yourself on the sharp rocks and when putting your weight on fragile lava formations that could crumble beneath you. The cove with the blowhole is the next cove east, across a rocky shelf strewn with deeply eroded boulders.

There's no better way to discover the blowhole's exact location than to listen for the characteristic *WHOOOOSH!* as it erupts. Once you've found the blowhole, just under 1/2 mile from the parking area, pick a spot from which to watch it and to enjoy the intricate natural sculptures around this area. It's quite a show!

Return the way you came.

Fretwork weathering.... Wind is the principal sculptor at Nakalele Point. It's responsible for those elaboratly layered and fluted formations around you as you sit watching the blowhole. But other agents are at work, too. Look closely at the faces of the boulders nearby. You'll probably notice on some of their faces a particularly lovely form of weathering: slender partitions of rock separating little hollows, all forming an intricate fretwork. According to *Maui: How It Came To Be,* this elegant "fretwork weathering" is the result of salt spray and of organisms that adhere to the rock, slowly dissolving it away as they grow. Their patient work has left us these treasures of lace in stone.

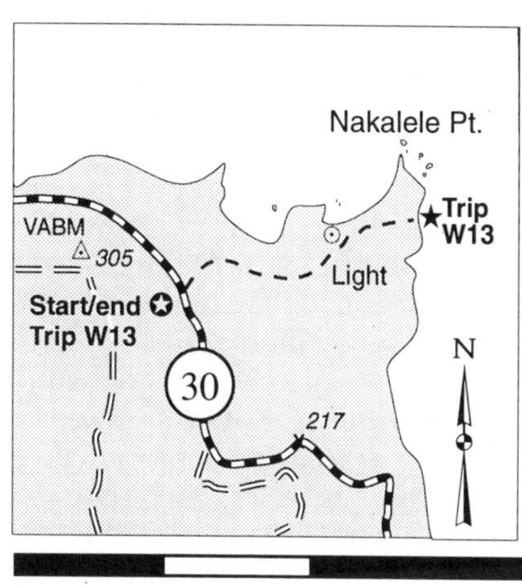

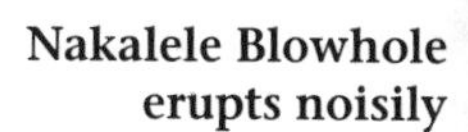
Nakalele Blowhole erupts noisily

Trip E1. Waikamoi Ridge

 **V** to **E** 	**Distance:** ⅓ to 1⅛ miles **Elevation gain:** 100′ to 205′ **Hiking time:** 10–30 minutes	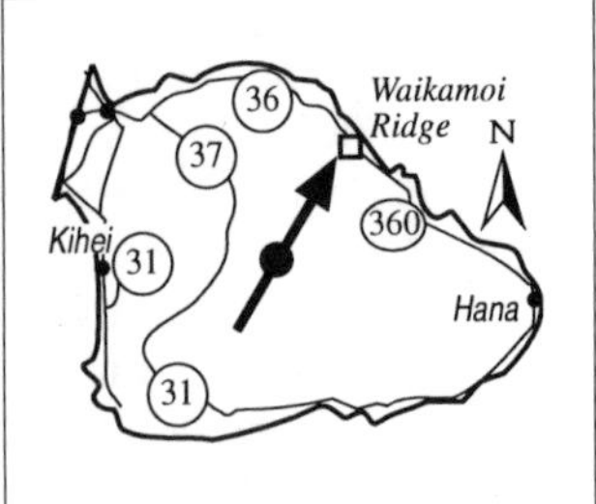

Topos: Optional: Keanae 7½.

Trail map (route approximated): At the end of this trip.

Highlights: The Waikamoi Ridge Trail with its two picnic shelters offers you an opportunity to hike without special permission into the rainforest that the Hana Highway "burrows" through. At one time, many of the plants along this trail were identified by signs that are now gone. However, the Division of Forestry and Wildlife hopes to restore the signs soon. Mosquitoes abound here; be sure to bring your jungle juice.

Driving instructions: From Wailuku, drive east on Highway 32, bearing southeast as it becomes Highway 36 (the Hana Highway). Continue on Highway 36 past the junction with Highway 37 and through Paia. Highway 36 becomes narrow, winding Highway 360 (still the Hana Highway), and all the highway mileage markers are reset to zero at that point. Between the 9-mile and 10-mile markers on Highway 360, pull into and park in a large turnout just below a ridge on the inland side of the highway, 29¼ miles from Wailuku. If the trailhead is unmarked, don't worry: if you were driving toward Hana and just nosed straight into this turnout, your car is probably pointing at the low bank which the trail initially ascends.

Permit/permission required: None.

Description. The Waikamoi Ridge Trail is a pair of nested loops, and you could start your hike in either direction. This description starts at what I think is the more obvious spot, where the trail leaves the parking area going uphill and east on a low bank. You reach a picnic shelter almost immediately, then follow the trail's left fork at the junction just beyond the shelter. You descend a little through huge eucalyptus trees wreathed in giant philodendrons (believe it or not, the philodendrons are just escaped houseplants). Look for the vivid red bracts of lobster-claw heliconia to your right. *Hala*, guava, white ginger, and *ti* line your path here.

Now the trail begins to climb, and you soon reach a junction where the left fork is a spur trail that leads about 10 yards to a concrete bench overlooking the bamboo-clad ridge across from you. (The spur trails aren't on the book's map.) There's a view of the coast to your left here. Back on the main trail, you pass sword fern and sweet fern under *hala* and eucalyptus as, ⅕ mile from the start, the trail begins to level out. A few more steps bring you to a second bench, and the trail soon forks again. You have a choice of making a shorter or a longer loop hike from this fork, as described below.

The shorter loop takes the righthand fork just beyond the second bench. You descend through dense forest past a sign that says QUIET TREES AT WORK, pass the junction with the trail to the picnic shelter, and shortly reach yet another junction (not shown on the book's map). The right fork takes you back to the parking lot in just over ⅓ mile from your start (the left fork is a dead end).

The longer loop takes the lefthand fork just beyond the second bench and climbs a little past strawberry guava. This section is overgrown, narrow, and slippery, and it has a steep dropoff on the right side. Nearing the ⅓-mile point, the trail levels out, makes a switchback, and climbs a little to a spur trail that goes a few yards to a third bench (the view from this bench is currently obscured by dense vegetation). To the right, the main trail goes through bamboo to a junction with an old jeep road. Turn left onto the jeep road to reach the upper picnic shelter, ½ mile from your start. The shelter itself sits under big mango trees, but someone has planted a row of ornamental cypresses across the road, adding a Mediterranean touch. After a rest and a snack here, retrace your steps back down the jeep road past the junction with the trail you came up on. To make a loop of it, you follow the jeep road downhill (north-northeast) past two more junctions with abandoned jeep roads and past some abandoned machinery, under a cover of bamboo, *kukui*, guava, *koa*, and African tulip trees. A locked gate and barbed wire at the end of the road keep you from going directly to the parking area. Circumvent them by bearing to your right (southeast) on a footpath which takes you to the parking area in a few steps.

Hikers who've taken the longer loop will probably want to double around to pick up the shorter loop, too, for a total hike of 1⅛ miles.

Along the Hana Highway....the "welcome mat" is seldom out for hikers. The East Maui Irrigation Company owns much of the land along the Hana Highway, and the company does not permit casual hiking on its land. This makes the Waikamoi Ridge Trail especially valuable as an opportunity to explore this rainforest!

Hikes along the Hana Highway.... The trip to Hana is much more enjoyable if you spend at least one night in Hana town itself (there are budget accommodations in Hana). This makes it possible for you to drive slowly, stop often, enjoy the sights, and take one or two of these hikes as you go. Trips E1 through E3 are described in terms of driving from Wailuku toward Hana because it makes sense to take those trips in conjunction with your drive to or from Hana town. However, you really need to stay in Hana town in order to have the time to enjoy most of the trips between Trip E4 and Trip E13. Those trips are described as "side trips from Hana town" for that reason.

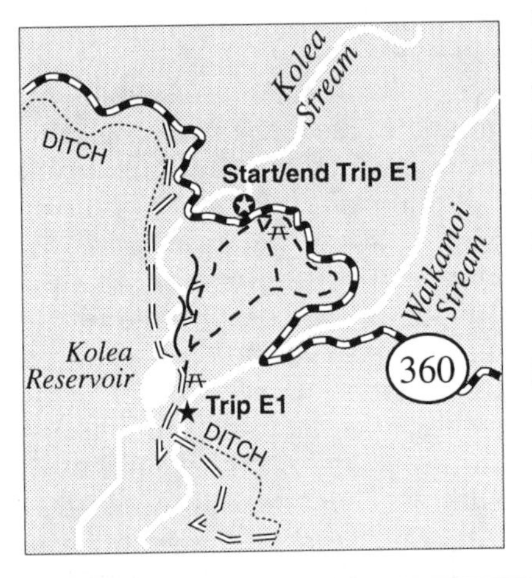

Yes, you can drive from Wailuku to Hana and back in one long day, but about all you'll have time for is driving, driving, driving!

Cascade on Keanae Arboretum Stream

Trip E2. Keanae Arboretum

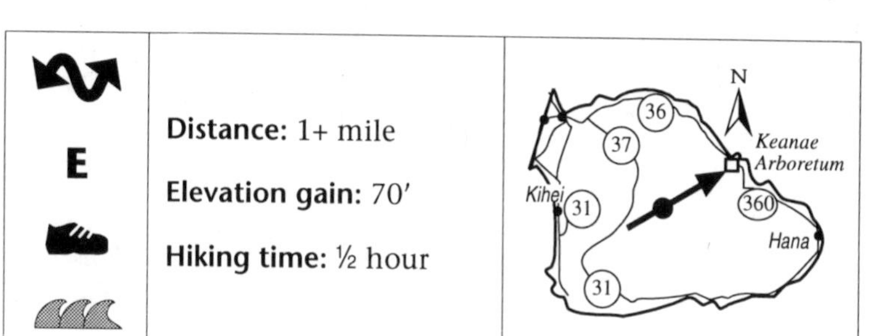

Topos: Optional: Keanae 7½.

Trail map (route approximated): At the end of this trip.

Highlights: Keanae Arboretum is a lovely tropical-valley walk you won't want to miss. There's an area of non-native tropical plants, including many ornamental plants you've probably seen but have not been able to identify. There's also an area of native plants, probably including ones you'd hoped to see in the wild but couldn't find or identify. Here, native and non-native plants are identified for you; what an opportunity to learn!

Driving instructions: Following the driving instructions of Trip E1 past Waikamoi Ridge. Continue east on Highway 360 past Kaumahina State Wayside, where you may want to stop to use the restrooms and to walk up the concrete path to enjoy some good views of the Keanae Peninsula. Around 6 miles past Kaumahina, look for a wide turnout on the inland side of the highway where a fence with a gate marks the boundary of Keanae Arboretum, 35½ miles from Wailuku. Park in this turnout or in another one across the highway.

Permit/permission required: None.

Description. Your hike starts at the gate, through which you pass to walk down an old road under a cover of *hau*, African tulip, and guava. Impatiens blossoms provide vivid spots of white, lipstick pink, and magenta under the dense tree cover. The road curves left to another gate, marking the start of the non-native plant section. Huge clumps of bamboo rise on your left, exotic palm trees on your right. Short side trails branching down to a stream invite you to explore plantings of heliconia, ginger, and other exotics.

A little before the ¼-mile point, you reach the native plant section. Many varieties of hibiscus are represented here. Look for breadfruit trees along the road. You may wonder about their huge, round, pale-green fruits or recall their historical connection to the infamous *Bounty* and Captain Bligh. But surely their most arresting feature is their immense, glossy, deeply lobed leaves.

A feature for which Keanae Arboretum is especially well-known is just ahead of you on this *ti*-lined avenue: many plantings of different kinds of dryland and wetland taro, the latter waving its elongated heart-shaped leaves over a series of gleaming ponds. The rocky road becomes a raised, rocky path as you skirt the taro patches.

Beyond the taro patches, you can follow the path, now a rough and muddy track, upstream past fragrant ginger to a spot where a little cascade spills into a pool shaded by guava and *kukui*. The track becomes little more than a slippery, muddy scramble over tangled roots after this pool, so this is a good place to turn around and return to your car, just over ½ mile from your start.

Breadfruit and taro.... The early Polynesian settlers brought with them to Hawaii a variety of breadfruit (*ulu*) that can be reproduced only from cuttings or shoots (it doesn't produce seeds, though many other varieties do). With only this one variety of breadfruit available in Hawaii, breadfruit was a seasonal rather than a year-round crop. Taro (*kalo*), of which the Hawaiians had many varieties, was a year-round crop in Hawaii, different varieties maturing at different times of the year. In Hawaii, taro became the staple starch. Elsewhere in the Pacific, there were many varieties of breadfruit, bearing fruit at different times of the year, so breadfruit became the staple starch.

Both cooked breadfruit and *poi*, the edible paste made from taro roots, seem to be foods you have to grow up with in order to enjoy. Try a bag of taro chips (sold alongside potato chips in most Hawaiian markets) even if you can't bring yourself to try *poi*. The chips will grow on you quickly. Don't think about calories as you stare into the empty bag, wondering how they disappeared so fast. Think instead of how you've made a sincere effort to enjoy taro; unlike most who try *poi* for the first time, you've probably succeeded!

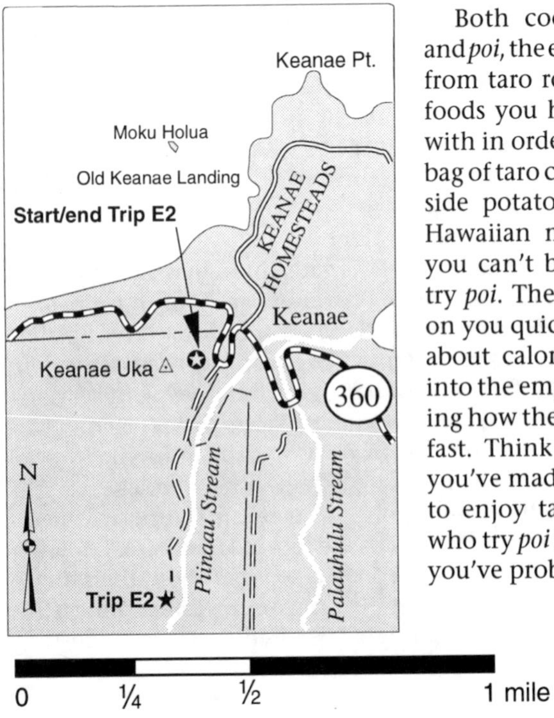

Trip E3. Puaa Kaa

V

Distance: Negligible

Elevation gain: Negligible

Hiking time: Negligible

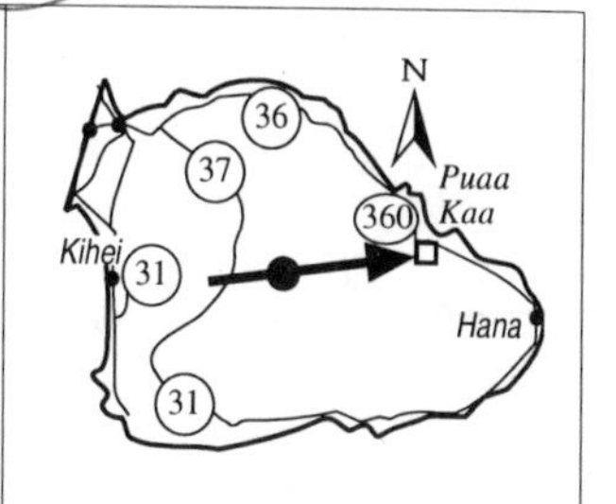

Topos: Optional: Nahiku 7½.

Trail map (route approximated): At the end of this trip.

Highlights: Two freshwater pools you can swim in, connected by a small cascade, and three picnic shelters, all in less than 2 minutes' walk from the highway, should tempt you to stay a while at Puaa Kaa. Puaa Kaa gets lots of visitors, but don't let that put you off.

Driving instructions: Follow the driving instructions of Trips E1 and then E2 past Keanae Arboretum for 2¼ more miles to the parking lot for Puaa Kaa. The parking lot is on the seaward side of the highway, 37¾ miles from Wailuku. The pools and picnic shelters are just across the highway from the parking lot.

Permit/permission required: None.

Description. The stream whose bridge you crossed just before you turned into the parking lot at Puaa Kaa divides Puaa Kaa into two sections: a southeast one with access from the southeast side of the stream to two picnic shelters and the upper pool, and a northwest one offering access from the northwest side of the stream to the lower pool and a third picnic shelter.

For the southeast section, you walk up a short rise through strawberry guavas to the first of two small picnic shelters. One picnic shelter is a few steps away, as is the upper pool. You can carefully pick your way across the stream to the other picnic shelter, which is on its west side. (As of this writing, it's easier to get to the west side of the upper pool area from the southeast section.)

There's no easy way from the southeast section to the lower pool, so it's better to return to the highway, cross the bridge, and get to the lower pool by taking the footpath on the northwest side of the bridge.

After your picnic and swim, retrace your steps to your car.

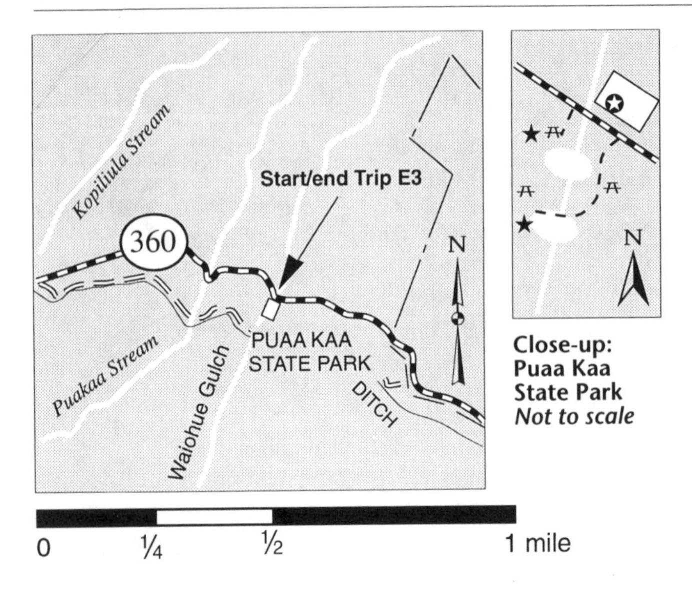

Puaa Kaa cascade

Trip E4. Ulaino Road Side Trip from Hana

M

Distance: 4 miles

Elevation gain: 150′ (upside-down trip)

Hiking time: 2 hours

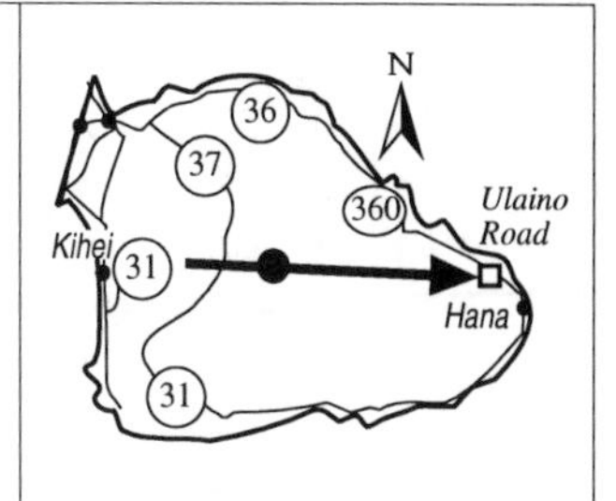

Topos: Hana 7½.

Trail map: At the end of this trip.

Highlights: The forest that lines this lovely old road includes many exotic flowering species, making it more colorful than other rainforest paths. At the end of the road, there's a cobblestone "beach" and fine coastal scenery. I'll give you some hints about the final highlight but leave you to discover it fully. The road part of this trip is suitable for travel by mountain bicycle as well as by Ankle Express.

Driving instructions: As I said earlier, I believe that most of the hikes in and around Hana town cannot be enjoyed in conjunction with a one-day trip to and from Hana, so plan to stay in Hana town. This is the first of several such hikes in this book—the side trips from Hana town. I'll give their driving instructions in terms of a reference point in Hana town: Hana Beach County Park, just seaward of the intersection of Ua Kea Road and Keawa Place in Hana. But first, you need to get to Hana town....

To get to Hana town and Hana Beach County Park. It's 54 miles from Wailuku to Hana town. To get to Hana Beach County Park, stay on Highway 360 past Puaa Kaa and the turnoffs to Hana Airport and Waianapanapa State Park. The highway forks just past the Hana Medical Center; the left fork is Ua Kea Road. Bear left on it and drive past the Hana Cultural Center to meet Keawa Place just where you can look left down to Hana Bay and Hana Beach County Park. Turn left and drive a short block down to the parking lot for the park. It's a convenient place to stop, relax, enjoy the view, and orient yourself to Hana town. When you've got your bearings, drive to wherever you're staying in Hana, note the distance, and adjust the driving distances given in this trip and Trips E5 through E13 accordingly. You probably won't need to drive at all to get to the start of Trip E10.

To get to the start of this side trip. From Hana Beach County Park, drive back on Ua Kea Road north past the Hana Medical Center, then north and west past the turnoffs to Waianapanapa State Park and Hana Airport. One mile west of the turnoff to Waianapanapa State Park, turn right (seaward) onto Ulaino Road. A sign on the highway directs you to Kahanu Gardens, which is down Ulaino Road. Drive down Ulaino Road to the end of the pavement, ¾ mile from the highway and 4¼ miles from Hana Beach County Park. Park off the road here where you won't block gates or driveways. (Yes, you could drive down Ulaino Road. But it is so delightful to walk on, and it soon becomes so rough and potholed, that you'll want to start your hike here.)

Permit/permission required: None.

Description. Be alert when walking on a road! In general, I recommend that when you are walking on a road, you assume that anyone operating a vehicle on that road is deaf, blind, and insane.

Follow the road generally northwest, initially along open pastures bordered by guava and *kukui*. In the deep grass bordering the road, you're likely to see the small, orange-y flowers of an upright *ilima*, the blue spikes of cayenne vervain, and the pink-and-orange flowerheads of lantana. Planes from nearby Hana Airport buzz overhead occasionally. As you near the ½-mile point, a row of tall *hau* trees brackets a cattle guard. You cross the cattle guard and soon ford a stream under huge mango trees just before reaching the gate of Kahanu Gardens (on your right, seaward). Look for dwarf poinciana trees, stunning in their brilliant red-and-yellow blossoms, across the road from the gate.

A little beyond ¾ mile, Ulaino Road passes through a magnificent forest of *kukui* and *hala* trees, punctuated by an occasional mango tree There is a lush understory of ferns, and ephiphytic ferns grow high in the trees. As the forest opens up around 1¾ miles, you pass some homes and ford a charming stream with several small cascades. The yards around the homes present a colorful display of ornamental ginger, variegated *ti*, heliconia, impatiens, and many other exotic plants. The road forks at a planting of the very symmetical Norfolk pine; take the left fork here.

Almost 2 miles from your start, the road dips down to a stream that's pooled behind a cobblestone barrier near its mouth. Across the pool, a cliff of black rock forms a wall almost hidden in the rich green of overhanging *kukui* trees. Deep in amongst the leaves you may glimpse seep springs feeding the pool. Turn seaward on the cobblestones and continue on the cobbles across the stream's mouth. The black lavas of the coastal cliffs, the intense blue of the turbulent sea, the mirror-like pool, and the vivid green of the coastal rainforest make an unforgettable picture.

Standing near the cobblestone barrier across the stream's mouth, look northwest across the stream and up the coast about 200 yards for the final highlight of this hike. Do you see it—the water falling over the cliff and down to the rocky beach? If tide and surf permit, you can pick your way across the barrier to explore this waterfall and what's at its base! (This last segment is up to you; the route shown on the book's map is just an approximation.)

When you can bear to tear yourself away from here, return the way you came.

Kahanu Gardens.... Kahanu Gardens, a branch of the National Tropical Botanical Gardens, is closed indefinitely because of funding cuts. The gardens' phone has been disconnected, and there is no forwarding number.

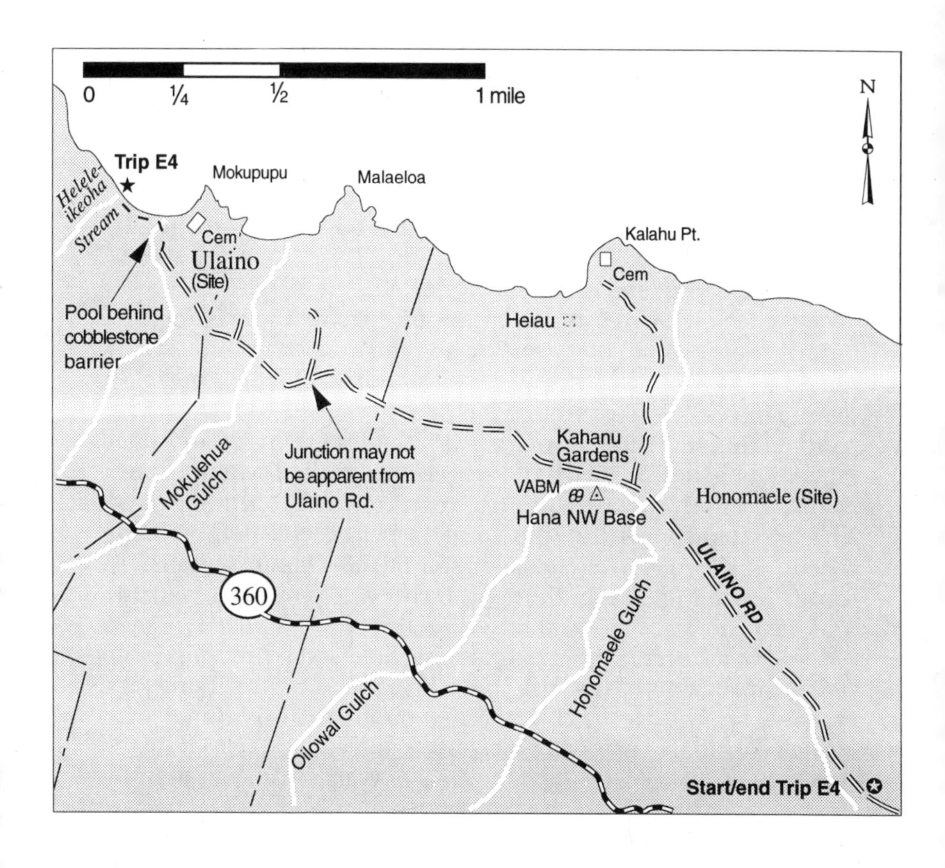

Trip E5. Waianapanapa Cave Side Trip from Hana

G
V

Distance: ⅕ mile

Elevation gain: Negligible

Hiking time: Less than 10 minutes

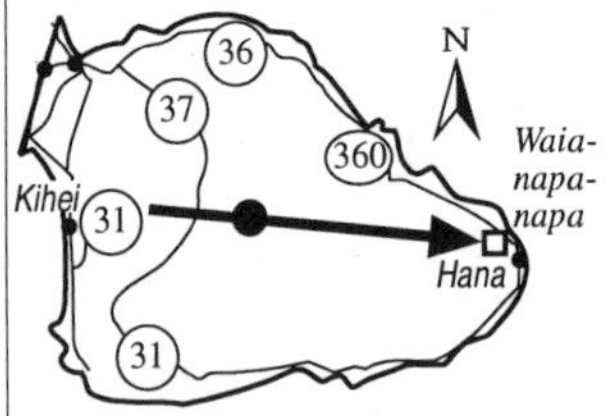

Topos: Hana 7½.

Trail map (route approximated): At the end of this trip.

Highlights: This very short loop trip offers a chance to look into a cave whose floor is a pool of water and which figures in a famous and tragic legend (below).

Driving instructions: From Hana Beach County Park, drive back on Ua Kea Road north past the Hana Medical Center 2½ miles to the marked turnoff for Waianapanapa State Park, on your right. Follow this one-lane road ½ mile seaward to the park, then turn left and follow a very potholed road a little less than ¼ mile more past the tent-camping area to a parking lot, just under 3¼ miles total. All Waianapanapa State Park trips in this book (E5 through E9) start from this area.

Permit/permission required: None.

Description. A sign on the seaward edge of the parking lot points left (north) to the cave. You descend a paved trail and stairs under dense *hau* to the first of two fern-draped openings into the cave. The pool you see through this opening is sometimes reddish-colored from the millions of tiny shrimp that live in it. Continue ahead along the impatiens- and ginger-lined path, ascending some stairs, to a short spur path leading to a second cave opening. Walk the few steps down the spur to get a better look through this opening. The cave is said to have a second, dry chamber reachable only by swimming across the pool, as Popoalaea and her attendant did (below).

Now, back on the main path, ascend the next set of stairs past ferns, ginger, and *ti*. The path soon curves back to the parking lot, passing a sign with the cave's legend on it (see also below). You *could* leave Waianapanapa now, but I hope you'll stay to walk to the nearby overlook to enjoy the view of Waianapanapa's beautiful black-sand beach and sculptured sea cliffs-maybe even to take some more hikes!

Popoalaea.... As related by Martha Beckwith in her classic *Hawaiian Mythology*, the chief Kaakea received the Hana chiefess Popoalaea as his wife as a reward for his victory in a series of games that tested his strength. Kaakea was a very jealous man, and he was particularly jealous of Popoalaea's fondness for her younger brother. Hence, he was all too ready to believe false rumors about her infidelity, and he began sharpening his axe to kill her.

Popoalaea fled with her attendant, took refuge in the dry cavern at Waianapanapa above the pool of water, and secretively visited a nearby village at night for food. Unfortunately, the villagers reported the mysterious visitors to Kaakea. Their exact hiding place was not easy to find, but one day Kaakea saw on the water of the pool the shadow of the fly whisk the attendant was waving for her mistress. (Some sources say it was the reflection of Popoalaea's *kahili*, the feather-crowned standard of the *alii*, that Kaakea saw.) Kaakea seized and murdered both women.

It's said that when the water in the pool turns reddish, it's red with Popoalaea's blood. Each morning, it's also said, rainbow colors (*anapa*) play over the pool as a sign of Popoalaea's innocence. What a sad fate, but what a beautiful spot in which to be remembered.

***Hala* trees at Waianapanapa**

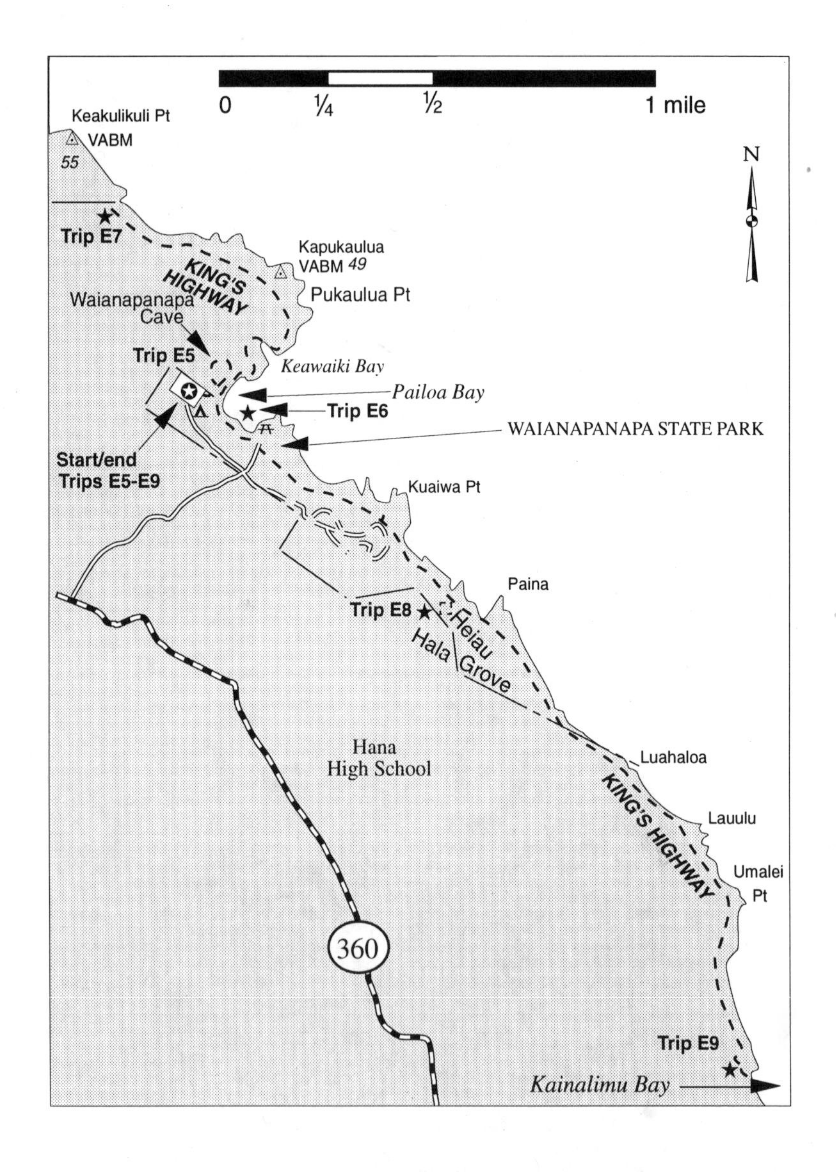

0
¼
½
1 mile
N
Keakulikuli Pt
VABM
55
Trip E7
KING'S HIGHWAY
Kapukaulua
VABM 49
Pukaulua Pt
Waianapanapa Cave
Trip E5
Keawaiki Bay
Pailoa Bay
Trip E6
WAIANAPANAPA STATE PARK
Start/end
Trips E5-E9
Kuaiwa Pt
Paina
Trip E8
Heiau
Hala Grove
Hana
High School
Luahaloa
KING'S HIGHWAY
Lauulu
Umalei
Pt
360
Trip E9
Kainalimu Bay

Trip E6. Waianapanapa Black-Sand Beach Side Trip from Hana

V

Distance: 1⁄10 mile

Elevation gain: 40′ (up-side-down trip)

Hiking time: Less than 5 minutes

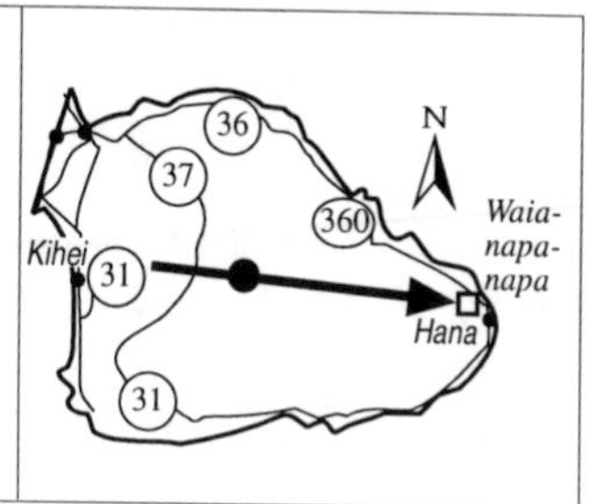

Topos: Optional: Hana 7½.

Trail map (route approximated): At the end of Trip E5.

Highlights: If you've been astonished at the beauty of Maui's many white-sand beaches, just wait till you see this gorgeous *black*-sand beach! A fair number of the people who gaze longingly at Waianapanapa's black-sand beach from the overlook near the parking lot seem unable to find their way down to it. Here's how to get to it.

Driving instructions: Follow the driving instructions of Trip E5.

Permit/permission required: None.

Description. From the seaward end of the parking lot, where the sign directs you left to the caves (Trip E5), turn right and head generally south on the path. Pause at the overlook of the black-sand beach to take in this glorious view. Among other lovely features, you'll count at least two natural arches in the cliffs cupping the beach. A few steps farther on, the path forks. The left fork here leads steeply down to the southeast end of the black-sand beach, which curves northwest away from the base of the path.

If you find the black-sand beach too crowded for your taste, there's a little black-*cobble* cove farther on. (The distance, elevation gain, and time given above don't include the jaunt to this cove.) Walk to the far end of the black-sand beach (away from the path you came down on). Here you'll find a little trail through the beach *naupaka*. Follow it upward through *hau, noni*, pink-flowered clover with sticky seeds, and sweet fern. After a brief level stretch, the trail descends to the black-cobble cove. Caution: swimming at Waianapanapa can be dangerous because of strong currents and high surf.

When you're ready, return the way you came.

Black-sand beaches....are rare anywhere in the world. Most beaches are of light-colored sand. In the tropics, that usually means that the sand is pulverized coral—a gift of the sea. Black-sand beaches are a gift of the land. Some form when hot lava flows enter the ocean, causing a steam explosion that blows the molten material into millions of glassy fragments. You'll find a very few beaches like that on the Big Island of Hawaii; walking on their coarse sand is like walking on tiny beads of jet. These beaches are short-lived, as there's no reliable source of new material to replace what the ocean and the wind carry away. The fragments are the result of a single steam explosion. The chances of another flow occurring in the exactly the same place and in the same way, yielding similar fragments to replenish the beach, are very remote. The once-famous black-sand beach at Kalapana on the Big Island is all but gone now, its glassy sands swept away or blown inland. (It also suffered major damage when its section of coast abruptly sank about 3 feet in the powerful earthquake of November 1975.)

Other black-sand beaches are the products of erosion—particles of dark-colored material weathered from the rocks at the ocean's edge. That's the source of this black-sand beach here at Waianapanapa and at a few other sites in the Hawaiian Islands. The patient work of erosion has created not only those lovely arches and sea stacks from the surrounding black cliffs but also this beautiful little beach. As you can see, there's plenty of material left to erode, so *this* black-sand beach will be here for a little while.

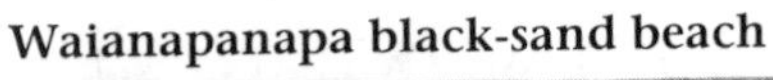

Waianapanapa black-sand beach

Trip E7. King's Highway (North) Side Trip from Hana

M

Distance: 2⅔ miles

Elevation gain: 160′

Hiking time: 1⅓ hours

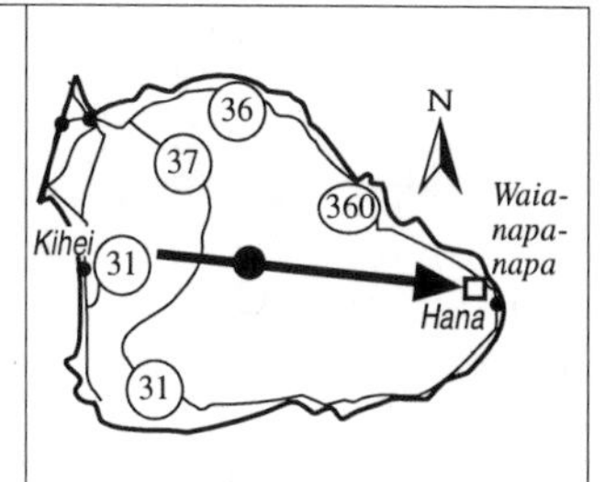

Topos: Hana 7½.

Trail map (initial route approximated): At the end of Trip E5.

Highlights: Scenery—the dramatic coastal scenery of the cliffs around Waianapanapa State Park and the sweeping views inland up the slopes of Haleakala. On your way, you visit the black-sand beach and black-cobble cove.

Driving instructions: Follow the driving instructions of Trip E5.

Permit/permission required: None.

Description. Follow Trip E6 down to the black-sand beach and over to the black-cobble cove. Cross the black-cobble cove and follow the trail as it climbs again, toward *hala* trees. With the help of a switchback, you're soon atop the cliffs in a region of twisted *aa* lava. The trail bears northeast through more *hala* and beach *naupaka* and follows the coast, passing high above bouldery Keawaiki Bay, where the waves surge in too forcefully for swimming. You pass through a forest of *hala* and find yourself in an open wilderness of *aa* lava, a landscape characteristic of the remaining coastal segments of the King's Highway (see below).

In ½ mile you reach a junction where you turn left (northwest); the right fork leads out to the remains of Kapukaulua VABM. If you pause for any length of time on this trail, you're apt to find your boots covered with a kind of ant that seems determined to conduct mass explorations of any stationary object. The rocks may be swarming with them, so keep your stops brief.

You pass a small shrine, where you may wish to respectfully add your own stone. Continuing through the *aa*, the trail dips into a deep gully where, offshore, remnants of the sea cliff stand isolated, washed in turquoise water and white foam. You come out of one gully to descend into another. On the other side of the second gully, the trail may be quite faint. A little exploring will soon reveal the trail, and you follow it—very rough now—to a cove whose beach consists of large, rounded cobbles. Pick your way across the cove on the cobbles, then climb back up to the cliffs on a steep, very loose track.

You presently climb a little, pass a narrow natural arch, and reach an anticlimactic end at the chain-link fence around Hana Airport, 1⅓ miles from your start. It's time to turn around and retrace your steps.

The King's Highway....is a remnant of old Hawaii, a trail around Maui established in prehistoric times for the king of Maui and his messengers and partly rebuilt in historic times. It's also called the *alaloa* or the Hono a Piilani Highway. Martha Foss Fleming, in *Old Trails of Maui*, estimated its original length at roughly 138 miles. Today, the hikable fragments are those that pass through *aa* fields here at Waianapanapa and east of La Pérouse Bay. Passage over the *aa* would have been very difficult if this trail had not been especially constructed. On easier terrain, the trail followed natural routes like beaches, and it has disappeared because there was never a *built-up* trail. Elsewhere, it's disappeared on account of erosion and neglect or been buried under newer construction.

Any lava field holds surprises no traveler needs. Fragile lava formations, such as thin ceilings over hidden lava tubes, can crumble underfoot, leaving you hanging in midair or, worse, falling. The King's Highway provides a safe passage through lava fields. The prehistoric Hawaiians invested a great deal of time and labor in building this roadway over the impossible jumble of the *aa* wilderness. As you'll find when you hike them, the waterless, shadeless *aa* fields can be brutally hot in the fiery sun. Imagine working to build the King's Highway in that heat, lifting and carrying the stones, placing them, and keeping the trailbed relatively level for all those miles.

These segments of the King's Highway can be demanding, for the *aa* rocks on the trailbed are loose and sharp. They roll around under your boots and make each step a little more work than you're used to. The trail makes no concession to the terrain. It simply marches as straight as it can steeply up, across, and steeply down the lava ridges and gullies. But look around you: what more could be done in this *aa* field without destroying it completely? Well done, I say!

Trip E8. Ohala *Heiau* Side Trip from Hana

E

Distance: 1½ miles

Elevation gain: Negligible

Hiking time: ¾ hour

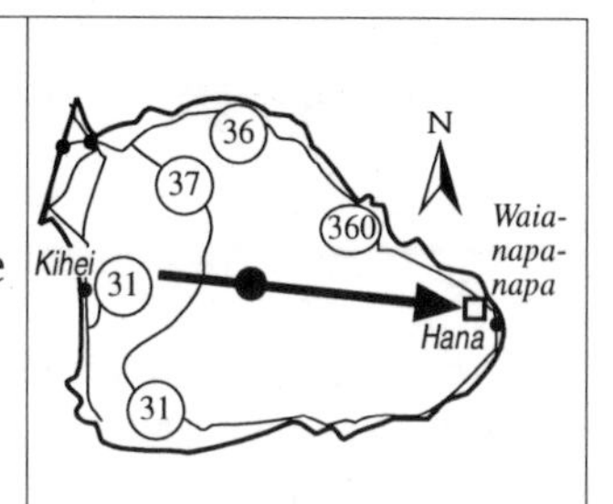

Topos: Hana 7½.

Trail map: At the end of Trip E5.

Highlights: Magnificent scenery as in Trip E7; the coastal scenery is perhaps even better on this trip. Your visit includes the well-known *hala* groves of Waianapanapa, a fine, noisy blowhole, and a *heiau*, too.

Driving instructions: Follow the driving instructions of Trip E5.

Permit/permission required: None.

Description. Follow Trip E6 from the parking lot to the point where the trail to the black-sand beach forks left. Take the right fork here, quickly passing the tent campground and then a cemetery in the shade of tropical almond trees, to yet another fork. Go left at this fork, and you'll soon reach some picnic tables. This is a good place to pause to enjoy the view: the fresh tropical green of Haleakala's slopes, the black of Waianapanapa's basalt cliffs, and the foam-streaked blue-green of the sea. Notice the column-like formations in the cliffs; you'll see formations like these often along this coastal walk.

Now you descend a little as the trail winds past *aa* flows and through beach *naupaka* and morning glory. Dense groves of *hala* trees rise just inland of the path; often, the path is plentifully strewn with their long, sawtoothed, pointed leaves and their chunky orange fruit. Use trails and even old roads strike off into the *hala* groves, but you stay on the coastal trail. Between ⅓ and ¼ mile, listen for the roar of a big blowhole that's just seaward off the trail. When it actually "blows" depends on tide and surf (some wave combinations aren't strong enough to make it erupt), and it may take you by surprise. Look for low-lying strands of *akulikuli* in the rocks along your path here.

Near ⅔ mile, you cross a cement-reinforced bridge. Soon after that, you descend steeply but briefly beneath a tree heliotrope. At the bottom of this descent, the path continues between the tree trunk and a black rock face. At ¾ mile, you reach signed OHALA HEIAU, a raised platform of black boulders. It's a picturesque spot, and you'll want to spend some time here. However, the lava field may be swarming with busy ants, so be prepared to defend your lunch.

When you're ready, retrace your steps from here. Or, if you feel the urge to go farther, continue toward Kainalimu Bay as described in the next trip.

***Heiau*, graves, and shrines....**These rugged and beautiful cliffs hold many sites of religious significance. Besides the *heiau* and the numerous small shrines, there are mounds of *aa* that may be ancient, raised graves. While it's a custom elsewhere to leave leaf-wrapped rocks as an offering at these shrines and *heiau*s, signs here ask you *not* to disturb the site by moving, removing, or wrapping any rocks.

There's a sense of the supernatural here in the presence of so much natural beauty; perhaps the sounds of wind and waves carry echoes of ancient prayers chanted at these solemn places. Please treat all *heiau*s, graves, shrines, and any offerings left at them with respect.

Beach *naupaka*

Trip E9. King's Highway South to Kainalimu Bay Side Trip from Hana

Distance: 5 miles

Elevation gain: Negligible

Hiking time: 2½ hours

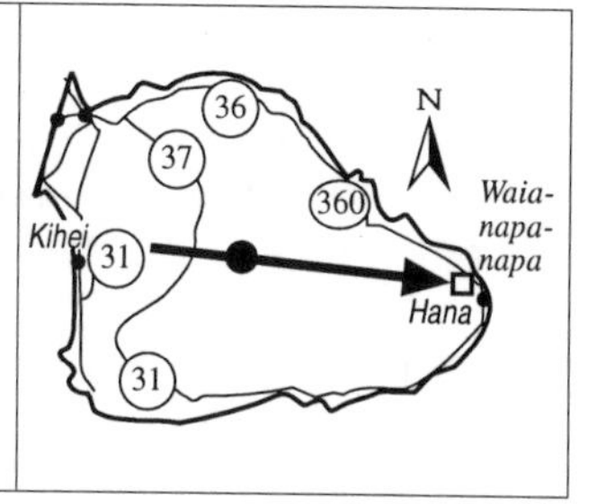

Topos: Hana 7½.

Trail map: At the end of Trip E5.

Highlights: More of the spectacular coastal scenery that makes Waianapanapa so unforgettable.

Driving instructions: Follow the driving instructions of Trip E5.

Permit/permission required: None.

Description. Follow Trip E8 to the *heiau*. A low rock wall stretching seaward from the *hala* grove keeps you away from the *heiau* proper. To continue your hike, pass through an opening in the wall near the wall's seaward end. A few yards beyond the *heiau*, a fence runs inland, perpendicular to the coast, and the King's Highway passes through it. Beyond this point, the King's Highway becomes rougher and fainter. At some points, you'll have to hunt around for it; please be careful in these sharp and sometimes unstable lava boulders. A telltale sign of the King's Highway that's particularly evident and useful here is a smooth boulder laid flat in the *aa* trailbed.

At a stretch of coast just over 1 mile from your start, look for a long sweep of coastal cliffs where the basalt columns are especially well-shaped, looking almost manmade-more about this below. Nearly 1⅓ miles from your start, you cross the end of a road that heads inland to your right; you continue along the King's Highway, which becomes even rougher now. The *aa*'s basic gray-black color is varied here and there by bands of red and brown and by whitish lichens, and the *aa* plain is broken by bizarre lava spires twisting skyward. Small ironwood trees grow here, their green foliage incongruously feathery and fresh against the dark, desolate lava.

Presently you cross a large field of smooth *pahoehoe* lava pocked by broken lava tubes and caves and invaded by beach *naupaka*. Here, you must follow ducks (small piles of rocks obviously set up by people) as the King's Highway is very indistinct. Don't follow them blindly, though; test your next foothold to be sure it's sound and will support you.

Nearing the 2½-mile point, you pass a sign that says WAIANAPANAPA STATE PARK 3 MILES (it isn't that far). The track soon dips into a buggy, tree-filled gully, where you may want a spider stick to get past some hiker-size webs and their occupants. The track bears left at the bottom of the gully and debouches at the cobblestone beach of Kainalimu Bay. Rest here, enjoy this wild, lonely bay, and then turn around and retrace your steps to your car.

Basalt columns.... When a lava flow forms a pond that cools slowly, it may crack into column-like shapes like those you see here along the Waianapanapa coast. Cooling lava shrinks, and cracks form as sections of rock shrink apart. These cracks tend to go from the top to the bottom of the cooling mass, producing the basic "column" effect. The cracks intersect, and columns with from three to eight sides form in the cooling mass. As every honeybee knows, a six-sided structure is the most efficient, and six-sided columns tend to predominate. A columnar formation is a spectacular sight when it's exposed to view. Columnar formations are said to be rare on Hawaii, so it's a special pleasure to see them here. (On the mainland, Devils Postpile National Monument in California's Sierra Nevada includes one of the better-known large columnar formations.)

King's Highway at Kanaio (see Trip E18)

Trip E10. Hana Bay Side Trip from Hana

Distance: ⅔ mile

Elevation gain: Negligible

Hiking time: 10 minutes

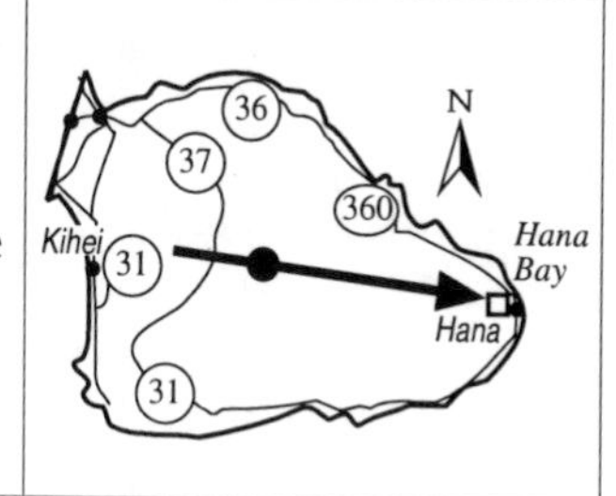

Topos: Hana 7½.

Trail map (route approximated): At the end of this trip.

Highlights: A morning walk around Hana Bay offers fine views of Hana from the wharf.

Driving instructions: This hike begins at Hana Beach County Park (see Trip E4).

Permit/permission required: None.

Description. Hana town is lovely, but it can get quite hot and humid. A long walk around Hana can be almost as debilitating as a walk through a steambath with hills. Add to this no sidewalks and streets with fast traffic that may come popping unexpectedly over the top of the hill you're walking on. I recommend that you keep your strolls in Hana town short, and restrict them to the early morning hours. With that caution, it's time to see Hana Bay.

Whatever direction you're facing when you get out of your car, it's hard to miss the prominent hill on the south side of Hana Bay, Kauiki (ka-oo-EE-kee) Head. Walk around the bay as it curves toward Kauiki Head. Follow the paved road as it bears left at the base of Kauiki Head at a little parking lot and out onto the wharf. Turn right where this first wharf meets a second wharf that runs almost at a right angle to it. Stroll out to the far end of the second wharf, a little over ¼ mile from your start, with a wonderful view of Hana town and its surroundings. A line of green-clad cinder cones marks one of Haleakala's rift zones. Nearer the town, a gray cross on sensuously shaped Puu o Kahaula honors the memory of Paul Fagan. When sugar production declined here and Hana's economy faltered in the 1940s, Paul Fagan helped revive Hana by introducing cattle ranching (Hana Ranch) and tourism (Hotel Hana-Maui). Grazing cattle dot the hillsides above the town now. And just in front of you, the blue waters of Hana Bay lap at the wharf.

Hana was one of the favorite places of the *alii*. Hana had everything, especially plenty to eat with little effort required to get food. The community maintained a lookout on Kauiki Head for schools of fish. Before Europeans came to Hawaii, Kauiki Head was covered with a native bunchgrass and could be climbed. Now, it's almost impossible to climb because of its dense cover of exotic plants. It's reported that the few who climb it get no reward for their effort: ironwoods block the view from its top.

Kauiki Head was used as a fortress; not surprisingly, it was the site of many battles. Hana is worth fighting over, and this isolated corner of East Maui has often been ruled by the Big Island of Hawaii. In 1754, the king of Hawaii conquered East Maui. Kahekili, then king of Maui, recaptured East Maui in 1775. The fortress at Kauiki Head did not fall in battle. Instead, Kahekili had to cut off the water supply to the fortress. When the fortress surrendered, Kahekili showed his contempt for the defenders by baking their bodies in earthen ovens.

As you'd expect, Kauiki Head also has its share of legends. One legend about the demigod Maui relates that long ago, the sky was so low that people couldn't stand straight. They even had to walk bent over. From the top of Kauiki Head, Maui pushed the sky up so that people could walk and stand upright.

Back at the little parking lot at the base of the wharf and of Kauiki Head, you may notice a rough use trail that heads seaward (left) from here out onto Kauiki Head, but don't take it. The trail used to lead to a plaque marking Queen Kaahumanu's birthplace, but the trail has been erased by a landslide. I recommend you not try to cross the slope, as it seems ready to give way again. It's unfortunate that you can't go out to pay your respects to Queen Kaahumanu any more because, as outlined in "Geology and History, Natural and Human" in this book, she became Kamehameha's favorite wife. After his death she was a leader in overthrowing the *kapu* that had been the basis of Hawaiian social structure. Here's something to think about: how would Hawaii's history have been different if the *kapu* been in force when the first missionaries arrived?

After having pondered that question, retrace your steps to your car.

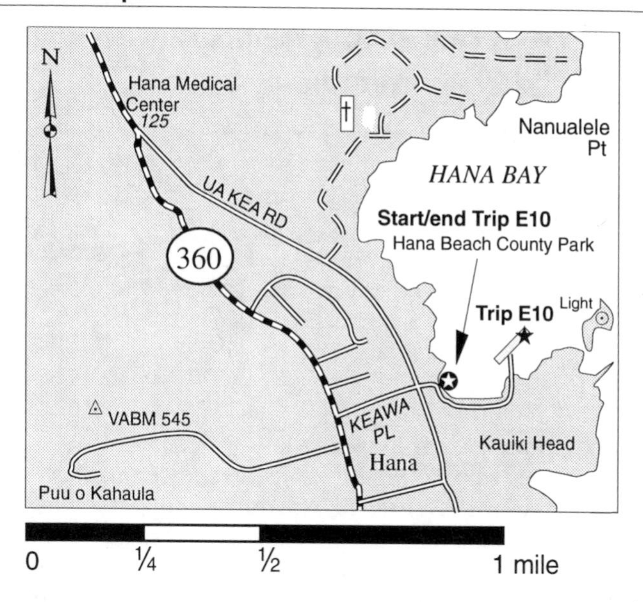

Cascade on stream along Ulaino Road

Trip E11. Oheo Gulch Pools (Kuloa Loop) Side Trip from Hana

V

Distance: Just under ⅔ mile

Elevation gain: 120′ (upside-down trip)

Hiking time: 20 minutes

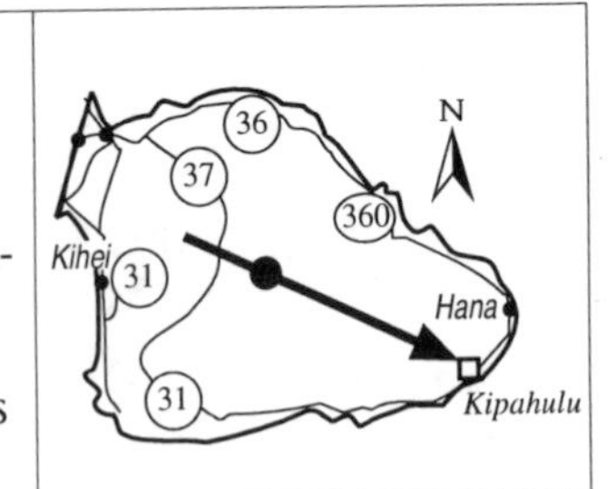

Topos: Optional: Kipahulu 7½.

Trail map (route approximated): At the end of this trip.

Highlights: A splash in Oheo Stream's famous pools is what most people come here for. This is the area that was once erroneously referred to as the seven sacred pools. In fact, there are more than seven pools, and there's no evidence that they were ever considered sacred. But there's more to enjoy than the pools: Don't overlook the marvelous coastal views here. You can often see the Big Island of Hawaii across Alenuihaha Channel. For the latest information on the Oheo Gulch area, call the Kipahulu Ranger Station at (808) 248-7375.

Driving instructions: From the intersection of Ua Kea Road and Keawa Place in Hana, drive uphill on Keawa Place and turn left onto the Hana Highway. From here, it's 10⅓ miles to the Kipahulu section of Haleakala National Park, which is where Oheo Stream is. At 7⅓ miles from Hana, you cross a bridge just inland of which beautiful Wailua Falls drops into a fine pool. You may be tempted to pull over onto the shoulder and walk back for a dip. On the road, you reach the park boundary, cross Oheo Stream, and follow signs a short distance to a dirt parking lot on the seaward side. In spite of its remoteness, enough people find their way to the Kipahulu section to fill this little parking lot to overflowing by midday. There are restrooms here but *no drinking water*. You must either purify any water you get from the stream or bring your own drinking water with you.

Permit/permission required: None.

Description. The marked trail to the lower pools begins at the northeast edge of the parking lot. Head downhill (east) toward the sea on a paved path, toward the ranger station and an information sign. You soon reach a junction (not on the map) where it's right to the ranger station and left to continue to the pools. The ranger station has interesting interpretive displays as well as books and maps. At the junction with the trail to Makahiku and Waimoku falls—the Pipiwai Trail, which branches left—go right to the pools. (This is the junction that's about ½ inch west of and slightly down from the star that marks the goal of this trip.) Almost immediately, you reach another junction (not on the map) where you go right again. Continuing to the pools, you stay on the wide, main trail, ignoring use trails that branch off. You pass Java plum and *kukui* trees, then cross a meadow dotted with clumps of *hala*. Soon you're on a bluff overlooking the ocean, next to the stone ruins of an old Hawaiian community. There are beautiful views up and down the coast and across Alenuihaha Channel south-southeast to the Big Island.

Now the trail curves left (north-northeast) toward the stream, and it's just a minute or so before you hear the sounds of merriment from the pools. At the next trail junction, just over ⅓ mile from the parking lot, the right fork is a spur trail leading to views of the coast and, uphill, of Oheo Gulch. You take the left fork, and another trail junction pops up almost immediately. The right fork here will take you down steep stairs to the lowest pool. From there, you can work your way upstream to the other pools (not part of this hike). The pools are generally quite crowded.

The left fork (that is, continuing on the main trail) takes you uphill to an area where railings allow you to safely enjoy the view over the stream and snap some photos. *Hala*, *ti*, and sisal clothe the steep slope below your viewpoint. Continuing, you presently curve away from the stream under tropical almond trees, almost reaching the road. You could close this loop on the road, but it's nicer to turn left and take the trail, now on stairs for a short stretch, back to the parking lot. You pass a junction where you continue ahead (the left fork goes back to the stone ruins you visited earlier on this hike).

At ½ mile you reach another trail junction (it's the first one you passed at the beginning of this hike). Here, you turn continue ahead and soon reach the parking lot, a little less than ⅔ mile from your start.

While paddling in the pools....keep an eye out for the water level. If it rises suddenly, that may indicate that a flash flood is imminent. Get out of the water immediately! You don't want to be swept downstream and drowned, much less be swept out to sea. It's said that the gray sharks around the mouth of Oheo Stream have acquired a taste for human flesh—a heck of a way to end your Maui vacation! But maybe sloshing around in the pools isn't all you're here for. You'd like to see some waterfalls! Read on—Trips E12 and E13 take you to splendid Makahiku Falls and then to enchanting Waimoku Falls.

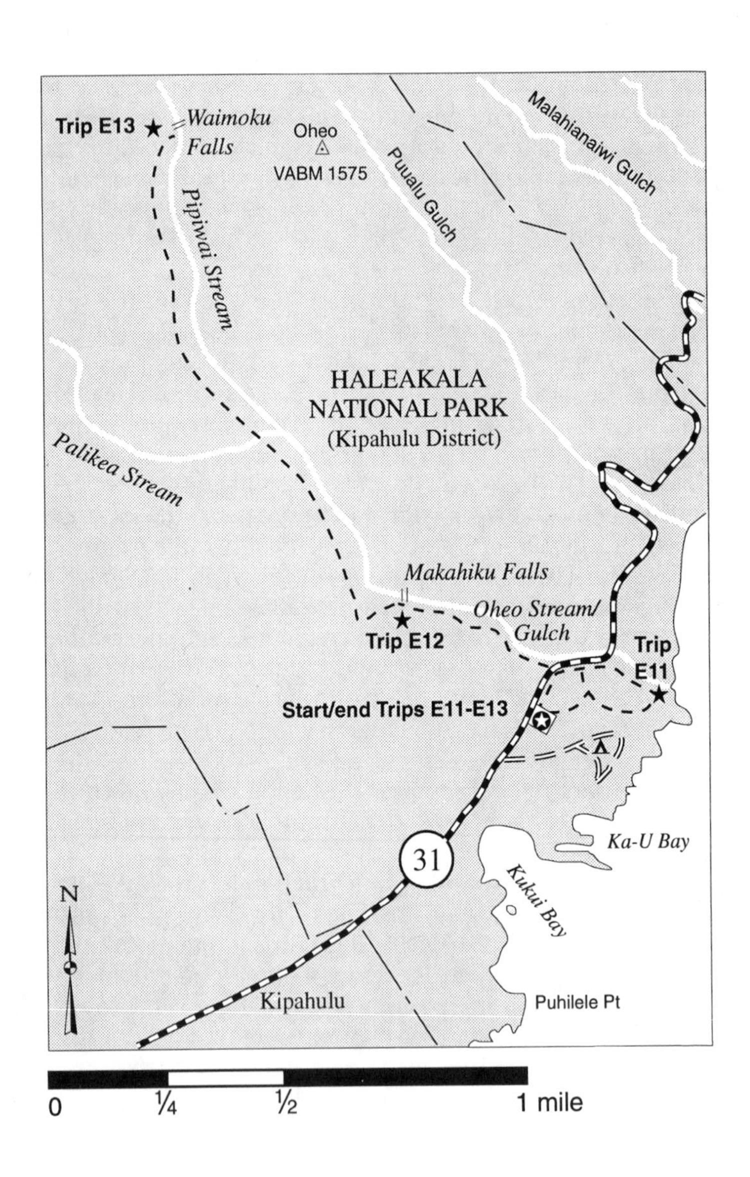
Trip E13
Waimoku Falls
Oheo VABM 1575
Puualu Gulch
Malahianaiwi Gulch
Pipiwai Stream
HALEAKALA NATIONAL PARK (Kipahulu District)
Palikea Stream
Makahiku Falls
Oheo Stream/ Gulch
Trip E12
Trip E11
Start/end Trips E11-E13
31
Ka-U Bay
Kukui Bay
Kipahulu
Puhilele Pt
N
0
¼
½
1 mile

Trip E12. Makahiku Falls Side Trip from Hana

E

Distance: ⅔ mile

Elevation gain: 250′

Hiking time: 20 minutes

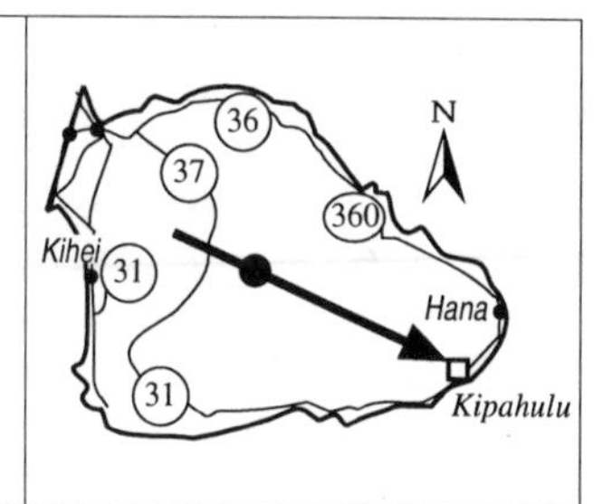

Topos: Kipahulu 7½.

Trail map (route approximated): At the end of Trip E11.

Highlights: An easy hike through the lovely hills and pastures upslope of the highway brings you to an overlook of spectacular Makahiku Falls. You can swim off the dust of the hike in the fine pools behind the falls. Note that it's possible for both falls, Makahiku and Waimoku, to be almost dry if there's been a drought. But you'll enjoy this hike even if the falls are barely dribbling.

Driving instructions: Follow the driving instructions of Trip E11.

Permit/permission required: None.

Description. You could head seaward toward the pools east of the highway and pick up the trail to Makahiku and Waimoku falls from that route (Trip E11). But there's a shorter route: From the parking lot, face the entrance to orient yourself and then go right, roughly parallel to and on the seaward side of the parking lot wall, to pick up a path that in a few yards leads you to a pedestrian crossing of the highway. Cross the highway and curve right to pick up the official trail, paralleling the highway briefly.

The trail shortly leads uphill under Java plum and on rocky footing to reach the edge of Oheo Gulch. The trail then bears left (west) along the south side of the gulch and climbs moderately through a dense forest of Christmas berry and strawberry guava. Many use trails branch off this main trail toward the rim of the gulch; keep your eyes peeled so you can stick to the main trail. The trail may be hard to follow at times, and you'll be thankful for the TRAIL signs the Park Service has posted here and there. You presently leave the forest at a WILDERNESS TRAIL sign for a track through an open stand of guava and Christmas berry, where there may be good guava-hunting—but watch your step as you thrash through deep weeds and across uneven ground.

You soon see a safety railing to your right, on the rim of Oheo Gulch. Sites along this railing provide excellent views of Makahiku

Falls. This is a good vantage point for a photo of the falls, too. Look for white-tailed tropicbirds soaring over the chasm. Near the upper end of the railing, a use trail leads down a small, damp, overgrown gully to the pools behind the falls. Even when the falls are nearly dry, you'll probably find enough water in the larger pools to splash around in. Enjoy your swim here, and please observe the cautions given for the lower pools in Trip E11.

When you're ready, return the way you came.

Kipahulu Valley.... You've been hiking in lower Kipahulu Valley on this trail. If you look at a topographic map of Maui, the immense Keanae and Kaupo valleys will probably catch your eye. You can see how they meet atop Haleakala to form Haleakala Crater. Now look to the east of Kaupo Valley, and you'll notice the deep "scoop" of Kipahulu Valley.

Kipahulu Valley is the result of distinct episodes of volcanism and stream-cutting. The first episode of volcanism built Haleakala. A second episode of volcanism covered the original volcano with new lavas. Rain soon sent streams radiating from the top of the shield volcano, cutting into it as they flowed. At Kipahulu, a stream carved a huge valley much deeper than the present one, cutting through both the newer and the older lavas. The next episode of volcanism sent new lava flowing down the huge valley, nearly filling it. A stream soon began cutting through the newest lava. Before this second stream could re-create the original valley by erosion, still more lava flowed from Haleakala, partly filling the newer valley. Now the present-day Palikea Stream, the western tributary of Oheo Stream, is scooping out the present Kipahulu Valley, while Pipiwai Stream, the eastern tributary of Oheo Stream, is scooping out a smaller side valley.

It seems likely that Palikea Stream will continue eroding Kipahulu Valley's headwall back toward Kaupo Valley and breach that wall, just as the streams forming Kaupo and Keanae valleys once breached their headwalls to create the crater—unless Haleakala erupts and fills Kipahulu again. In the meantime, a dense rainforest fills upper Kipahulu Valley, and many rare species of birds and plants flourish only there. Upper Kipahulu Valley is a scientific reserve closed to the public so that it can be protected, preserved, and studied.

The dense growth of the upper valley soaks up the abundant rain, releasing it in streams and springs and ensuring a good water supply for the settled areas below. The lands of Kipahulu are very productive. They once supported a large population and were, like Hana, fought over by the *alii*. Kipahulu was gradually abandoned as the center of commerce on Maui shifted to Lahaina in the early nineteenth century.

Trip E13. Waimoku Falls Side Trip from Hana

Distance: Just under 4 miles

Elevation gain: 560′

Hiking time: Just under 2 hours

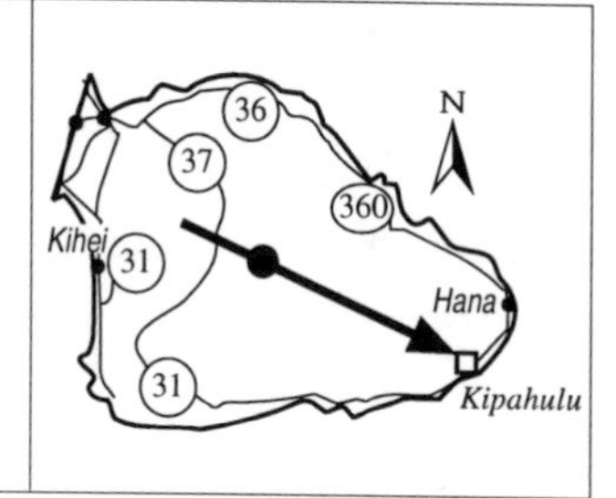

Topos: Kipahulu 7½.

Trail map (route approximated): At the end of Trip E11.

Highlights: After your visit to Makahiku Falls, you continue uphill to Waimoku Falls. Along the way, you pass through stands of giant bamboo so dense that what little light filters down to you seems tinted green. Waimoku Falls is lovely, but the pool at its base is too shallow to swim in.

Driving instructions: Follow the driving instructions of Trip E11.

Permit/permission required: None.

Description. Follow Trip E12 to Makahiku Falls. If you want to swim, Makahiku Falls is a fine place to do so (Waimoku Falls isn't). Back on the main trail, you soon bear north past some banyan trees. Your progress between here and the 1-mile point is apt to be slower than usual if you like guavas, for trees bearing abundant fruit line this stretch.

Nearing the 1-mile point, you cross an open area and descend slightly to pass through a fence and into a dense growth of guavas. A sign warns FLASH FLOOD AREA DO NOT CROSS DURING FLOODING and another warns you that it's a difficult trail ahead. Whatever the other hazards may be here, you're in very real danger of getting beaned by falling guavas as you stand reading these signs. Mosquitoes are sure to be a problem from here on, if they haven't been already, so apply that jungle juice now.

In a few more steps, you reach and cross Palikea Stream (a tributary of Oheo Stream) and, bearing left to pick up the trail on the other side, scramble up very steeply under guavas and mangoes, negotiating a few short switchbacks. Soon you're walking between walls of giant bamboo. Wooden walkways help you across boggy spots in and between these bamboo forests; watch out for missing planks. As you walk out of this first bamboo stand, clumps of fragrant yellow ginger line your path and the long ribbon of Waimoku Falls is straight ahead in the distance.

You descend the now-damp trail to another stand of bamboo, emerging from it into *kukui, ti, mamaki,* and thimbleberry. Now a third bamboo forest closes in on your trail, which is often on a boardwalk from now on, the route seeming to have just been hacked through the giant stalks. As you grope through the twilight of the dense stand, a breeze may rattle the stalks, playing random percussion music on them, and rustle the leaves, making a thin accompaniment with their whisperings.

On the other side of the bamboo, you cross a streamlet (watch the poor footing). In a few more yards, the trail becomes less distinct as you cross several channels of Pipiwai Stream flowing from Waimoku Falls, which you can see just ahead. Follow the trail or the channels a few more steps to the shallow pool at the waterfall's base, almost 2 miles from your start. Waimoku Falls is cradled in a deep little amphitheater with sheer walls to which cling mosses and ferns. Its base is surrounded by shattered rock; there's a real danger of rockfall here. The principal cascade is on the left side, but smaller cascades slip down the walls on every side. Bands of solid lava rock alternate with looser bands of consolidated ash or clinker, layer upon layer up the amphitheater walls. Spray from the waterfall cools and dampens everything.

Rest awhile and enjoy this lovely sight. When you're ready, return the way you came.

Waterfalls at work.... In Hawaii, the terrain tends to consist of alternating layers of resistant lava and less resistant material, such as consolidated ash or clinker. The layers you see alternating in the amphitheater walls at Waimoku Falls are an example. A stream wears through the softer layer faster and cascades over the remaining harder layer. The force of the falling water wears away the rock at the base of the falls, forming a pool. Undercut by that process, rock above the pool succumbs to gravity and falls away, shattering at the base of the falls. This process wears the stream's channel farther and farther back into the slope. Over eons, the stream cuts its gorge back toward its headwaters. Because harder and softer layers alternate, many streams form a chain of waterfalls on their long descent to the sea. A waterfall like Waimoku may be—and in this case *is*—just one in the chain.

Trip E14. Kaupo to Haleakala Park Boundary

S

Distance: 6½ miles

Elevation gain: 2730′

Hiking time: 3¼ hours

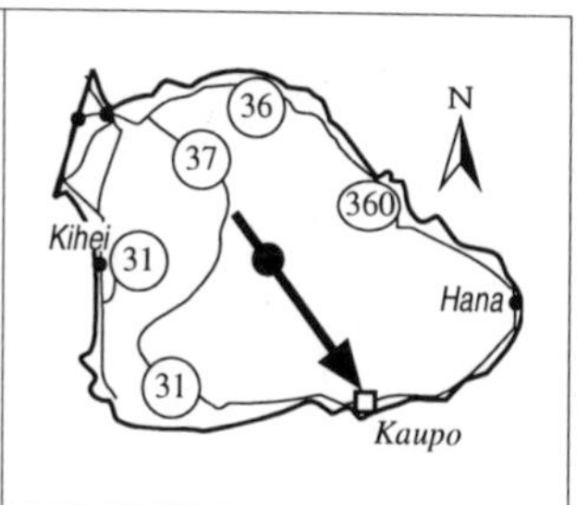

Topos: Kaupo 7½.

Trail map (route approximated): At the end of this trip.

Highlights: The sweeping views down Haleakala's southern slopes from this steep, breezy, very strenuous trail defy words. The scene upslope to Kaupo Gap's mountain-guarded portals is just as stunning. A few miles east, scores of people crowd into the Kipahulu District parking lot to visit the pools and waterfalls of Oheo Gulch. But here at remote Kaupo, where there are no typical tourist attractions, you'll probably have the trail all to yourself.

Driving instructions: You can't get to Kaupo from Kipahulu in the average rental car. As mentioned earlier, much of the road between Kaupo and Kipahulu is unpaved and extremely rough. It's subject to washouts, landslides, and closures. If you must take it, check with the highway department first to see if it's open. If it's open, then tackle it only in a high-clearance 4WD vehicle with plenty of gas and well-stocked with food and water.

There's no gas until distant Keokea, but you can get food and drink at the Kaupo Store at Kaupo. The store is open Monday through Friday from about 9:30 A.M. to 5:30 P.M. and stocks cold drinks, snacks, other simple supplies. The store also has a restroom. It's a family venture, the owners are delightful people, and a visit to the Kaupo Store is not to be missed. Call ahead to verify the hours (808-248-8054).

The better approach is from Ulupalakua, though it's a long and, beyond Keokea, a very slow drive. Allow at least 2 hours each way for this drive and have a full tank of gas before you start out. When the Kaupo Store is open (see above), you can get food and drink there; otherwise, take them with you. I'd prefer to have recommended that you make this a side trip from someplace closer than Wailuku. But there are few accommodations—try bed-and-breakfast services to find a place in Kula—and no legal campgrounds on the route between Kahului and the campground at Kipahulu. So it's drive, drive, drive; hike, hike, hike; drive, drive, drive. It's worth it!

From Wailuku, drive east on Highway 32 to Highway 36. Take Highway 36 southeast and then northeast to Highway 37. Turn onto Highway 37 southeast through Pukalani; stay on Highway 37 where Highway 337 departs toward Haleakala's summit (both times). Follow it southeast, then south and southwest, through the rolling green slopes of "upcountry" Maui (Kula, Waiakoa, Keokea, and Ulupalakua Ranch). Keokea is your last chance for gas!

Beyond Ulupalakua Ranch, the road is renumbered as Highway 31 and bears east. It becomes much narrower; you may wish to pull over to let others pass from time to time. The speed limit along here is 15 mph. You descend gradually to the coast, and the pavement ends a little before Kaupo. You pass the Kaupo Store (see above) between mile markers 34 and 35. *Please do not park for your hike at the Kaupo Store!* By all means resupply there, but you can then drive another 1.6 miles and 720 feet up to the real trailhead. In 0.1 mile beyond the Kaupo Store you pass a private driveway and reach an unpaved road. Turn left onto the unpaved road, which is narrow and rough but passable. Follow the road uphill for 1.5 miles, to its end where there is a fork: right to a house, sharply left to a grassy area where there's informal parking for a few cars and beyond that a stone wall. Bear left and park as best you can—it's pretty uneven ground—51.5 long and beautiful miles from Wailuku. Don't block the right fork or the house. There's a trailhead sign for Haleakala National Park near a gate in the stone wall.

Permit/permission required: None.

Description. Following the road, you walk from the parking lot toward the trailhead sign and through the gate in the stone wall. A sign a few yards past the gate advises you that you may go no farther on the road but must pick up the trail to your right (northwest). It's slow going on this indistinct, rough, overgrown foot trail as you pass juniper, mango, castor, silk oak, and a smelly trash heap. Because the path is faint, numerous little TRAIL signs help point it out—but be aware that the signs are oriented to help people hiking *down* this trail from Haleakala "crater," not those hiking *up* it! This part of the trail can be tough, but the rewards—the views ahead—are worth the trouble, I think. Many use trails and cow paths crisscross the area, petering out in the thickets and adding to the confusion. If you find yourself bushwhacking for more than 10 feet, you've lost the true trail; backtrack before you get lost in the dense growth off-trail. Your goal is to reach the old 4WD road shown on the map as "Kaupo Trail."

You cross an intermittent stream (may be dry) and ascend a slope, bashing your way through the undergrowth. You climb over a stile and begin working your way uphill through Christmas berry. You walk up a north-trending gully that's booby-trapped with use trails, cow paths, and lantana clumps overgrown with morning-glory vines. The little TRAIL signs are hard to see here. As you near the head of the gully, look for a particularly tall silk oak about 50 yards off the trail to the right (I hope it's still standing) and look straight ahead for a broad clump of swamp mahogany. To escape the gully, aim for a **Y** junction where you're above the point on the trail that's abreast of the silk oak and about 25 yards below the clump of swamp mahogany. Don't take the left fork, which is a cow path that meanders into dense lantana thickets! Turn right (east) on a shady trail that may be a little overgrown at first but which soon becomes quite distinct. Following that track, you presently reach a barbed-wire fence with a hiker's pass-through. Beyond the fence, you soon meet the 4WD road.

Down the road to the right, a sign on a gate advises DO NOT ENTER. You turn left toward a national-park sign half-hidden in the vegetation (the distance it gives to the park's boundary is too short). In spite of the road's steepness and rockiness, it's a big relief from the bushwhacking you've been doing and offers great views and cool breezes after it breaks free of the trees that here overhang it. You may see tracks branching off the road. Don't take them; stick to the road. Be alert for any vehicles-vehicles are infrequent, but traction on this steep, rocky road can be poor.

At 1⅝ miles, the road forks, and a crumpled sign currently suggests you should take the right fork downhill—don't. Take the left fork uphill past a water tank. You'll want to stop often to catch your breath on this steep climb and to enjoy the marvelous views in every direction.

As you approach the 2⅝-mile point, the road forks twice. Take the left fork both times. At the 2⅝-mile point, the maw of cloud-filled Kaupo Gap opens far uphill, and the peak named Haleakala rises on the Gap's west side. A patch of bare, red soil looms ahead of you. The road turns to parallel the patch of soil, carrying you into the shade of some *koa* trees, remnants of the forest that once clothed the upper slopes of Haleakala. You pass a water tank on your left.

At 3¼ miles, you reach another road junction and again take the left fork (ahead). In a few more yards, amid plants uprooted by wild pigs, you reach the fence that now surrounds much of Haleakala National Park. A little flat spot with some avocado trees offers you a resting spot just outside the fence. Just inside the fence, a handsome grove of *koa* trees beckons you. If you go through the gate, please be sure you close it, even if you have to stamp down the grass to do so!

This trip ends here at the boundary of Haleakala National Park. Retrace your steps from here to your car. (Hikers who want to continue to Paliku Cabin should have a *Nahiku* 7½' topo and should reverse the steps of Trip H7.)

The road to Kaupo.... Cool, green "upcountry" is a treat for the eye and a welcome change from the heat of Lahaina and Kihei. The eucalyptus-shaded fields and rolling green hills with their views down to the sea will seem very familiar if you've spent any time along the coast of central California.

A drastic change occurs after you pass Ulupalakua: the green pastures of "upcountry" soon disappear, and you find yourself driving through a landscape scorched, barren, and colorless in the fierce light. You drive past the sunstruck Lualailua Hills and between the grazing lands of huge ranches. Cattle, stupefied by the heat and dazed by the glare, sag against splintering chutes and huddle in the pitiful shade of leafless *wiliwili* trees. Along the road, apple-of-Sodom's yellow fruit dangles fat and deadly from its withered parent.

These parched slopes once supported sizeable human populations. Not far from the Lualailua Hills and upslope of the highway lie the ruins of Kahikinui, where a thousand or more people once lived. *Maui: How It Came To Be* notes that there are more than 140 house-sites in ruins between Ulupalakua and Kaupo. This area was heavily populated when Cook arrived in Hawaii in 1778. But soon after, the goats, cattle, and pigs descended from those brought by Europeans began stripping the land of its vegetation. It was naturally arid to start with; now, with insufficient vegetation to trap and retain what little moisture fell, it became a desert. The damage continues today; a way to successfully control the animals still hasn't been worked out (except for Haleakala's fences).

Now the road begins a definite descent to the coast, snaking in and out of the narrow throat of deep Manawainui Gulch. As you approach Kaupo, the green of trees softens the harsh landscape. Stretches of paved road alternate with unpaved road; then, a little beyond Nuu, the pavement ends for good. Sections of the road between here and Kaupo are covered with smooth beach pebbles that offer poor traction on the uphill side of some small rises. Don't fight it if you lose traction; roll back down and try another route up. The sound of pebbles ricocheting off the underside of a rental car may strike terror into your heart. At last you pass lonely, picturesque St. Joseph's Church and, a little farther on, reach the Kaupo Store. Kaupo is beautifully green, swept clean by strong breezes, and tranquil in a way you're not likely to find elsewhere on Maui. Unlike Hana, Kaupo remains truly remote, difficult to reach, and little-visited.

Enjoy your hike, then leave quietly, thankful that there's still a place like Kaupo.

Continued on the map at the end of Trip H7

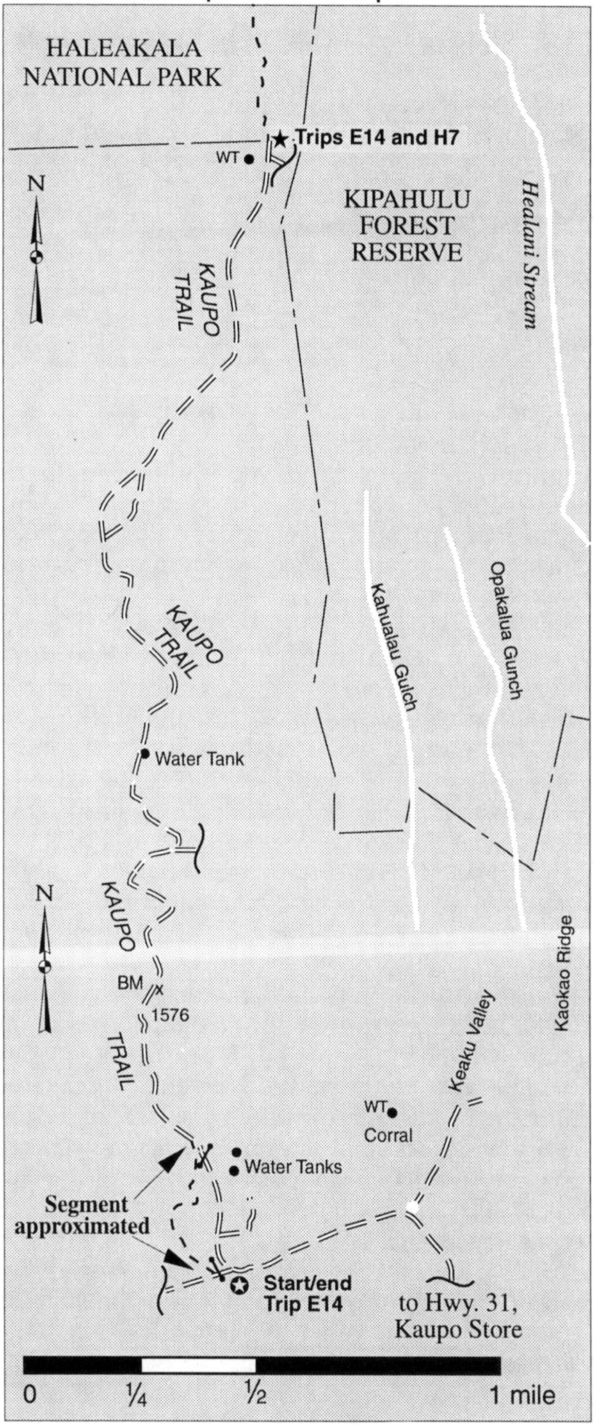

HALEAKALA
NATIONAL PARK

Trips E14 and H7

WT

N

KIPAHULU
FOREST
RESERVE

Healani Stream

KAUPO
TRAIL

KAUPO
TRAIL

Kahualau Gulch

Opakalua Gunch

Water Tank

N

KAUPO

BM
x
1576

TRAIL

Kaokao Ridge

Keaku Valley

WT

Corral

Water Tanks

Segment
approximated

Start/end
Trip E14

to Hwy. 31,
Kaupo Store

0 ¼ ½ 1 mile

Trip E15. Fuchsia Wall Side Trip from Polipoli

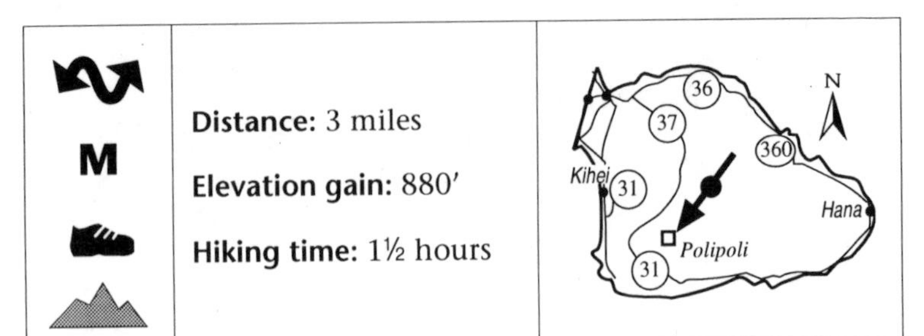

Distance: 3 miles

Elevation gain: 880′

Hiking time: 1½ hours

Topos: Optional: Lualailua Hills, Makena 7½.

Trail map: At the end of this trip.

Highlights: I have a surprise for you at the end of this trip, and I don't want to spoil it *here!* Okay, just a hint: flowers and birds.

Be aware that you may have to share Polipoli's trails with mountain bikers, a situation I regard as hazardous to and unpleasant for hikers.

Driving instructions: Polipoli State Park is so remote, partly because of the poor road to it, that it's almost mandatory that you stay overnight there. From Wailuku, drive east on Highway 32 to Highway 36. Take Highway 36 southeast and northeast to Highway 37. Take Highway 37 southeast through Pukalani and past the first (northern) junction with Highway 377 to the second (southern) junction with Highway 377, 19 miles. Turn onto Highway 377 (a very hard left) and drive ⅓ mile more to a junction with currently unmarked Waipoli Road on your right. It's the first road on your right that has a STOP sign. Turn right onto Waipoli Road.

Getting to Polipoli will take you another hour from here. Drive uphill on this road, ignoring side roads and driveways on your right. The road becomes quite steep, narrow (one lane; be alert for oncoming vehicles), and winding (one hairpin turn after another). Cattle graze alongside it; watch out for cattle straying onto the road. After 6 miles from the start of Waipoli Road, the pavement ends and the road, though less winding and steep now, is quite rough (protruding rocks and roots; sometimes deep dust, sometimes hard, slippery clay). Your rental-car company does not want you to drive this section, but, with care, it is just passable to ordinary passenger vehicles. The road forks 9½ miles from its start; bear right on the fork that dips downhill, negotiating a particularly rocky hairpin on the remaining ½ mile to Polipoli State Park's picnic and camping area. Park here, 29⅓ miles from Wailuku.

Permit/permission required: None.

Description. From the campground, backtrack a few steps through the parking lot and up the road to the side road that turns off north-northwest toward the cabin (left if your back is to the campground). You descend this barely discernable road, ducking under the vehicle barrier if it's closed. Soon you reach the cabin and curve around it on the road, then pass through an opening in a fence. At ⅕ mile, you reach an obscure junction where you go right (northeast) onto a footpath, not left onto the road (which is currently marked THIS IS NOT A TRAIL). The footpath is the start of the Redwood Trail.

The damp path descends gently under conifers—look out for exposed roots on the path and for overhanging dead, cone-studded branches! This profusion of dead branches still on the tree, as well as the many fallen trees, gives the path that oppressive feeling of decay so characteristic of this forest. You twine down into the forest, eventually bearing west. Around ⅔ mile, look out for false trails leading northwest and south—you continue west for now. Not far beyond, a spur trail leads uphill on your left to one of Polipoli's must-miss shelter huts (see below). Just beyond ¾ mile, you reach a junction with the Tie Trail. Here, you and the Redwood Trail turn right and go north-northeast. Again, be alert for false trails as the Redwood Trail bears north.

Eventually, the Redwood Trail curves west. At 1⅓ miles, you reach an apparent junction with a false trail. The Redwood Trail with you on it continues ahead (southwest now; you'd have to make a hard right turn north-northeast onto the false trail). A few more steps bring you to the muddy, hydrangea- and fuchsia-filled yard of the decaying, garbage-filled "ranger's cabin" and then to a junction with the Boundary and Plum trails.

Turn right (northwest) onto the Boundary Trail and follow it past tall fuchsias—the "Fuchsia Wall"—for just under ⅕ mile to some logs near the boundary fence, 1½ miles from your start. Have a seat here and look around you. The brilliant red sepals of the purple fuchsia blossoms have attracted one of Hawaii's native birds, the red *apapane*. At times, this wall of fuchsias seems almost alive with fluttering *apapane* sipping from the blossoms. In the evergreens behind you, look for a small greenish bird that gives a single *chirp!*, probably the Maui creeper (it's hard to spot until it moves).

Sooner or later, you have to tear yourself away from the Fuchsia Wall and retrace your steps.

Polipoli State Park....is a wonderful resource for the people of Maui but not for visitors from the mainland. The people of Maui enjoy camping and hunting (pigs and goats) in its extremely dense, fog-bound forest of non-native trees: coast redwood, Oregon ash, cedar, eucalyptus, etc. For the people of Maui, that forest is a unique novelty.

That forest is one of the principal reasons why I think Polipoli is *not* a wonderful resource for *mainland* visitors. At the risk of offending the people of Maui, I see no reason at all for a visitor from the mainland to drive for hours on Maui to see a sickly forest consisting almost entirely of mainland species. Your time in Hawaii is limited, so spend it seeing things representative of Hawaii, not of the mainland!

There are three memorable hikes from Polipoli in this book: this one, E15, the Fuchsia Wall (which incorporates the forgettable Redwood Trail); E16, Kahua Road; and E17, Skyline Trail, which is also accessible from the summit of Haleakala. The other trails, including the hike known as the Polipoli Loop, are summarized in Appendix B of this book and are not worth your trouble, as explained below.

Polipoli's trails were in poor condition when I first hiked them. Recently, mountain-biking groups have volunteered to improve them, but that means that these single-track trails must now serve mountain bikers, too. My experience is that hikers and bikers cannot safely and pleasurably share single-track trails. In my opinion, this development makes Polipoli's fragile trails even less attractive for hikers. Polipoli's trails are being bulldozed out of existence by wild pigs, and there's not much anyone can do about it. Trails in the heart of the dense, non-native forest are very faint under their thick blankets of fallen needles and twigs and are further obscured by a maze of crisscrossing use trails. In the fog or in the dark—forget it! At their best, they would still be uninteresting: you can't see much besides a dense network of dead twigs ahead of you. Potential views at the occasional openings are often concealed by the daily fogs. Most of Polipoli's trails don't appear as trips in this book for these reasons.

The plum trees some sources mention as a Polipoli attraction are mostly gone—shaded to death in the incredible overgrowth that, together with Polipoli's normal daytime fog, makes it twilight at high noon under the redwoods, ash, cedar, eucalyptus, etc. The overgrowth of the forest is largely due to the spacing of the original plantings in the 1930s by the Civilian Conservation Corps. It's hoped that as stronger trees crowd out and kill weaker trees, a healthier, more open forest will eventually take the place of the present one.

If you do hike in the heart of Polipoli, make sure you get back to your camp or your car before sunset. The brief Hawaiian twilight is as dark as night there, a bright moon can't penetrate the forest except at rare clearings, and a flashlight is no substitute for daylight in that dense growth and on those faint trails. (You should still carry one, anyway.)

Staying at Polipoli. Polipoli State Park is very remote, very wet, and very cold compared to the rest of Maui. (It lies in a local low spot within Haleakala's inversion-layer cloud bank.) Your choices when you stay overnight there are its tiny tent-campground or its one cabin (reserved through the Division of State Parks; book well in advance). Drinking water is available only at the tent-campground and the cabin. The shelters along the trails do not merit your consideration. They are either windowless wooden huts with no light, no water, four dirty wooden bunks, and dirt—I mean loose dirt!—floors, or they are claustrophobic caves. Your tent is a palace compared to those shelters.

Your tent must be waterproof, as it rains frequently at Polipoli and is always damp there. You'll need a warm sleeping bag, rain gear, and plenty of warm clothing. The nearest lodgings are in Kula on Highway 377, but even from there, it's an hour-long grind each way to/from Polipoli.

White hibiscus

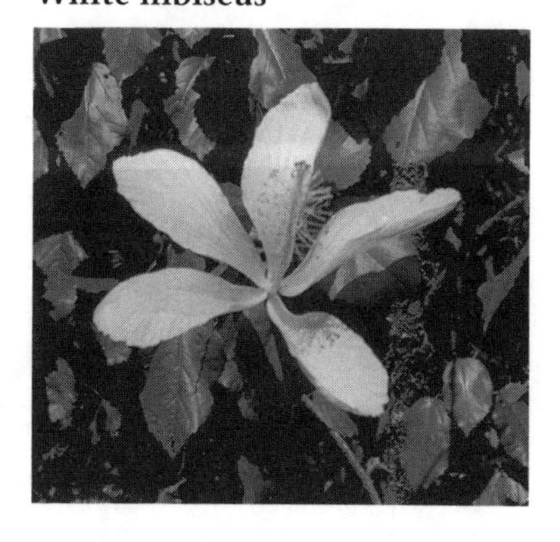

Continued on map at end of Trip E17

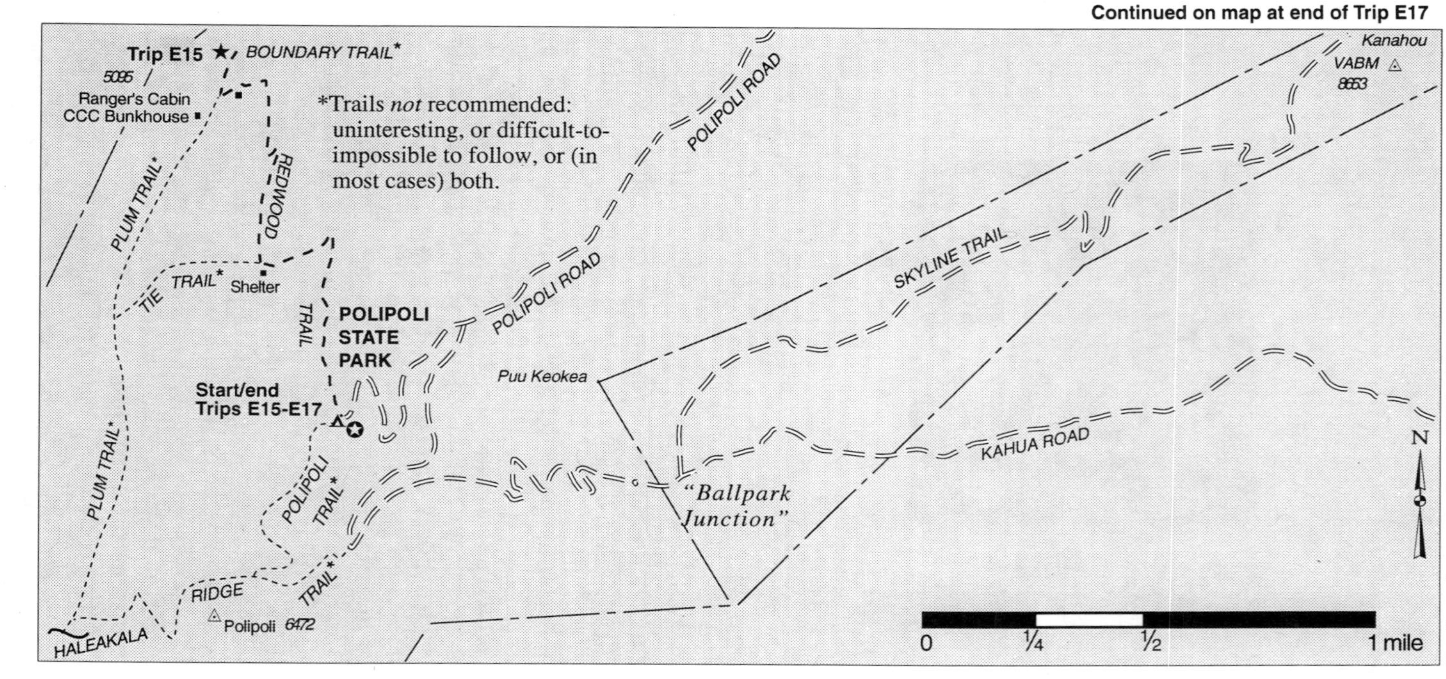

Continued on map at end of Trip E16

Trip E16. Kahua Road Side Trip from Polipoli

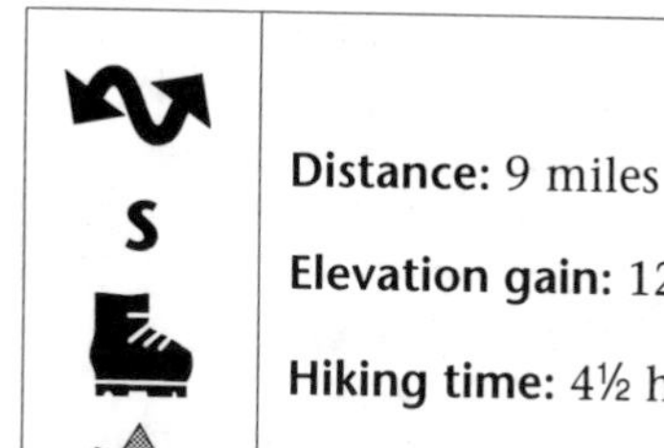

Distance: 9 miles

Elevation gain: 1210′

Hiking time: 4½ hours

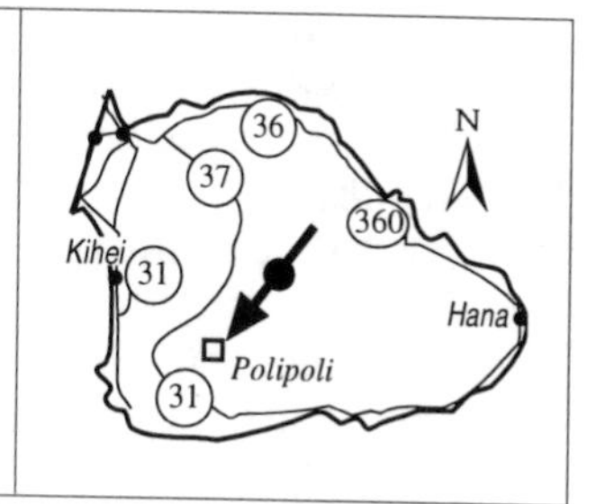

Topos: Lualailua Hills 7½.

Trail map: Starts on the map at the end of Trip E15; ends on the map at the end of this trip.

Highlights: Easy going through native scrublands on an old 4WD road with views upslope to Haleakala's summit region and downslope to the ocean (weather permitting). This is by far the most enjoyable of the trails that are accessible *only* from Polipoli State Park (more below). Kahua Road is a fine choice for mountain bicycles, too.

Driving instructions: Not applicable if you're already camped at Polipoli State Park. Otherwise, follow the driving instructions of Trip E15.

Permit/permission required: None.

Description. You could start this trip on Polipoli's poor trail system, but I found it much more enjoyable to start on the road. I think you will, too. Get an early start so you can enjoy the views before the fog moves in (it will probably be in a layer just below the road).

Walk back ½ mile on the road you drove in on, to the fork where you turned right to get down to Polipoli. Take the other fork here (a sharp right) and continue uphill. The elbow of a hairpin turn at 1 mile from the start offers wonderful views over the ocean to Molokini and Kahoolawe, even a glimpse of the Big Island of Hawaii, if cloud-cover permits. One of Polipoli's trails, the Haleakala Ridge Trail, meets the road at this elbow.

Volcanic material lies exposed in the road cut, in some places as stacks of wafer-thin orange, black, and tan layers. Near 2 miles, you reach a fork in the road at what's called Ballpark Junction. (The Civilian Conservation Corps men who planted the present forest in the 1930s used to play softball on this flat, open spot.) Kahua Road is the righthand fork, which you take (the lefthand fork is Skyline Trail to Science City atop Haleakala—see Trip E17).

On Kahua Road now, you ignore roads bearing left and right off Kahua Road just beyond Ballpark Junction, and also ignore any tracks leading away from the road, which rises very gently as it heads generally east. The non-native forest soon disappears, and native plants begin to dominate, particularly red- and white-berried *pukiawe*, red-fruited *aalii*, and red-berried *ohelo*. Be sure to look up at that wonderful line of cinder cones along Haleakala's southwest rift zone from time to time—quite a sight! The road passes through flows of rough *aa* lava as clouds move constantly across the slopes, now hiding, now revealing, but always leaving a strip of blue sky somewhere. Cool breezes make this exposed road quite pleasant. Here and there, masses of concrete lie broken where there's been an unsuccessful attempt to smooth the road's rough surface. You'll also notice the occasional rain-collecting station's roofs and tanks.

A little less than ½ mile from Ballpark Junction, you reach a fence with two vehicle gates, one pedestrian gate, and a sign that says HAWAIIAN HOME LANDS KAHIKINUI. There's a hunter's check station on the seaward side of the road just beyond the fence. Go through the pedestrian gate, being careful to close and latch it behind you. Continue your hike; be sure to stay on the road.

A little past 3 miles, the road begins an almost imperceptible descent, cutting through low ridges of brown *aa* that extend like misshapen fingers toward the distant sea. Scrub and bracken fern happily colonize them. It's not long before you can see a bit of the white towers and domes of Science City, the research complex atop Haleakala, uphill and to the left (northeast), if weather permits. The slopes below Science City are streaked with colors: brick reds, browns, deep maroons, tans, touches of pink and orange, and the green of vegetation.

You've been seeing lots of *aa* lava, but just past 4 miles, there's a smooth *pahoehoe* lava flow. A little farther on you'll find Kahua shelter (on the left side of the road; water available outside) and a pit toilet and Kahua cone (on the right). The deteriorating road passes behind Kahua cone and ends at a trashed-out grassy area 4½ miles from Polipoli. A footpath, the Kahikinui Trail, takes off east-southeast from here through the lava fields; its start is marked only by a couple of metal poles (more about the Kahikinui Trail below).

From here you retrace your path back to Polipoli.

Kahikinui Trail....is an interesting and very rugged use trail. It's so remote that if you wish to explore it, you should backpack out to the end of Kahua Road and camp near Kahua shelter, sharing its pit toilet and drinking water supply with anyone staying in the shelter. That would give you time to really enjoy the Kahikinui

Trail. Check with the Division of Forestry and Wildlife for permission to camp out there (or, at least, assurance that it's okay to do so).

I explored the Kahikinui Trail for about 1½ miles, probably as far as Manawainui Gulch, but not to its end (at least another ½ mile), for lack of time. There were not enough landmarks I could recognize in order to better determine my location at my turnaround point.

The use trail leads across the pleated southern slopes of Haleakala some 5000 to 6000 feet above the scorched countryside through which Highway 31 passes as it goes from Ulupalakua to Kaupo. This is a hunting area, and trash from hunting parties litters the track. The trail occasionally becomes quite hard to follow, so you need to orient yourself with the large cairns (piles of rocks) built on the larger ridges. At times you need to employ your boulder-scrambling skills. You climb over one lava ridge and descend into the gully beyond it, climb out of the gully onto the next lava ridge and descend into the next gully....That might seem monotonous, but something interesting unfolds: the farther you go, the larger and deeper the gullies are, and they begin to hold pools and even streams of water. The floors of the deeper gullies are very smooth in contrast to the rough *aa* of the ridges, and there are interesting formations in some of them. As the gullies become more moist, they provide a niche where soil has accumulated and red-flowered *ohia* trees have taken root. Successive niches seem to support a wider variety of plants. I don't know what you'll find at its end or how you'll know you've reached the end. A current rumor says that the Kahikinui Trail may be extended even farther, perhaps by volunteers, but for now the Kahikinui Trail is near the bottom of the priority list.

See the supplemental information at the end of Trip E14 for a brief look at the ecology and history of these slopes.

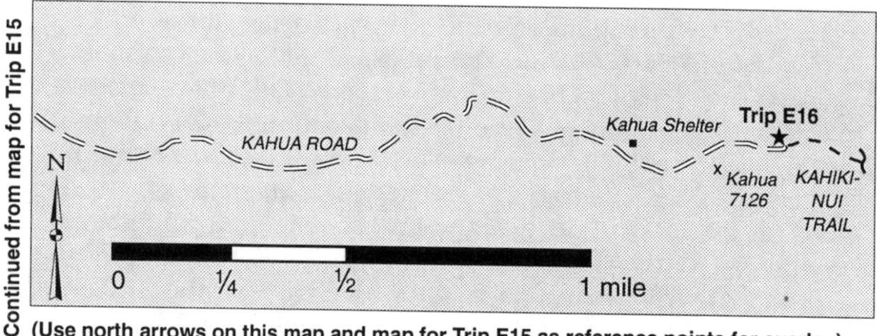

(Use north arrows on this map and map for Trip E15 as reference points for overlap)

Trip E17. Skyline Trail Side Trip from Polipoli

Distance: 13 miles

Elevation gain: 3730′

Hiking time: 6½ hours

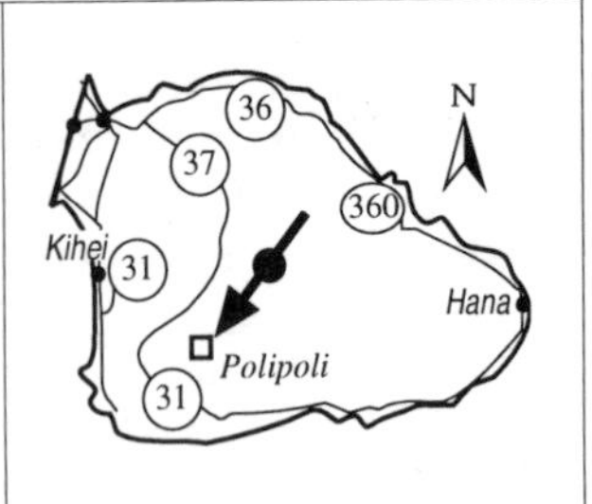

Topos: Lualailua Hills, Kilohana 7½.

Trail map: Starts on the map at the end of Trip E15; ends on the map at the end of this trip.

Highlights: This thrilling walk up Haleakala's southwest rift zone to Science City, the research complex atop Haleakala, offers sweeping views along Haleakala's slopes and down over the isthmus to West Maui (weather permitting). The contrast between the overgrown Polipoli region at the start and the lava moonscape at the top is startling. Nearing the top, the road wanders among cinder cones and vents—at least one big vent opens almost at your feet. Most of the Skyline Trail is now closed to motorized traffic, so it makes an outstanding hiking and mountain-bicycling trail. *This* would be the way to bike down Haleakala—no dodging the stream of passenger vehicles! Of course, you can also hike or bike the Skyline Trail down from Science City and then back up (see the end of Trip H17).

Driving instructions: Not applicable if you're already camped at Polipoli State Park. Otherwise, follow the driving instructions of Trip E15.

Permit/permission required: None.

Description. Follow Trip E16 to Ballpark Junction. Take the left fork and climb moderately past orange-berried *pilo*, yellow-flowered *mamane, pukiawe, ohelo,* bracken fern, and dubautia. Note the dubautia, with its composite brush of yellow florets. It's a relative of the silversword (hard to believe, but it's true; more on this following Trip H10). One-quarter mile beyond Ballpark Junction, you pass the upper end of the new Mamane Trail (not on map), a hiking-and-mountain-biking trail that's still under construction and that I haven't hiked and don't plan to (I don't like sharing single-track trails with mountain bikes). The Mamane Trail veers off to the left, north-northwest, but you go right (ahead), staying on the road that's the Skyline Trail.

The Skyline Trail stays on the northwest side of the rift zone most of the time. On the ridge to your right, the line of red-brown cinder cones marches along the rift itself. Early in the morning, you have breathtaking views downslope across "upcountry," where plantings of conifers look like so many toy Christmas trees. You'll notice the occasional rain-catching station, too (roof, tanks). Many roadside cuts display colorful layers of volcanic soil. It's possible you'll see wild pigs here, along with ring-necked pheasants. Non-native evening primrose (large, loose, yellow flowers) and thistle put in an appearance, too.

You can't help but notice as you rise higher and higher that the vegetation becomes smaller and sparser. At 3¾ miles you pass around a gate that bars further travel to motorized vehicles, and soon the larger shrubs disappear. Nearing 5 miles, only *pukiawe* remains, in low, compact mounds. Up here, the ground is covered with red, gray, orange, and pink volcanic cinders. On them lie raw chunks of red and black-red rock—"lava bombs," masses of lava ejected from the adacent vents. Here and there between the heaps of lava grow strange little alpine meadows of tough straw-colored grasses, low dubautias, and diminutive bracken ferns. The jagged mouths of vents gape north and east of you. As tempting as it may be, exploring lava fields off-road or off-trail can be hazardous without a knowledgeable guide. You could unknowingly step right through the fragile roof of an unseen lava tube. Mountain-bicyclists should carefully control their speed on this section, where the roadbed consists of very loose material.

As you approach Science City, avoid turnoffs to its facilities and continue generally northeast toward Red Hill, which is Haleakala's summit. You leave Kahikinui State Forest Reserve at 6 miles and pass around the upper road-closure gate just before 6½ miles. Another few steps bring you to the Skyline Trail marker for the upper (Science City) end. Depending on your fancy and the weather, you may want to find a spot in the cinders near here to rest, enjoy the available views, and have lunch. Or you may want to continue carefully up the road to the observation shelter at Red Hill, visible straight ahead now (additional mileage and elevation gain not included in the figures for this trip).

When you're ready, retrace your steps back to Polipoli.

Why are Puu Kukui and Haleakala so different?... As you walked up from Polipoli, you probably had good views of West Maui until the daily cloud layer formed. Puu Kukui, the volcano that created West Maui, is one of the wettest spots on earth, as its deeply eroded contours brilliant with dense rainforest growth attest. For rainfall, Puu Kukui (5788 feet) rivals Kauai's Mt. Waialeale (5148 feet), which is considered by some to be the rainiest spot on earth. Puu Kukui and Mt. Waialeale have features in common that make them so rainy. Continuing on the Skyline Trail, you then walked up through scrublands and into the alpine desert near the top of Haleakala, where only a few low plants are tough enough to survive. How different Puu Kukui and Haleakala are! But why? In *Hawaii: A Natural History*, Sherwin Carlquist gives an explanation that I've tried to summarize here.

First, an oversimplified look at the air over Hawaii: The Hawaiian Islands tend to have daytime inversion layers 50% to 70% of the time. In these inversion layers, the air gets warmer as it rises (the land heats it). The top of the inversion layer is at 5000 to 7000 feet. Above, there's cooler air. Second, the incoming winds, both trade and kona, pick up a great deal of moisture on their long sweep across the open ocean to Hawaii. The winds rise, warming instead of cooling as they rise, until they encounter the cooler air at the top of the inversion layer. There their moisture condenses as rain.

If the mountain is rounded and its summit is at about the height of the inversion layer, the moisture-laden air rises gradually. The moisture condenses as it rises up and over the summit. There's time for rain to fall on the windward and leeward sides as well as on the summit.

That doesn't happen with Puu Kukui and Waialeale, even though both summits are at about the height of the inversion layer. Both mountains have rainfall concentrated near the summit and have dry leeward sides because both mountains are *not* rounded. They're gashed on all sides by deep, narrow valleys that have very steep headwalls. The moisture-laden winds rush into those valleys and fly up the steep headwalls so rapidly that the air mass is almost at the summit when the moisture condenses very abruptly. Most of the rain falls on the summit ridge and just beyond the summit, effectively concentrating the rainfall in a relatively small region. Immense swamps lie just beyond these summits.

If the mountain is significantly higher than the inversion layer, the rain falls largely on the windward side, leaving both the summit and the leeward side dry. This is the case with 10,023-foot Haleakala. You can almost see the top of the inversion layer around Haleakala. A cloud layer typically forms in the morning and surrounds the mountain at about 5000 to 7000 feet on most sides. Polipoli State Park at 6200 feet on the western slopes lies within this cloud belt, and it is usually very foggy, often rainy, by mid-morning. Above the inversion layer lie the drier scrublands and the alpine deserts you walk through on the Skyline Trail.

The Skyline Trail, with its views of Puu Kukui, offers a fine lesson about Maui's "weather makers" and their effects—a lesson you can take with you to help you better understand the other Hawaiian islands, too.

Continued from map at end of Trip E15

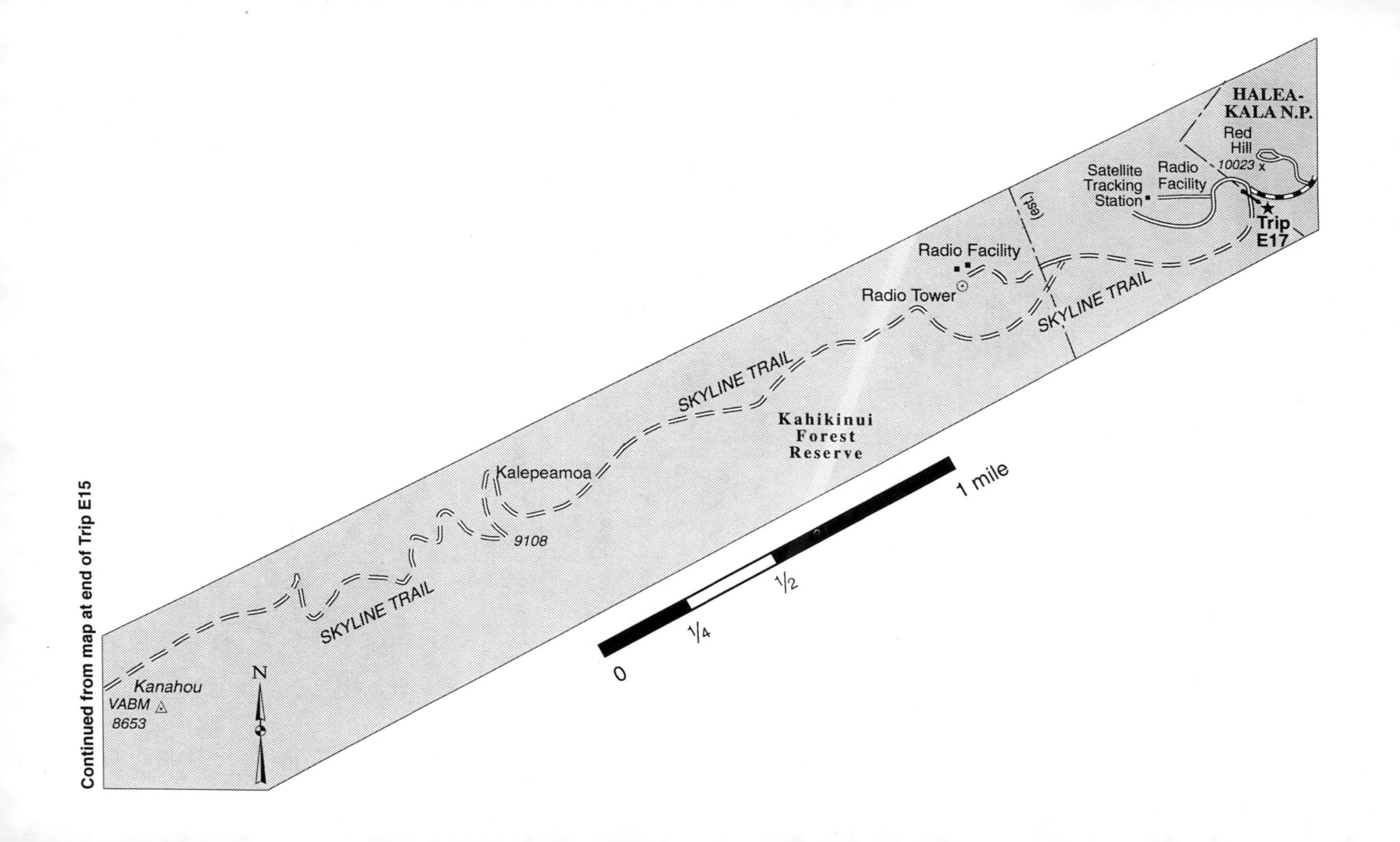

Trip E18. King's Highway to Kanaio

Distance: 4 miles

Elevation gain: 40′

Hiking time: 2 hours

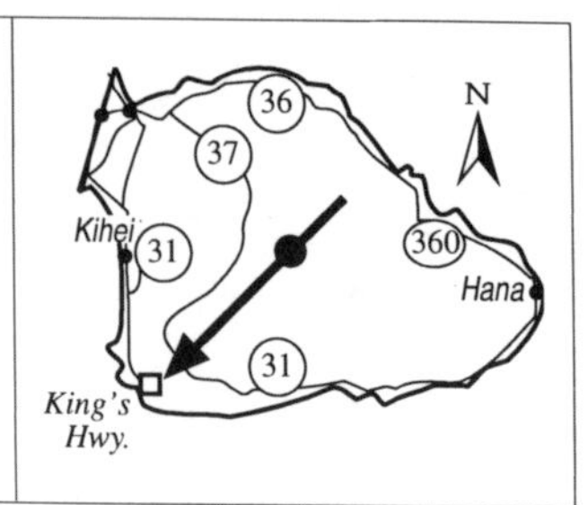

Topos: Makena 7½.
Trail map: At the end of this trip.
Highlights: An unforgettable panorama: the dazzling turquoise-blue of the water along this coast as seen across the tormented *aa* landscape left by Haleakala's most-recent eruptions.

Driving instructions: From Wailuku, drive south on Highway 30 to its junction with Highway 31 to Kihei, Wailea, and Makena. Turn left onto Highway 31 and follow it past Maalaea Beach and Kealia Pond. As you pass the northernmost condominiums in Kihei, the highway swings slightly inland at a junction with South Kihei Road, 8½ miles from Wailuku. Turn right onto South Kihei Road and follow it south through Kihei. As you approach Wailea, you turn inland (left) a short way on Okolani Drive, then right on Wailea Alanui. You pass several large resorts and golf courses as the road becomes Makena Alanui. As you near the end of the Makena Golf Course, the road becomes very narrow, and thickets of *kiawe* stretch away on either side of the road. You pass a couple of dirt roads leading seaward to Puu Olai (Trip E19). The road is alternately paved and unpaved now—more often paved—and bobs up and down. You may not be able to see traffic on the other side of these "mounds," so exercise caution. The road presently dips down to skirt Ahihi Bay and then crosses the base of Cape Kinau to a small parking area just below Puu o Kanaloa at the northwest end of La Pérouse Bay. From here the "road" is impassable to all but the stoutest 4WD vehicles and to the Ankle Express, so park here to begin your hike, 23¼ miles from Wailuku.

Permit/permission required: None.

Description. The heat from the sun, reradiated by the dark lava rocks along this route, can be intense, and there is no fresh water. From the parking area, pick up the extremely rough 4WD road that bears southeast over *aa* and under *kiawe* to skirt La Pérouse Bay—don't take the spur road that goes south to the sea. There are wonderful views over the blue-green bay toward Kahoolawe and up the slopes of Haleakala, down which streams of rough, dark lava have poured. The road soon becomes sandy and begins winding in and out of tiny, rocky coves under a natural archway of *kiawe*. Inland, growing *kiawe* pushes apart the lichen-speckled boulders of old stone walls.

The road becomes alternately rocky and sandy, and *hau* and *noni* appear as you pass the ½-mile point and reach a little beach. At a junction (not on the map) on the far side of the little beach, take the right (south-southeast) fork through an open area of reddish *aa* and past a square stone enclosure seaward of your route. Where the road bears seaward to the light on Cape Hanamanioa, a little more than ⅔ mile from your start, you notice a stone wall on your left (inland). Look for a pedestrian opening with a vehicle barrier in the wall and turn left (inland) through the pedestrian opening. Walk about 100 feet to the Hoapili Trail, built in its present form by Governor Hoapili in 1824–1840. (Remember that these lava flows date from about 1790, so they may have destroyed an earlier King's Highway here. See Trip E7 for some background on the King's Highway.) Na Ala Hele, the Hawaiian trail-support organization, has rebuilt Governor Hoapili's "King's Highway" here, and you turn right onto it.

The going is pretty rough now, as the trail consists of *aa* chunks laid to form trailbed but not cemented together, so that they wobble a little under your boots. The *aa* wilderness stretches away on all sides, often blocking ocean views. Its origin in the lava flows on the slopes above could hardly be more obvious. *Is this what an ant feels like in a gravel bed?* you may wonder. Still, the tortured rocks are not without their beauty. They are, after all, the raw material from which time and erosion will fashion new, fertile plains. Some of the rocks ring almost bell-like beneath your feet. Stop to examine them. The broken fragments sometimes reveal delicate, marbled colors and bubble chambers. Grays and browns predominate, but surprising tints appear when you look closely: soft oranges, deep purplish reds, brick reds, ochres, pinks, and the white of lichens called "Hawaiian snow." Rarely, you may see a smooth lava "bomb."

Two miles from your start, you descend very abruptly to a marvelously picturesque, *kiawe*-shaded cove along a coast locally known as Kanaio. There is a trashy campsite here, and a 4WD road comes down to it on the far side. Still, it's a fine place to rest and have lunch. The King's Highway continues a few coves farther on, but this trip ends here. Retrace your steps when you're ready.

Beyond Kanaio.... You may want to explore Kanaio a little more before you leave. If you continue along the shore, you'll hear the *WHOOOOOSH!* of a small blowhole if the tide is high enough. (I'll let you have the fun of hunting for it.) Your trail is a 4WD road now; as you approach a ruin on a small point, it turns inland. At a junction with another jeep trail, one that goes inland, you bear right (east), staying along the coast. It becomes rockier and, at 3 miles, dips abruptly down through a stone wall toward the sea.

I cannot recommend the next stretch to Kanaloa. The King's Highway has not been rebuilt here and is extremely rough and hot. You are permitted to backpack this route and to camp along this coast from Kanaio east to Kanaloa, but I can't recommned that, either. There's no fresh water, and the few potential campsites are full of junk.

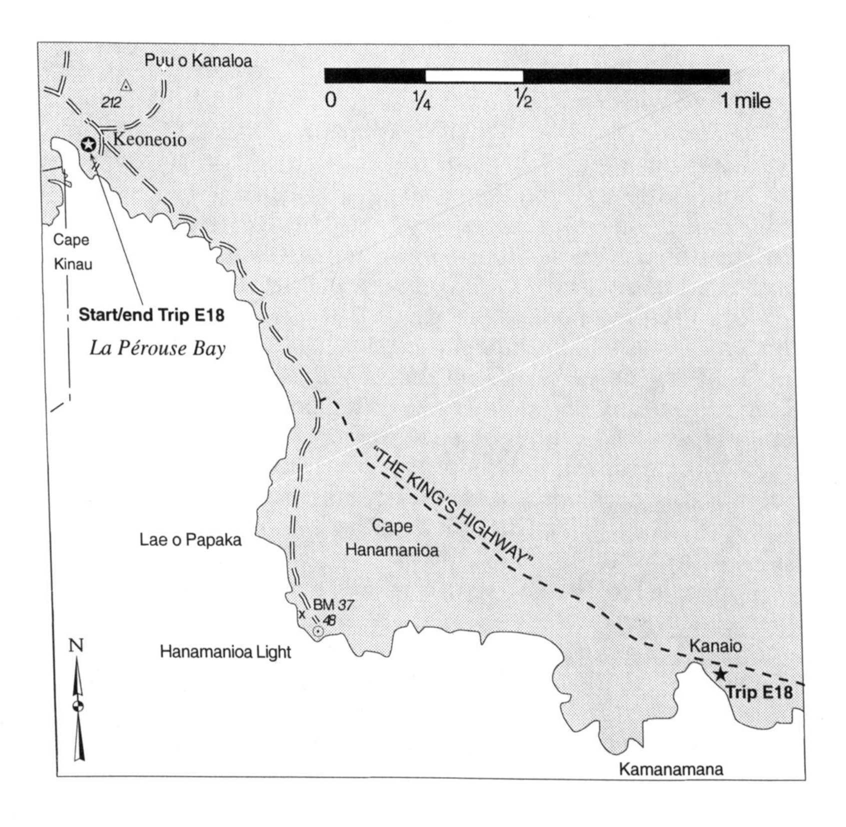

Trip E19. Puu Olai

M

Distance: 1½ miles

Elevation gain: 480′

Hiking time: ¾ hour

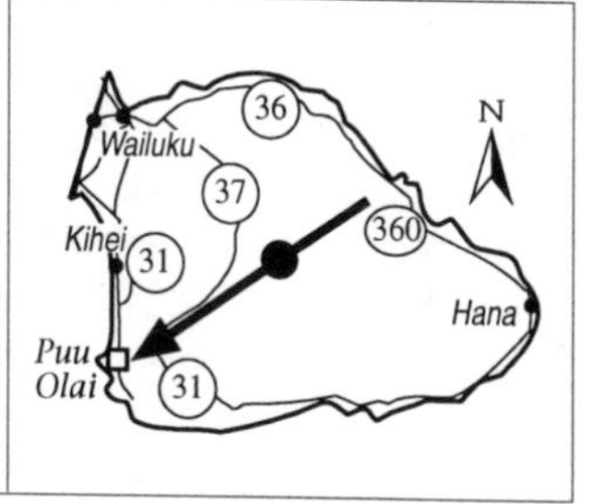

Topos: Optional: Makena 7½.

Trail map (route approximated): At the end of this trip.

Highlights: Superb views from one of the two summits of this little tree-topped cone, plus an opportunity to visit two beautiful beaches.

Driving instructions: Get an early start; the parking lot for this popular area is often full by 10 A.M. Start as described in the driving instructions of Trip E18, but don't go all the way to La Pérouse Bay. Instead, as you drive south from Kihei, look for the prominent cone—Puu Olai—that sticks out into the ocean; you can't miss it. A paved road comes in from the north to join your road, now named Makena Alanui, at a very sharp angle on your right, just as the main road turns away from Makena Golf Course. As you come abreast of Puu Olai, pass the road that heads seaward along Puu Olai's north side. Look for the paved road that heads seaward along Puu Olai's south side to Makena State Park (it may not be marked as such on Makena Alanui). Follow this access road for ⅓ mile to a paved parking area, just under 20½ miles from Wailuku. You can't drive all the way to the beach any more, so park here. The beach is locally called Big Beach; on maps, it's often shown as Oneloa Beach; and now it's Makena State Park. Vandalizing cars is a growth industry here, so be sure to take all your valuables with you.

Permit/permission required: None.

Description. Walk past the vehicle gate at the beach end of the parking lot, then down the remaining road, and bear right past the defunct, elevated restroom, toward the handsome red cliffs framing the north end of the beach. The little point extending from the base of Puu Olai is right ahead of you; walk to its face. Here you'll find a steep use trail hidden in the cliff. You scramble steeply up the low cliff with the help of some natural handholds. When you're atop the cliff, take the time to look back and enjoy the view of Big Beach from here. Side trails lead out onto the point to tidepools, and a wide trail leads northwest (ahead) to Little Beach.

You, however, want the very steep use trail on your right that climbs northeast along Puu Olai's southern slopes. Take this trail upward—*upward!*—on loose, cindery soil, through *koa haole* and *kiawe*. Past the ⅓-mile point, the grade eases a little, then steepens again as you pass through weeds, and finally eases for good at an open spot a little over ½ mile from your start.

Here, atop Puu Olai's southeast summit, you have fabulous views southwest to Molokini and Kahoolawe, northwest to West Maui, southeast to Haleakala, and south to the southwest rift zone and Cape Kinau. Now you begin the loop part of this trip by following the use trail north past a slight depression and through scrub, to a fork. Take the left fork, which passes a cement marker (possibly the remains of the benchmark shown on the topo), descends to a saddle, and then climbs to Puu Olai's northwest summit. Though it's slightly higher, this summit's views are obscured by *kiawe* and the southeast summit. Follow the track across this summit as it descends west and then south around Puu Olai's *kiawe*-filled vent. At the low point, you meet a track coming uphill from the west, but you continue south around the crater, ascending to the open spot on the southeast summit.

Retrace your steps down Puu Olai—slippery on this steep grade and loose soil. From here, you can retrace your steps to lovely Big Beach (left as you face the ocean). If you turn to your right, the trail leads to Little Beach in a few dozen yards.

When you're ready, return the way you came, just over 1½ miles total (not including going to Little Beach).

Little Beach.... *Hawaii's Secret Beaches* says that Little Beach is "Hawaii's most well known nudist beach because of the numerous arrests here of nudists." It is beautiful, and, though nudity is officially illegal here because it's in a state park, you'll find people sunning and swimming with and without swimsuits. If nudity offends you, it's best not to go to Little Beach. Nudity isn't legal anywhere in Hawaii, and the law, which once winked at it in a few remote places, is increasingly intolerant of it today.

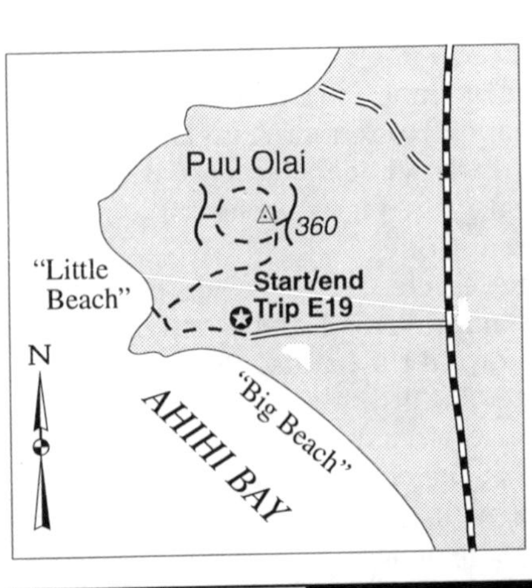

Trip E20. Polo Beach

V

Distance: ⅔ mile

Elevation gain: Negligible

Hiking time: 20 minutes

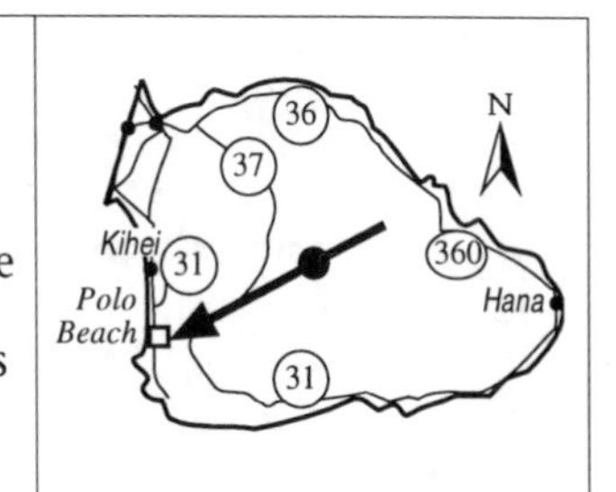

Topos: Optional: Makena 7½.

Trail map (route approximated): At the end of this trip. There is no trail as such; you walk along the beach as you please.

Highlights: This trip: 1. Gives you an excuse to visit a perfectly lovely beach and to potter around a bit on it, enjoying the views and looking at the plants, maybe sunning and swimming, too. 2. Gives you legitimate grounds for subsequently claiming that you were on a *hike* the whole time, so it's okay to stop for ice cream on the way back to the condo.

Driving instructions: Start as described in the driving instructions of Trip E18. Beyond Kihei, after you've gone briefly uphill and then past some big resorts, keep your eye on the signs pointing to beaches. Turn right where the sign points you seaward to Polo Beach, just over 17 miles from Wailuku and just beyond an elaborate, turreted hotel. It's a block to the end of this short street, where you turn right into the parking lot for Polo Beach. The walkway to the beach is at the far end of the parking lot.

Permit/permission required: None.

Description. Descend the short flight of stairs to the beach and continue walking ahead to the black boulders at the north end of the beach. Chairs, lounges, and umbrellas dot the beach; they belong to the luxury hotel whose grassy lawn extends to the edge of the low bluffs backing this cove. There's a splendid view of West Maui as you go. Several kinds of seaweed grow on just these few boulders; how many of them can you identify? (Sea lettuce was the only one I could identify.)

On the low, sandy bluff backing the beach, you'll find *akulikuli*, beach vitex (*pohinahina*), beach *naupaka* (*naupaka-kahakai*), and *ilima papa*—a nice little collection of naturally occurring plants for an area as developed as this one is. These plants are indigenous to Hawaii's beaches and to many other tropical Pacific coastlines, having arrived in Hawaii without human assistance. For example, the white fruits of beach *naupaka* are buoyant and tolerant of saltwater, so ocean currents can disperse them from one shoreline to another. According to *Hawaiian Coastal Plants and Scenic Shorelines*, development has taken a heavy toll on Hawaii's beach vitex plants, so it's good to see them flourishing here. *Kiawe* trees and tree heliotrope, both introduced species, grow atop the bluff.

It's only a few steps to the other end of the beach, where you can continue walking by stepping over trailing morning-glory vines and then crossing the black-pebble and white-coral beach of a little cove. A use trail leads from here through *kiawe* to another pebbly cove that offers a fine view of Puu Olai, whose two summits are quite distinct from this vantage point. Out to sea, tiny Molokini lies in front of Kahoolawe, an island sacred in Hawaiian mythology—more about Kahoolawe below.

Return to the beach after taking in these fine views, and retrace your steps to your car when you're ready.

Kahoolawe.... Kahoolawe is too small and too arid to support a substantial population, but small family groups inhabited it well into historic times. It became a thriving cattle ranch in the first half of this century. One day after the Japanese attack on Pearl Harbor, the U.S. Navy seized Kahoolawe, dispossesed the ranch owners, and began using the island for target practice. After a long and bitter struggle between the U.S. Navy and Hawaiian groups determined to see the desecration stopped, Congress finally voted in 1990 to return Kahoolawe to Hawaii. Its restoration will be a fascinating project for those lucky enough to participate and an interesting story to follow for the rest of us.

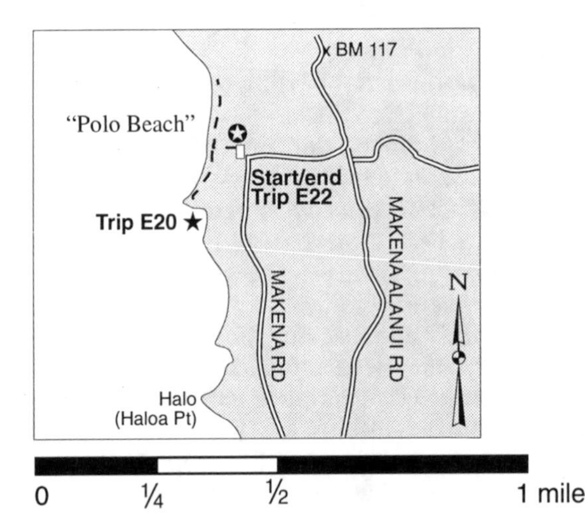

Trip E21. Kamaole County Beach Park 2 and 3

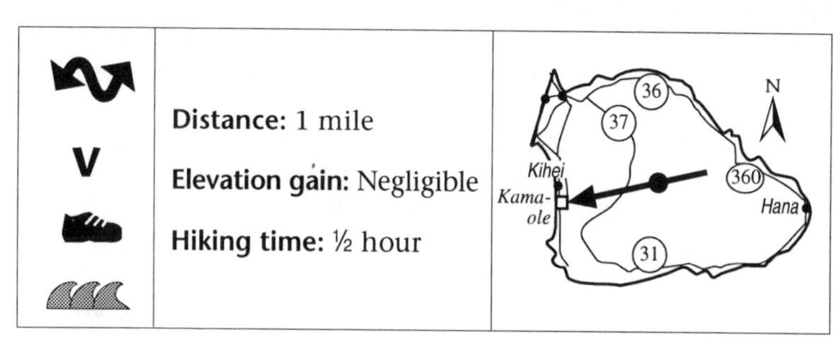

Topos: Optional: Puu o Kila 7½.

Trail map (route approximated): At the end of this trip. There is no trail as such; you walk on the beach or on the grass as you please. Just how far you actually walk depends on whether you stick to the beach, detour to the grass, and so on.

Highlights: Views, picnic facilities, restrooms, a children's playground, plenty of sandy beach to stroll on and stretch out on, plenty of grass to move onto when that midday Kihei breeze picks up—Kamaole has lots to offer. There are 3 beaches in this park (Kamaole Beach County Parks 1, 2, and 3) separated by private property that you can skirt by walking along the tide-line. Each beach is worth a visit, but I've arbitrarily limited this hike to beaches 2 and 3 because a mile's walk seems just about right for this area. This trip is better in the morning—you'll avoid the midday wind.

Driving instructions: Start as described in the driving instructions of Trip E18. In Kihei, keep your eyes peeled after you pass Kalama Beach County Park (seaward side) and Kihei Town Center (a shopping center). First you'll pass Kamaole 1, then some resorts and shopping malls, then Kamaole 2, and finally you'll reach Kamaole 3. Park near Kamaole 3 if possible (this trip starts at the south end of Kamaole 3) or Kamaole 2, 13–13⅓ miles from Wailuku, depending on where you park. If you come to a left-hand, uphill jog, you've gone too far; turn around.

Permit/permission required: None.

Description. Start your walk at the south end of Kamaole 3 (left end as you face the ocean). Stroll north (toward West Maui, looming in the distance) on the beach if the wind permits, on the grass if it doesn't. *Kiawe*, palms, and monkeypod trees shade the grass, where you'll also find tables, grills, restrooms, water, and playground equipment. At the north end of Kamaole 3, you'll need to be on the beach, or to detour to it, to circumvent a *kiawe*-covered point the top of which is marked PRIVATE PROPERTY. A use trail along the low bluff below the point allows you to walk around to Kamaole 2 without trespassing. If tide and surf permit, you can walk out on the rocks here, exploring tidepools as you go—best not to do this barefooted!

Soon you're at the sandy south end of Kamaole 2, whose beach is somewhat longer. The pleasant grassy area of Kamaole 2 has no facilities but is brightened by morning glory, beach *naupaka*, autograph tree, and bougainvillea. As you stroll north, the grassy area ends where the buildings begin. The beach stretches farther in front of the buildings, and you may wish to check out Kamaole 1, while others will want to turn around here. Now that you've had a good look at Kamaole, it's time to make your really big decisions: where to stretch out in the sun, and whether to have your picnic lunch now or later. They're tough decisions when you have so many good choices. Maybe you should think it over as you amble back toward Kamaole 3, retracing your steps. In any case, you won't be in any hurry to get back to your car for a while. Enjoy your stay!

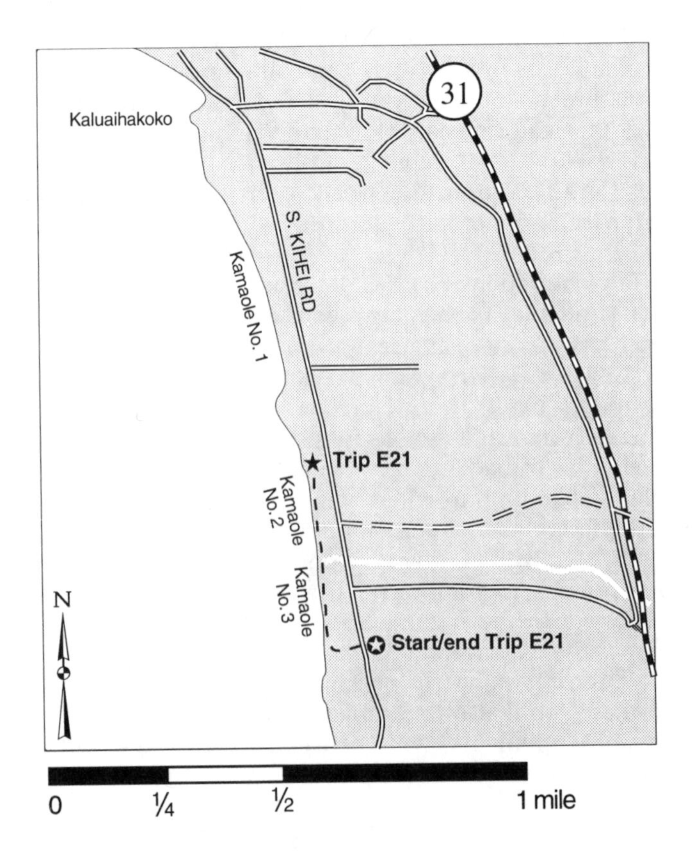

Trip H1. Hosmer Grove Nature Loop

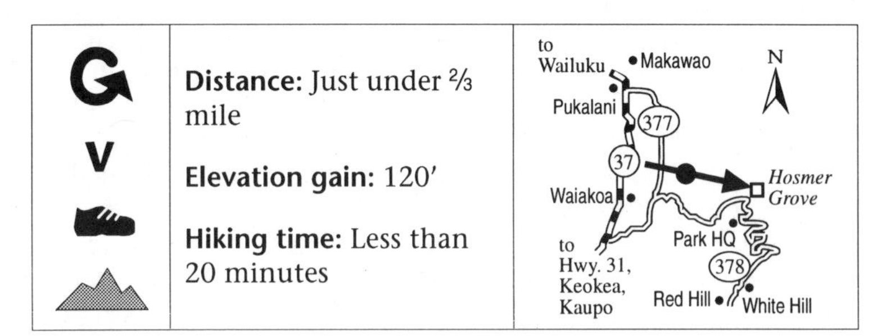

Topos: Optional: Kilohana 7½.

Trail map (route approximated): At the end of this trip.

Highlights: A number of native and introduced plants grow together here, and many of them are marked with numbered stakes so that you can identify them with the help of a brochure that should be available at the first numbered station. The brochure also has historical information and poses some intriguing questions about this area. It's a fine little hike even if the brochure isn't available. Birders should bring their binoculars and plan to take advantage of the birding opportunities midway along the trail. Best in the early morning, as clouds and rain often move in by midmorning.

Driving instructions: From Wailuku, drive east on Highway 32 to its junction with Highway 36 (Hana Highway). Take Highway 36 to its junction with Highway 37 (Haleakala Highway). Take Highway 37 through Pukalani—last chance for gas and groceries—to the first junction with Highway 377. Turn left onto Highway 377, which is now the Haleakala Highway, and follow it through the green pasturelands of eucalyptus-shaded "upcountry" to its junction with Highway 378. Turn left onto Highway 378 (*it's* now the Haleakala Highway) and follow it uphill on its zigzagging course toward Haleakala's summit. Just after you cross the park boundary, a sign points left down a side road to Hosmer Grove and its campground, just under 30 miles from Wailuku. Turn left here and follow the side road past a spur road (to a radio facility) to the side road's end in ½ mile at the Hosmer Grove parking lot 30½ miles from Wailuku.

Cattle on the road are hazards drivers must watch out for. Many areas on the slopes along Highways 377 and 378 below the national park are pastures. There's no fence to keep the cattle that graze there from wandering onto the road, so of course they do. You're especially likely to find them on the road in the evening and at night. Be ready to stop for them. They'll amble off the road if you'll give them time.

Permit/permission required: None.

Description. Hosmer Grove, at 6800 feet, is not only high but potentially windy, cold, and wet. Be prepared with warm clothing that insulates when wet, with rain gear, and with shoes that will grip on slippery terrain. And take it easy if you're unaccustomed to hiking at higher altitudes!

Walk toward the trees, past the picnic pavilion, and pick up the path, paved at first, that leads away from the parking lot. As it bears north, you pass an information sign explaining that Hawaii's first territorial forester, Ralph S. Hosmer, planted this grove, now named in his honor, in 1910. The grove consists (like Polipoli) largely of continental species. Hosmer wanted to see if they would flourish here and support a timber industry. Fortunately, they didn't do well enough to compete with imported timber. As the pamphlet you'll pick up at the first station asks, "Do you think Haleakala would be a National Park today if the experiment had succeeded?"

You promptly cross a stream on a bridge. Exotic eucalyptuses dominate this first part of the grove. Red-berried *pukiawe*, a typical member of the native shrubland that is the natural cover of these slopes, struggles to survive beneath the huge, exotic trees. A procession of other exotics, beginning with sugi cedars, soon takes over from the eucalyptuses. The native shrubs beneath them are more interesting: *aalii, ohia lehua, mamane,* and more *pukiawe.*

Soon you reach an open spot where a bench overlooks a gully and an expanse of native shrubland slopes. Break out your binoculars and your bird-identification guides here and settle down for a look at native and exotic birds. When you move on, you're out of the grove proper and in native Hawaiian shrubland. A few seedlings of the exotic species may sprout here, but the Park Service is committed to pulling them up in order to allow the native plants to flourish. Otherwise, the naturally low native plants here would be shaded to death by the dense, towering exotics—as most of them have been in the grove you just left.

The Park Service must wage its fight in favor of native species and against exotics not only for plants but also for animals. The upper slopes of Haleakala are now completely fenced so that the Park Service can remove the non-native goats and pigs they find inside the fence with some confidence that another batch of goats and pigs won't immediately invade the park in their place. Inside the fence, native plants are recovering. However, a new threat confronts the park: rabbits have been appearing near the fence.

The trail soon curves back toward the campground. Near the end, false trails crisscross the main trail, but don't let them distract you. The trail returns to the end of the road you drove in on. Stay to picnic and enjoy the scenery!

Waikamoi Preserve.... The Nature Conservancy owns and manages Waikamoi Preserve, a native near-rainforest area next to Hosmer Grove. Waikamoi Preserve protects many rare and endangered native birds and plants. Birdwatching is the preserve's main attraction for the visitor. Access is by permit only, and travel is allowed on foot only.

The Nature Conservancy conducts guided hikes from Hosmer Grove into the preserve on a regular basis, currently the second Sunday of each month. Call the preserve manager at (808) 572-7849 to reserve a place on their hike. You'll probably get a recording. I've been assured that the preserve manager does return all calls, but you will need to be within reach of your phone to catch that call.

The National Park Service also conducts "cloud forest" hikes in the preserve, currently on Monday, Thursday, and Friday mornings. Call the Park Service at (808) 572-9306 to get the latest information. Reservations are not required. Once in a while, the hike may be canceled because of inclement weather, or for lack of a ranger to conduct the hike, or because too few people showed up (the hike requires a minimum of three people for safety). I recommend that you also call the Park Service the morning of the hike, as early as possible (they're in the office by 7 A.M.), to be sure it hasn't been canceled for either of the first two reasons. Hosmer Grove is probably hours away from where you're staying. There's a problem here: how can you get to Hosmer Grove in time for the hike without starting from your hotel well before 7 A.M.? You probably can't. Suggestion: take this book with you and drive toward Hosmer Grove but stop in, say, Pukalani for breakfast and call the Park Service around 7 A.M. from there. You'll still have time to get up to Hosmer Grove safely if the "cloud forest" hike is still on. Or, if it's been canceled, you'll have time to choose and take another hike.

You will need to make special arrangements directly with the preserve manager for any other access to Waikamoi Preserve.

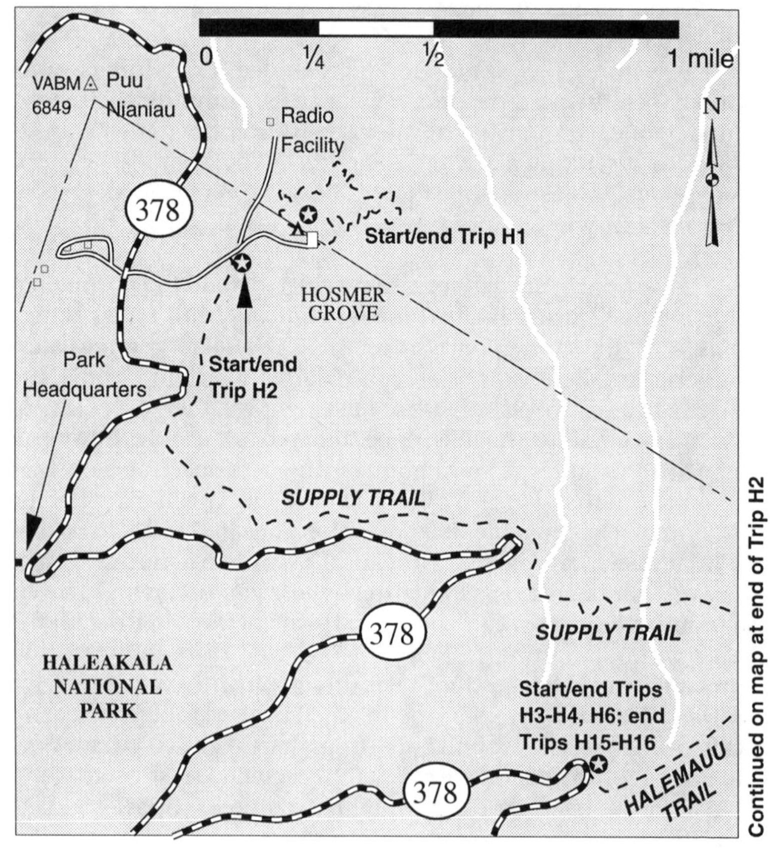
0
¼
½
1 mile
N
VABM 6849
Puu Nianiau
Radio Facility
378
Start/end Trip H1
HOSMER GROVE
Park Headquarters
Start/end Trip H2
SUPPLY TRAIL
378
SUPPLY TRAIL
HALEAKALA NATIONAL PARK
Start/end Trips H3-H4, H6; end Trips H15-H16
378
HALEMAUU TRAIL
Continued on map at end of Trip H2

Trip H2. Supply Trail to Crater Rim

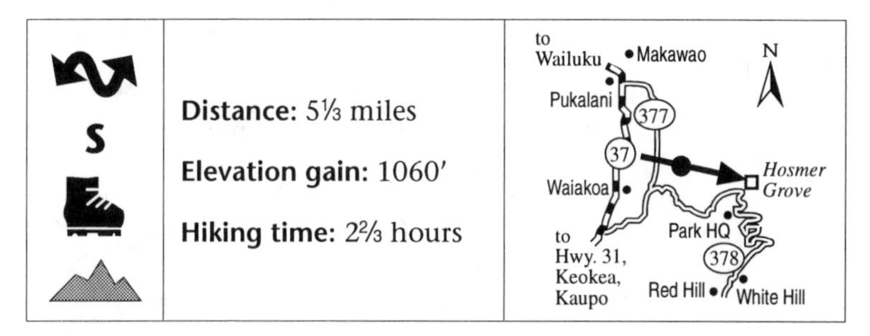

Topos: Kilohana 7½.

Trail map: Begins on the map at the end of Trip H1; ends on the map at the end of this trip.

Highlights: This is the trail mule trains take to resupply the cabins in Haleakala's crater. For the hiker, it offers a close-up look at the native shrublands and breathtaking views downslope to East Maui's northeast coast (weather permitting) and, at its upper end, into the crater itself.

Driving instructions: Follow the driving instructions of Trip H1. Park at Hosmer Grove.

Permit/permission required: None.

Description. Walk back down the road you drove in on, past the spur road to the radio facility, ⅕ mile to the signed trailhead that will be on your left (south-southeast) in a wide, shallow, scrub-filled gully. Pick up the trail here and follow it uphill through *mamane, pukiawe, ohelo*, and *kukaenene*. Nearing ½ mile into this hike, the highway swings to the east and comes very close to the trail but is separated from it by a gully. You shortly cross a lava-floored gully just above a steep dropoff and pass a sign listing the park's rules (on your right). Alien, yellow-flowered evening primrose grows here; you'll see it far too often along the trails as well as along the roadside.

The trail bears east toward another gully, down whose steep, rocky sides water from seep springs drips. Just beyond ⅔ mile, you cross a section of flat, black lava, where rainwater may have pooled in the shallow depressions. Hosmer Grove and the radio facility are visible downhill to the north—convenient reference points. As the trail bears southeast, a highway bridge looms ahead to your right. The highway will be just above you, on your right, for a while. Do your best to ignore it as you make a brief, rocky descent, pass through a stone wall, and cross another section of lava. *Ohia lehua* trees grow here, leaning over the shallow pools in the rock. You meet a rather impressive pipeline and cross over it where it runs under the trail.

At 1½ miles, just as it comes within yards of you, the highway switchbacks away from you at last. You cross a closed-off road (not shown on the map or the topo) and pick up the trail directly on the other side of it. You pass a rain shed ahead and some water tanks on your left.[1] On this last segment before you descend to the crater's rim, you'll want to pause often to take in the magnificent views down Haleakala's northeast slopes all the way to the sea, if the cloud cover permits. You cross intermittent streams, gullies, and a couple of culverts; a fern-lined intermittent streambed at 2 miles is especially pretty. Just beyond 2 miles, there's a meadowy area where the tramping of many feet and hooves has worn multiple tracks deep into the soft soil. Footing is spongy here.

You meet the Halemauu Trail at 2½ miles from your start, where a sign points you left to the CRATER. (On your way back, go right down the SUPPLY TRAIL at this junction.) Turn left onto the rocky Halemauu Trail, where *mamane* and a silvery, native shrub geranium line your route. You're descending now, and in a few steps you reach a gate in Haleakala's protective fence. Pass through the gate, being sure it closes behind you. A couple of switchbacks bring you down to a sweeping crater view just before the trail makes a third switchback. This is your destination for this hike. Find a perch here where you can spend some time to watch the show. On your left, Koolau Gap opens. Clouds often fill it, drifting across the crater floor. Shifting clouds may reveal a feature for a moment, then hide it again while parting to show another feature. The green, spire-studded cliffs of Leleiwi Pali (*pali* means cliffs) fall steeply away at your feet to a meadow that's more than a thousand feet below. On your left, the Halemauu Trail snakes down, down, down the steep ridge that juts into the crater, and the crater walls rise again across Koolau Gap. Eastward, fantastically colored cinder cones dot the crater floor.

It's hard to leave this awesome sight, but you can console yourself with more of those fine views toward the coast as you retrace your steps back to Hosmer Grove.

Crater trips overview.... Visualizing the crater's trail system can be difficult, especially as you're taking your first look at it over the crater rim. It's helpful to think of the network of maintained trails in Haleakala's crater as forming a sloppy letter **Y**, knocked over onto its left side, with a crooked tail, as shown in the not-to-scale drawing below. One arm of the **Y** starts at the trailhead for the Halemauu Trail. The other arm of the **Y** starts at the trailhead for the Sliding Sands Trail. There are a couple of maintained spur trails, and there are three maintained interconnecting trails between the Sliding Sands and the Halemauu trails in the vicinity of Kawilinau. The Sliding Sands and

[1] The topo shows a rain shed and water tanks on your right (west), but they are now on your left (east).

the Halemauu trails meet not far from Paliku Cabin/Campground to begin the tail of the **Y**. Just past Paliku Cabin/Campground, the tail turns almost 90° south toward Kaupo village.

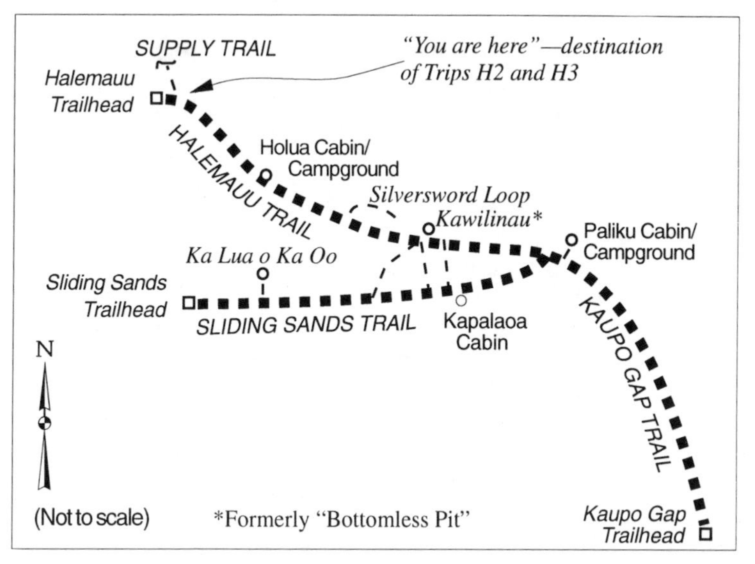

Visualizing the Crater Trails

The trips in this book describe a variety of dayhikes and backpacks in Haleakala's crater covering the current network of maintained trails. There's a trip to each of the cabins/campgrounds and a unique dayhike from each cabin/campground. Call the Park Service about taking one of their guided hikes—a wonderful new program you shouldn't miss. See Appendix A for information on permits and cabin reservations. See the note following Trip H4 for the importance of staying on the maintained trails.

Dayhikes from the crater's rim. Trips H4, H10, H11, H12, and H15 are dayhikes from the crater's rim. The most comprehensive trip is strenuous Trip H15 down the Sliding Sands Trail, through the crater, and out on the Halemauu Trail (requires a car shuttle). It's one of the best hikes in this book and on Maui.

A note on the Sliding Sands Trail. Some people consider the Sliding Sands Trail to be too difficult to hike out on because of its "loose" surface. However, hikers in good shape may not agree. The surface has been consolidated to some extent by years of being hiked on; that's certainly the way I found it. My friend Ray Brouillard, who backpacked in and out on the Sliding Sands Trail, reports that he had no problem hiking out. Others report similar experiences. The bottom line: if you're fit, don't let the reputation of the Sliding Sands Trail deter you!

To Holua Cabin/Campground. Trip H4, which you can make as either a dayhike or a backpack, takes you to Holua Cabin/Campground in the northwest corner of the crater. Trip H4 is teamed with Trip H5, which is a dayhike from Holua Cabin/Campground to Kapalaoa Cabin.

To Kapalaoa Cabin. Trip H12, which you can make as either a dayhike or a backpack, takes you to Kapalaoa Cabin. Trip H12 is teamed with Trip H13, which is a dayhike from Kapalaoa Cabin to Holua Cabin/Campground via a somewhat different route from that taken by Trip H5. Or you can reverse part of Trip H5 to make it a dayhike from Kapalaoa Cabin.

To Paliku Cabin/Campground. Trip H6 builds on Trip H4 to take you down the Halemauu Trail from Holua Cabin/Campground to Paliku Cabin/Campground. Trip H6 is teamed with Trip H7, which is a dayhike from Paliku Cabin/Campground down Kaupo Gap to the park's boundary. Trip H7 thus complements Trip E16, which is a dayhike from Kaupo village up Kaupo Gap to the park's boundary. Trip H14 takes you down the Sliding Sands Trail to Paliku Cabin/Campground with an optional night at Kapalaoa Cabin. It's certainly feasible for the sturdier hiker to backpack all the way to Paliku in one day from either the Halemauu or Sliding Sands trailhead because it's mostly downhill. The trip out—uphill—will be more enjoyable if you stay the night at Holua Cabin/Campground or Kapalaoa Cabin.

The grand crater tour. Trip H16 is "the grand crater tour." You visit each cabin or cabin/campground on a three-night shuttle trip between the Sliding Sands and the Halemauu trailheads. Sturdy early-birds will be able to make morning dayhikes on some of the other crater trails from Holua Cabin/Campground or from Kapalaoa Cabin (e.g., Trips H5 and H13) and still hike out of the crater in the afternoon.

Kaupo Gap. The backpack from either the Sliding Sands or the Halemauu trailhead all the way across the crater floor and down Kaupo Gap almost to Kaupo village requires an extremely long shuttle. Most visitors will find that shuttle to be very difficult to arrange. You may not camp beyond Paliku Cabin/Campground, and there is no readily available water along the way, not even in Kaupo village. Also, the layout of the crater trails and the short time you're allowed to stay in the crater (3 nights maximum in any 30-day period) means you'll have to choose between the Halemauu and Sliding Sands trails. It's just not practical to see the entire crater *and* hike out down Kaupo Gap. That's why I treated Kaupo Gap in two trips, Trip E16 from Kaupo village up to the park boundary, and Trip H7, a side trip from Paliku Cabin down to the park boundary. You won't need a shuttle, and you'll have more time to enjoy the crater or Kaupo Gap or both.

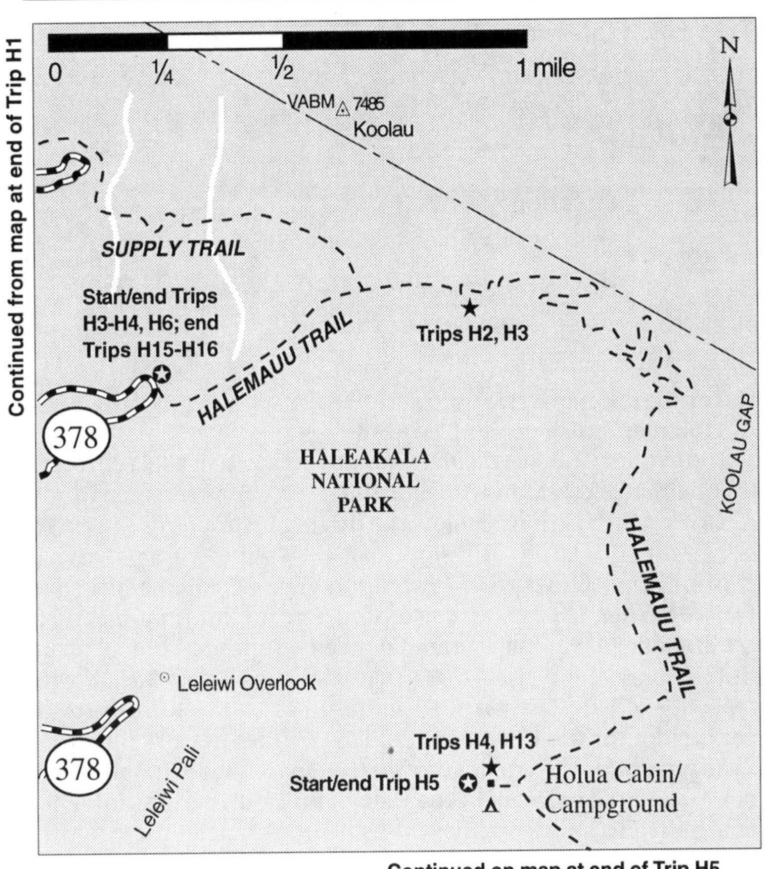

Continued from map at end of Trip H1

Continued on map at end of Trip H5

Haleakala Crater as seen from the Visitor Center at White Hill

Trip H3. Halemauu Trail to Crater Rim

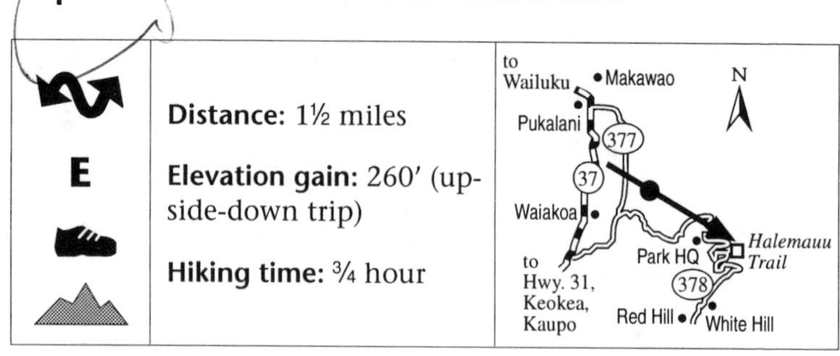

Distance: 1½ miles

Elevation gain: 260′ (up-side-down trip)

Hiking time: ¾ hour

Topos: Kilohana 7½.

Trail map: At the end of Trip H2.

Highlights: The spectacular view down into Haleakala's crater is the main attraction on this short hike.

Driving instructions: Follow the driving instructions of Trip H1 but don't turn off at the side road to Hosmer Grove. Instead, continue up Highway 378 toward the Visitor Center, a little over ¾ mile farther. It's a good idea to stop here for information and to get any books and maps you may need. (Topos are not available there or anywhere else on Maui as of this writing.) Back on the road, it's a little less than 3½ more miles to the turnoff to the parking lot for the Halemauu Trail, 34¼ miles from Wailuku.

Several *nene,* the endangered native goose that is the state bird of Hawaii, used to frequent the Halemauu Trail's parking lot. Their antics used to amuse many visitors. Unfortunately, there may be no *nene* at the parking lot any more. Most of the *nene* that used to hang out there got run over by cars, and the Park Service moved the others to safety. The Park Service is now trying to keep the *nene* away from roads and trailheads. Maybe you'll meet some *nene* down in the crater; see below for more about them.

Permit/permission required: None.

Description. The start of the Halemauu Trail is a little deceptive: you'd expect it to lead straight away from the parking lot east toward the crater rim. But in fact, it starts off southeastward, passes an information sign where you may find brochures on the park, and finally angles northeast at a little gully. (Remember this for your return.) Descending gently, you contour briefly around Haleakala's slopes through native shrubland. Yellow-flowered *mamane,* red-berried *ohelo,* and a white-flowered native shrub geranium add interest to the trail. If the weather permits, you'll have some fine views downslope all the way to the ocean, some 7700 feet below and many miles away.

As you near the ⅔-mile point, you meet the supply trail from Hosmer Grove (Trip H2). From here, you continue ahead on the Halemauu Trail through the gate to the crater-rim viewpoint as described in Trip H2, just under ¾ mile from your start. When you can tear yourself away, retrace your steps.

Nene.... This handsome, non-migratory goose is believed to have descended from the migratory Brant and Canada geese that occasionally winter over in the Hawaiian Islands. Unlike their ancestors, the *nene* aren't waterfowl. One of the *nene*'s adaptations to this dry habitat is feet that are only partially webbed.

There were once as many as 25,000 *nene* in the islands. But by the early 1950s, it was estimated that there were only 30 wild *nene* left. Their habitat had been destroyed by the deforestation that had left so much of Hawaii stripped of her native trees. Introduced animals, particularly mongooses and cats, had destroyed *nene* eggs, chicks, and nesting adults. Concerted efforts in Hawaii and in England have enabled the *nene* to survive in captivity. *Nene* have been reintroduced into the wild here at Haleakala National Park, on the Big Island at Hawaii Volcanoes National Park, and on Kauai in the lowlands around Lihue. It's not known whether they can successfully reestablish themselves in the wild, because the introduced animals that prey on them haven't been controlled.

Nene "honk" like other geese, but you're more likely to hear another of their calls, a cow-like "moo." Here at Haleakala, they are filling a sort of ecological niche, but in their own *nene* style. On the mainland, the campground beggars are typically ground squirrels, bluejays, and raccoons—the latter two are out-and-out thieves. Haleakala's *nene* aren't thieves, but they're accomplished beggars. If you find them hanging around the cabins and campgrounds in the crater, look out! They'll come running for a handout when you unzip your daypack or pull some trail mix out of your pocket. You must be hardhearted and not feed them. (It's both the law and common sense, so they won't become dependent on people supplying food.) However, you will probably feel as guilty as I do when one of them stands there in front of you, eyeing your sandwich hopefully and mooing as if to say, "I'm endangered, I'm adorable, feed me!" Just hang onto your goodies. You'll be off the hook just as soon as someone else unzips a daypack or pulls out some trail mix!

Trip H4. Halemauu Trail to Holua Cabin Dayhike or Backpack

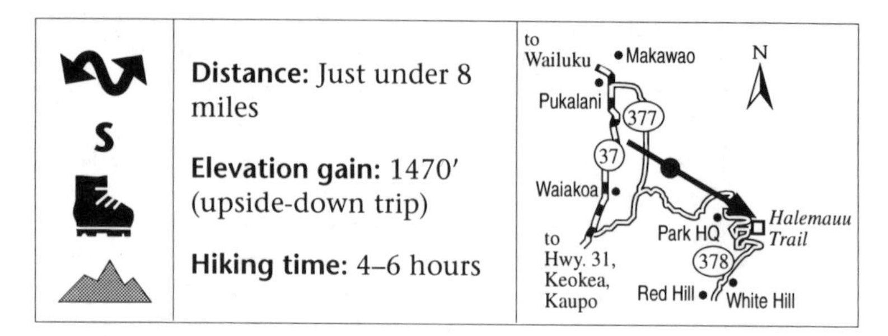

Distance: Just under 8 miles

Elevation gain: 1470′ (upside-down trip)

Hiking time: 4–6 hours

Topos: Kilohana 7½.

Trail map: At the end of Trip H2.

Highlights: The awesome view from the Halemauu Trail at the crater rim, which is the destination of Trips H2 and H3, is just the beginning of *this* breathtaking scenic adventure down into the northwest corner of Haleakala's crater. This trail is so beautiful and so well-engineered that the return trip uphill can be as enjoyable as the descent if you take the time to appreciate it. While it's described below as a dayhike, you can also do it as a backpack if you can get permission to stay at Holua Cabin or the adjacent campground.

Driving instructions: Follow the driving instructions of Trip H3.

Permit/permission required: None for a dayhike. Required for an overnight stay at Holua Cabin (by reservation only) or at the adjacent campground; see Appendix A.

Description. Follow Trip H3 to the crater rim and take in the view. Now continue your zigzagging way down the Halemauu Trail, sometimes indistinct here because of multiple crossing tracks. Watch your step if it's been raining, as these rocks can be very slippery. It's not long before you cross a narrow saddle where, if the cloud-cover permits, you have dizzying views into the crater on your right and down Haleakala's green northern slopes to the sea on your left—one of the very best viewpoints on this or any other hike in this book!

Soon you're negotiating carefully engineered switchbacks as you descend Leleiwi Pali to the crater floor. The grade is moderate to gentle, and the views are always spectacular. Stop often to enjoy them! One long switchback carries you around the other side of this ridge for a look down Koolau Gap. Seep springs dampen the black rock of the *pali*, which provides a perfect backdrop for the jewellike colors of the *amauu* fern. Mature *amauu* fronds are a bright green, while young fronds are a bright red. Together, set against the black rock, they're a sight you'll never forget. The red pigment is said to protect young fronds against the intense radiation at these altitudes.

You reach the crater floor at a stock gate in a little less than 3 miles from your start. Pass through the fence and please close the gate behind you. You may have expected to be on a dry, cinder-covered crater floor like the ones you see in most photographs of the crater. But here, the crater floor is a broad meadow of tall, waving grasses, nourished by the moisture in the clouds that flow through Koolau Gap. The trail is sometimes hard to see in the high growth, so watch your step and beware of half-hidden rocks. Bizarre, twisted peaks of half-vegetated lava rock rise out of the meadow here and there.

Holua Cabin sits atop a plateau on the opposite (south) side of this meadow. Follow the trail across the meadow, on the other side of which the trail rises gradually up the lava plateau in a few lazy switchbacks. You reach a **T**-junction atop the plateau, just under 4 miles from your start. The Halemauu Trail turns sharply left (southeast) here toward the Silversword Loop, Kawilinau (formerly "the Bottomless Pit"; the park wants to restore Hawaiian names to all named features wherever possible), and Paliku Cabin. You turn right to Holua Cabin, which is just a few steps away, sitting on a tidy, grassy flat. There's water, a picnic table, a toilet, and a few semi-resident *nene* here. If you're staying the night in the campground, it's 120 feet farther up the plateau on a short, steep spur trail that goes off to the left, past the water tap, as you face the cabin.

Return the way you came.

Crater trails.... The system of maintained trails leading down into and through the crater follows routes through this delicate ecosystem that are safe for you and for the environment. Going off the maintained trails can be physically hazardous and can damage the ecosystem, particularly in the extremely sensitive western part of the crater. Please don't step off the trail even to photograph the silverswords. You could be trampling and killing tiny silversword sprouts you can't even see. You'll find silverswords growing right next to the trail in several places, especially on the spur trail to Ka Lua o Ka Oo (Trip H11), so stepping off the trail is unnecessary. There aren't as many maintained trails as there used to be, "thanks" to cuts in the funding for national parks. But trust me on this: there's more than enough to explore on the remaining maintained trails to keep you busy for the few days you're permitted to spend in the crater. Haleakala National Park hopes to start maintaining more trails and to reopen closed ones over the next few years. Stick to the maintained trails, spare the environment, spare yourself injury, and help keep Haleakala beautiful.

Trip H5. Holua Cabin/Campground Side Trip to Kapalaoa Cabin

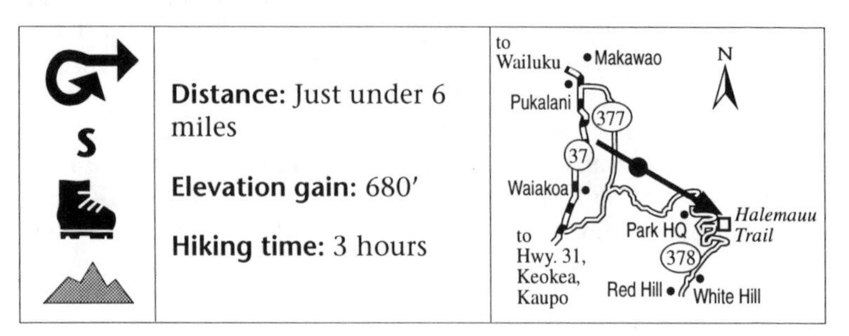

Topos: Kilohana, Nahiku 7½.

Trail map: At the end of this trip.

Highlights: This delightful semiloop takes you to the famous Silversword Loop and through some of the most colorful volcanic areas in the crater. It's one of several dayhikes you might take while staying at Holua Cabin/Campground. See the note at the end of Trip H2 for more ideas on crater dayhikes and backpacks.

Driving instructions: Not applicable.

Permit/permission required: None for the side trip, which is a dayhike. Required to stay at Holua Cabin or the adjacent campground (see Trip H4 and Appendix A).

Description. Trip H4 has gotten you to Holua Cabin. This trip starts from the **T**-junction in front of Holua Cabin and bears southeast on the Halemauu Trail. You ascend gradually past a pit that is the open mouth of a lava tube and then through low ridges of jagged brown lava whose outcrops are crusted with a white lichen and whose protected hollows hold plants. At first you'll see *mamane, aalii,* sword ferns, and bracken ferns.

But soon the terrain becomes drier, and *ohelo, pilo, pukiawe, kukaenene,* dubautias, and even a few silverswords appear. Lava cinders crunch under your boots. On either side of the trail, islands of fantastically shaped lava twist and twirl up from beds of black and red cinder. Sometimes the clouds from Koolau Gap drift in, leaving you alone in a misty world of goblin forms. At other times, you can see far across the crater to the cliffs enclosing it and to the red, brown, and black cinder cones that dot its floor. Pause often to look around you. It's one of earth's most striking landscapes, often referred to as a moonscape.

One mile from Holua, you reach the first of two junctions with the famous Silversword Loop. It's less a loop than a ¼-mile diversion from the Halemauu Trail. Veer left onto the Silversword

Loop at this first junction for just over ¼ mile and then rejoin the main trail. When you've been around the Silversword Loop and come back to the Halemauu Trail, turn left to continue south on this dayhike.

Back on the Halemauu Trail, you descend briefly on soft, fine sand and walk through a red-tinged Mars-scape of bizarre lava rocks. Cinder cones rise on either side of the trail, and you soon reach another junction, just under 2 miles from your start at Holua Cabin/Campground. Both the left and the right forks here will get you to Kapalaoa Cabin and the Sliding Sands Trail, but take the left fork east toward Kawilinau (formerly "the Bottomless Pit") for now.

As you approach Kawilinau, you see a natural, if somewhat sloppy, bull's-eye of soft reds, grays, golds, and oranges ahead on the southeast slope of an unnamed cone. The slopes are a deep red with dots of fiery red and a brilliant splash of gold and orange at the saddle with Halalii cone. Orange, red, and lavender along the trail contrast with the dark brown slopes to your left, while on your right, pinks, golds, and reds spill into Halalii cone's vent. A lively brick red splashes up one slope, vivid orange another; nearby, there's a pit of shattered gray and red-brown rock. Grasses and dubautia make their homes here, adding a dash of green.

Now you know why this area is referred to as "Pele's Paint Pot." No subdued watercolors here—these are bold tempera colors, the result of minerals in the volcanic rock. Sulfur compounds are responsible for the yellows, iron for the reds. Fenced-off Kawilinau is not bottomless; according to a sign, it's 65 feet deep. Its depth may be forgettable, but its colors are memorable: pinks and reds burst from its throat; golds and grays tint its edges.

Ignore the unmarked side trail that leads south away from Kawilinau (it's just a shortcut over the saddle between Halalii and Puu Naue to the trail you'll be returning on). Instead, continue generally eastward around Puu Naue, past brown-black cinder cones whose slopes are daubed with patches of orange and red. Ahead looms Puu Mamane, its northern slopes green with vegetation, its southern slopes bare red cinders.

Now you pass through a cinder-strewn landscape as desolate as any you've seen; silverswords grow high on the slopes to your right. Soon, the bare, reddish cone of Puu Nole rises ahead on your right, Puu Mamane on your left. You pass a couple of use trails down which you have views of Kapalaoa Cabin.

At the next marked junction, between Puu Mamane and Puu Nole, you turn southeast (right) toward Kapalaoa Cabin on the easternmost Sliding Sands-Halemauu spur trail. The green-clad *pali* behind the cabin dominate the scenery as you begin a descent between Puu Naue and Puu Nole. As you approach the red slopes of another cone, you see that they have a sparse cover of bracken fern and silversword. A group of silverswords grows where the trail brushes past a ridge extending from the cone. Jagged chunks of rock protrude through the sand here, looking like the spine of a prehistoric monster half-buried in the sand.

You level out on black sand that's tinged with lavender and strewn with red and orange cinders; soon you reach a junction with the Sliding Sands Trail. Turn left (east) here for a few steps to Kapalaoa Cabin, 1¼ mile from Kawilinau. Here you'll find a toilet, a picnic table, water, and *nene* anxious to help you polish off that granola bar. There's no tent-campground here: water at Kapalaoa Cabin is limited to precipitation collected from the roof, and there's not enough to support both a cabin and a campground.

The trail that goes north immediately in front of Kapalaoa Cabin is not a maintained trail, so you go west ⅓ mile, past the junction with the trail you descended on, to the next marked trail junction. Turn right (northwest) here onto the middle Sliding Sands-Halemauu spur trail toward Holua Cabin.

You head toward Puu Naue through bunches of a native alpine tussock grass—a sort of meadow and just about the last thing you'd expect to see in this lava wilderness. The grass ends as you pass a red-cinder hillock, and you traverse a region of black and reddish sand and of lava frozen as it oozed across the landscape. The rocks here are riddled with holes left by gas bubbles and brushed with subtle hues from cream through orange, red, and black.

You cross a spine of lava, climb past a miniature butte of red rock, and level out amid reddish cinders and black boulders. A remnant of a *pahoehoe* flow, markedly smoother than the *aa* you've been passing, appears on your left. The trail is plain ahead of you, winding up to the saddle between Ka Moa o Pele and Halalii cones. Ka Moa o Pele's huge red vent gapes at you, its edges dusted with ochre and gray. You pass more *pahoehoe*, cross a stretch of black cinders, and abruptly enter a region of light-colored cinders—white, tan, pink-orange—on which sit isolated lava bombs.

The light-colored cinders end as abruptly as they began, and you're soon on the saddle between Ka Moa o Pele and Halalii cones at the junction with the spur trail around Halalii, a little under 1 mile from Kapalaoa Cabin. Head northwest (right) past a little, squarish vent called Pele's Pig Pen to the junction where, earlier, you turned off to Kawilinau.

Bear left (northwest) on the Halemauu Trail here and retrace your steps to Holua Cabin to end this beautiful dayhike.

Continued from map at end of Trip H2

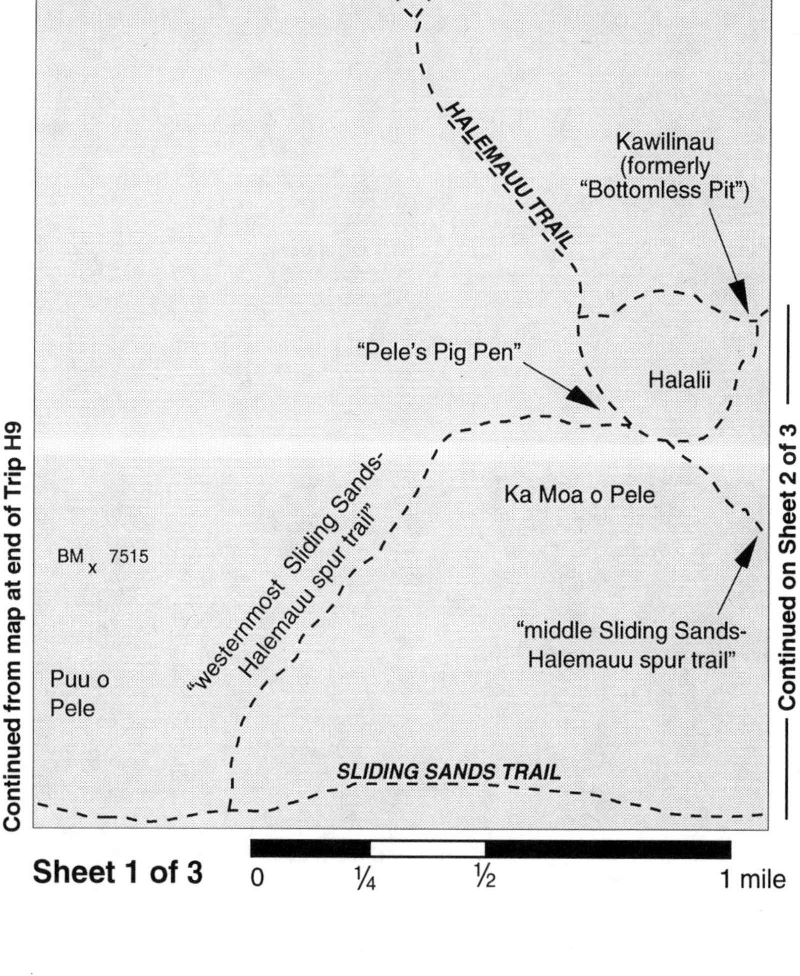

Sheet 1 of 3

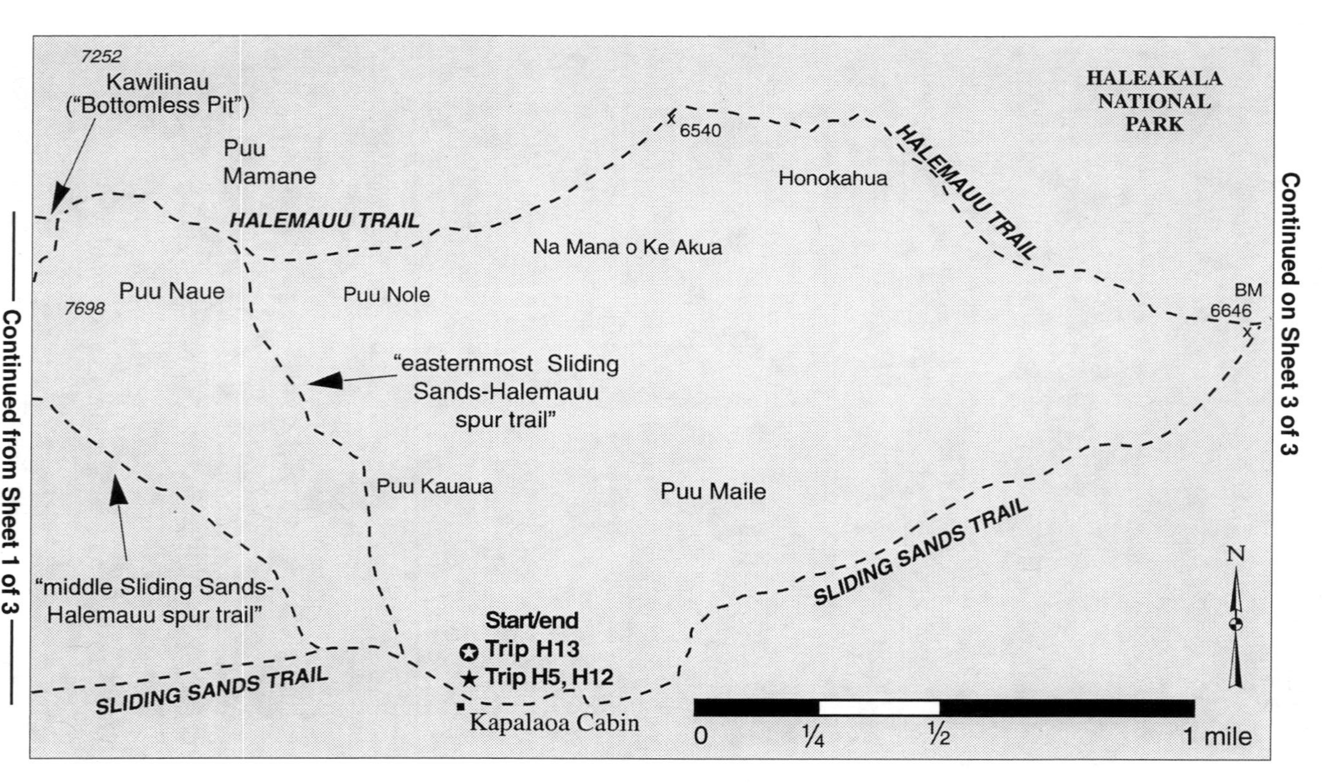
Continued on Sheet 3 of 3
HALEAKALA NATIONAL PARK
7252
Kawilinau ("Bottomless Pit")
Puu Mamane
6540
Honokahua
HALEMAUU TRAIL
HALEMAUU TRAIL
Na Mana o Ke Akua
Puu Naue
7698
Puu Nole
BM 6646
"easternmost Sliding Sands-Halemauu spur trail"
Puu Kauaua
Puu Maile
SLIDING SANDS TRAIL
"middle Sliding Sands-Halemauu spur trail"
Start/end
Trip H13
Trip H5, H12
SLIDING SANDS TRAIL
Kapalaoa Cabin
N
0
1/4
1/2
1 mile
Continued from Sheet 1 of 3

Sheet 2 of 3

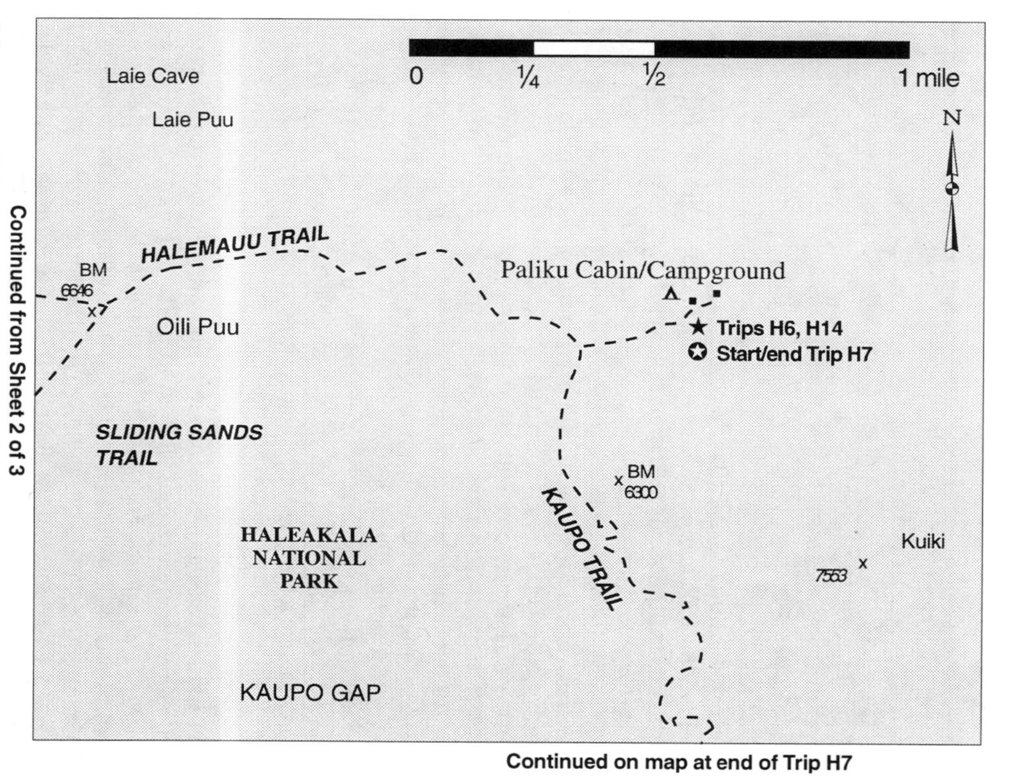

Continued on map at end of Trip H7

Continued from Sheet 2 of 3

Sheet 3 of 3

Trip H6. Halemauu Trail to Paliku Cabin/Campground Backpack

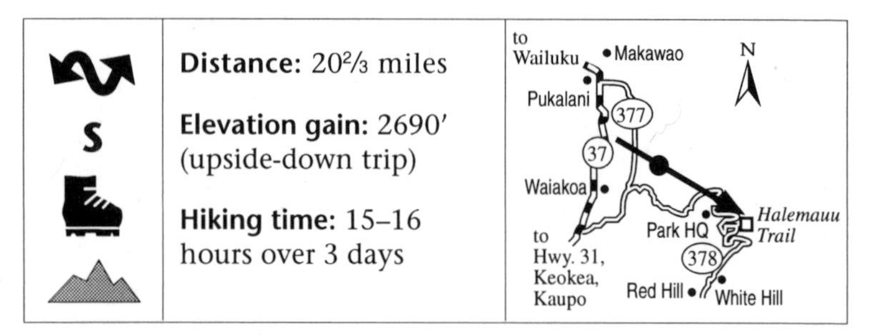

Distance: 20⅔ miles

Elevation gain: 2690′ (upside-down trip)

Hiking time: 15–16 hours over 3 days

Topos: Kilohana, Nahiku 7½.

Trail map: Begins on the map at the end of Trip H4; continues and ends on the maps at the end of Trip H5.

Highlights: The soft, green beauty of the *pali* and meadows near Holua Cabin/Campground and around Paliku Cabin/Campground contrast marvelously with the vivid mineral colors and harsh aridity of the crater backcountry that separates them.

Driving instructions: Follow the driving instructions of Trip H3.

Permit/permission required: Haleakala National Park permit required to stay overnight at Holua Cabin/Campground or Paliku Cabin/Campground or both. See "Getting Permits and Permission" and Appendix A.

Description. You can organize this trip in a number of different ways depending on the permits you're able to get and whether you want to take a layover day. Clearly, going all the way to Paliku in one day and all the way out in one day is the most strenuous version. I've described an easier version below: you go all the way to Paliku in one day—mostly downhill—and take two days to walk out, staying one night at Holua Cabin/Campground.

Day 1 (10⅓ miles). Follow Trip H4 to Holua Cabin/Campground. From there, follow Trip H5 to the marked junction between Puu Mamane and Puu Nole, where Trip H5 turns right (southeast) toward Kapalaoa Cabin. Bear left (ahead; east) toward Paliku Cabin/Campground at that junction. You presently reach a saddle where a low, vegetated hill rises ahead of you. As you continue, the cliffs around the crater begin to assume a softer, greener look. Soon you're gazing across an almost-African landscape, where the *veldt* is shrubs and bracken rather than grass, dotted by green *kopjes* whose tops sport tree-sized *mamane* rather than the airy African acacia. You descend gradually onto the veldt, and you presently see what looks like a dry wash ahead. It is a wash, and the trail leads down to it. In some places, the trail is right in the wash; in others, where the bottom of the wash is very rocky, the trail leads you around its edges.

At the foot of shrub-covered Oili Puu, you reach the junction of the Halemauu and Sliding Sands trails. Turn left (northeast) here toward Paliku Cabin/Campground, abandoning the wash and following a path sometimes over *pahoehoe* and sometimes worn deeply through the shrub-and-bracken plain. The troughs of the grey-black *pahoehoe* ripples are sometimes highlighted by a delicate trace of red color.

At a junction with the trail heading down Kaupo Gap, you can just glimpse Paliku Cabin to the northeast. It's surrounded by trees and nestled at the foot of lushly green *pali*, sometimes framed in a rainbow by late-afternoon light refracted through a fine rain. Bear left (northeast) on the side trail ¼ mile to Paliku Cabin/Campground, 6⅓ miles from Holua Cabin/Campground. The spur trail to the campground is on your left a few dozen yards before you get to Paliku Cabin. *Nene* patrol the picnic area in front of the cabin and the adjacent campground, mooing for a handout. Not far from Paliku cabin, there's a rangers' cabin (almost hidden) and a meadow where horses graze. It's a lovely place to stay, and you'll probably want to spend two nights here in order to take Trip H7.

Day 2 (6⅓ miles). Reverse your steps from Paliku Cabin/Campground to Holua Cabin/Campground.

Day 3 (Just under 4 miles). Reverse your steps from Holua Cabin/Campground to the Halemauu trailhead.

Why the great variations in the amount of vegetation?...You'll no doubt have noticed the great variation in the amount of vegetation in the crater. What a contrast the arid volcanic landscapes around the Silversword Loop and Kawilinau make with the meadows around Holua Cabin/Campground and Paliku Cabin/Campground! One factor is the difference in precipitation the different parts of the crater receive. In general, the crater floor near Koolau Gap (Holua Cabin/Campground and the meadow) shares the moisture of East Maui's rainy northern coast, which flows through Koolau Gap. The crater floor here is just within the inversion-layer zone. Above Paliku Cabin/Campground, there's a notch in the slim ridge still separating Kipahulu Valley from Kaupo Gap and Haleakala's crater. Moisture from the very wet Hana-Kipahulu coast pours through this notch, nourishing Paliku. By contrast, the southwest edge of the crater is on the dry, leeward side of the island and is high above the inversion-layer zone. Annual rainfall in the crater varies from 20 inches there to 200 or more inches at Paliku!

But rainfall variations alone aren't enough to explain the differences. An annual rainfall of 20 inches a year is more than enough to sustain a cover of vegetation in many areas of the world. However, in order for that vegetation to flourish, the soil must retain the water it receives. The crater's cinder cones, remnants of its last phase of volcanic activity, have made the crater both a visual delight and an inhospitable desert. Their eruptions covered most of the crater with a porous layer of cinder and ash, reported to be 3000 feet deep in some places. That layer allows whatever precipitation falls to percolate right through it. Little water is retained, except in isolated pockets, to feed plants. Nooks like Paliku escaped those cinders. Unlike the cinder deserts, their older, more-consolidated soils retain life-giving water and create these green oases.

Trip H7. Paliku Cabin/Campground Side Trip to Park Boundary

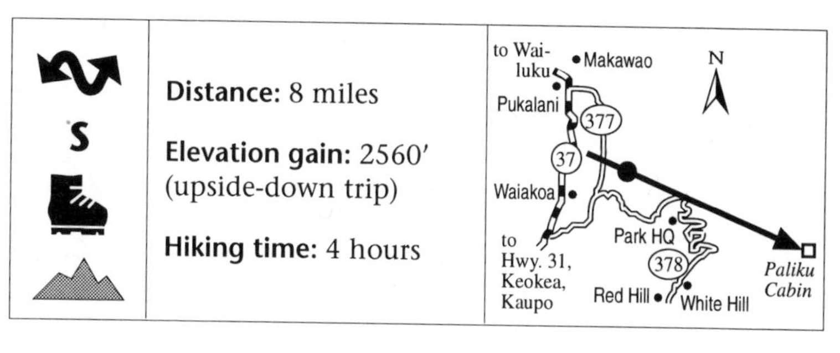

Topos: Nahiku, Kaupo 7½.

Trail map: Begins on Sheet 3 of 3 of the map at the end of Trip H5; ends on the map at the end of this trip.

Highlights: A fascinating descent through scrubland, forest, and meadow, with fine views downslope to the coast around Kaupo village. This trip complements Trip E14.

Driving instructions: Not applicable.

Permit/permission required: None just for this side trip, but you must have permission to stay in the crater as described in Trips H4 and H6.

Description. Trip H6 or H14 brought you to Paliku Cabin/Campground. To begin this trip, retrace your steps from Paliku Cabin/Campground to the junction with the trail that goes down Kaupo Gap. Turn left (southwest) toward the dark peak, Haleakala, that guards the west side of Kaupo Gap. (Haleakala peak is too far south and west of the trail to appear on the book's maps.) Opposite, Kuiki peak watches Kaupo Gap's east side. The trail presently veers south and begins a descent on a cindery surface through the scrub you've come to recognize as typical of this region. Look for some almost-tree-sized *aalii* shrubs here. In ½ mile from Paliku, you begin a series of cinder-covered switchbacks. White-flowered *ulei* grows here, as do many splendid *amauu* ferns. Down you go, leveling out in a little forest, then emerging into a meadow of waving grasses through which you follow the trail to the edge of this bench. Here, you may be startled to realize that the blue vastness ahead of you is only half sky. The lower portion is the sparkling ocean, so far away that it blends into the sky.

You switchback briefly down to another bench and another meadow. From here, you make a delightful descent over an old, built-up trail whose supporting lava-rock walls are covered with a thick white fluff of lichens. Spikes of small, blue-flowered vervain sway along the trailside. Now you reach a third bench, pushing your way first through blackberry and then through dense grass. The sheer walls of Kaupo Gap loom high on your left.

Rounding a curve, you find yourself walking south along the west side of a gully whose shady east side is well-clothed in native plants, including *ohia* trees, *amauu* ferns, and *mamane* shrubs. As you veer west and then south, the view opens up again, and you see some fine *koa* trees down in the gully. On the rocks to your right, look for the low, trailing *kukaenene* with its shiny black berries.

The next series of switchbacks offers breathtaking views down to Kaupo and the sea, west to Haleakala peak, and back up to the misty *pali*. The trail becomes very rocky, and with so many loose rocks, it's wise to pause when you want to enjoy the scenery. You leave the rocks at a little clearing in the now-predominant *koa*. The terrain has become drier as you have descended, as you can see from the shrubbier forms of the *mamane* and *pukiawe*. Soon the trail becomes rocky again, and you resume descending on switchbacks under the shade of *koa* trees. At a little emerald meadow, pause to check the gentle slope ahead and slightly to your right (south-southwest) to see where the trail resumes, as it all but vanishes in the lush grass here. Make your way across the meadow and pick up the trail again as it rises briefly on the low ridge, then follows the ridge generally south through scrub, becoming quite rocky and sometimes steep. Soon you begin a series of grassy switchbacks that bring you to the protective fence of the Kaupo Gap Study Area.

Now you descend moderately on a track that's more often grass than rock. The slopes ahead of you frame distant, square-shaped Kamanawa Bay west of Kaupo village. At an apparent fork, either fork will do, but watch your footing on the deep grass. It makes a spongy surface to walk on and conceals some loose rocks. You pass a National Park boundary sign on the other side of which is a sign announcing that you're now on Kaupo Ranch's private property. Soon you cross a gully above some *koa* trees and, as the track grows faint, duck into a lovely grove of *koa* just before the park's protective boundary fence. Remember that if you do go through the fence, you must be sure the gate shuts securely behind you, even if you have to trample the grass down to make it close.

Retrace your steps to Paliku Cabin/Campground when you're ready. (To continue to Kaupo, reverse the steps of Trip E14.)

Maui and Haleakala peak.... Shelters, platforms, and a *heiau* are said to be located on Haleakala peak, signs that it once had religious significance. One source speculates that Haleakala peak may be the site of the demigod Maui's mythical encounter with La, the sun. There are many versions of this myth, but all agree that long ago, the lazy sun moved across the sky so quickly that the day was very short. La arose from his resting-place reluctantly, hurried as fast as he could through his work of lighting and warming the earth, and rushed home to his leisure without a thought for the long nights that people had to endure. The day was far too short for Maui's mother, the goddess Hina, to dry her *kapa*, the bark cloth characteristic of Polynesia. Hina asked Maui to find a way to dry her *kapa*. Here on Hale-a-ka-La, the House of the Sun, Maui prepared ropes and hid so he could surprise La as he rose, climbing over the walls of Haleakala crater like a spider, one leg—ray—at a time. As La put each leg over the *pali*, Maui lassoed it. He held La captive until La promised to move across the sky more slowly. Even then, some accounts say, Maui left a few of the ropes on La's legs. You can see them trailing off into the sky just before the sun sets.

The island of Maui is unique in Polynesia: it is the only island named for a deity. Maui was a great mischief-maker, and legends about his escapades (or "strifes") occur throughout Polynesia. Martha Beckwith reported in *Hawaiian Mythology* that Maui legends in Hawaii tend to be "minutely localized." East Maui, West Maui, the Big Island of Hawaii, Oahu, and Kauai all have their own versions of the same Maui exploit, placing the exploit's location somewhere on that island. For East Maui, Maui's tricks usually occur near Kauiki at Hana; for West Maui, near Kahakuloa. Haleakala isn't one of the sites Dr. Beckwith records in association with Maui's legends. Still, legends are fluid, and Haleakala certainly seems appropriate as a poetic, if not entirely traditional, site for Maui's capture of La.

Continued from Sheet 3 of 3 of map at end of Trip H5

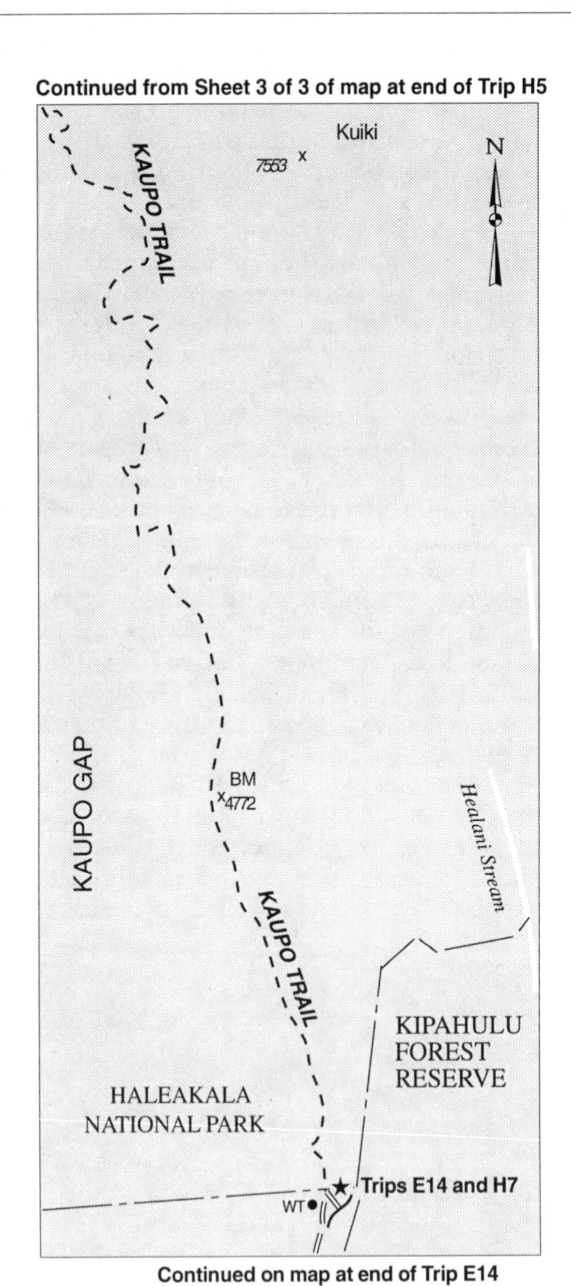

Continued on map at end of Trip E14

Trip H8. Kalahaku Overlook Mini-loop

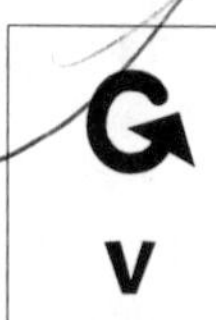

Distance: ⅕ mile

Elevation gain: 40′

Hiking time: Less than 10 minutes

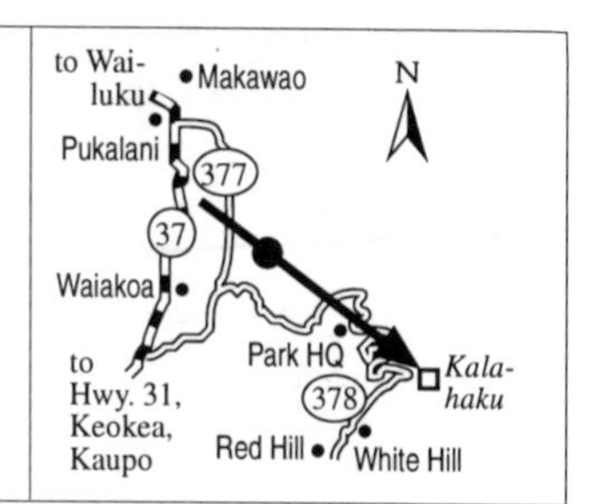

Topos: Optional: Kilohana 7½.

Trail map (route approximated): At the end of this trip.

Highlights: This brief trip offers fine crater views and a visit to a little garden of silverswords in just a few brief minutes of walking with little elevation gain. Non-hikers, this is the Haleakala trip for *you!*

Driving instructions: Follow the driving instructions of Trip H4 past the Halemauu Trail turnoff. Continue up the highway to the Visitor Center at White Hill, 40⅓ miles from Wailuku, *deliberately driving past the turnoff for the Kalahaku Overlook*—all but invisible when driving up the highway. You're not allowed to turn off here when you're going uphill. Turn around in the parking lot at the Visitor Center and drive back down the highway just over 1½ miles to the turnoff for the Kalahaku Overlook, well-marked for downhill traffic. Turn right here and follow the spur road to the parking area, 42 miles from Wailuku. (It's 38¾ miles from Wailuku plus the slightly over 3 miles you drove to the Visitor Center and back.)

Permit/permission required: None.

Description. Near the end of the spur road, a paved path leads up to an overlook shelter. Taking this path, you climb with the help of some stairs past a sign explaining the impact non-native animals have had on native plants and animals. Don't take the path that branches to the right at a junction here; instead, continue ahead to the shelter on the crater rim. There's a magnificent crater view from the shelter, and interpretive signs explain the many crater cones you can see below to the east and southeast. To the west, you can see West Maui.

It's hard to leave this view, but when you're ready, retrace your steps to the exotic-animal sign. Turn left at the junction here and follow the paved path down a gentle descent with a short flight of stairs to the road. Cross the road and descend the stairs that are just a little to your right. Turn left at the bottom of the stairs and follow the paved path along the silversword viewing area. You can't walk out into the silversword garden, but you can walk back and forth here to see how the light brings out the silvery patina on these remarkable plants.

The path winds back up to the road, where you turn left (north) and retrace your steps back to your car.

The Brocken specter....is a natural light show in which you are both audience and star: your shadow on a cloud bank below you, surrounded by a rainbow ring. It's often seen at Haleakala, particularly from Leleiwi Pali (for example, Leleiwi Overlook, just down the highway). Afternoon sunlight behind you casts your shadow onto the clouds drifting through Koolau Gap. The light around your shadow is reflected back from the cloud by the water droplets that make it up. Like tiny prisms, these water droplets also refract the light into the familiar colors of the rainbow. You see the rainbow effect as a colored halo around your shadow. You don't believe that's your shadow? Wave your arms and watch the shadow follow suit. Worldwide, seeing the Brocken specter used to be rare; nowadays, airline passengers frequently see the Brocken specter from the airplane. Still, it's much more exciting when the rainbow-circled shadow is yours, not the airplane's! The phenomenon is named for Brocken Mountain in Germany, where it was first described.

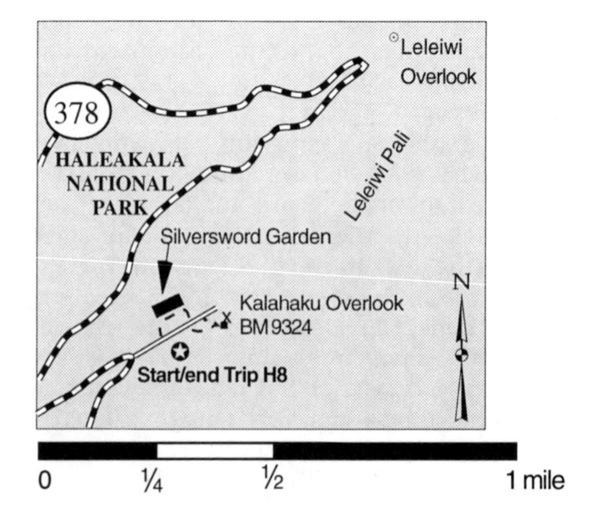

Trip H9. White Hill

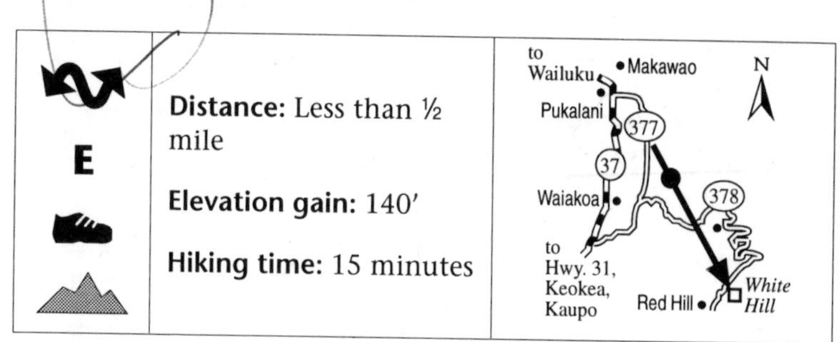

Distance: Less than ½ mile

Elevation gain: 140′

Hiking time: 15 minutes

Topos: Kilohana 7½.

Trail map (route approximated): At the end of this trip.

Highlights: The awesome panorama from the top of White Hill is something you won't forget. White Hill's summit is one of the favored places for watching sunrise at Haleakala, too. So is the Visitor Center, but it's usually crowded with those who came unprepared to wait in the icy dark. The vigil demands plenty of warm, windproof clothing—don't forget that warm hat and those gloves or mittens, either.

Driving instructions: Follow the driving instructions of Trip H3 past the Halemauu Trail turnoff and continue up the highway to the Visitor Center at White Hill, 40⅓ miles from Wailuku.

Permit/permission required: None.

Description. The trail up White Hill begins near the Visitor Center building, to its right as you face the building from the parking lot. It's a gentle but rocky grade; if you're coming here in the frigid predawn darkness, you'll need a flashlight to keep yourself on the trail and to avoid tripping over the rocks. The trail winds almost 360° around the hill as it rises to the summit, where a few tough dubautias live. From here, you have superb views in all directions once it's light. To the southwest sits Haleakala's high point, Red Hill (Trip H17). Southeast, you look over the crater walls to the summits of Mauna Kea and Mauna Loa on the Big Island of Hawaii, many miles away across the ocean. To the west, you have amazing views of the Isthmus and West Maui. And below you to the east, steep cliffs fall away into the crater. Perhaps the crater is clear of mist and dramatic with its cinder cones and sheer walls, or perhaps it's filled with clouds through which the cones push their dark heads. Nothing but the thin air separates you from the crater, making you feel almost as if you had wings and were soaring high above it.

It's hard to retrace your steps from here. After you've done so, but before you leave, stop in at the Visitor Center to enjoy the exhibits, browse for another book, and get your questions answered by the ranger on duty.

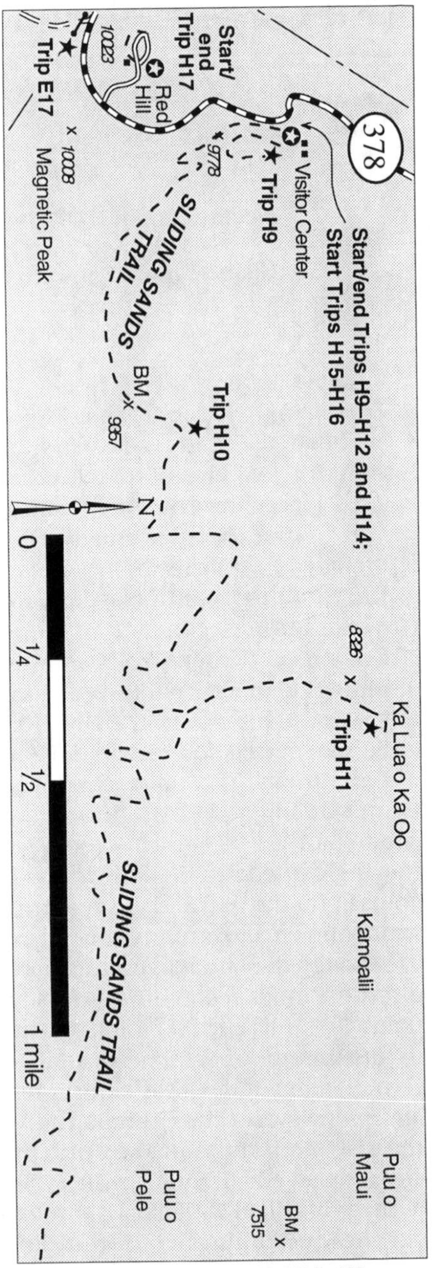

Continued on map at end of Trip H5, Sheet 1 of 3

Trip H10. Sliding Sands Trail to "Rock Garden"

M

Distance: 2 miles

Elevation gain: 560′ (upside-down trip)

Hiking time: 1 hour

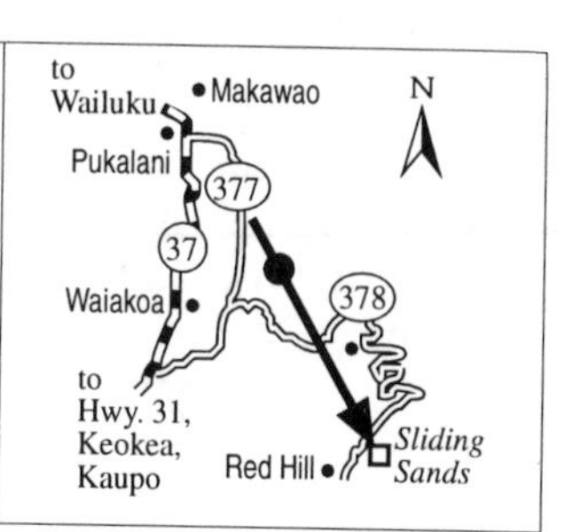

Topos: Kilohana 7½.

Trail map: At the end of Trip H9.

Highlights: This relatively short descent on the famous Sliding Sands Trail offers you a chance to experience hiking in Haleakala's crater and to enjoy some wonderful crater views.

Driving instructions: Follow the driving instructions of Trip H9. The Sliding Sands Trail is on the side of the parking lot nearer the highway (away from the Visitor Center building).

Permit/permission required: None.

Description. Pause at the trailhead sign to read its information and to pick up one of the park's brochures on hiking trails. Now that you're fully informed, follow the path away from the parking lot, briefly paralleling the highway. You're at the crater rim in a little over ⅛ mile. You can't help but pause and think, *How vast and lifeless the crater seems from here!* Ahead, the Sliding Sands Trail stretches away along the cindery crater wall, dwindling till it seems little more than a scratch in the dark sand. Specks moving on the distant scratch will turn out to be your fellow hikers. Down in the crater, clouds drift in and out among the brown and red hulks of distant cinder cones, constantly changing the view. Far, far away at the east end of the crater, Kaupo Gap breaks the stark crater walls, mists ebbing and flowing through it. Perhaps you had thought you could easily orient yourself here; now, the crater's immensity may seem almost intimidating and its shifting clouds may defy your attempts to positively identify the landmarks that seemed so obvious from the Visitor Center.

The well-graded trail is pleasant walking, and you're soon descending, negotiating a couple of switchbacks, and looking forward to your next photo stop. You presently drop into the shallow depression between a low ridge on your left and the crater wall. At the next switchback, just under 1 mile from your start, you come upon a handsome formation of red-brown rock around which grow a number of bright green shrubs with cheery little puffs of yellow flowers. This striking natural arrangement of forms and colors is what I've called the "rock garden." These are dubautias, specifically *Dubautia menziesii*, one of the plants most characteristic of this arid landscape (more about them below). Other dubautias grow in and around Haleakala, but this particular one, with its small, stiff, succulent leaves arranged rather formally in fours, is especially conspicuous because it seeks no shelter, growing instead in the most exposed places. A few stunted *pukiawe*, another hardy native shrub, grow here, too, but the dubautias are really the show.

When you're ready, retrace your steps.

Dubautias and their relatives.... Botanists believe that the endemic dubautias (*Dubautia*) and their showier endemic relatives, the silverswords (*Argyroxiphium*) and *iliau* (*Wilkesia*), share a common ancestor with the present-day tarweeds of California. The common California tarweed is a daisy-like annual plant, not particularly showy, competing with many other mainland species for survival and having few opportunities to radiate into different environmental niches.

The tarweeds that reached Hawaii, probably as bristly seeds stuck to birds' feathers, have undergone one of the most amazing adaptive radiations to be found in the Hawaiian Islands. As their common ancestor was adapted to dry locations, it's not surprising to find dubautias, silverswords, and *iliau* in arid places. But many dubautias have evolved into shrubs and trees of the rainforests. One dubautia even grows on the summit of Kauai's Mt. Waialeale, possibly the rainiest spot on earth. Another rare dubautia is a vine in Kauai's *koa* forests.

The Haleakala silversword occupies the extremely arid, bright alpine environment. The Kau silversword grows in a moist region on the slopes of Mauna Loa on the Big Island of Hawaii. More amazing still are the silverswords and greenswords (like silverswords but lacking silvery hairs) that grow in bogs like the one on Puu Kukui, the highest point on West Maui and another of the rainiest spots on earth.

The shrubby dubautias and the rosette-shaped silverswords are so closely related that they can hybridize naturally. *Plants and Flowers of Hawai'i* includes a photograph of one such natural hybrid, between the *Dubautia menziesii* you see here at the "rock garden" and the Haleakala silversword, *Argyroxiphium sandwicense*.

The *iliau*, one of only two members of its genus, occupies a moderately dry, scrubby forest niche around Waimea Canyon on Kauai. It's rare, but it doesn't seem to be an endangered species.

Apparently, the only major environmental niche the dubautia-silversword-*iliau* family doesn't occupy in the Hawaiian Islands is the lower coastal region—but it's one of the principal niches occupied by their California tarweed relatives and their presumed common ancestor. Perhaps that niche was already fully occupied when the ancestor of the dubautia-silversword-*iliau* family arrived, so the adaptable family went on to evolve into forms that occupy virtually every other niche in Hawaii.

Dubautia

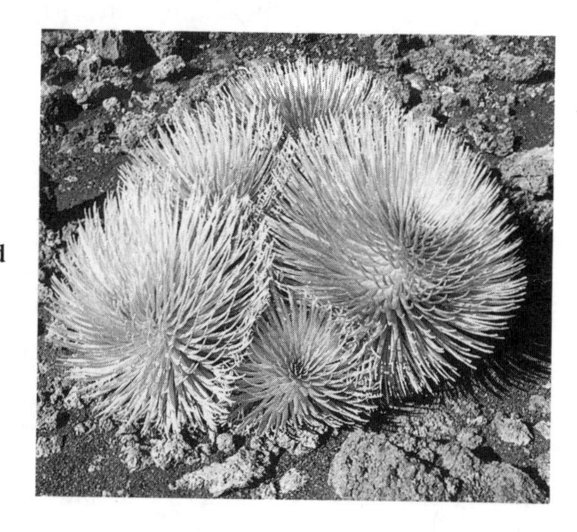

Silversword

Trip H11. Sliding Sands Trail to Ka Lua o Ka Oo

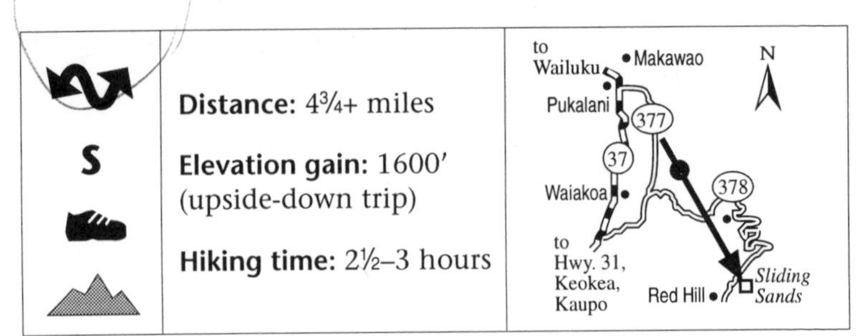

Topos: Kilohana 7½.

Trail map: At the end of Trip H9.

Highlights: Ka Lua o Ka Oo ("Kalua O Ka Oo" on the topo, "Ka Luu o ka Oo" on a park brochure) is one of the most colorful cones in the crater. The way it's tucked into the steep ridge below Red Hill means there's very little climbing required to get to its top. As a bonus, the spur trail from the Sliding Sands Trail to Ka Lua O Ka Oo presently has one of the best concentrations of silverswords to be found in the crater, several growing so near the trail that there's no excuse or need for stepping off the trail to get your own silversword photograph. A park brochure may be available for this hike; check at the trailhead. It says that "Ka Luu o ka Oo" means "the plunge [luu] of the digging-stick [oo]."

Driving instructions: Follow the driving instructions of Trip H9.

Permit/permission required: None.

Description. Follow the Sliding Sands Trail down to the "rock garden" as described in Trip H10. Continue down the ridge, where views of the crater open up again as you switchback away from the "rock garden." Silverswords appear along the trail as you approach the junction with the spur trail to Ka Lua o Ka Oo. The junction is set amid jagged lava formations, and you turn left (north) here toward the cone.

The spur trail makes a short, steep, rough descent at first. Then it levels out and curves around the steep but shallow depression below Red Hill and White Hill, revealing a landscape of red-brown cinders enlivened by the shining gray-white of silversword rosettes and the sprightly green of dubautia shrubs. Climbing a little, the spur trail leads right to the edge of the cone, from which a use trail bears left around the cone's deep, brightly colored vent. Bluish-gray rocks dot the scene, and splashes of mineral colors stain the vent's throat and edges: reds, pinks, tans, blacks, oranges, golds, yellows, chocolates, and lavenders. Oh, for a wide-angle lens to capture all these wonderful colors at once!

As you enjoy this spectacle, Haleakala's clouds may drift in and drizzle on you, then float out, leaving the cone awash in sunlight, then swirl in again. Photography hint: in *Haleakala: A Guide to the Mountain*, the authors advise shutterbugs to meter off the ground, not off the too-bright sky, to avoid underexposures of crater scenery.

Too soon, it's time to return the way you came—almost all uphill now—to your car.

Meadow and cinder cones west of Kapalaoa Cabin

Trip H12. Sliding Sands to Kapalaoa Cabin Dayhike or Backpack

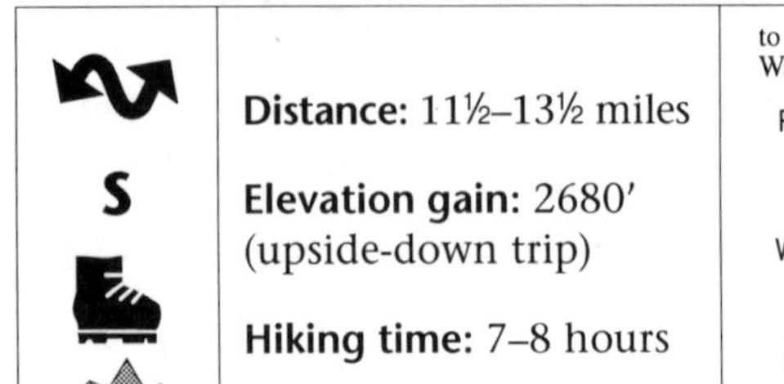

Distance: 11½–13½ miles

Elevation gain: 2680′ (upside-down trip)

Hiking time: 7–8 hours

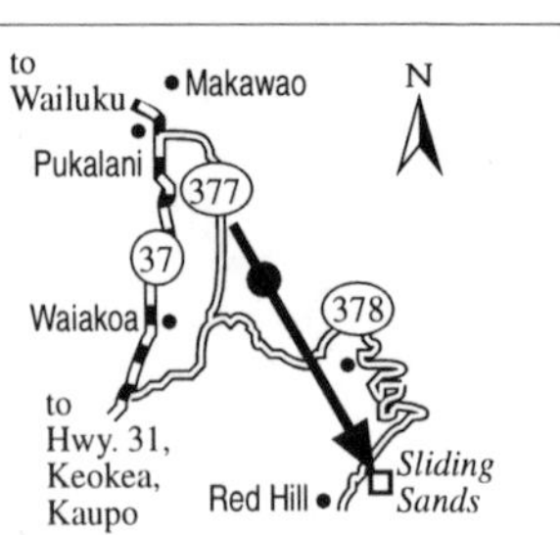

Topos: Kilohana, Nahiku 7½.

Trail map: Begins on the map at the end of Trip H9; ends on the map at the end of Trip H5.

Highlights: All the visual delights of Trips H10 and H11, plus a visit to Kapalaoa Cabin's tiny oasis. Crater views on the way back from Kapalaoa Cabin are especially stunning. I've described this trip as a dayhike, but you can also do it as a backpack if you can get a reservation for Kapalaoa Cabin.

Driving instructions: Follow the driving instructions of Trip H9.

Permit/permission required: None for dayhike. Required for an overnight stay at Kapalaoa Cabin (by reservation only); see Appendix A. There is no campground at Kapalaoa Cabin, so it's the cabin or nothing.

Description. Follow Trip H11 to Ka Lua O Ka Oo, but on your return to the junction with the Sliding Sands Trail, turn left and continue east down the trail. You come around some rocks to see wonderful colors on the adjacent hillsides—pinks, reds, and lavenders. As Puu o Pele looms ahead, you pass through an area of silverswords and presently begin hiking over rocks—chunks of *aa*—instead of the cinders you've been on till now. This area, which appears to be a dull, dark, monochrome from above, reveals itself to be full of subtle colors and intriguing textures. The view back up the Sliding Sands Trail from here is very striking.

You bear east-southeast past heaps of brick-red cinder near the top of Puu o Pele, then zigzag down, down, down its sides to a junction with the westernmost spur trail going north to Holua Cabin/Campground and the Halemauu Trail. Dark-brown Puu o Maui, the highest cone in the crater, is off to the north on one side of the spur trail, reddish Ka Moa o Pele on the other. South of you, on the crater walls, there's a patch of bracken fern. When it turns orange-gold in the fall, you may wonder if you've stumbled upon a field of California poppies in bloom. Here, 4 miles from your start, you bear right (ahead) toward Kapalaoa Cabin.

An unexpected delight, an alpine meadow of tussock grasses, grows along the Sliding Sands Trail between here and Kapalaoa Cabin. As you continue east, Ka Moa o Pele recedes, and you're able to see Halalii, Puu Naue, and Puu Nole cones to the north. You pass two more junctions with spur trails northward to Holua Cabin/Campground and the Halemauu Trail, but you persist eastward to Kapalaoa Cabin. The third junction is only 1⁄10 mile from Kapalaoa Cabin, which is perched on a small, grassy platform just south of the trail, dwarfed by the scrub-covered *pali* rising behind it. A picnic table, pit toilet, and water are available here, a little over 5¾ miles from your start (6¾ miles if you detoured to see Ka Lua o Ka Oo). It's a wonderful place to rest, enjoy your lunch, and take in the awesome crater views. Resist the temptation to share your lunch with the engaging and shameless *nene* beggars here!

Retrace your steps to White Hill when you must; be sure to allow plenty of time for the steep pull up the hill.

Did the old Hawaiians come up to Haleakala crater?...There's no evidence that anyone ever lived permanently high on Haleakala or down in its crater, but there are ruins of stone shelters that the old Hawaiians used for temporary shelter while they were up here. The Hawaiians found the necessities of life in the ocean, on the coastal plains, and on the lower mountain slopes, not in the alien harshness of this high mountain. Yet there's plenty of evidence that the upper slopes and crater of Haleakala were ceremonially and economically important. The note at the end of Trip H7 mentioned the heiau on Haleakala peak. A survey of Haleakala (Emory, 1921, reported by Kirch in *Feathered Gods and Fishhooks*) lists "[58] terraces and platforms..., [9] groups of open stone shelters, 'several hundred' cairns, and a section of an ancient paved road....Several of the terraces and cairns proved to contain burials." Slingstones found on the crater floor suggest that the Hawaiians came up here to hunt birds. They also came to Haleakala to mine its outcrops of fine-grained basalt, which was an excellent material for making adzes (cutting tools used chiefly for shaping wood). Radiocarbon dating of charcoal from one of the stone shelters shows people were here perhaps as early as the eighth century. The ancient paved road, which once connected Wailuku and Hana but has almost disappeared now, may indicate that the Hawaiians preferred the arduous climb up and down Haleakala to the tortuous coastal routes.

Trip H13. Kapalaoa Cabin Side Trip to Holua Cabin/Campground

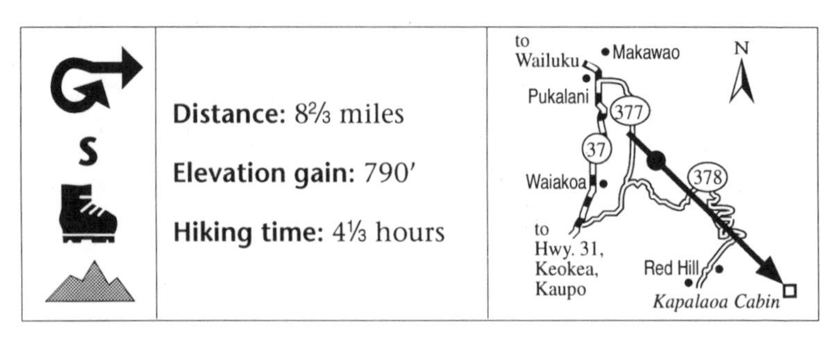

Topos: Kilohana, Nahiku 7½.

Trail map: At the end of Trip H5.

Highlights: Many of the same scenic joys that highlight Trip H5 highlight this trip, too. However, this trip returns to Kapalaoa Cabin on the westernmost of the three maintained spur trails between the Sliding Sands and Halemauu trails. The return leg, passing between Puu o Maui and Ka Moa o Pele, offers a different experience of the crater floor from that offered by Trip H5.

Driving instructions: Not applicable.

Permit/permission required: None for this dayhike. Required to stay at Kapalaoa Cabin (see Trip H12 and Appendix A).

Description. From Kapalaoa Cabin, retrace your steps ⅓ mile west to the junction with the middle (second) maintained spur trail linking the Sliding Sands and Halemauu trails, as described in Trip H5. Follow this spur trail northwest to the saddle between Ka Moa o Pele and Halalii as described in the next-to-last paragraph of Trip H5. (I've chosen this spur trail because it offers such a stunning view of Ka Moa o Pele's vent as you walk it this direction.)

On the saddle, go right on the spur trail that heads around the east side of Halalii—uninteresting until it meets the Halemauu Trail on the saddle between Halalii and Puu Naue at Kawilinau in Pele's Paint Pot. Turn left (west) on the Halemauu Trail through the dazzling colors of Pele's Paint Pot and follow it west and then northwest to the Silversword Loop, reversing part of the description of Trip H5. You can pick up the Silversword Loop now or on your way back from Holua Cabin/Campground. Continue northwest, still reversing Trip H5's description, to Holua Cabin/Campground. The scenery opens westward before you, and the meadow below Holua Cabin contrasts sharply with the forbidding lava wilderness you're traversing.

After enjoying your lunch at beautiful Holua Cabin, retrace your steps to the junction where the Halemauu Trail turns left (east) toward Pele's Paint Pot. Here, you bear right, past Pele's Pig Pen. At the junction just beyond Pele's Pig Pen, you turn sharply right and begin climbing the northern slopes of Ka Moa o Pele to a saddle between it and an unnamed cone to its north. Enjoy the view from this saddle before descending west and then southwest on the red slopes of Ka Moa o Pele. The dark brown slopes of Puu o Maui rise on your right (west). As the trail levels out, you enter a choppy, frozen "sea" of lava whose stony waves have crests of gray and orange rock and troughs of black sand.

You leave the lava "sea" behind as you approach a junction with the Sliding Sands Trail, where bracken, *mamane*, and yellow-flowered, alien evening primrose grow. At this junction, turn left (east) onto the Sliding Sands Trail and follow it back to Kapalaoa Cabin as described in Trip H12 to end a satisfying and highly varied hike.

Ideally....you'd stay two nights at Kapalaoa Cabin to enjoy this side trip at a leisurely pace. If you can't get a permit for two nights, an alternative is to get an early start, stash most of your gear at Kapalaoa Cabin, take this side trip with a daypack, and pack out when you get back to Kapalaoa Cabin—before the next party arrives, you hope. Another choice, if you can get the necessary permit, is a backpacking variation on Trip H15: backpack down the Sliding Sands Trail as far as Kapalaoa Cabin, take one of these lovely spur trails to Holua Cabin/Campground (where you'll stay), and then pack out on the Halemauu Trail. However you manage it, I hope you won't miss the beauty of the central crater.

Kapalaoa Cabin

Trip H14. Sliding Sands Trail to Paliku Cabin/Campground

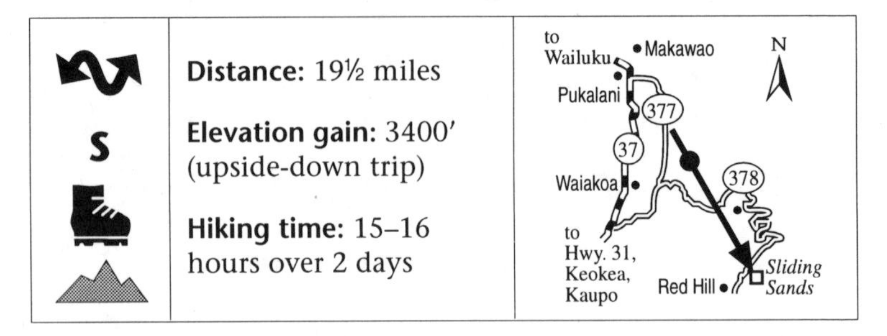

Topos: Kilohana, Nahiku 7½.

Trail map: Begins on the map at the end of Trip H9; continues on the map at the end of Trip H5; ends on the map at the end of Trip H6.

Highlights: The beauty of the Sliding Sands Trail is yours to enjoy until, at Olii Puu, you pick up the Halemauu Trail for the different, but equally beautiful, stretch to Paliku Cabin/Campground.

Driving instructions: Follow the driving instructions of Trip H9.

Permit/permission required: Required for an overnight stay at Kapalaoa or Paliku Cabin or both (by reservation only) or at the campground adjacent to Paliku Cabin; see suggestions at the end of this trip and details in Appendix A.

Description (strenuous trip):

Day 1 (9¾ miles). Follow Trip H12 to Kapalaoa Cabin. On this trip, you can skip the detour to Ka Lua o Ka Oo (add just under 1 mile out and back and 150' elevation gain if you're determined to see it).

After a rest on Kapalaoa Cabin's lawn, you continue east on the Sliding Sands Trail into scrub country, where you soon begin a gentle descent as the trail bears northeast. Puu Maile, visible to the northeast when you left Kapalaoa, is soon hidden by a ridge of *aa*, and there's a dry wash to the southeast. The trail presently levels out amid rocks some of which are a lovely soft, dark, pinkish-red color. The trail becomes dusty as it passes through more scrub and bracken.

It's not long before Oili Puu comes into view ahead to the northeast as you descend moderately to steeply over some fairly stable rocks and through a region of scrub and jagged vents. A few curious little "buttes" stand a few feet above the general terrain here. A couple of them seem to be the products of spatter lava, but one, standing north of the trail and isolated in a flow of *pahoehoe*, appears to be a tiny columnar basalt formation (see Trip E9 for a discussion of this type of formation).

Your descent becomes more gradual as Paliku's meadow becomes visible to the east, only to be hidden by Oili Puu as you begin crossing a broad lava field. Ridges of *aa* are separated by narrow channels of green scrub—mostly *aalii*, *ohelo*, and *pukiawe*. Kaupo Gap opens on your right (east), but the challenge of negotiating the loose *aa* may keep you from appreciating it.

You leave the lava field on cinders dotted by *pukiawe* and evening primrose and shortly reach the junction of the Halemauu and Sliding Sands trails. Turn right (northeast) here at the foot of scrub-covered Oili Puu and follow Trip H6 to Paliku Cabin/Campground.

Day 2 (9¾ miles). Retrace your steps to the Sliding Sands trailhead.

Logistics.... The easier way to do this trip is to stay a night at Kapalaoa Cabin. If you want to stay overnight at Kapalaoa Cabin and can get a reservation for it, your trip will probably be easier if you backpack in directly to Paliku Cabin/Campground (downhill) and then stay at Kapalaoa Cabin on your way out (uphill).

Paliku Cabin

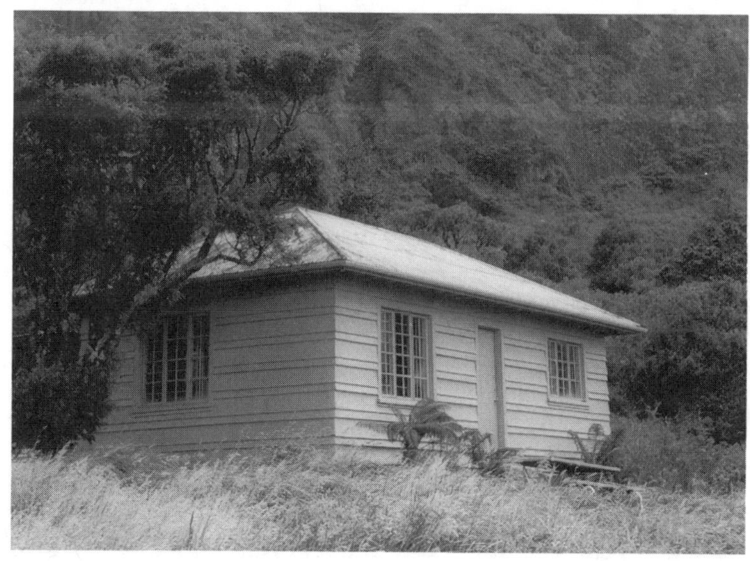

Trip H15. Sliding Sands Trail to Halemauu Trail Adventure

Distance: 13 miles

Elevation gain: 1680′ (upside-down trip)

Hiking time: 7–8 hours

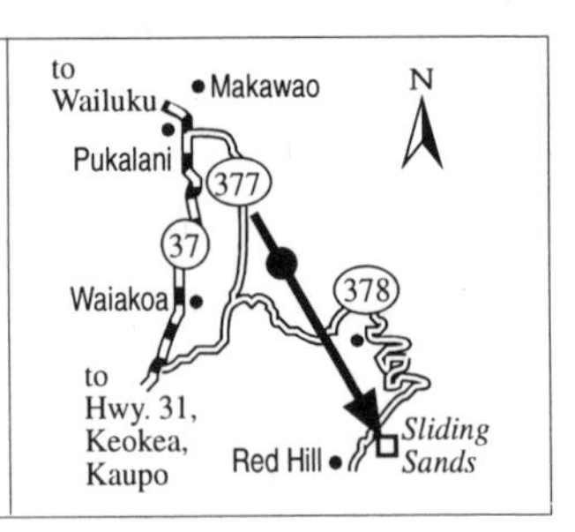

Topos: Kilohana, Nahiku 7½.

Trail map: Begins on the map at the end of Trip H9; continues on the map at the end of Trip H5; ends on the map at the end of Trip H2.

Highlights: This is, I believe, the single finest dayhike in Haleakala's crater—make that the single finest dayhike on Maui. It's as complete a crater adventure as you can enjoy without staying overnight in the crater. By all means allow time for detours to Ka Lua o Ka Oo, Kawilinau and Pele's Paint Pot, and the Silversword Loop! Take plenty of color film, and budget your time so that you can take advantage of the multitude of photo opportunities along the way.

Note that while this trip is described as a dayhike, you can also do it as a backpack if you can get permission to stay at Holua Cabin/ Campground.

Driving instructions: This trip is a shuttle, so leave one car at the Halemauu Trail by following the driving instructions of Trip H3. Then, following the driving instructions of Trip H9, drive to White Hill to start your adventure at the Sliding Sands Trail.

Permit/permission required: None if done as a dayhike. See Appendix A for information on cabins and camping in the crater.

Description. Follow Trip H12 down the Sliding Sands Trail, detouring to visit Ka Lua o Ka Oo, to the junction with the first of the three maintained spur trails to the Halemauu Trail, 4¾ miles including the detour. Here, with Puu o Pele above you to the west and with Ka Moa o Pele ahead of you to the northeast, you turn left (northeast) onto the spur trail through the bracken, *mamane*, and evening primrose that grow around this junction.

Follow the spur trail northeast and then east, reversing part of Trip H13, through the choppy lava "sea" and up the red slopes of Ka Moa o Pele. You descend to the point just east of and above

Pele's Pig Pen on the saddle between Ka Moa o Pele and Halalii. Turn right and follow the trail around Halalii, going left at the next junction, to Kawilinau. Turn left (west) onto the Halemauu Trail at Kawilinau for a short walk through the intensely colorful area called Pele's Paint Pot.

At the next junction, on the west side of Halalii, you turn right (northwest) toward the Silversword Loop and Holua Cabin/Campground. Now you reverse the steps of part of Trip H5, detouring to see the Silversword Loop if you wish. The amount of vegetation increases as you rise toward Holua Cabin/Campground, where you'll welcome a chance to rest. This area seems especially green and flourishing after the colorful but barren regions of the crater you've been traveling through since leaving White Hill. All too soon, the pressure of time obliges you to resume your trip, reversing the steps of Trip H4 down the ridge, across the meadow, and up Leleiwi Pali to the crater rim.

At the crater rim viewpoint that's the destination for Trips H2 and H3, you can't help but pause for one final, long look at the stupendous world of Haleakala's crater. Continuing, you now enjoy views downslope to East Maui's north coast on your way to the Halemauu trailhead and your shuttle car. At last you can shed your pack, change into tennies, and ease your weary body into a soft car seat.

Sure, you're tired. But what's being tired compared to being dazzled by Haleakala's splendors?!

Shuttle, anyone?... How do you set up a shuttle for a group that's sharing just one rental car? It's easy if you've made sure your group includes at least one non-hiker who doesn't mind driving the hikers around. Perhaps that's not so easy. Other options: rent another car for the necessary period; take the trip with an organized group whose arrangements include the shuttle; or, if you have friends on Maui, arrange for one of them to pick you up.

But let's assume you're limited to one car and have no other options. What if everyone wants to hike? What if there's only the one of you? Forget taking the trip as a shuttle. Instead, select a midpoint along the trip and take an out-and-back hike from each end of it to your midpoint. This has some real advantages: You get to enjoy the trip twice as much; you won't have to make any complicated arrangements; you won't have to hold yourself to a schedule for meeting a ride; and you won't keep anyone waiting and worrying at the other end.

Trip H16. Grand Crater Tour (Backpack)

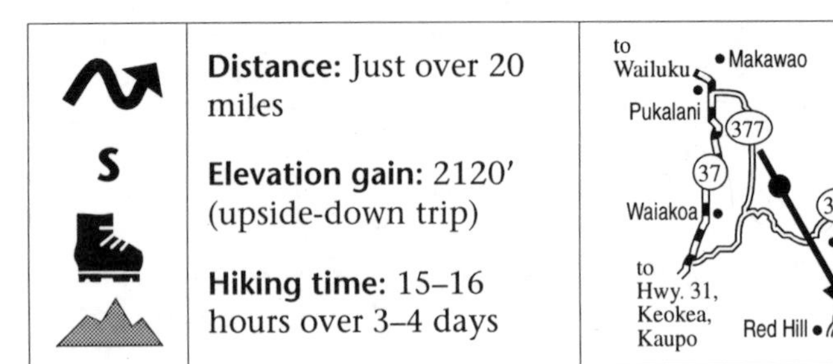

Distance: Just over 20 miles

Elevation gain: 2120′ (upside-down trip)

Hiking time: 15–16 hours over 3–4 days

Topos: Kilohana, Nahiku 7½.

Trail map: Begins on the map at the end of Trip H9; continues on the maps at the end of Trips H5 and H6; ends on the map at the end of Trip H2.

Highlights: You see virtually every one of the finest crater features that maintained trails take you to. On the way, you sample the comforts of the cabins or campgrounds, or both, depending on the mix of reservations and permits you're able to get. The easiest trip, described below, is possible only if you can get a reservation for Kapalaoa Cabin for your first night. Otherwise, combine Days 1 and 2 to go directly to Paliku Cabin/Campground on your Day 1 as described in Trip H14, and consider spending two nights at Paliku Cabin/Campground. That would allow you to take Trip H7, too.

Driving instructions: This trip is a shuttle like Trip H15, whose driving instructions you should follow.

Permit/permission required: Required for an overnight stay at any of the cabins (by reservation only) or at the campgrounds adjacent to Paliku and Holua cabins; see Appendix A.

Description (easiest trip):

Day 1 (just over 5¾ miles). Follow Trip H12 from the Sliding Sands trailhead to Kapalaoa Cabin.

Day 2 (4 miles). Follow Trip H14 from Kapalaoa Cabin to Paliku Cabin/Campground.

Day 3 (6⅓ miles). Reverse the steps of Day 2 of Trip H6 from Paliku Cabin/Campground to Holua Cabin/Campground.

Day 4 (just under 4 miles). Reverse the steps of Trip H4 from Holua Cabin/Campground to the Halemauu trailhead. Early birds will find that it's possible to take Trip H5 before packing out.

Trip H17. Red Hill Mini-hike

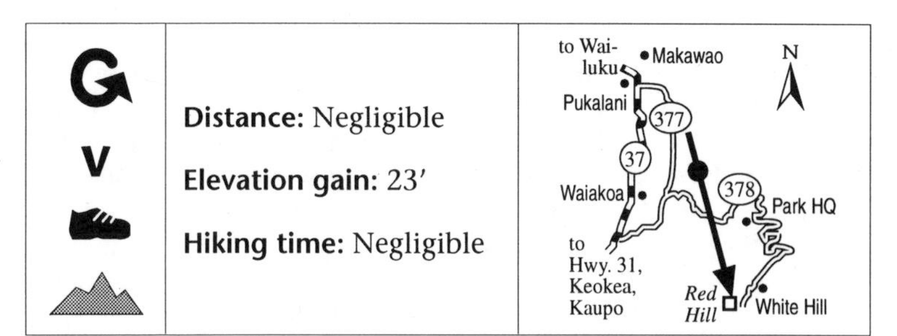

Topos: Optional: Kilohana 7½.

Trail map (route approximated): At the end of Trip H9.

Highlights: Red Hill (Puu Ulaula), 10,023 feet high, is the highest point on Haleakala and, therefore, on Maui. The parking lot itself is at 10,000 feet! The views from Red Hill are superb. The air is pretty thin at this altitude, so take it easy. Make this an early morning visit so that the cloud bank that normally forms by midmorning won't obstruct your view.

Driving instructions: Follow the driving instructions of Trip H9 past the Visitor Center turnoff at White Hill and continue all the way up Highway 378 past the turnoff to Science City to the parking lot for the observation shelter at the very top of Haleakala.

Permit/permission required: None.

Description. From the parking lot, climb the stairs to the enclosed observation shelter, where marked stations point out features of the nearly-360° view from here. Mauna Kea and Mauna Loa on the Big Island of Hawaii, many miles away to the south-southeast, are particularly striking from Red Hill. Magnetic Peak, right next door in the southeast, is reputed to be so full of iron that it interferes with compass readings. The view southwest and west over Science City, the Isthmus, and West Maui is unparalleled.

The sight of Science City is even more striking from outside the shelter, so follow the little path outside the shelter. The white domes and buildings of Science City and the barren red-brown clinker of Haleakala's summit region combine to make a landscape so stark, so surreal, and so alien that you may think you've strayed onto the set of a science-fiction movie or been translated to Mars like Edgar Rice Burroughs's hero John Carter. But please don't step off the path. Despite its apparent lifelessness, there is life in this harsh environment, and a careless step can too easily crush seedlings and tiny creatures hidden in the clinker.

From here, take the other stairs down to the parking lot and return to your car.

Skyline Trail.... Remember that you can reverse the directions for the Skyline Trail, Trip E17 in this book, and take it from Science City, just below Red Hill. That will make it an upside-down trip, but getting to the Skyline Trail from Science City rather than from Polipoli will be more practical for many people, because the road to Polipoli is awful, while the road to Red Hill is quite good.

Your best bet is probably to leave your car parked here at Red Hill and carefully walk back down the road to the turnoff for Science City. The Skyline Trail branches off from the Science City road just a little past the National Park boundary sign. This would add ¾ mile and 100 feet of elevation gain to your Skyline Trail hike or mountain-bicycle trip. You could more than compensate for that by turning around at Ballpark Junction instead of going all the way to Polipoli. Sturdy cyclists who can set up the shuttle may be interested in continuing all the way down from Polipoli to Highway 377 and meeting their shuttle ride in Kula.

Cones in Haleakala Crater. In the distance, Mauna Kea and Mauna Loa on the Big Island of Hawaii.

Bibliography

Beckwith, Martha. *Hawaiian Mythology.* New Haven: Yale University Press (for the Folklore Foundation of Vassar College), 1940. Reprint. Honolulu: University of Hawaii Press, 1970, 1976.

Bisignani, J.D. *Hawaii Handbook.* 2nd ed. Chico, California: Moon Publications, Inc., 1989.

Carlquist, Sherwin. *Hawaii, A Natural History.* 2nd ed., 2nd printing. Lawai, Kauai: National [formerly Pacific] Tropical Botanical Garden, 1980, 1985.

Chisolm, Craig. *Hawaiian Hiking Trails.* 3rd ed. Lake Oswego, Oregon: The Fernglen Press, 1989.

Clark, John. *Hawaii's Secret Beaches, A Guide to Twenty-Four Hawaiian Beaches.* Honolulu: Tongg Publishing.

Day, A. Grove, and Carl Stroven, Eds. *A Hawaiian Reader.* Appleton-Century-Crofts, 1959. Reprint. Honolulu: Mutual Publishing Company, 1984.

Day, A. *Grove. Hawaii and Its People.* New York: Duell, Sloan and Pearce, 1955.

Epidemiology Branch, State Department of Health, State of Hawaii. "Leptospirosis in Hawaii." October 1, 1987.

Fleming, Martha Foss. *Old Trails of Maui.* Sponsored by William & Mary Alexander Chapter, Daughters of the American Revolution, 1933. (Obtained through the courtesy of Mr. Don Reeser, Superintendent, Haleakala National Park.)

Hargreaves, Dorothy, and Bob Hargreaves. *Hawaii Blossoms.* Japan: Dorothy and Bob Hargreaves, 1958. Reprint. Lahaina: Ross-Hargreaves.

——. *Tropical Trees of Hawaii.* Kailua: Hargreaves Company.

Hawai'i Audubon Society. *Hawaii's Birds.* 4th ed. Honolulu: Hawai'i Audubon Society, 1989.

Hill, Mary. *Geology of the Sierra Nevada.* Berkeley: University of California Press, 1975.

Joesting, Edward. *Hawaii, An Uncommon History.* New York: W.W. Norton & Company Inc., 1972.

Kepler, Angela Kay. *Maui's Hana Highway, A Visitor's Guide.* Honolulu: Mutual Publishing Company, 1987.

Kepler, Cameron B., and Angela Kay Kepler. *Haleakala: A Guide to the Mountain.* Honolulu: Mutual Publishing Company, 1988.

Kirch, Patrick Vinton. *Feathered Gods and Fishhooks: An Introduction to Hawaiian Archaeology and Prehistory.* Honolulu: University of Hawaii Press, 1985.

Kyselka, Will, and Ray Lanterman. *Maui: How It Came To Be.* Honolulu: University of Hawaii Press, 1980.

Levi, Herbert W., and Lorna R. Levi. *Spiders and their Kin.* New York: Golden Press, 1987.

Macdonald, Gordon A., Agatin T. Abbott, and Frank L. Peterson. *Volcanoes in the Sea, the Geology of Hawaii.* 2nd ed. Honolulu: University of Hawaii Press, 1986.

Mack, Jim. *Haleakala: the Story Behind the Scenery.* 4th printing. Las Vegas: KC Publications, 1979.

Merlin, Mark David. *Hawaiian Coastal Plants and Scenic Shorelines.* 3rd printing. Honolulu: Oriental Publishing Co., 1986.

——. *Hawaiian Forest Plants.* 3rd ed. Honolulu: The Oriental Publishing Co., 1980.

Mrantz, Maxine. *Women of Old Hawaii.* Honolulu: Aloha Publishing, 1975.

Pukui, Mary Kawena, Samuel H. Elbert, and Esther T. Mookini. *The Pocket Hawaiian Dictionary.* Honolulu: University of Hawaii Press, 1975.

Smith, Rodney N. *Hawaii: A Walker's Guide.* Edison, New Jersey: Hunter Publishing, Inc.

Sohmer, S.H., and R. Gustafson. *Plants and Flowers of Hawai'i.* Honolulu: University of Hawaii Press, 1987.

Winnett, Thomas, and Melanie Findling. *Backpacking Basics.* 3rd ed. Berkeley: Wilderness Press, 1988.

Woolliams, Keith. *A Guide to Hawaii's Popular Trees.* 2nd ed. Aiea, Hawaii: Island Heritage Publishing, 1988.

Appendix A. Camping on Maui

Backcountry camping accessible on foot

Backcountry camping that's accessible only on foot is practical for the tourist from the mainland only in Haleakala crater (Haleakala National Park). You must have a permit to stay in the campgrounds or cabins in the crater. You may not camp in the crater outside of the campgrounds or cabins. Your stay in the crater is limited to 3 nights per month, whether in cabins or campgrounds or a combination of cabins and campgrounds. Your stay at any one location in the crater is limited to 2 consecutive nights; for this purpose, a cabin and its adjacent campground (if any) count as different locations.

Crater campgrounds. There are two tent-campgrounds in the crater, one near Holua Cabin (6960') and the other near Paliku Cabin (6380'). Permits for tent camping in the crater are issued only in person at Park Headquarters (or, for very early starts before Park Headquarters opens, at the Visitor Center near the summit) and only on the day you begin your trip. There are quotas, so be prepared to modify your itinerary or come back another day if the quotas are filled. There is no fee. The crater can be cold (my thermometer read 40° F one clear morning after a rainy night at Holua Campground), windy, and rainy, so you must be prepared with a rainproof tent, warm clothes, rain gear, and a stove that you can start and keep going in wind and rain. A friend who thought he wouldn't need his whole tent in Hawaii and who went into Haleakala crater with only the rainfly for shelter was very cold, very soggy, and very sorry. The ranger who issues your permit will ask about your preparedness.

Crater cabins. There are three cabins in Haleakala Crater: Holua Cabin, Kapalaoa Cabin, and Paliku Cabin. Only one party as a unit may use a cabin at a time; a cabin holds up to 12 people. The cabins have tables, benches, bare bunkbeds (you'll still need your sleeping bag), and a kitchen with potable running water, a wood stove and wood (or those logs made from chips), and cooking and eating utensils. There is no electricity or lanterns; bring your flashlight and candle lantern. Each cabin also has an outhouse. Applying for a cabin is complicated; write the Park Superintendent (address below) to find out what the latest procedure is for applying. Applying doesn't guarantee you'll get to rent a cabin. Who actually gets to rent a cabin is decided by lottery; you'll be notified of the results. *Get your information and start the application process early!*

People sometimes cancel their cabin reservations on the spur of the moment. It's remotely possible that you'll get a night at a cabin just because you happen to be at the Park Headquarters counter when someone cancels a reservation. Don't count on it, though.

Haleakala National Park's address is:

Haleakala National Park
Box 369
Makawao, Maui, HI 96768
(808) 572-7749 (recording of general information)
(808) 572-9177 (recording of camping and cabin information)
(808) 572-9306 (park headquarters; 7:30 A.M. to 4:00 P.M. Hawaii Standard Time)
www.nps.gov/hale/

Other (outside Haleakala). There are two other possibilities for those who are desperate to do some backpacking, though these sites are also accessible by 4WD vehicles. See the supplemental information following Trips E16 and E18.

Car camping

Maui doesn't offer much car camping—the kind of camping where you drive up, pay your bucks, pick a space, park your car, and pitch your tent there and live out of it (or live out of your parked vehicle). For those who enjoy car camping, there is a list below of the places you can car camp on Maui. This information is largely from other sources, such as the agency in charge; I've verified the information for only a couple of these places.

Car camping at Haleakala National Park is limited to Hosmer Grove (just off Highway 378, which goes to Haleakala crater's principal trailheads and to Haleakala's summit) and Kipahulu (the coastal section of the park, south and west of Hana). No permit is required. Camping is free. Camping at Hosmer Grove is limited to 25 persons (organized groups are limited to 15 persons). However, there may be no one to see that the limit is observed. The result may be that Hosmer Grove, so peaceful by day, will be jammed full of people by nightfall. Those who can't cram into the campground may try to sleep in their cars along the road! A stay at Hosmer Grove may be less than idyllic. Camping at Hosmer Grove and Kipahulu is limited to 3 nights per month. Trailers are permitted in the parking lot of Hosmer Grove. RVs are not permitted at either site.

Car camping at the state parks is by permit only and for a maximum of 5 consecutive nights in any 30-day period. Permits are free. They are issued Monday through Friday, 8 A.M. to 4 P.M., at the Division of State Parks office in Wailuku. The person appearing to apply for the permit must provide proper identification for each person in the party who is 18 years old or older. "Proper identification" means a driver's license or passport. You may also apply by mail at least seven days in advance of your proposed trip by writing to the Division of State Parks. When applying by mail, include a copy of the proper identification for each person in the party who is 18 years old or older. Trailers and RVs are not permitted in Maui's state parks. For the state parks, write or call:

Department of Land and Natural Resources
Division of State Parks, Maui District
P.O. Box 1049
Wailuku, Maui, HI 96793
(808) 244-4324 (or (808) 243-5354 for camping and cabin reservations)

Car camping on Division of Forestry and Wildlife lands. At present, there are no car-campgrounds in areas managed by the Division of Forestry and Wildlife.

Car camping at Maui County's parks. Two of Maui County's parks allow car camping. It's limited to a maximum of 3 consecutive nights at one campsite. Permits are required. There is a fee per night. Obtain permits by mail from:

Department of Parks and Recreation, County of Maui
1580 Kaahumanu Avenue
Wailuku, Maui, Hawaii 96793
(808) 243-7389

Car camping on West Maui. As of this writing, private Camp Pecusa (below) offers the only car camping on West Maui. However, a public car-campground is in the planning stage for West Maui. Look for news of it when you get your packets of information from Maui's public agencies.

Private. Car camping is possible at one private campground, Camp Pecusa. This is an Episopalian Church campground on the beach at Olowalu, but they allow the general public to camp there for a fee as long as there's room. Write or call:

Camp Pecusa
800 Olowalu Village
Lahaina, HI 96761
(808) 661-4303

The following table summarizes the car-camping opportunities.

Name	Type	Nearest Town	Amenities; Restrictions
Hosmer Grove	National Park	Kula	Grills, tables, potable water, picnic pavilion, toilets. Tents only in campground proper; trailers permitted in parking lot Rainy. Free. No permit required. Stays limited. At 6800'.
Kipahulu	National Park	Hana	Grills, toilets, and tables. No potable water. Tents only. Free. No permit required. Stays limited. Near sea level.
Waianapanapa	State	Hana	Potable water, picnic tables, outdoor showers, barbecue grills, toilets. Tents or campers. Free. Permit required. Stays limited. Near sea level.
Kaumahina	State	Between Paia and Hana but not near anything	Restrooms, picnic tables, outdoor grills. Off Hana Highway in rain forest; no beach. Free. Permit required. Stays limited. Near sea level.
Polipoli	State	About an hour from Kula, Waiakoa	Potable water, restroom, picnic tables, shelters. Tents only. Dark and rainy. Free. Permit required. Stays limited. At 6200'.
H.A. Baldwin	County	Paia	Restrooms and outdoor showers. Tents only. Fee. Permit required; see above. The camp ing area abuts the highway. *Not recommended.* Stays limited. Sea level.

Name	Type	Nearest Town	Amenities; Restrictions
Rainbow Park	County	Paia	Restrooms. Tents only. Fee. Permit required; see above. Stays limited. Elevation unspecified; estimated at 800'.
Camp Pecusa	Private	Olowalu	Fee. No limit on stays. May be only camping on West Maui. Sea level.

Cabins

The following areas offer cabins, which you should reserve (or try to reserve) months in advance.

Haleakala National Park. There are three backcountry cabins in Haleakala National Park in the crater. See "Backcountry camping accessible on foot" at the front of this section.

State parks. There are 12 cabins at Waianapanapa State Park (very popular) and one cabin at Polipoli State Park (popular). There is a fee per person per night, and your stay is limited to a maximum of 5 consecutive nights in any 30-day period. Write or call the state parks at the address or telephone number given above. I think the trail shelters in Polipoli are not worthy of your consideration; see the note following Trip E15.

Private. Camp Pecusa also has a few cabins, for which they charge a modest fee. Write the camp at the address given above or call the telephone number also given above.

Appendix B. Hikes You Won't Find Here and Why

You may have read articles on the following hikes, seen them mentioned in other books, or noticed them on topos. Some are in this book under different names. Some are closed because landowners no longer give permission to hike them. Others have become unsafe; don't let your vacation end in the emergency room! Finally, I judge that some are too remote and boring to be worth your time.

West Maui/Isthmus

Iao Valley State Park—Poohahoahoa, Nakalaloa, and Kinihapai streams; Tableland Trail. Regarding the streams, a spur trail goes partway up Poohahoahoa Stream; see Trip W8. Otherwise, these are trailless; reputed to be difficult, rugged, and slippery where you have to walk in the streambed; subject to flash flooding. Wailuku Agribusiness now considers the Tableland Trail (formerly Trip W8 in this book) off-limits to hikers and doesn't issue permits for it; you are trespassing if you hike it. Please don't!

Kealaloloa Ridge. See "Lahaina Pali Trail," below, for a new trail in this area.

Lahaina Pali Trail. May not yet be completed. Na Ala Hele will tell you how to find it if you call them at (808) 871-2521. I'm waiting until the trail has been completed and parking is available at both ends.

Lahaina "L." See Trip W11 to David Malo's grave.

Puu Kukui. Closed to casual hikers. The Nature Conservancy now helps the landowner, the Maui Land and Pineapple Company, manage the swamps on the slopes and summit of Puu Kukui. Access is severely restricted, to protect rare native species, the ecosystem, and the watershed. The survival of endangered species and fragile ecosystems is much more important than the recreational wishes of our numerous and mobile species. We can so easily go somewhere else to hike—and just about anywhere else sounds better than Puu Kukui, anyway. One source describes Puu Kukui as having been "the most exhilarating and interesting" hike on Maui and describes the hiker's condition on this trail as "...soaked to the skin and chilled to the bone." Okay, all of you who came to Maui to get soaked to the skin and chilled to the bone, raise your hands!...That's what I thought. (Apparently, the reason for going to the top of Puu Kukui was to enjoy the views—views seldom available because of the cloud cover.)

Cross Above Wailuku. Wailuku Agribusiness no longer grants permission to hike to this landmark.

Huluhulupueo Stream. The bridge described as the starting point is over the Waihee River. Huluhulupueo Stream is a tributary of the Waihee River, joining it over a mile upriver from the bridge. I found no parking on or near the bridge. Access to the river from the bridge and highway is blocked by barbed wire, KEEP OUT signs, somebody's yard, and steep concrete abutments. Try Trips W2 and W9 for streamside hikes on West Maui.

East Maui *(except for Haleakala National Park, which you'll find below)*

Twin Falls. Formerly Trip E1 in this book and sometimes found in other books, this area is private property on both sides of the highway, and the owner doesn't want us hiking on it. The owner tries to keep the land posted, but the NO TRESPASSING signs are frequently vandalized, often missing. Vandalizing of cars parked around here is a serious problem.

Keanae Village. With all due respect to Keanae, the village isn't particularly interesting. I found a NO TRESPASSING sign between me and the one thing I thought *might* have been interesting. Also, if the people of Keanae wanted to make a tourist showplace of their village, there'd be signs on the highway inviting us to come on down and visit—but there aren't. There's a restroom near the end of the peninsula, and you might want to take some photos of the coast from there. That's about it.

Blue Pool. See Trip E4, Ulaino Road.

Hana Town. Hana isn't a particularly good "walking" town, as explained in Trip E10, because it's hilly, hot and humid, and lacks sidewalks. See Trip E10 for a walk in Hana.

Red-Cinder Beach. Formerly Trip E12 in this book. The unmaintained path to the red-cinder beach has suffered enough erosion that I think it is no longer safe for most hikers. The footing on the steep part is terrible because of loose cinders and other rubble, and the steep part has become very narrow as material has sloughed off the cinder cone here. (Recall that the landslide that made Kaahumanu's birthplace inaccessible is just on the other side of this cone.) A fall from this part of the path would surely lead to grave injury, maybe to death.

Helio's Grave. Trail reported to be too dangerous to hike on any more.

Polipoli State Park. With all due respect to the people of Maui, there is little at Polipoli State Park for the visitor from the mainland. See the discussion following Trip E15. About specific trails, alphabetically:

Boundary Trail. An oppressive, dark, and very dull trail made irritatingly hard to follow by the number of thoughtless use trails that crisscross it. Northeastern part damaged by pigs and dirt bikes.

Haleakala Ridge Trail. Crisscrossed by use trails; dull. See Polipoli Loop, below.

Kahua Road. Worthwhile. See Trip E16.

Mamane Trail. Under construction but must be shared with mountain bikers—ugh! See Trip E17.

Plum Trail. Oppressive, dark, and dull. The plum trees have died from lack of light and from competition. See Polipoli Loop, below.

Polipoli Loop (Polipoli, Haleakala Ridge, Plum, and Redwood trails). This hike is an old standard, but I found it oppressive, dark, and dull. Here's a condensed description of it in case you have a lot of time to kill: Loop; moderate; tennis shoes okay; mountains, 3½ miles, 880' elevation gain (upside-down trip), 1¾ hours. This hike starts on the Polipoli Trail near the west edge of the campground. You leave the campground on that trail, under oppressive overgrowth, climb steeply but briefly to a 3-way junction, and turn right (west) onto what turns out to be the Haleakala Ridge Trail. The trail presently turns into the Plum Trail, which you follow past an intersection with the Tie Trail and past the abandoned Civilian Conservation Corps bunkhouse to a junction with the Boundary and Redwood trails. Turn right on the Redwood Trail and reverse the steps of Trip E15 back to the campground. You may want to take the Boundary Trail to the Fuchsia Wall before turning onto the Redwood Trail.

Polipoli Trail. Oppressive, dark and dull. See Polipoli Loop, above.

Redwood Trail. Oppressive, dark, and dull. Unlike any mainland stand of coast redwoods I've ever seen—and not a change for the better. See Trip E15 and Polipoli Loop, above.

Skyline Trail. Worthwhile. See Trip E17.

Tie Trail. Oppressive, dark, and dull.

Upper Waiakoa (Waiohuli) Trail. Severely damaged by feral pigs; may be impassable.

Waiakoa Loop Trail. Badly damaged by feral pigs; may be impassable.

Puu Pimoe. Ulupalakua Ranch no longer gives permission to hike here.

Piiholo Hill. Haleakala Ranch no longer gives permission to hike here (they've leased it to another party who doesn't give permission, either).

Haleakala National Park

This book covers all the *maintained* trails in Haleakala National Park as Trips H1 through H17. A number of trails that used to be maintained aren't any more and should be considered unsafe. Particularly in the western part of the crater, the maintained trails represent the only environmentally safe way through a very fragile ecosystem. Safety—yours and the ecosystem's—dictates that you stick to the maintained trails. There are more than enough maintained trails in and around Haleakala to keep you busy, including enough crater trails to keep you hopping for the maximum 3 nights/4 days you can spend in the crater.

Appendix C. How I Got Distances, Elevations, Times, and Trail Maps

I estimated distances primarily by time, knowing that I hike 2 miles/hour and backpack at 1⅓ miles/hour. I compared the distances I got by time with distance values supplied by the agencies in charge of the trails. In a few cases, I also had distance data from plots I'd made from the topos. When those distances were close, I felt satisfied with the distance I'd estimated by time. I usually rounded the distances off to the nearest ¼ or ⅓ mile.

I got most driving distances by rental-car odometer, which was consistent to within ±1/10 mile over routes I drove repeatedly. When I had not started from Wailuku, I added or subtracted the distance from my starting point to Wailuku. I found that in a some cases I did not get usable odometer data; in those cases, I used data from the University of Hawaii Press map of Maui.

I determined elevation from topos and with an altimeter. Where I had altimeter data, I looked for close correspondence between those values, topo values, and any values supplied by the agency in charge of the trail.

Trail times are based on the time I actually spent in motion on the trail.

I made the trail maps by first scanning relevant pieces of the USGS topos into a computer. I put the resulting digitized topo information that applied to a trip or a set of trips into the bottom layer of a multiple-layer electronic drawing. I then traced selected topo information onto transparent electronic upper layers. I deleted the scanned data before I saved out the finished maps in a format compatible with the desktop publishing program I used to lay out this book. I left out the elevation contours because they would have taken me too long to draw and because they would have made these gray-scale maps too busy. I added, deleted, or modified topo information that I knew had changed. My choices of conventions for trails, roads, boundaries, etc., primarily reflect the software's capabilities.

Many trails on Maui do not appear at all on the topos or in usable form on any official agency map. For them, I approximated the route based on field notes and sketches and any agency information I could find.

Index

Acknowledgments

I'm deeply grateful to Thomas Winnett, president and editor-in-chief of Wilderness Press, for his encouragement, help, advice, and endless patience.

My thanks to all the readers who took the time to write me and to give me the benefit of their experience in using this book. I tried to put your information to good use, and I hope it's reflected in the pages of this second edition. Please keep up the good work!

I am very much indebted to Jerry Schad. His use of icons to help summarize hikes in his outstanding *Afoot and Afield* series of hiking guides for Southern California (available from Wilderness Press) inspired me to create and use icons in this series of guides.

Spokespeople for Maui's Division of Land and Natural Resources, for Na Ala Hele, for the Hawaii Nature Center, and for Haleakala National Park were very helpful, too. Thank you.

I'm grateful to another valuable source of information: the people who operated the places where we stayed. They were always ready with plenty of local knowledge and advice.

I hope I have accurately and adequately reflected the information these people provided. Any misunderstanding or errors are my responsibility.

——K.M.

East Maui +
Iao State Park
Hikes

> 1 day

Haleakala 1 day

Hana 1 day

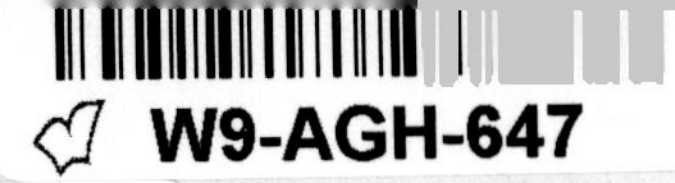

P... RSON

"Melanie Dickers... ed childhood fairy tale with wit, heart-thumping action and wonderfully endearing characters. Her mastery of faith-woven tales enveloped in the charm of a true storybook world simply can't be beat. It's enchanting from once upon a time to the very end."

—Kristy Cambron, author of *The Ringmaster's Wife* and the A Hidden Masterpiece series

"Dickerson breathes life into the age-old story of Rapunzel, blending it seamlessly with the other YA novels she has written in this time and place . . . The character development is solid, and she captures religious medieval life splendidly."

—*Booklist* on *The Golden Braid*

"Readers who love getting lost in a fairy-tale romance will cheer for Rapunzel's courage as she rises above her overwhelming past. The surprising way Dickerson weaves threads of this enchanting companion novel with those of her other Hagenheim stories is simply delightful."

—Jill Williamson, Christy Award–winning author of the Blood of Kings trilogy and the Kinsman Chronicles, on *The Golden Braid*

"Life in 1384 is depicted nicely in this well-written novel that shows kindness and honesty can help form allies in unexpected places. It is a very enjoyable journey into medieval England."

—Historical Novel Society on *The Silent Songbird*

"[*The Silent Songbird*] will have you jumping out of your seat with anticipation at times. Moderate- to fast-paced, you will not want this book to end. Recommended for all, especially lovers of historical romance."

—*RT Book Reviews*, 4 stars

"A terrific YA crossover medieval romance from the author of *The Golden Braid*."

—*Library Journal* on *The Silent Songbird*

"*The Piper'*... mption. Kat and Steffa... e very satisfying en...

... *wist* and

"A sweet s...

"In this fantastic retelling, Dickerson brings to life a completely new aspect of the medieval era . . . Discover castles, battles, beliefs, and injustices alongside Wolfgang and Mulan . . ."

—HOPE BY THE BOOK ON *THE WARRIOR MAIDEN*

"Christian fiction fans will relish Dickerson's eloquent story."

—*SCHOOL LIBRARY JOURNAL* ON *THE ORPHAN'S WISH*

"*The Goose Girl*, a little retold fairy tale, sparkles in Dickerson's hands, with endearing characters and a charming setting that will appeal to teens and adults alike."

—*RT BOOK REVIEWS*, 41/2 STARS, TOP PICK! ON *THE NOBLE SERVANT*

"Dickerson is a masterful storyteller with a carefully crafted plot, richly drawn characters, and a detailed setting. The reader is easily pulled into the story. Does everything end happily ever after? Read it and see! Recommended for young adults and adults who are young at heart."

—*CHRISTIAN LIBRARY JOURNAL* ON *THE NOBLE SERVANT*

"When it comes to happily-ever-afters, Melanie Dickerson is the undisputed queen of fairy-tale romance, and all I can say is—long live the queen!"

—JULIE LESSMAN, AWARD-WINNING AUTHOR OF THE DAUGHTERS OF BOSTON, WINDS OF CHANGE, AND HEART OF SAN FRANCISCO SERIES ON *THE BEAUTIFUL PRETENDER*

"I couldn't stop reading! Melanie has done what so many other historical novelists have tried and failed: she's created a heroine that is at once both smart and self-assured without seeming modern. A woman so fixed in her time and place that she is able to speak to ours as well."

—SIRI MITCHELL, AUTHOR OF *FLIRTATION WALK* AND *CHATEAU OF ECHOES*, ON *THE BEAUTIFUL PRETENDER*

"Melanie Dickerson does it again! Full of danger, intrigue, and romance, this beautifully crafted story [*The Huntress of Thornbeck Forest*] will transport you to another place and time."

—SARAH E. LADD, BESTSELLING AUTHOR OF THE CORNWALL NOVELS

The Golden Braid

Other Books by Melanie Dickerson

The Dericott Tale Novels

Court of Swans

Castle of Refuge (available June 2021)

The Fairytale Romance Series

The Healer's Apprentice

The Merchant's Daughter

The Fairest Beauty

The Captive Maiden

The Princess Spy

The Golden Braid

The Silent Songbird

The Orphan's Wish

The Warrior Maiden

The Piper's Pursuit

The Peasant's Dream

The Medieval Fairy Tale Novels

The Huntress of Thornbeck Forest

The Beautiful Pretender

The Noble Servant

The Regency Spies of London Series

A Spy's Devotion

A Viscount's Proposal

A Dangerous Engagement

The Golden Braid

MELANIE DICKERSON

Thomas Nelson
Since 1798

Published in Nashville, Tennessee, by Thomas Nelson. Thomas Nelson is a registered trademark of HarperCollins Christian Publishing, Inc.

Thomas Nelson titles may be purchased in bulk for educational, business, fund-raising, or sales promotional use. For information, please e-mail SpecialMarkets@ThomasNelson.com.

Publisher's Note: This novel is a work of fiction. Names, characters, places, and incidents are either products of the author's imagination or used fictitiously. All characters are fictional, and any similarity to people living or dead is purely coincidental.

ISBN: 978-0-7852-4037-2 (trade paper)

Library of Congress Cataloging-in-Publication Data

Dickerson, Melanie.
The golden braid / Melanie Dickerson.
pages cm
Summary: In medieval Hagenheim, Germany, seventeen-year-old Rapunzel asks God for guidance as she tries to dutifully serve and obey her unpredictable mother, yet fulfill her dream of learning to read and marrying.
ISBN 978-0-7180-2626-4 (hardback)
[1. Mothers and daughters--Fiction. 2. Love--Fiction. 3. Christian life--Fiction.] I. Title.
PZ7.D5575Go 2015
[Fic]--dc23

2015020898

Printed in the United States of America

21 22 23 24 25 LSC 5 4 3 2 1

The Golden Braid

Chapter One

Late winter, 1413, the village of Ottelfelt,
Southwest of Hagenheim, the Holy Roman Empire

Rapunzel, I wish to marry you."

At that moment, Mother revealed herself from behind the well in the center of the village, her lips pressed tightly together.

The look Mother fixed on Wendel Gotekens was the one that always made Rapunzel's stomach churn.

Rapunzel shuffled backward on the rutted dirt road, "I am afraid I cannot marry you."

"Why not?" He leaned toward her, his wavy hair unusually tame and looking suspiciously like he rubbed it with grease. "I have as much land as the other villagers. I even have two goats and five chickens. Not many people in Ottelfelt have both goats and chickens."

She silently repeated the words an old woman had once told her. *The truth is kinder than a lie.*

"I do not wish to marry you, Wendel." She had once seen him unleash his ill temper on one of his goats when it ran away from him. That alone would have been enough to make her lose interest in him, if she had ever felt any.

He opened his mouth as if to protest further, but he became aware of Mother's presence and turned toward her.

"*Frau* Gothel, I—"

"I shall speak to you in a moment." Her mother's voice was icy. "Rapunzel, go home."

Rapunzel hesitated, but the look in Mother's eyes was so fierce, she turned and hurried down the dirt path toward their little house on the edge of the woods.

Aside from asking her to marry him, Wendel's biggest blunder had been letting Mother overhear him.

Rapunzel made it to their little wattle-and-daub structure and sat down, placing her head in her hands, muffling her voice. "Father God, please don't let Mother's sharp tongue flay Wendel too brutally."

Mother came through the door only a minute or two later. She looked around their one-room home, then began mumbling under her breath.

"There is nothing to be upset about, Mother," Rapunzel said. "I will not marry him, and I told him I wouldn't."

Her mother had that frantic look in her eyes and didn't seem to be listening. Unpleasant things often happened when Mother got that look. But she simply snatched her broom and went about sweeping the room, muttering unintelligibly.

Rapunzel was the oldest unmarried maiden she knew, except for the poor half-witted girl in the village where they'd lived several years ago. That poor girl drooled and could barely speak a dozen words. The girl's mother had insisted her daughter was a fairy changeling and would someday be an angel who would come back to earth to punish anyone who mistreated her.

Mother suddenly put down her broom. "Tomorrow is a market day in Keiterhafen. Perhaps I can sell some healing herbs." She began searching through her dried herbs on the shelf attached to the wall. "If I take this feverfew and yarrow root to sell, I won't have any left over," she mumbled.

"If you let me stay home, I can gather more for you."

Her mother stopped what she was doing and stared at her. "Are you sure you will be safe without me? That Wendel Gotekens—"

"Of course, Mother. I have my knife."

"Very well."

The next morning Mother left before the sun was up to make the two-hour walk to Keiterhafen. Rapunzel arose a bit later and went to pick some feverfew and yarrow root in the forest around their little village of Ottelfelt. After several hours of gathering and exploring the small stream in the woods, she had filled two leather bags, which she hung from the belt around her waist. *This should put Mother in a better mood.*

Just as Rapunzel reentered the village on her way back home, three boys were standing beside the lord's stable.

"Rapunzel! Come over here!"

The boys were all a few years younger than she was.

"What do you want?" Rapunzel yelled back.

"Show us that knife trick again."

"It's not a trick." She started toward them. "It is a skill, and you will never learn it if you do not practice."

Rapunzel pulled her knife out of her kirtle pocket as she reached them. The boys stood back as she took her stance, lifted the knife, and threw it at the wooden building. The knife point struck the wood and held fast, the handle sticking out perfectly horizontal.

One boy gasped while another whistled.

"Practice, boys."

Rapunzel yanked her knife out of the wall and continued down the dusty path. She had learned the skill of knife throwing in one of the villages where she and Mother had lived.

Boys and old people were quick to accept her, an outsider, better than girls her own age, and she tried to learn whatever she could from them. An old woman once taught her to mix brightly colored paints using things easily found in the forest, which Rapunzel then used to paint flowers and vines and butterflies on the houses where she and Mother lived. An older man taught her how to tie several types of knots for different tasks. But the one skill she wanted to learn the most had been the hardest to find a teacher for.

She walked past the stone manor house, with the lord's larger house just behind it and the courtyard in front of it. On the other side of the road were the mill, the bakery, and the butcher's shop. And surrounding everything was the thick forest that grew everywhere man had not purposely cleared.

Endlein, one of the village girls, was drawing water from the well several feet away. She glanced up and waved Rapunzel over.

Rapunzel and her mother were still considered strangers in Ottelfelt as they had only been there since Michaelmas, about half a year. She hesitated before walking over.

Endlein fixed her eyes on Rapunzel as she drew near. "So, Rapunzel. Do you have something to tell me? Some news of great import?" She waggled her brows with a smug grin, pushing a strand of brown hair out of her eyes.

"No. I have no news."

"Surely you have something you want to say about Wendel Gotekens."

"I don't know what you mean."

Endlein lifted one corner of her mouth. "Perhaps you do not know."

"Know what?"

"That your mother has told Wendel he cannot ever marry you because the two of you are going away from Ottelfelt."

Rapunzel's stomach turned a somersault like the contortionists she had seen at the Keiterhafen fair.

She should have guessed Mother would decide to leave now that a young man had not only shown interest in her but had declared his wish to marry her. The same thing happened in the last two villages where they had lived.

Rapunzel turned toward home.

"Leaving without saying fare well?" Endlein called after her.

"I am not entirely sure we are leaving," Rapunzel called back. "Perhaps Mother will change her mind and we shall stay."

She hurried down the road, not even turning her head to greet anyone, even though the baker's wife stopped to stare and so did the alewife. She continued to the little wattle-and-daub cottage that was half hidden from the road by thick trees and bushes. The front door was closed, even though it was a warm day for late winter.

Rapunzel caught sight of the colorful vines and flowers she had only just finished painting on the white plaster walls and sighed. Oh well. She could simply paint more on their next house.

Pushing the door open, Rapunzel stopped. Her mother was placing their folded coverlet into the trunk.

"So it is true? We are leaving again?"

"Why do you say 'again'? We've never left here before." She had that airy tone she used when she couldn't look Rapunzel in the eye.

"But why? Only because Wendel said he wanted to marry me? I told you I would not marry him even if you approved of him."

"You don't know what you would do if he should say the right thing to you." Her tone had turned peevish as she began to place their two cups, two bowls, pot, and pan into the trunk.

"Mother."

"I know you, Rapunzel. You are quick to feel sorry for anyone and everyone." She straightened and waved her hand about, staring at the wall as though she were talking to it. "What if Wendel cried and begged? You might tell him you would marry him. He might beg you to show him your love. You might . . . you might do something you would later regret."

"I would not." Rapunzel's breath was coming fast now, her face hot. It wasn't the first time Mother had accused her of such a thing.

"You don't want to marry a poor, wretched farmer like that Wendel, do you? Who will always be dirty and have to scratch out his existence from the ground? Someone as beautiful as you? Men notice you, as well they might. But none of them are worthy of you . . . none of them." It was as if she had forgotten she was speaking to Rapunzel and was carrying on to herself.

"Mother, you don't have to worry that I will marry someone unworthy." Rapunzel could hardly imagine marrying anyone. One had to be allowed to talk to a man before she could marry him, and talking to men was something her mother had always discouraged. Vehemently.

Mother did not respond, so Rapunzel went to fold her clothes and pack her few belongings.

As she gathered her things, she felt no great sadness at the prospect of leaving Ottelfelt. She always had trouble making friends with girls near her own age, and here she had never lost her status as an outsider. But the real reason she felt no regret was because of what she wanted so very badly, and it was not something she could get in tiny Ottelfelt.

Rapunzel was at least nineteen years old, and she could stay in Ottelfelt without her mother if she wanted to. However, it would be difficult and dangerous—unheard of—unless she was married, since she had no other family. But if they went to a large town, there would certainly be many people who knew how to read and might be willing to teach her.

"Mother, you promised someday you would find someone who could teach me to read. Might we go to a large town where there is a proper priest who knows Latin, a place where there might dwell someone who can teach me to read and write?" She held her breath, watching her mother, whose back was turned as she wrapped her fragile dried herbs in cloths.

Finally, her mother answered softly, "I saw someone in Keiterhafen this morning, someone who . . . needs my help with . . . something."

Rapunzel stopped in the middle of folding her clothes, waiting for Mother to clarify the strange comment.

"And now we will be going to meet him in Hagenheim."

Her heart leapt. Hagenheim was a great town, the largest around.

She tried not to sound eager as she asked, "Isn't that where you lived a long time ago, when Great-Grandmother was still alive?"

"Yes, my darling. Your great-grandmother was the most renowned midwife in the town of Hagenheim—in the entire region." She paused. "Someone I once knew will soon be back in Hagenheim after a long stay in England."

"I don't remember you saying you knew anyone who went to England. Is it a family member?"

Her mother turned to Rapunzel with a brittle smile. "No, not a family member. And I have never mentioned this person before. I do not wish to talk about it now."

The look on Mother's face kept Rapunzel from asking any more questions. Mother had never had friends, and she had never shown any interest in marrying. Although she could marry if she wished. She was still slim and beautiful, with her long, dark hair, which had very little gray.

Later, as Rapunzel finished getting her things ready to tie onto their ox in the morning, she hummed a little song she'd made up. Mother enjoyed hearing her songs, but only when no one else was around.

When night fell, Rapunzel sang her song as Mother finished braiding Rapunzel's long blond hair. Mother smiled in her slow, secretive way. "My precious, talented girl."

Rapunzel embraced her and crawled under the coverlet of their little straw bed.

The next day Rapunzel trudged beside her mother down the road, which was nothing more than two ruts that the ox carts had worn deep in the mud that had then dried and become as hard as stone. She led their ox, Moll, down the center between the ruts, careful to avoid stepping in the horse and ox dung. Their laying hens clucked nervously from the baskets that were strapped to Moll's back.

Night began to fall. Rapunzel lifted her hand to her face and rubbed the scar on her palm against her cheek absentmindedly. She'd had the scar, which ran from the base of her thumb to the other side of her hand, for as long as she could remember. The skin over it was smooth and pale, like a long crescent moon.

"How much farther to Hagenheim, Mother?"

"At least two more days."

Rapunzel didn't mention what she was thinking: that a band of robbers could easily be hiding in the trees at the side of the road. It was not safe for two women to be traveling alone, although they had never been attacked in all the times they had moved from one village to the next.

They had also never traveled so far. They normally only journeyed a few hours.

When the moon was up and shining brightly, and they had not encountered any other travelers for at least an hour, Mother said, "We will stop here for the night."

Rapunzel guided the ox off the road and among the dark trees.

They made a small fire and prepared a dinner of toasted bread, cheese, and fried eggs.

After making sure the ox and hens had food, and after putting out their fire, Rapunzel and Mother lay close together, wrapped in their blankets. Rapunzel sang softly until Mother began to snore.

The next day was uneventful and the unusually warm weather continued. The sun shone down on Rapunzel's head and shoulders as she plodded along at the speed of the ox and to the sound of the chickens' clucking and squawking. Occasionally she amused herself and Mother with her songs, but she always stopped singing when someone came within listening distance. Her mother had warned her not to let strangers hear her beautiful voice or see her golden, ankle-length hair, which Rapunzel kept covered with a scarf and sometimes a stiff wimple. But Mother had never explained why. Perhaps she just didn't want Rapunzel attracting attention to herself for the same reason she didn't want her singing or speaking to men, young, old, or in-between.

On the second day of their journey, two travelers caught up with them, leading two donkeys that pulled a cart loaded and covered by burlap, with one of the men riding on the tallest lump on the back of the cart. As they passed by to Rapunzel's right, the man leading the donkeys smiled. "Pardon me, but would you know how close we are to Hagenheim town?"

"We should reach it by tomorrow night." Rapunzel noticed a big scar on the side of his face. "You may reach it sooner since you are moving faster."

"Thank you, kind maiden." He nodded.

Mother turned to stare hard at something just behind them. The second man stared pointedly at their bundles and baskets tied to Moll's back. When the man's eyes darted to hers, the hair on the back of her neck stood up at the look in his eyes and the strange smile on his face.

"A good day to you." He spoke politely, and they moved ahead until they rounded a shady bend in the road and disappeared.

She sighed in relief, until her mother said in her irritable tone, "Don't speak to strangers, Rapunzel. You know it is dangerous."

"He only asked a simple question. Besides, he didn't look dangerous."

"Dangerous men are the ones who take care not to look dangerous."

Clouds encroached on the sun, sending a shadow creeping over her shoulder. As they entered the double shadow of the trees that hung over the curve in the road, the cart that had passed them a few moments before sat idle several feet ahead. Its two owners were nowhere in sight.

Rapunzel felt a sensation like bugs crawling over her skin. She put her hand on her belt, where she usually kept her knife, but it was not there. She must have left it in their food bag when she put everything away after their midday meal. Should she stop? Or speed up?

Before she could decide, she heard footsteps running up behind her. She spun around just as the man who had smiled at her earlier reached his hands toward her. And he was still smiling.

Chapter Two

Mother screamed. The scarred man clamped his hand over Mother's face.

"Get away!" Rapunzel yelled. While her head was turned, the smiling man closed the gap between them and grabbed her hands. She screamed, and the man with the scar on his face yelled, "Shut her up!"

He grabbed her face, his fingers biting into her cheek, smothering her screams.

She had to get free, had to help her mother. She yanked a hand up and slammed her fist into the grinning man's throat. Next she brought her knee up and struck him between his legs.

He released her, let out a strangled cry, and sank to the ground.

She ran to her mother. The scarred man was choking her. "No!" Rapunzel screamed.

He looked down at his partner, who lay on the ground, coughing weakly and moaning.

Rapunzel stepped forward and slammed her fist into the scarred man's throat. She tried to knee him between the legs, but he shifted Mother in front of him.

Rapunzel clawed at his hands with her fingernails. But instead of letting Mother go, he grabbed Rapunzel's wrist with one hand and squeezed so hard she cried out.

She used her other hand to claw at the hand that held Mother's throat. Mother was struggling against him, but her lips were turning blue and her movements were slow and weak.

The scarred man was breathing out curses and threats, but Rapunzel renewed her efforts, slamming her fist into his face until he finally let go.

Mother coughed and sputtered, leaning forward as she gasped for breath.

The scarred man grabbed both Rapunzel's hands and twisted her arms behind her. He hissed in her ear, "I will kill you."

The smiling man got to his feet and caught hold of her mother. Rapunzel yelled and lunged at him, but the scarred man held her fast.

The smiling man continued to grin. "You put up quite a fight. What have you got on that ox besides those chickens? Any gold or silver?"

Mother rasped out, "I've a Saracen charm that will cause your extremities to turn black and shrivel up." She began chanting as though in a foreign tongue.

"Shut up, old woman." The scarred man behind her jerked Rapunzel's arms, making her shoulders burn more. "Get some rope and tie her up," he growled.

"O Father God, send your angels," Rapunzel whispered under her breath. "Send your archangel with his flaming sword." Her heart pounded. What would these men do to her and her mother? Would they steal their chickens and few household belongings and then leave them alone? Would they do something even more dastardly than robbing them of their possessions once they realized they had no gold or silver?

The smiley one was still breathing strangely after her attack, and the scarred one had bloody scratches on his hands from her fingernails, a sight that sent a thrill of satisfaction through her.

A sound broke through her consciousness. Horse's hooves!

"Help!" Rapunzel yelled until the scarred man covered her mouth again.

The two men exchanged a look.

Suddenly, he let go of her, then shoved her so the ground rushed up to meet her.

Rapunzel hit the dirt so fast she didn't have time to get her hands underneath her. She landed on her left shoulder and the side of her head. A sharp pain pulsed through her eye, then everything went dark.

Gerek urged his horse into a full gallop in the direction of the scream. Another scream, this time louder, sent a chill through him. Donner, always ready for a full-out gallop, seemed to revel in the wind whipping through his mane as his hooves flew over the ground, eating up the road with his powerful legs.

When they rounded a bend, two women were lying in the dirt. He pulled back on the reins. "Whoa!"

Donner slowed before halting beside them. The older woman sat between the ruts holding the head and shoulders of a young woman in her lap.

"What has happened here?" Gerek dismounted and came toward them.

His breath stuck in his throat at how beautiful the young woman was. Her eyes were closed. Dirt and a small trickle of blood marred her temple, but he couldn't imagine she was dead, as her cheek glowed with color and her lips were unusually pink.

"What happened?" He knelt beside her.

"She struck her head on the ground," the older woman said. "You have frightened away our attackers, but if you hurry, you might catch them." The older woman hooked her thumb over her shoulder to the north, the direction of Hagenheim.

There was nothing he could do for the girl, so he leapt onto Donner's back and gave the horse his head again.

After racing around another slight curve in the road, he caught a glimpse of a cart before it disappeared into the trees.

Gerek guided his horse off the road, drawing his sword as he entered the woods.

Two men ambushed him with knives. Their eyes flicked to his drawn sword and they halted. One man turned and ran left, the other right.

The first one looked the most dangerous, so Gerek went after him. Donner had to wind around trees and step over bushes and limbs, while Gerek kept his head low to prevent being knocked off his horse's back.

Had he lost the man? He halted his horse and listened. He heard heavy breathing but was uncertain of the direction from which it came. He guided Donner forward and found the man hiding behind a tree trunk.

"In the name of Duke Wilhelm of Hagenheim, I order you to give yourself up to me."

The man's shrewd eyes trained themselves on Gerek as he dismounted.

"I have done nothing wrong."

"You and your companion attacked those two women in the road."

The man was silent. His expression was quite strange, as if he couldn't stop smiling.

"Down on your knees, lout, or I shall knock you unconscious the way you did that poor maiden."

The man complied.

"Now put your hands on your head." Gerek quickly grabbed the rope in his saddlebag and tied the man's wrists together. Then he tethered him to Donner's saddle.

The man's eyes were defiant and sullen, but he was smiling.

Gerek remounted his horse and made his way back to the road where he had left the two women, his prisoner forced to follow behind on foot.

He found the women where he had left them. The pretty one was sitting up and her eyes were open.

Even with dirt on her face and dress, she took his breath away. Her eyes were a dark blue, her hair a golden blond, although it was tightly braided and mostly covered by a cloth that had fallen askew.

The older woman was dabbing at the blood and dirt on the girl's forehead. "Cover your hair," she hissed.

The maiden started stuffing her braid back inside her head covering. She looked up and her gaze immediately fell on the man whose hands were tied to the back of Gerek's saddle. She drew back.

Gerek dismounted and bowed before the two women. "My name is Sir Gerek. I am a knight in the service of Duke Wilhelm of Hagenheim. Can you tell me if this man is one of your attackers?"

"Yes," the young one said. "The one who shoved me has a scar on his face, like this." She drew a line down her cheek.

"I am sorry I was not able to capture both of them," Gerek said, "but I shall warn the other knights and guards in Hagenheim to be looking for a man with a scar. Did he have any other distinguishing marks?"

She bit her lower lip. "He had a gap between his front teeth. Mother, do you remember what he looked like?"

"He looked like a fiend. They grabbed us and choked us and talked of stealing our chickens and doing us harm. Look what they did to my daughter!"

The beauty said, "He had brown hair and was only a little taller than me, but his scar was very evident."

"He was ugly," the woman added.

"Please allow me to thank you," the young one said, "for saving us from those two evil men. If you had not come when you did, they surely would have stolen everything we have."

Gerek nodded. "It is my duty, as a knight pledged to Duke Wilhelm, to protect all the people of the region of Hagenheim. I shall take this cur to see justice done." He stepped closer to her. "May I help you up?"

Her mother quickly moved between him and the girl. "No. She doesn't need your help." And she proceeded to haul the young woman to her feet.

Gerek took a step back at her rudeness. Most mothers, when they discovered he was one of Duke Wilhelm's knights, smiled and simpered and nearly threw their daughters at his feet.

The woman began brushing the dust from the girl's clothing. The girl swayed.

"Are you well?" Gerek tried to get a better look at the girl's eyes. Sometimes one could see by a person's eyes if the head injury was serious or not.

"I am well." She didn't look at him, but she placed a hand on her mother's shoulder to steady herself.

He could not leave them until he made sure the maiden would not fall over as soon as she started to walk. "Where do you live? Were you traveling someplace?"

"We are on our way to Hagenheim," the girl supplied, as the mother was quite tight-lipped. "How much farther is it?"

"It is at least another day's walk, and you do not look able to walk." He sensed her mother would never allow her to ride on Donner's back with him.

"We do not need your help," the mother barked. "We wish to travel at our own pace."

"The two robbers left a cart and two donkeys near the side of the road when I was chasing them. The donkeys and cart might still be there. Your daughter could ride in the cart the rest of the way to Hagenheim."

"My daughter is not your concern."

He stared at her with his mouth open. "Are *you* not concerned for her? She has suffered an attack and a blow to the head and should not be walking."

She scrunched her face and raised her nose in the air, turning away. "She is not your concern," she repeated.

He was getting quite tired of this woman's refusal of his help. Before she could protest, he took the young maiden's arm, led her to Donner's side, and lifted her onto the horse's back so that she was sitting sidesaddle.

The girl's mother sputtered. "What are you doing? Get away from her!"

He held on to her long enough for her to get her balance and grab hold of the pommel. "Are you secure?" he asked, still holding on to her elbow. "You will not fall if I release you?"

"No." She finally met his eye. Her lips pursed in a tight line, she did not smile, and she did not thank him.

He pulled on Donner's reins and they started down the road.

His prisoner followed behind the horse, remaining silent. The mother's expression was surly as she urged her ox forward.

They moved slowly and no one spoke. Gerek couldn't help thinking about the girl. In all his travels around the Continent—in Burgundy, Normandy, Silesia, Aquitaine, Castile, and Bavaria—he couldn't recall a more beautiful maiden. But it was quite strange to see one her age—at least eighteen or nineteen—unmarried. Especially one so beautiful. Possibly she was widowed.

But he shouldn't be wondering about her. He was still stinging from them rejecting his help.

When they reached the cart, they found it as it had been left by the robbers, except that one of the donkeys was missing. The other culprit must have returned long enough to untie the donkey and ride away on it.

Before the mother could object, Gerek quickly helped the maiden down from the horse.

"Feeling better?" he asked.

"*Ja*, I am well. Only a slight headache."

He should not be staring into her eyes, as he was aware of her mother scowling at them.

He closed his eyes for a moment. She was only a peasant, after all. "I shall accompany you the rest of the way to Hagenheim. That is my destination anyway."

She started to say something, but her mother cut her off.

"Not necessary. You may go on your way, knowing you have saved two women from evil men." Her tone was sarcastic.

"I deem it necessary." He glared down at the woman. "I shall accompany you the rest of the way, whether you wish it or not."

She sized him up with a long stare, then turned away. The young woman, in the meantime, had climbed onto the back of the cart. She no longer met his gaze.

He would not pay any more attention to either of them. He would make sure they made their journey safely, and he would never have to see either one of them again.

Chapter Three

Rapunzel's cheeks burned at the way her mother was treating this knight after he had saved them from their attackers and so courteously helped them. He did sound a bit arrogant in his reply to Mother, but she had been equally rude and had not even told him their names.

Her mother never liked to tell strangers—or anyone else, for that matter—anything. She had often warned Rapunzel, "You should not talk to people. Don't tell any more than is necessary."

"Why, Mother?" But her mother would give her a vague answer, something about curious people being dangerous people or how their business was no one else's business. She must have absorbed some of her grandmother's—Rapunzel's great-grandmother's—strangeness. Mother had told her some odd stories about her.

But this knight, Sir Gerek, was not at all like the men she had known in the villages where she'd grown up. She couldn't understand why Mother would treat him the same way she had treated all of those "unworthy" men.

In fact, Sir Gerek was different from head to toe. Dressed defensively, he wore a leather vest that was quilted with some sort of thick material—an article of clothing that knights wore to protect themselves from arrows and sword blades. She had never seen one until now. In fact, she had never seen a knight until now. A sword swung at his hip, and high leather shoes came almost to his knees. His hair fell to his shoulders but was clean, neat, and evenly cut. It was swept off his forehead, well above his black eyebrows.

His eyes were brown, his hair dark, and he was taller than perhaps any man she had ever seen before. His lips and chin were well-formed and masculine. When she was fighting off their attackers and heard his horse's hooves coming toward them, her first thought was that he was the sword-wielding angel she had prayed for, sent by God to protect them.

He was also handsome. But her mother had taught her not to regard fairness of face, especially in men. It was a tool they used to manipulate weak-willed women into giving them what they wanted.

Would Duke Wilhelm and the rest of his knights look as magnificent as this man? But she would not allow herself to be awed by their appearance. Men could not be trusted, as Mother so often told her.

Thinking about that reminded her that she should find her knife as soon as they stopped again and make sure she carried it with her. Their knight protector had made her feel safe, but that was foolish. She should not assume she could trust him any more than she could trust the lord's son who had tried to attack her when she was fifteen—an incident that seemed to prove right her mother's warnings.

The shaky feeling in her limbs subsided as she rode on the back of the cart. Even the pain in her head subsided, unless she touched the lump where she'd fallen.

The knight was traveling just to her right with his prisoner walking behind him. Mother led the way, her posture stiff, her pace quick.

Rapunzel shifted to a more comfortable position on the bundles. They were lumpy but not terribly uncomfortable, and she wondered what was inside them.

While watching the leaves of the trees overhead, Rapunzel's eyes began to feel heavy. When she opened them, the sun was sinking low. Soon it would be dark and they would be forced to stop for the night.

The knight slowed his pace until he was beside her on his horse. "Are you well?"

The expression on his face was pained. Did it bother him to have to speak to a peasant girl? Or was he sincerely concerned?

"Yes, I thank you." She glanced over her shoulder. Her mother was watching them.

He must have noticed, too, because without so much as a nod, he turned to face forward.

She studied him out of the corner of her eye. Had he been to distant lands? Did he know how to read and write? Perhaps he had not learned. He probably did not know how to read at all. He may have studied only fighting and war skills. He may have killed men with the very sword that hung from his belt.

But even if he did not know how to read, he might know someone, a priest perhaps, who could teach her, someone she could work for in exchange for reading lessons. She should ask him before he left them or, as was more likely, Mother chased him away.

Darkness slowly began to close in on them, and when the last of the sun's light was fading, Sir Gerek spoke. "We will sleep here for the night."

He guided his horse off the road, his prisoner following behind him. Would Mother refuse to be led by him?

She seemed to hesitate, then followed slowly, leading the donkey and cart, as well as their ox with all their belongings, off the road behind Sir Gerek.

Rapunzel grabbed the sides of the cart as it rocked from side to side, bumping over the ruts and into the soft, grassy, uneven ground. The smell of loamy forest dirt and leaves surrounded her, a fresher scent than the animal dung that frequently assaulted her on the road.

When the cart halted, she scrambled down and helped Mother

unhitch Moll so she could eat, as well as the donkey that had pulled the cart. They took their water flasks to a stream nearby and refilled them.

Rapunzel stayed close by her mother's side but kept glancing at Sir Gerek. He filled a water flask for the prisoner and allowed him to drink. He did not untie his hands, but did untie him from the back of his horse's saddle and led him into the cover of the trees, no doubt so they could relieve themselves.

Did she have the courage to ask the knight about teaching her to read? The memory of the lord's son in Wagsburg who had tried to get her to go with him to his father's barn, the look of evil intent on his face, came back to her. Her mother had told her stories about men and the unsuspecting, unprotected, gullible women they convinced to lie with them, or who they lured into the woods where no one could hear them scream.

Perhaps she wouldn't speak to him after all.

Gerek kept an eye on his prisoner. The man wore that smile on his face, which was more an odd expression than an actual smile, his lips curling upward at the corners and his teeth showing. He didn't speak, and Gerek was in no mood to talk to him either, so he ordered him to hurry so they could get back to the two women who would be sleeping nearby.

Just thinking of them put him in a grumpy mood. He had never escorted or protected anyone less grateful. The mother had done nothing but glare at him, and the daughter usually avoided making eye contact, even when talking to him. He didn't need their gratitude. As a knight, he would do his duty in protecting Duke Wilhelm's people, grateful or not.

When they returned, he tied the prisoner's rope to a tree and quickly built a fire.

The two women kept to themselves, and after he had fed his prisoner, the man fell asleep, snoring as he lay on his side, facing the fire.

Gerek lay watching the dying flames lick up the last of the sticks he had gathered. He was nearly asleep when he heard a voice, a melody so unearthly and beautiful he glanced up at the sky, expecting to see heaven opened and an angel of music. But all he saw were a few stars winking above him through the leaves.

The sound was coming from beyond the fire, from the direction of the two women who had chosen to sleep a distance away. He thought he had heard every song that was sung in the Holy Roman Empire, as many troubadours, *Meistersingers*, and minstrels as he had encountered in his travels. But this was not any song that he recognized.

He closed his eyes. The melody wrapped around his chest, which ached with the beauty of it, even though he couldn't quite make out the words.

His mother was only a hazy figure now in his memory, as he had last seen her when he was seven years old. He had a memory of her leaning over him. It was nighttime, and she was singing to him. Her voice was sweet and soft and gentle, just like this one. Her song had filled his chest with a beautiful aching love, and now, listening to the song, he was filled with a similar, sweet ache.

It must be the young maiden who was singing. The voice was too young and clear to belong to the older woman. Where had she learned such a song?

How strange it was that two women would be out walking alone on the roads for such a distance. Tomorrow he would ask them where they came from and what their names were. And if they didn't tell him, he would threaten to take them to Duke Wilhelm under suspicion that they were indebted servants who had run away from their rightful lord.

He listened closely to the melody of the song, trying to memorize it. If only she would sing a little louder.

His prisoner made a noise in his sleep like a pig snorting.

The singing ceased. The man rolled over and started breathing heavily again. Gerek waited, holding his breath, but the singing did not resume.

He stared up the stars, letting the melody of the song and the sweetness of the voice play over and over in his memory. It was haunting, lingering, beautiful.

He slept lightly, waking every time his prisoner moved, which was often. By morning he was glad the night was over so he could get his prisoner to Hagenheim and turn him over to the gaoler to await justice.

While he kept a close eye on his prisoner and prepared to depart, the two women were already packed up and leaving. The young maiden was looking back at him as they started toward the road.

So they were leaving without him, were they? Well, why should he care? Let them get attacked by robbers again.

He and his prisoner set out, too, but instead of the sky becoming lighter, it seemed to be getting dark again. He could smell rain in the air as a chill stole over him. It had been unusually warm, as it was still late winter, but rain would bring colder weather.

He kept at a slow pace, with his prisoner walking behind, occasionally complaining about his feet or being thirsty. Gerek made sure he had what he needed, but he mostly ignored his complaints. If the prisoner thought Gerek was too kind, he would be more likely to do something sneaky.

Suddenly the wind began to pick up, and then, just as quickly, it became still. Thunder rumbled in the distance.

"Now I will get wet," the robber grumbled.

Gerek kept on his same steady pace. Just as he noticed a strange feeling in the air, a crack of lightning split the stillness, so loud it seemed to numb his ears. Gerek's horse leapt, all four hooves off the ground, then reared and pawed the air.

Gerek fought to control the horse and stay mounted. When his hooves were all back on the ground, the horse snorted and danced to the side.

The lightning seemed to have come from just ahead of them. Gerek urged his horse forward at a trot, forcing his prisoner to walk fast to keep up.

"Are you trying to kill me?" he protested.

But Gerek did not slow the pace. He pictured the beautiful young maiden with the unearthly voice lying on the ground, felled by the lightning strike.

After a few moments, he caught a glimpse of them up ahead. The young woman turned to glance behind her. Her eyes were wide, but she looked unhurt.

His prisoner began breathing heavily behind him and mumbling curses. Gerek slowed his horse.

The young maiden's mother grumbled at the ox and donkey, flicking them lightly with a makeshift whip to make them walk faster. Another clap of thunder came from farther away.

A fat drop of rain landed on his nose. Another crack of lightning split the air, even closer than the first one. Donner danced and snorted, still unsettled, when a hare darted out across the road directly in front of him.

Gerek braced himself as Donner neighed and reared. Gerek leaned forward and pulled back on the reins. His horse reared so high, Gerek started falling backward.

A dull snap. The saddle girth must have broken. The saddle was sliding. Gerek couldn't gain any leverage to push himself free. He hit the ground on his right side just before the big warhorse fell on top of him.

A sharp pain in his ankle broke his consciousness, but he ignored it. He had to see where his prisoner had gone.

Donner scrambled to get up. Every time the horse attempted to heave his big body, it allowed Gerek to wriggle a little way out. He twisted around to see the prisoner pull Gerek's long knife out of his saddlebag.

Gerek's sword was underneath him. He tried to get his hand on the hilt. Just as his horse made it to his feet and freed Gerek, the prisoner lunged at him with the knife.

Gerek blocked the man's arm. He lay at an awkward angle and could not reach the knife in the man's hand. Another moment and the prisoner would be able to jab the knife between Gerek's ribs.

The girl yelled. The prisoner hovered over Gerek with that strange, angry smile. He raised the dagger, aiming for Gerek's throat.

Something flew past, above Gerek's head. The hilt of a knife was sticking out of the prisoner's upper arm.

The prisoner cried out, dropping Gerek's dagger and grabbing at the knife that protruded from his arm. Then he turned and ran, disappearing into the trees.

Gerek turned to see who had thrown the knife that had saved him. The young maiden stood staring at him, the rain dotting her dress and head covering and starting to drip down her face. That's when he realized it was raining.

The prisoner had escaped. His heart sank.

Donner was stamping his hooves, as if testing his legs. With his left hand, Gerek pulled himself up to stand. When he came to his feet, his ankle collapsed beneath him. He fell back to the ground.

The ankle bone was broken.

Chapter Four

Rapunzel dropped to her knees beside Sir Gerek. "I think he's gone. Where are you hurt?"

Mother called, "Rapunzel! Get back here."

She hovered over him as the rain began to fall in large, hard, cold drops, soaking into her clothes and through her hair to her scalp. He was cringing and holding his arm close to his body. She tried to shield his face from the rain by leaning over him. He gasped and struggled to sit up.

"What may I do to help?"

"Bring my horse to me."

She went and caught the horse's reins. The animal was so much larger and more high-spirited than a mule or donkey that she was careful to stay as far away from it as the extent of the reins would allow.

"Help me up," he said, reaching for her with his left hand, keeping his right arm against his stomach. He grabbed her arm, and she braced herself to accept his considerable weight. Then he grasped her shoulder and rasped out something unintelligible under his breath. He leaned heavily on her.

"I don't think you can mount your horse," she said, stating the obvious. "Come and lie on the back of the cart."

His face contorted, and he looked deathly pale. "No, I can ride."

The rain was coming down so hard, it was running down her

cheeks and sending a chill down her spine. She pulled the horse a bit closer, pleased the animal kept its teeth to itself.

She supported Sir Gerek's weight as he put his left foot in the stirrup. He cried out as he threw his right leg over the saddle and boosted himself up.

He leaned forward over the pommel, his eyes closed.

"Are you sure you are well enough to ride?" She had to speak loudly to be heard over the steady roar of the rain as well as the frequent thunder.

He did not move. Finally, he straightened a little. "Let us go." He turned his horse around.

Rapunzel held up her skirts from the mud that was quickly forming and hurried to where her mother stood beside the donkey and cart.

Mother was scowling at her. "What are you doing? He does not need your help."

"Mother, he does. He is injured. He could barely mount his horse."

"That is not your concern."

"Where is your Christian charity? He is a noble knight who saved us from those robbers."

Mother wouldn't truly leave the poor knight to lie on the ground, hurt. After all, her mother had taken Rapunzel in when she was alone and helpless.

Sir Gerek rode forward, so Rapunzel and her mother led their donkey and ox forward as well, doing their best to ignore the rain.

After a few minutes, he rode up beside her. "Would you do something for me?" He looked quite pale. Water dripped from the ends of his hair and ran down his face.

"What is it?"

"Would you put my foot into the stirrup?"

It was the injured foot, his right foot. She tried to use care as she took his booted foot in one hand and his heavy metal stirrup in the other and slipped it inside.

She thought she heard him groan, but with the rain coming down so hard, it was difficult to tell. His face was stiff and his eyes closed. He continued to hold his right arm against his stomach.

They kept up a steady, if slow, pace. When it finally stopped raining, a cool breeze set in. Rapunzel shivered. She was soaked straight through to every inch of her skin. Nothing had been safe from the heavy rain. And now she was plodding down the muddy road in cold, wet skirts. But Sir Gerek must have been the most miserable. He was slumped forward on his horse, his head hanging low.

The longer she walked in her wet clothing, the more uncomfortable she felt, and the more she realized the day was not getting warmer, but colder.

"Rapunzel," her mother called. "Come here."

Rapunzel left Sir Gerek's side and went to join her mother where she was leading the caravan of ox, donkey, and cart.

"Rapunzel, we must get out of our wet clothes now that it's stopped raining. Get your extra dress and go change in the shelter of those trees there."

Rapunzel retrieved her clothing from the bag on the back of the ox, which had been kept dry by their oiled tarp. She changed quickly and emerged from the trees feeling more comfortable.

Sir Gerek had stopped with them and was waiting, motionless, on top of his horse. While Mother was changing, Rapunzel approached him. "Do you have extra clothing in your saddlebag?"

His lips were a strange shade of blue. Finally, he said, "If I dismount, I don't know if I will be able to get back on again."

She wasn't sure what to say.

"I believe the bone in my ankle is broken, and so is my arm."

"How long will it take to get to Hagenheim?"

"I'm not sure we will make it by nightfall. The rain slowed us down."

"Is there anywhere nearby you might stop for help?"

He shook his head.

"Truly, there is a simple solution to this difficulty. You must get down, let my mother help you change your clothing, and allow us to bring you to Hagenheim in the cart. You cannot continue the entire journey on horseback, and you must get out of those wet clothes. You will freeze."

"I shall go on as I am."

"That is foolish," she said. He was too arrogant and prideful to accept their help.

He grunted.

They did indeed go on, as Mother came back and insisted they get on their way again.

When they had continued on for another hour or so and it was midday, Mother announced it was time to stop and rest and eat a bit of food.

Rapunzel had been trying not to speak to Sir Gerek unless he spoke to her first, but when they stopped, she went over to him.

"Sir Gerek, you are still wet. Can I persuade you to change your clothing now?"

"Perhaps I will. I need to let Donner feed. Will you . . . ?" He looked down at his boot, which was still in the stirrup.

She extricated his foot as gently as possible. He made no sound, but his face was tense as he then pulled his leg over—and disappeared on the other side of the horse with a *whoosh* and a *thud*.

Chapter Five

Rapunzel hurried around the horse. Sir Gerek was lying on the ground, not moving.

"Sir Gerek? Can you hear me?" His eyes were closed, but his breathing was harsh and loud.

He opened his eyes just a slit. "Will you go find a stick, a tall, sturdy one, and bring it to me?"

Rapunzel was already hurrying toward the trees. Mother was taking out their food and water and frowning at her.

It took her a few minutes, but she finally found a stick that should hold Sir Gerek's weight. Then she hurried back to where he still lay on the ground.

After handing him the stick, she said, "I shall find some dry clothes in your saddlebag."

After locating the clothes, she turned around, and he was sitting up looking at her. Her breath fluttered in her throat.

She never would have imagined herself showing so much concern for a *man*, and it made her a bit sick in her stomach to think of helping him change his clothing. But he was nearly helpless, after all. However, if he behaved in the slightest way inappropriately toward her, insinuating anything unseemly, she would leave him right there on the road, in the mud.

"I don't think I can change, but thank you for your efforts." He was still breathing hard.

They had to help him. "Mother! Mother, come here." Rapunzel motioned. "Come and help Sir Gerek."

Her mother came toward them, a cautious look on her face.

"Mother, we cannot leave him like this." She thrust his dry clothes at her. "Please, help him get dressed." She said a little silent prayer that her mother would not refuse.

"I can dress myself," he grumbled.

Mother said nothing but reached toward him.

A look like fear came into Sir Gerek's brown eyes. "Frau, there is no need—" But before he could say anything more, Mother had knelt beside him, taken hold of his wet woolen tunic, and pulled it up. His eyes widened and he held his arms up, keeping his injured left arm crooked at the elbow. Mother slipped the wide-neck tunic over his head, then threaded the sleeve up, hardly touching the injured arm.

Underneath his tunic he wore a fine linen garment, but it was also wet, so Mother took it off in the same way.

Quickly, trying not to look at his bare chest, Rapunzel slipped the dry tunic over his head. But she saw that would not work, so she took it off and put his injured left arm into the sleeve first, then put it over his head and let him put his right arm in. Rapunzel had caught a glimpse, beneath the dark hair on his forearm, of the large bruise and the swelling.

Now that his upper body was dry, Mother was examining his leg.

"Are you a healer?" he asked, his leg stretched out in front of him.

Mother grunted as she got onto her knees and bent over. "I am a midwife, but I have been called upon, on occasion, to treat wounds." She looked at his leg, encased in his leather boot up past the middle of his calf, and his thick woolen hose, which was tucked into his boot. But his leg was so swollen, it seemed to be stretching the boot.

She took out her own table knife from a pouch she wore around her waist and began cutting a slit down the side of his boot.

"*Ach!* What are you doing?"

"Your leg is swollen too much. The boot must come off." Soon she had split it all the way down, and she slipped it off his foot. "The hose has to come off too. Rapunzel, go take the donkey and ox to the side of the road where the grass is green. Sir Gerek has to take off his clothes."

"Yes, Mother." Rapunzel moved quickly, not wishing to embarrass either Sir Gerek or herself. No one could say no to Mother when she was in this mood, not even a strong and powerful knight like Sir Gerek. Besides, he needed their help, and he finally seemed ready to admit it.

Rapunzel heard a few grunts and growls behind her, followed by Mother's sharp voice giving orders. Even though it might cause him pain and a bit of embarrassment, at least he would be dry and more comfortable.

Rapunzel unhitched the donkey and led him and the ox to a patch of lush, green grass off the road. She quickly hid herself deeper among the trees to take care of her own needs, then stood, speaking soothingly to the donkey and ox.

She supposed she would have to name the donkey since Sir Gerek said they could keep him. They would also keep whatever was in the cart he was pulling, and she wondered again what might be hidden underneath all the burlap.

"Rapunzel, hitch the donkey back up and bring the cart over here. Sir Gerek is going to ride on the cart."

A deep grumbling came from their direction. No doubt Sir Gerek was protesting such a decision. But even he had been doubtful that he would be able to mount his horse again once he was down. It would surely be better for his broken bones to ride in a cart than on a horse.

She grasped the donkey's bridle and tugged until she was able to turn him around and lead him toward Sir Gerek.

He had risen to his feet and was leaning on the stick Rapunzel had brought him. His hair was dark and wavy with rain, but at least he looked dry everywhere else, and he was no longer shivering.

She hurried the donkey along and finally drew the cart up beside him. Mother had gone into the woods, perhaps to relieve herself, so Rapunzel stood waiting to see if she could help him.

He leaned heavily on the stick as he hop-stepped to the back of the cart. Instead of sitting down or climbing onto the back, he looked down into her face.

Her heart thudded against her chest as she stared up into his brown eyes. He was tall and powerful looking, yet his smooth skin and absence of wrinkles around his eyes told her that he was barely older than she was. His hair looked soft and clean, which in itself set him apart from most other men.

But looking into his eyes was a bit like looking into the sun. It was impossible to do for more than a few seconds.

She looked down at the cart. The piles of burlap were still wet. "Let me put something down for you, something dry." She hurried to pull out her own blanket from underneath the oiled tarp. She quickly spread it out.

He sat on the piles of burlap, where she'd lain herself the day before after her head injury. He gradually pushed himself up with his good leg until he could stretch out his broken leg on the hemp cloth sacks. He lay back and closed his eyes, his face once again tense, his jaw twitching as he clenched his teeth.

No doubt all the movement made his injuries more painful, and her stomach writhed in sympathy.

"I'm tying your horse to the back of the cart," she called to him. Fortunately, the horse did not seem to object to her doing so. "Is there anything else I can do?"

He said nothing for a moment, then, in a gruff voice, "No."

Oddly relieved that he was being terse, she hurried back to the donkey, her shoes slipping and sliding in the mud. She tugged again on the animal's bridle.

Mother was waiting for her on the road ahead with their ox.

Rapunzel braved her mother's wrath by walking close beside the cart and saying to him, "Is Hagenheim where you live?"

"Yes, on the castle grounds."

"I have never had a broken bone. It must hurt immensely."

"I have had broken bones before," he said, his voice low. He lay on his side, his right arm lying against his stomach. He was no longer cringing in pain. "It doesn't hurt so much if you can lie still." He lifted his brows. "But that's hardly possible when riding in a donkey cart, is it?"

"I suppose not, with all the jostling. I will try not to let him pull the cart over too many holes."

After a short silence, he said, "There is a healer in Hagenheim at the castle, Frau Lena. If we can reach the castle, she will be able to set the bones."

"Set the bones?" She was not so much interested in how to treat a broken bone as she was with hearing him speak. His voice was warm and low, and his speech more refined than the men in the villages.

"She makes sure the bones are in place so they will grow straight. Then she splints them with sticks or blocks of wood."

"How do you know the bone is broken? Can you feel it move?" She shivered at the imagined sensation.

"Sometimes. Frau Lena says if it swells a lot, it's probably broken."

"I know your leg is badly swollen. Is your arm swollen?"

Instead of answering her, he looked down at his arm. He pulled up the sleeve of his loose tunic. The sunbrowned skin of his arm was bruised and the middle of his forearm was swollen.

"Why did your horse rear up like that? Do horses often fall backward on their riders?"

"No, not often." He made a wry frown. "He is new. My last horse broke a leg. This one is still more skittish than I would like. He was nervous from the lightning strike. But he reared because a hare ran out in front of him. Now I have a useless arm and a leg that won't bear my weight. And all because of one small hare and a skittish horse."

She nodded.

"Not to mention that the man who attacked you and your mother is now free." He closed his eyes and his jaw twitched again.

"How long do you think it will take your broken bones to heal?"

"Six weeks at least."

Mother was tugging on the donkey's rope as it had decided to stop in the middle of the road. Seeing Rapunzel looking at her, she shook her head no. Rapunzel sent her mother a slight shrug and smiled.

After Mother persuaded the donkey to move, Rapunzel continued to walk alongside the injured knight in the cart. After all, what harm could the man do with a broken arm and leg?

He was looking at her. "How did you ever learn to throw a knife like that?"

"From some boys in my village when I was a young girl. I like to learn things, and growing up, I rather enjoyed learning boyish things, like archery and knife throwing." Perhaps she was talking too much, but he looked interested. She had never had the opportunity of speaking with a knight before. She may as well make the most of it and learn all she could.

"You saved my life today, with your boyish skills." He gave her another one of his wry half smiles that made her insides flutter. "Will you tell me your name?"

"Rapunzel."

"Is your head better after your fall yesterday, Rapunzel? Sometimes head injuries can take a long time to heal."

"I am feeling well today, I thank you."

"Rapunzel." He grunted, whether as a reaction to her name or in response to the jostling of the cart, she did not know. "I have not heard of anyone named that."

"It is unusual, I know. My mother named me after the plant. She once told me she found me in the rapunzel patch in her garden when I was a baby. I am not certain that was true, but someone did leave me with her when I was a baby. They must have known she and her grandmother were midwives."

Unable to contain her curiosity, she asked, "Have you ever been in any battles or traveled to distant lands?"

"I have participated in many mock battles, but never a real one. And yes, I have traveled to distant lands."

"Are the people very strange in other places? Do they have colored skin, and do they speak in strange tongues?"

He smiled. It was brief and slight, but it was a smile. "I have only traveled around the Continent, and most of the people speak French, which I have learned. The people have fair skin, like ours. But I have met some Saracens who have very dark skin."

"Forgive my questions. My mother says a curious man is a dangerous man."

"I'm sure your mother is right, in some cases. But I have always thought a curious man was a knowledgeable man."

Those in the villages where she had lived had sometimes laughed at her curiosity and desire to learn. Perhaps it was not something to be ashamed of at all.

"How exciting to know another language besides German. Is French very difficult to learn?"

"Not so difficult, if you are forced to speak it in order to communicate with people."

The breath stilled in her throat. "Do you know how to read and write? In German?"

"I do."

Her heart beat faster. Did she dare ask him to teach her? Could she be so bold?

Her mother's sharp eyes were on them. She would get a thorough scolding when the knight was gone. Asking him to teach her to read would anger her mother even more. Mother would surely prevent his teaching her anything. How could she ever spend time learning from him without Mother knowing about it? No, she had better wait and find someone else in Hagenheim to teach her.

For the moment, she was enjoying just looking at his face. With his handsome features, his sword, and his finely stitched clothing, he was like an exotic creature. If he told her he was a prince from a foreign kingdom, she would have believed him.

Finally, she broke the silence by asking, "Do you know how to read in any other languages besides German?"

"I read and write in German, French, English, and Latin."

"Truly?" She suddenly was painfully aware of her own ignorance. What must it be like to have such learning? She must seem like the most ignorant peasant to him. He was the son of some nobleman, a baron or earl or duke, and only his code of chivalry and courtesy as a knight in the service of the noble Duke of Hagenheim could have induced him to stoop to help her and her mother, to travel and protect them from harm.

But she had saved his life. Perhaps he would be grateful enough to teach her a bit about languages and reading. Now that he would be laid up in bed for six weeks with a broken leg . . . Gratitude and idleness could be the perfect combination.

Her heart beat wildly at the thought of getting what she had wanted for so long. Her greatest hope and wish was to learn to read so she would no longer feel like an ignorant peasant. Would he agree to teach her?

Sir Gerek was staring. She probably looked strange as she shifted from shame at her own ignorance to great joy.

He said softly, "What was that song you were singing last night?"

"Singing? Perhaps it was someone on the road." She turned away so he couldn't read her face.

"No, it was not." He sounded irritable. "Do not lie. It was you."

Rapunzel took a deep breath and huffed it out. "Is it unlawful to sing?"

"Of course not."

"If you must know, I always sing at night for my mother. But she doesn't like for me to sing in front of other people." She lowered her voice to make sure her mother couldn't hear her.

"What was the song? I've never heard it before."

"It is my own song." Rapunzel felt her face growing warm again. Her mother had made her keep her singing and songs a secret for so long, it was strange to admit to someone.

"I made it up."

"You wrote it?"

"I have never written it down, but I created the words and the tune." She wanted to ask him if he liked it.

He didn't say anything for several moments. Then he said, "You do not know how to write?"

She shook her head. "I have always wanted to learn."

"Then you are not from Hagenheim?"

"No. My mother and I lived in Ottelfelt, and before that, we lived in Frankendorf. We are free women, and my mother doesn't like to stay in one place very long. But she lived in Hagenheim before, when I was a baby." Then a thought struck her. "Why did you say that I must not be from Hagenheim? Do all Hagenheim townspeople know how to read?"

"Our Lady Rose, the wife of Duke Wilhelm, started a school for the children of Hagenheim. Anyone who wishes to attend, girls and boys, are taught to read and write in German and Latin."

"Oh!" Such a thing seemed too wonderful. "This Lady Rose must be a very generous person."

"She is a great and noble lady." He said the words quietly but with great feeling.

"This Lady Rose . . . does she have children?"

"She has several children. They are mostly grown now, except for two young boys and a little girl."

She must be nearly forty. Too old for Sir Gerek to be in love with, surely.

"She is a very motherly woman," he went on. "She can never turn away a child in need, no matter how dirty or cast away."

As it should be. Rapunzel was disposed to like this Lady Rose very much.

"Perhaps Lady Rose," he said, "would find an older child who would be willing to teach you to read."

Excitement fluttered inside her. "I . . . But I would have nothing to give to them in exchange. My mother and I are very poor."

He shrugged. "Or you could attend classes with the smaller children."

That was not a very appealing thought. Still, if it was the only way . . .

The cart wheels suddenly dropped into a particularly deep hole. Sir Gerek let out a cry of pain as the cart jostled violently, tossing him one way and the other as the wheel bumped in and then out of the deep rut.

"Oh no," Rapunzel said. "I should have been making sure the donkey stays away from the holes." She checked ahead to see if there were any more holes she might steer him away from.

He groaned. "It's going to be a long day."

Chapter Six

Gerek bit back a groan for the fiftieth time. His leg had grown enormous while he was sitting on his horse. Now that he was able to stretch it out on the cart, the swelling had gone down a bit. Even though he had experienced some pain and embarrassment at the older woman forcing him to strip his clothes off, at least he was wearing dry clothes again and no longer felt like an icicle.

The young maiden, Rapunzel, walked along beside him, talking to him every so often. She had a mistrustful air about her that was irritating, given the fact that he had saved her life. But it was to her credit that she longed for a chance to learn languages and to read. Lady Rose would love to teach her, no doubt, but she did not have time, as she was busy enjoying her children and grandchildren.

Twilight was descending and they were still far from Hagenheim. It was too dangerous to travel after dark when he was injured and unable to fight off robbers. "Rapunzel," he called to the maiden.

She appeared at the side of the cart.

"There is a monastery off this road. The lane is just ahead. We can spend the night there."

"I shall tell Mother." And she disappeared again.

A short time later, they turned down the lane that would take them off the main road to the monastery buildings.

As eager as the woman was to get rid of him, he would not be surprised if they left him there with the monks and went on in the dark without him.

The monks brought them in and offered their hospitality, but immediately separated Sir Gerek from the women. He was helped onto a litter by a large lay worker and dragged away to a smaller building next to the monks' dormitory. He caught one small glimpse of Rapunzel looking back at him, and then she was gone.

Gerek awoke the next morning and tried to roll over—until he realized he couldn't move his leg or his arm. The monastery's healer was quite eager to set Gerek's leg and arm and splint them. Now he was weighted down with enormous blocks of wood on two sides of his leg and two sides of his arm, wrapped with strips of cloth and tied together. His whole body ached, and he wasn't sure he didn't have a broken rib or two, due to a sharp pain in his side.

The room where he had slept was bare except for Gerek's saddlebag on the floor and the tiny, low cot that was built for a shorter man. The pale light of the sun was just beginning to peek in the high window.

The door creaked open. *Let it be food.* Gerek was starved for a decent meal.

"Andrew! My old friend."

"Sir Gerek. They told me you were here." Andrew looked different with his tonsured head and brown robe, but Gerek knew his face better than his own.

"It is good to see you."

Andrew came near and clasped his arm. "It is good to see you, too, my friend, but not so broken up. What happened?"

Gerek repeated the tale of his injuries. He also told of his prisoner escaping after nearly slashing Gerek to death with his own dagger.

"You are never to repeat this," Gerek told him, "but I was actually saved by the young maiden I'd rescued the day before. She threw her knife and it struck him in the arm, and he ran off."

Andrew hung his head, shaking it slowly back and forth. They had been squires together, had trained together as knights, and then Andrew had suddenly decided to enter the monastic life.

Andrew raised his brows at Gerek. "Sounds like you owe this maiden a knife, as well as your life."

"You always did have a way of getting right to the point." Gerek smiled, but it was a rueful one. Andrew was right. He should have planned to at least replace the peasant girl's knife. It might have been the only one she had. "You don't happen to know where she is?"

"She and her mother left before dawn."

Gerek moved to get out of bed, then was stopped by the weight of his splinted leg. He couldn't even walk.

"Don't worry." Andrew must have read his thoughts. "God will repay her for saving your life."

But Gerek did not like owing anything to anyone, especially someone much poorer than he was. When he was well, he would go to the Hagenheim market, buy a good knife, and find her and give it to her. After all, how hard would it be to find someone with a name like Rapunzel?

"The abbot says you may stay here until you have recovered. Our healer, Brother John, is quite good."

Gerek examined the splints on his arm and his leg. They were well done. "What a thing to have happen—a broken leg and a broken arm. I'll be as useless as a candle in a rainstorm."

"You can improve your mind and your spirit by reading inspired writings." Brother Andrew smiled. "And we'll move you to a more comfortable room. It won't be so bad."

They spoke for a while longer, and Gerek gave Andrew the news of the other knights that he asked about. Then a servant brought Gerek his breakfast, and Andrew promised to come back later.

While he ate, Gerek contemplated the next six weeks. He would have few people to talk to, nowhere to go, and nothing to do, as the healer had ordered him not to stand on his leg for at least three weeks, and for the next three weeks after that to only have limited movement. He would have no choice but to do what Andrew suggested and find some things to read.

Even so, it was going to be a very long six weeks.

Rapunzel stared openmouthed at the place where Mother had announced they would live. It was the tiny house that her mother had shared with her grandmother. Rapunzel could clearly see why no one was living there—no humans, that is. The thatch on the roof was falling in and had obviously been leaking. Filth of various descriptions littered the floor, including animal droppings, and spiderwebs decorated every corner.

Mother grabbed the short little broom she had brought with her and sent Rapunzel out to gather broom straw to make a second broom. Soon they were both sweeping out the leaves and dirt that had accumulated over the past sixteen or seventeen years, since, after her grandmother died, Mother had taken Rapunzel and moved to the first village.

They worked steadily all day, with Mother reminding her in a determined tone of every little find or victory.

"Now that we have cleaned the floors, we'll do the walls."

"Now that we have cleaned out the hearth, we'll build a fire."

"Now that we have a fire, we'll cook some pottage."

"Oh, look at this blanket. It used to be yours when you were little."

Rapunzel drew near and examined the piece of cloth. "Yes, I remember it. It is dirty, but you can see the embroidery here. It's a lamb, but when I was little, I thought it was a dog."

Mother gave Rapunzel a strange look, her eyes becoming round. It was almost a look of fear. "How do you remember that? You haven't seen this blanket since you were three years old."

Rapunzel shrugged. "I remember holding it to my cheek every night while I cried."

"Yes." Mother's voice sounded distant. "But that was because you didn't like the dark or nighttime and used to cry yourself to sleep. But it was only for a while. After a few months, you stopped."

"Isn't that when I started making up songs?" Rapunzel hoped to distract her mother. When she got that far away look in her eye and that sound in her voice, she became agitated and would yell or say strange things.

"Yes, you did start making up songs when you were about four." The smile returned to Mother's face. "You always had such a talent for singing and songs and painting pretty pictures. There was never any child as wonderful as my Rapunzel." She squeezed Rapunzel's shoulder and went to the next task—brushing down the cobwebs from the walls, corners, and ceiling.

Rapunzel sighed, glad she could take her mother's mind off whatever had made her get that look.

When they had gotten the house in livable condition, they decided to open the bundles that had been on the cart belonging to the thieves.

Untying the cloth bags, they found mostly food—containers full of lard and salted pork, bags of flour, kegs of oil, with rags and old clothes covering everything as though to disguise it. But underneath everything else, wrapped in rags, lay bundles of old swords.

Mother exclaimed over the food supplies, overjoyed to have

gotten them for nothing, but Rapunzel couldn't help wondering. "What do you suppose those two men were doing with so many swords? And with so much food? There's enough here to feed an army."

Mother shrugged. "They were probably taking it to sell at Hagenheim's *Marktplatz*. It is ours now."

"But aren't you afraid those men will come for all this?" Rapunzel lifted a sword, turning it over in her hand. She glanced at Mother. Her lips were parted, her eyes narrowing as she stared at the weapons.

Mother suddenly took the sword from Rapunzel's hand and wrapped it back up with the other ones, then picked up the bundle.

"What are you doing?"

Mother walked to the back door. "I'm burying these. Get the shovel."

Rapunzel helped her mother dig a long, shallow trench in the dirt behind their little house and bury the weapons. Was Mother afraid of the men coming to find them? Or did she have other plans for the swords?

That night they lay awake on their straw beds with a stool pushed in front of the door to hold it shut since they hadn't had a chance to repair it yet. Rapunzel sang one of her songs. When she finished, Mother was still awake, still stroking Rapunzel's long braid.

Instead of singing another song, Rapunzel thought about the knight who had protected them, Sir Gerek. She liked remembering his face. What would it be like to have a man like him fall in love with her? Of course, as a noble knight, having been born into a noble family, he was much too proud to ever marry anyone lower than the daughter of a baron. That was how men like him made their fortunes. When there was no war in which they could pillage and plunder or endear themselves to the king, they married someone wealthy.

But she still wanted to remember his face. And his voice and manner. And the way he was dressed and the way he sat on his horse. Although now he wouldn't be sitting on a horse for quite a while.

"Mother?"

"Yes, *liebling*?"

"Who do you expect that I shall marry?" She tried to make her tone as light as possible. "You haven't liked any of the young men who have shown an interest in me. Who would be my ideal husband?"

Mother's hand ceased stroking Rapunzel's hair. A heavy silence descended between them. Since Mother was behind her, Rapunzel imagined that hard look that sometimes came over her face.

"My darling," her mother finally said, her hand heavy on Rapunzel's head, "men only want to take advantage of someone as innocent and sweet as you are. I have not met a one of them that I would trust with my darling Rapunzel. Besides, aren't you content? Just the two of us, taking care of each other? What do we need with a . . . *husband*?" She said the word as if it were *snake* or *monster*.

A shiver went down Rapunzel's back. She had always believed that someday she would marry, that her mother couldn't mean to keep her from getting married. If a good man, especially a free man with a bit of land or a job in town, asked to marry Rapunzel, her mother would give her approval. It was the way of the world. Everyone got married.

But her mother had never married. Encouraging her to be cautious around men seemed sensible. But could Mother intend to prevent her from marrying?

"Darling, men will only hurt you, pretend to love you, and then leave you when they feel they've made a conquest of you. I don't want that to happen to you, Rapunzel."

"Did that happen to you?"

For a moment she didn't answer, but then she said, "I was just as innocent and trusting as you are, when I was your age or a little younger . . . Yes, that is what happened to me. But I am strong now, and I will not allow it. That is a pain you need never feel. I shall protect you . . . always." Mother started stroking her hair again.

A strange weight entered Rapunzel's throat. She coughed and then wiggled into a more comfortable position on the makeshift bed. Poor Mother. Something *had* happened, something she had never gotten over. She must have been brokenhearted, abandoned by the man who had pretended to love her, as she had said. But would Mother never trust anyone again? Would she truly "protect" Rapunzel until she was too old for anyone to want her?

She wouldn't worry about it tonight. Besides, she was about to get what she'd always wanted. While Mother was telling the monks that she was a midwife and impressing them with her piety so that they would recommend her to any pregnant women who might come their way, Rapunzel had asked a young monk who was walking nearby if they had any work for her to do at the monastery in exchange for reading lessons. He had looked quite thoughtful, then told her he would go and ask someone higher in authority, for her to wait there.

Rapunzel had waited nervously, not wanting Mother to know what she was doing. Miraculously, Mother was visiting the privy when the young monk came back.

"We need someone to help clean the rooms where the female travelers stay," he said, "and the abbot prefers it be a woman. If you can come every two days and clean and perform a few other chores, I will teach you."

"Oh, thank you, Brother . . . ?"

He bowed. "Brother Andrew."

Now if Mother would make a trip into town tomorrow to buy what they needed or to try to find midwifery business, Rapunzel would walk back to the monastery, which was even closer than the town of Hagenheim to their little home, and perhaps have her first reading lesson.

Chapter Seven

Gerek was now in a slightly larger room, closer to the chapel where the monks prayed five times a day. He lay listening to the monotone chants, prayers, plainsong hymns, and repeated scriptures.

Only his third day and already he was sick of reading. Now he was awkwardly polishing his sword with one hand, making the best use of the fingers of his left hand that peeked out of the splint on his broken arm.

He sighed in frustration but kept working.

A knock came at the door.

"Come in."

Andrew stuck his head in. "Do you need anything?"

"A new leg and a new arm. That is what I need."

Andrew nodded. "Speak to God. Perhaps . . ." He raised his eyebrows and shrugged.

Gerek growled. Why would God give him a new arm and leg, or even miraculously heal his old ones? They would likely be healed on their own in six weeks. "God must have more important things to attend to." Besides, God probably wanted to teach him patience.

"While you wait for your miracle," Brother Andrew went on cheerfully, "I have a task for you, to keep you from becoming too dull and frustrated."

A task? When his friend didn't elaborate, Gerek asked, "What could I possibly do with two broken limbs?"

"Something that will be easy for a man of your learning. How many languages do you know?"

"Four."

"Well, I only need you to teach someone to read their native German. That will not be difficult for you, and it's something you can do while lying down—or sitting with your leg propped up."

"Who is to be my student?" Gerek eyed Andrew, who was fidgeting and not meeting his eye. He had a feeling he wouldn't like Andrew's answer.

"Someone very eager to learn, I assure you. In exchange for working here at the monastery—and we do very much need her to clean the rooms where the female visitors stay—she wishes to be taught to read."

"She? You wish me to teach a woman?"

"She is not just any woman, she is the very woman to whom you owe your life."

"My mother is dead, Andrew." Gerek infused his voice with the growling tone that made most squires' eyes round with fear and sent maidservants skittering for cover.

"I was not speaking of your mother, Sir Gerek. I was speaking of the young woman who saved you from the prisoner who escaped and nearly carved out your heart with your own dagger two or three days past."

Gerek stared at him and expelled a loud burst of air. "No. I won't do it."

"Why? It is the perfect way to repay her for saving you."

"As far as I am concerned, she was repaying *me* for saving *her*. No. I emphatically refuse."

"But why?"

Gerek blew out another noisy breath, hesitating. "Have you seen the girl, Andrew?"

"Yes."

"Then you have seen how . . . fair she is."

"She is very comely, it is true."

"Do you not see the problem?"

Andrew shrugged and shook his head.

"What sort of monastery is this?" Gerek sat up straighter, and his sword that he had been polishing slipped with a loud clatter onto the stone floor. "Why don't you teach her?"

"I must keep my vow of chastity. Being alone with a beautiful young maiden would not suit our abbot, nor be conducive to my vow."

"Andrew, I do not wish to succumb to temptation any more than you do. I have taken a vow of chastity as well, a vow never to know a woman before marriage, and I have promised *myself* that I will never marry a peasant girl. I shall marry an heiress or widow with a large estate, or marry into a noble family who can make my fortune. So, because of this, I have no less claim to the vow than you do."

"I could argue that, and I believe my brother monks would agree with me, brother knight." Brother Andrew failed at hiding his grin. "You need only leave your door open when she is here. The brothers passing by your room will keep you from breaking your vow with the maiden."

"I happen to know her mother would not approve of her learning to read from me, and I do not want to teach her!"

He chuckled and shook his head. "You always were overly excitable."

Andrew's words struck him like an accusation. His first inclination was to defend himself and demand why Andrew would say such a thing. But instead, he studied his friend's face. Andrew couldn't know about Gerek's father. Gerek had never told any of the other knights. He tried to push back the memories that were invading his thoughts and making his face and neck feel hot and prickly. Was he his father's son?

"You have nothing else to do," Andrew explained calmly, "but if you are so adamant about not teaching her, I suppose I could find an older monk to do so."

Before he could stop himself, Gerek asked, "Which older monk?" In his experience, a monk's age did not necessarily end his lasciviousness.

"Oh, any monk over the age of thirty should do."

Gerek sputtered, then cleared his throat.

"You are not afraid," Andrew said, "that the maiden will try to seduce you, are you?"

"Are you afraid she will try to seduce you?"

Andrew shrugged. "I am much more handsome than you."

Gerek glared at him.

"And since you have too much self-control to seduce *her*, I believe you are the safest person to teach her."

Gerek growled. Why did his life have to be so frustrating? Was God preparing him for some huge, sacrificial quest? "I suppose I can make an attempt at teaching her. But if for any reason it seems a bad idea, I will end it."

"Of course. But do not worry. Your vow of chastity should remain safe." Andrew hid his mouth behind his hand.

Andrew was laughing at him. Gerek wanted to tell his old friend that he was not treating him nobly, as befitted a knight who was nearly killed trying to protect the people of the Hagenheim region from brigands and thieves. But Andrew might tell him he was being excitable again.

He did not want to teach the maiden to read, but she might give up after a lesson or two, thinking it was too hard. Or her strange mother would force her to cease them. He couldn't imagine her mother would approve of Rapunzel learning to read, especially from him, since she seemed to have a special dislike of him from the moment she saw him.

Brother Andrew soon left and returned a few minutes later with Rapunzel. Her hair was completely hidden by an opaque wimple, but her cheeks were pink and she was smiling. However, when she saw Gerek, the smile faded.

"Rapunzel, I believe you know Sir Gerek van Hollan, a noble knight of Hagenheim. He has agreed to teach you to read, so I will leave you two to your studies." Andrew ducked out of the room before either of them could say anything.

The coward.

Chapter Eight

Rapunzel stared at him, her mouth open. She had expected to see an older monk, or perhaps a bedridden invalid, but to find Sir Gerek here . . . "Brother Andrew is forcing you to teach me, isn't he?"

He looked up at her through his eyelashes as he lay on the low bed. "I don't mind telling you . . . yes, he is forcing me to teach you."

Rapunzel crossed her arms. She wanted to tell him she'd rather not learn to read than to be taught by someone who did not wish to teach her. She imagined herself leaving the room and slamming the door. But if she did that, she might be giving up her one chance to learn to read.

Closing her eyes, she reminded herself that Mother would only be gone a few hours and Rapunzel had already spent at least two hours cleaning the monastery rooms.

"I can only stay an hour, so let us get this lesson started."

"Why can you only stay an hour?" he asked. "Is it because your mother doesn't know you're here?" He raised his brows at her.

Was he trying to make her feel bad? To make her go back home?

"Yes, if you must know, but I am not leaving. I will stay right here for an hour."

He made a grunting sound, then turned, leaning over the side of the narrow cot, and picked up a large book.

Rapunzel was breathing hard. She focused on his splinted leg, which was stretched out on the low bed, and his splinted arm, bent at the elbow and lying across his stomach. Looking at them helped her feel a bit of pity for him, and her breathing gradually returned to normal.

"Since I saved your life from that brigand who was about to slit your throat"—she lifted her head an inch or two higher—"I would think you would want to teach me, to repay me."

When she deigned to glance down at him, he was glaring up at her from half-closed eyes.

"If I had not first saved you from said brigand, you would not have needed to save me from him."

She put her hands on her hips. "Why can't you just be grateful and stop being arrogant?"

"I am a knight in Duke Wilhelm's service. I am not accustomed to being bullied by a novice monk and a peasant girl."

"You are insufferable!"

"Why can't *you* just be grateful," he shot back, "and . . . be quiet."

"Be quiet? Oh, yes, I'm sure that's what you think all women should do. You probably think a clout or two to the head once or thrice a day would do them good too." She tried to calm down, to take slower breaths. Did she sound like an imbecile, arguing with a knight over who should be the most grateful? But when she looked back down at him, he had turned a shade paler.

"No." The arrogant look was completely gone from his face. He stared down at the book in his lap, away from her, and spoke softly. "That is not what I think. I do *not* think women should be struck. Ever."

Why had her words created such a reaction? She waited to see what he would say next, to give a clue as to why his demeanor had changed so.

"Won't you bring that stool over here so we can begin?"

Rapunzel stared. He looked earnest, actually meek, so she complied.

Sir Gerek stared down at the book and frowned. "Do you know how to read any words at all?"

"No," she admitted. "I don't know any words."

"This is a copy of the Holy Writ that I commissioned—"

"What? You have a copy of the Holy Writ? How did you get it? I've never seen one before."

Now that she was sitting and they were at the same level, he stared into her eyes.

"As I was saying," his voice was quiet, and he spoke slowly, "it is a copy of the Holy Writ that I commissioned from the monks at this same monastery." He opened the book.

"You are not going to teach me to read using the Bible, are you?" Rapunzel leaned away from the large tome. "A priest once told me that people who have not said their vows or been consecrated to God should not interpret the Bible for themselves. I do not want to be excommunicated."

Gerek frowned. "You will not be excommunicated."

"How do you know? A woman in Heidelberg was ordered beaten by the bishop, and she only saw a vision and said she heard the voice of God. If I were to read God's words . . ."

Sir Gerek sighed very loudly. "Listen. You are not considered a heretic just for reading the Bible. I have been reading it for years and—"

"But you are a man! A knight noble born. I am a woman, and a peasant woman at that. Will you swear an oath that you will not tell anyone I read the Holy Writ?"

"I don't even know if you will learn to read it. Now stop with your ignorant fears and let me begin before you have to go."

Rapunzel's cheeks burned at his calling her fears "ignorant." She pressed her lips together and watched him turn the pages.

He pointed to the open page. "See this? It's the first missive to Timotheus written by the apostle Paul. See this word? It says

'Timotheus.' The first letter is *tay*." He pointed with his large forefinger at a mark on the page. "And there is another *tay* there."

"But that doesn't look like the other *tay* you pointed to."

"That was a *tay* at the beginning of someone's name. These *tays* are not at the beginning of a sentence and are not names or nouns, and therefore they are small *tays* and not big *tays*."

Rapunzel fought to understand the seemingly random thing he was telling her. Why would you call something a *tay* and something else a *tay* when they looked completely different? Perhaps he was lying to her, trying to confuse her. But she had little choice but to trust him.

"Each letter makes a sound," he continued. "This letter *tay* sounds the same as these other *tays*. All *tays* make the same sound."

"Oh. You said this word is 'Timotheus' and this is a book in the Bible?"

"Yes. Now this word is—"

"Is this written in German? I thought the Bible was only written in Latin."

"Yes, but occasionally you can find someone who will translate it into German for you."

She wouldn't tell him, but she was impressed that he would spend his money on Scripture books and then carry them around with him.

"This is not the entire Bible. It is only the parts that were written after Jesus came. I do not have the Old Testament writings in German, except for what is in my Psalter."

"Is the Bible very expensive?" she asked.

"Yes, and when I have a home of my own, I shall commission a copy of the entire Bible, all the holy writings."

"But even this much must have been very costly. The illuminations are very bright and color—"

"Yes, now pay attention. This word is "Pavel." See? It is the first word of the first verse in the first missive to Timotheus."

"What sound does this letter make?" Rapunzel pointed to the second letter in the word *Timotheus*.

He sighed, then made the sound. He pointed to each letter and made the sound, which might have made her laugh, hearing him saying, *"Tuh, ee, mm, oh, tuh, ee, oo, ss,"* if she had not been afraid of offending him. Then he went back to the beginning of the word and made the sound of each letter, but a bit faster than before.

"So I only have to remember what sound each letter makes and I will be able to read?"

He shrugged and nodded.

She wanted to ask him more questions but forced herself to tuck them away for later.

"The first three words are: 'Pavel, an apostle.'"

"Will you teach me the letters?"

"Yes, of course. But I will need something to write on and a writing instrument. I can get those from Brother Andrew. Do you think you can find him?"

Rapunzel jumped up and hurried out. When she found Brother Andrew in the large garden behind the dormitory, he was hoeing around some young plants. He agreed to find the implements they needed, and Rapunzel went back to Sir Gerek's room. She opened the door without knocking, and he gave her a piercing stare. "Do not enter this chamber until you have knocked and have been invited to come in."

"I was just here, and you knew I was returning, so I didn't think it necessary—"

"Do not do it again. You must not be careless around men. It is very unwise."

Rapunzel huffed. "If there is one thing I am not," she said, trying to infuse her voice with cold dignity, "it is careless around men."

He narrowed his eyes, his brows lowering to create a crease

across his forehead. "Very well." He continued speaking about the first verse of the missive to Timotheus, but Rapunzel could not understand what he was saying—something about words being put together to form ideas and different words having different meanings, depending on what order they were in or what the words around that word meant. It all sounded like gibberish.

"I think you've made my brain hurt." Rapunzel rubbed her temple.

"If you don't want to continue, I understand. It will only get more difficult."

"I will not give up and I *will* learn to read. That is, *if* you are a good enough teacher."

He gave her that narrow-eyed look again.

Just then, Brother Andrew came in the door—without knocking or announcing himself—and said, "I brought you a slate and some chalk rock. I can probably get someone to make a wax board for you, if you'd rather have that."

Rapunzel took the small slate, which was about as big as her two hands, and the chalk from Brother Andrew. "Thank you very much."

"And I can bring you a bit of parchment and a quill, but the abbot is not very free with parchment. It's rather expensive."

"I have a bit in my supplies," Sir Gerek said. "I need it so that she can have a permanent copy of the alphabet to memorize."

After Brother Andrew left, Gerek asked her, "What makes you want to learn to read so badly? Most people never learn."

"Do you mean most people of my peasant class? Or most women?"

He shrugged. "It is only a question. Why do you want to learn? What use will it be to you?"

He was probably thinking she could have little need for reading. She would probably never even be able to afford a book. "I have a use for it." But since she had already confessed to him that she liked to make up songs . . . "I wish to write down the words of my songs."

"Only the words? There is a way to write music as well as words. Did you not know?"

"I did not know." The blood was rising to her cheeks at how ignorant he must think her, but she was glad to know this. Once she learned to read and write, she would also want to learn to read and write music. She had always wanted to learn to play an instrument, but that had seemed an even less likely dream than learning to read.

The door was darkened again and Brother Andrew stood there, holding out a small square of parchment. "This is a list of the letters in the German language. You may have it if you wish." And then he was gone again.

Rapunzel stared down at it. She did not know what any of the letters were, except for the *T*.

"I will tell you the sound each letter makes. You will have to memorize them all before you can begin to read."

"I can do that. I am very good at memorizing."

He told her very quickly what each letter sounded like. When he asked her to tell which ones she remembered, she got almost all of them correct.

"Very good." His smug look had disappeared.

He held up the Bible text and asked her to sound out the first few words.

"I already know that the first three words are 'Pavel, an apostle' because you told me that." She stared at the words, sounding out each letter. "*Puh. Ah. Vuh. Eh. Ll.* Pavel. I did it! I see how it works now." Rapunzel did the same with the next two words and was able to sound them out and see how the letters made the words. Then she tried the fourth word. Sir Gerek had to help her with that one since she had already forgotten some of the letters' sounds. Finally, she sounded it out. "*Uh. Vuh. Of. Yuh. Eh. Ss. Oo. Ss.* 'Jesus.' I did it. 'Pavel, an apostle of Jesus!'"

"Keep reading."

With help from Sir Gerek, Rapunzel read the next word and the next. Finally, she had read the entire first sentence. "'Pavel, an apostle of Jesus Christ by the command of God our Savior and of Christ Jesus our hope, To Timotheus my true son in the faith: Grace, mercy, and peace from God the Father and Christ Jesus our Lord.'"

"What does it mean?"

"It's a greeting, from a letter. Pavel is greeting his friend Timotheus."

"Oh. I've never had a letter. Is this how people greet someone in a letter, by telling their name?"

"Usually they greet the person they are writing first, and then at the end they write their own name. I suppose letters were written differently in those days, with the writer introducing himself first."

How exciting! If she received a letter, she might actually be able to read it. Of course, who would write one to her? Her mother had never learned to read. But now that she could read, *what* would she read? She had no books, nothing with words written on it. She would worry about that later.

"Oh." How long had she been sitting with Sir Gerek? Rapunzel jumped up, knocking over the stool. "I mustn't be late. Mother might not let me come back." She put the stool back where she had gotten it. "Fare well, Sir Gerek!" she called and ran out the door.

Chapter Nine

Mother brought back some bread, some oats for the pottage, and a few other things they needed. She had also found some pregnant women who might be interested in her services.

"Did you find the person you were looking for?" Rapunzel asked her. "The one who was coming back from England?"

Mother concentrated on putting the leftover oats away. "No, he is not in Hagenheim yet. What have you been doing while I was gone, Rapunzel? I thought you were going to paint some of your pretty flowers and vines and birds on the walls today?"

"I suppose I was . . . thinking of other things." Rapunzel hated deceiving Mother, but it seemed the only way she would be able to take reading lessons.

"Making up a new song?" She patted Rapunzel's cheek. "I don't know how you think of them."

Rapunzel shrugged and smiled. "I don't know either."

Together they made a plum pie and some fried pork. "Meat is as plentiful as ever in Hagenheim," Mother said. "The butchers sell everything here—pork, goose, pheasant, chicken, and even some beef. Are you pleased we came here, Rapunzel?"

"Yes, of course, Mother. Are you pleased?"

"Not missing your old friends in Ottelfelt, are you?"

"No." Rapunzel sighed. "I don't think I was ever friends with anyone the way other people are. Most of the other girls my age thought my paintings and songs were strange. They thought *I* was strange."

"They were just jealous. Forget about them."

That was Mother's solution to everything—to forget about it. Perhaps it was better to put out of her mind anything that bothered her, but she was more likely to brood about it, to consider how she could make it better, how she could change it, or how it might affect her in the future. She kept thinking that if the villagers had thought she was strange—and they often spoke of how strange they thought Mother was—then wouldn't the people of Hagenheim think them both strange as well? Not that she cared what most people thought, but it would be nice to have at least one friend, someone to talk to and confide in.

Her mother would just say, "You have me. Why do you need friends?" But she didn't always want to tell her mother everything. At the moment, she had to keep her reading lessons a secret. If Mother found out she was seeing Sir Gerek, spending time alone with him . . . it was too terrible to contemplate, after all the times her mother had warned her of what men would do to her if she was ever alone with them. It would not matter that Sir Gerek had one broken arm and one broken leg. He still would not seem safe to Mother.

Mother just didn't understand what it was like to be young and to want to do things, to learn things, to meet new people. Mother was content to speak only with Rapunzel, to be always with her.

What if she never did make a close friend? Was she destined to be alone with her mother until one of them died? To never marry or have children?

At least she had her reading lessons. Learning to read felt like the greatest thing that had ever happened to her. It *was* the greatest thing that had ever happened. Now she could write down her songs on paper and keep them forever. Learning to read would prove that she was just as worthy as any lord's son or daughter. She could prove she was just as significant, just as intelligent, just as worthy of love and acceptance as anyone else.

Besides, who knew what learning to read could lead to? She might even get some kind of occupation in town with her new skill.

How strange that it was Sir Gerek who was teaching her—against his will, she ought to remember. She really owed more gratitude to Brother Andrew for giving her a job cleaning at the monastery and for forcing Sir Gerek to teach her. And why shouldn't he? He should want to help her since she saved his life from that evil brigand. She sighed.

"Rapunzel? Didn't you hear me? I said the pottage is burning. Take it off the fire."

"Sorry, Mother. I must have been thinking."

"You think too much, my dear. Thinking only makes one sad."

"Not if one is thinking joyous thoughts."

"What joyous thoughts are you thinking?" Mother gave her an intense stare.

Rapunzel shrugged. "Me? I'm only thinking . . . about Hagenheim. Perhaps I will get my first glimpse of it soon. I've never seen a walled city before."

"I shall take you tomorrow if you like."

"Oh, I'm in no hurry. Now that we live here, I can see it anytime."

Mother gave her a suspicious glance before continuing to slice the bread for their meal. "I hope you are not thinking about that boorish knight we met on the road to Hagenheim."

"I wouldn't call him boorish." He was a little rude and arrogant, but after all, he was a noble knight. She supposed he had a reason to be arrogant. "No, of course I'm not thinking of him, Mother. But he did save us from those robbers."

"And then you saved him from his own prisoner who was about to kill him. If he hadn't been so careless as to let his prisoner get loose and steal his own knife, you wouldn't have had to save him."

"He wasn't careless. It was not his fault his horse fell on him."

"I say it was. He should have better control over his horse or get a new one."

It was impossible to win an argument with Mother, so Rapunzel said nothing more.

Later, while they ate their meal of pottage and bread and plum pie, Rapunzel asked, "Have you seen any of your old friends since we came back? Any people you know? You must know a lot of people since you grew up here."

"There is no one here I care to speak to."

"Do you have any relatives—cousins or aunts or anything?"

"Your great-grandmother did not like any of her living relatives, so we never saw them. 'They are all cruel and deceitful,' Grandmother would say. She said they would only hurt us, so we stayed away. I never met any of them." She smiled. "I'm sure it was for the best."

"Perhaps, but sometimes I wish we had some family, people we could talk to." *People I belong with. People who would love me.*

"You mustn't be discontent, my darling." Mother's face and eyes were cold. "You have everything you need. At least you aren't an orphan, without a mother to take care of you."

It was at the forefront of Rapunzel's thoughts to say that she was nineteen years old. She was too old to need a mother to care for her. But she knew from experience how angry that would make Mother.

"Tomorrow I will be going to Hagenheim to speak to more people about my midwifery skills. You may come with me if you wish."

"Thank you, Mother. I may. Or I may stay home and work on a new song."

"As you wish, darling."

At least Rapunzel had her next reading lesson to look forward to. The thought of unlocking the secrets of an entire book made her giddy and light-headed. She didn't want her mother to see. "I'm going outside for a few minutes."

"Very well, darling, but don't stay out after dark."

"Yes, Mother."

The next day Rapunzel hurried through the thickly wooded area and a small sheep pasture to the monastery that lay beyond. She had the small piece of parchment in her pocket with all the letters written on it. It was her most prized possession. She patted her pocket as she made her way toward the pale stone walls of the monastery buildings. She could see the garden, half hidden from view, and someone bending over, working in the soil.

When she reached Sir Gerek's door, she remembered his command that she knock and wait to be invited in. She huffed but knocked, then waited. After all, she had no desire to see Sir Gerek in any state of undress.

"Come in."

Rapunzel opened the wooden door. Sir Gerek was sitting up, a book across his lap. His arm was still bundled awkwardly and resting by his side and his leg equally big and awkward in its splint.

He looked up at her with a half scowl. "Back so soon? I would not have thought your mother would allow it."

Rapunzel bit her lip to keep from retorting something she might regret. Why did he have to spoil her mood? "Yes, I am back. But I need you to refresh my memory of some of these letters, please." She sat primly on the stool beside him and held out the list of letters.

They went over the letters two more times, until Rapunzel was certain she would not forget them again. Then Sir Gerek turned back to the passage they had been reading the day before. He allowed her to sound out some more words, and this time she read several sentences aloud.

"I would like to read the New Testament and the Old Testament."

"You'll have to learn Latin. The portions of the Old Testament that I own are in Latin."

The smug look on his face made her long to say something that would erase it. "You'll just have to teach me, then."

That did it.

"I was only asked to teach you to read German, not Latin." The scowl on his face did not frighten her, but why was he always so grumpy?

"Very well, we shan't discuss it now." She might as well not argue with him. She could take up the Latin cause later.

She went back to reading the text in the enormous book, which was so large it lay across both their laps so they each could see the words.

Her reading sounded halting and broken and slow, and she sometimes had to reread passages to understand the meaning. But she kept going and finally came to this passage: "'I urge, then, first of all, that petitions, prayers, intercession and thanksgiving be made for all people—for kings and all those in authority, that we may live peaceful and quiet lives in all godliness and holiness. This is good, and pleases God our Savior, who wants all people to be saved and to come to a knowledge of the truth.'"

What a freeing thought—that, perhaps, she didn't have to do great exploits for God, didn't have go on long, painful pilgrimages or suffer in some way.

"Is that all we have to do to please God? Only to pray for all people and to live a peaceful life in godliness and holiness?"

Sir Gerek quirked one brow up. "Jesus said the greatest

commandment is to love God with all your heart, and the second greatest is to love your neighbor as yourself."

Rapunzel had heard a traveling friar teach that several years before. She eyed Sir Gerek from a new angle. Perhaps, behind his arrogance, he was not so terrible. He was only a man, after all, and she should not expect him to be perfect in temperament as well as principles. Though he had seemed perfect, in a physical sense, the first time she saw him—strong in body, handsome of face, and mighty in a fight—his arm and leg had been broken by a simple accident on horseback. Now he lay fairly helpless on the bed, barely able to stand on his own.

But he was rude, arrogant, and grumpy. Why should she overlook those things? Perhaps because of what Pavel said, she should pray for Sir Gerek.

She still didn't like Sir Gerek very much, but she did need him to teach her to read and to allow her to read his books since she had none of her own. Perhaps he needed her too.

"Does anyone besides me come to talk to you every day? I would think you would be grateful for the opportunity to teach me, to break the monotony of your routine."

"Read on, if you please," he said with a frown.

"You are going to give yourself wrinkles with all that frowning. You're only, what, twenty-five?"

"Twenty-four."

"And are you now growing a beard?" The stubble on his chin, jaw, and above his lip had grown quite thick since she first saw him.

"I think I will. It makes me rather more intimidating, don't you think?" He rubbed his whiskered jaw.

"Frightening, you mean? Yes, rather like a bear or a wolf."

His expression, lowered brows and curling lip, caused a laugh to bubble up in her throat. Rapunzel covered her mouth with her hand.

"I'll have you know, when I traveled with Duke Wilhelm's eldest son, Valten, to all the best tournaments, ladies often told me how handsome I was."

"Women are notoriously poor judges of character." She wasn't sure why she said that, except that she wanted to aggravate him.

"What does character have to do with being handsome?"

"Exactly."

He eyed her askance, out of the corner of his eye, then took a slow breath. "Are you going to read, or are we going to keep talking until your mother gets home?"

Rapunzel cleared her throat and kept reading. The second and third chapters were short, and it ended with what seemed like verses from a song:

> *"'He appeared in the flesh,*
> *was vindicated by the Spirit,*
> *was seen by angels,*
> *was preached among the nations,*
> *was believed on in the world,*
> *was taken up in glory.'"*

She especially liked that part. Perhaps she might memorize it or think of some tune to go along with it.

"Tired of reading?"

"Just a moment." She read it through again in a whisper this time. Then she turned and looked at the first chapter again.

"What is this 'law' he keeps talking about?"

"The Jewish law, of course."

Rapunzel raised her brows at him.

"The rules that the Jewish people followed, the law of Moses, keeping the Sabbath day holy, tithing all of their crops, all those sorts of laws."

"Oh." She remembered a question she had had for a long time now. "A friar once came to my village, and he said that we are all equal because we are Christians. You are a noble-born knight, I am a peasant, and Andrew is a monk, but we are all the same to God. Is this true? Is that what the Bible says?"

Sir Gerek scowled. "Are you sure you are not staying too long again?"

"Very well." She closed the book and pushed it onto his lap. "Is there anything you need before I go?"

"No, thank you."

She nodded primly. Just as she reached the door, she glanced back at him. "But I shall return very soon."

Chapter Ten

Rapunzel accompanied her mother the next day to Hagenheim. Her mother was beginning to seem suspicious of why she was not eager to see the largest town Rapunzel had ever been near. So she and Mother set out for the town market.

As they approached the town gate, Rapunzel stared up in awe at the brick wall around the town. People were coming and going through the opening, which was guarded by two men. The guards were dressed similarly to Sir Gerek, each with a sword on his hip, but were not nearly as handsome.

Rapunzel followed her mother, who ignored the guards and walked through. Rapunzel glanced at the one nearest her. He pinned her with a severe look. His expression was even more frightening than Sir Gerek's scowl. She expected him to grab her by the arm and order her to stay out of Hagenheim since such a rustic peasant girl, as poor and unsophisticated as she, did not belong in a grand town like Hagenheim. But he said nothing, and she walked on through.

Rapunzel was wearing her brown wool kirtle, which laced up to her neck. She wore the outer sleeves, which were tied on with leather laces, over the white sleeves of her underdress. She had never thought about it before, but her clothes must look rather drab and ugly compared to most of the other dresses around her.

She shrank as far into her head-covering shawl as she could.

She peeked out of the sides but tried not to draw attention to herself. Everyone on the streets of Hagenheim appeared as different from the villagers she had grown up amongst as if they were from another world. Their clothing was made of the brightest and prettiest of colors—and that was only the men! The women wore fabrics of more variety than she had ever seen. Some looked soft and shimmery, like the smooth surface of a lake, and some of the veils were light and airy as a cloud and hardly covered their hair at all. One woman wore peacock feathers in her headdress, so elaborate it must have cost a year's wages.

Most of the women her age only partially covered their hair, or they left it entirely bare. She drew in her breath to see one, and then another and another, grownup maidens wearing their hair loose and uncovered or braided to keep it out of their eyes. She saw shoes that were wondrously strange, that curled up at the toe.

Suddenly, she realized she had lost Mother. She searched through the crowded street for her mother's familiar back and finally spotted her. She ran, losing sight of her again as more people passed between them, but finally caught up. She touched her mother's sleeve and held on to it as she allowed herself to take in the fine buildings surrounding her.

Such tall buildings, with windows on each of the three or four levels, and the upper floors jutting out over the lower ones, over the very street. What would it be like to live in such a sturdy looking house, with so many windows and so many floors? They also had chimneys. The hovel she shared with Mother only had a pit in the middle of the floor for the fire and a hole at the top of the roof for the smoke to go through. Having a place in the wall for the fire and a chimney going up through the roof worked much better, she had been told, for helping the smoke go out instead of circulating through the house and making everything black and smelly.

Everywhere she looked was a new, interesting sight. Some of the buildings had carvings in the wood timbers, of faces or animals, or even words and numbers. Other buildings were made of half timbers, but instead of plaster or wattle and daub, they were surrounded by red bricks and mortar in interesting, angled designs. They towered even higher than the other buildings.

A lady riding sidesaddle on a white horse passed by. She kept her eyes focused ahead. On the back of her head was a tiny gold caul with all her hair stuffed inside—she must have had very thin hair—but with its mesh design, did nothing to actually cover her hair.

Rapunzel suddenly bumped into someone. "Oh, excuse me. I was not looking—"

The young woman backed away from her, lifted her nose in the air, and twisted her perfect, plump lips into a look of repulsion as she stared at Rapunzel.

On the lady's head was a gold circlet trimmed with a white veil that was so thin and delicate, she could see the girl's lustrous blond curls underneath it, not to mention that several long wavy curls hung outside the veil and across her shoulders. Her bright-red dress was trimmed in fur at the neckline, sleeves, and hem. She was beautiful and looked to be about the same age as Rapunzel.

"You oafish girl," she said, looking down. "I hope you did not soil my slippers." She shook her hand at Rapunzel, as if to shoo her away.

Another woman, dressed much less showy, pulled on her arm. "Come, Rainhilda. The horses are ready."

The woman, Rainhilda, deigned to give one more backward glance. "Ignorant peasant girl. Must be from the village." She didn't even lower her voice. "Look at her dress! And her hair—or lack thereof." She snickered behind her hand and the woman beside her turned to stare, as did several others nearby.

Rapunzel rushed away, her face burning and her stomach

churning. Of course, anyone could see by Rapunzel's clothing and her wide-eyed stares that she was poor and had never been outside her rustic village.

"That is Rainhilda," Mother pointed out, drawing Rapunzel to her side.

"Did you hear what she said?"

"No, I was talking to those women over there. Did she say something to you?"

"No." Rapunzel kept her head down, still feeling the sting. "Is she one of Duke Wilhelm's daughters?"

"No, but she is as proud and haughty as if she were. Her father is only a knight, but he is very rich and has no sons. Rainhilda has an enormous dowry."

"She isn't married, then?"

"No. She wanted to marry Duke Wilhelm's oldest son, Valten, but he ended up marrying the orphaned daughter of one of the duke's former knights. Everyone was surprised, but she is beautiful beyond compare and is pregnant with his first child." Her mother's lip curled, as if she did not like him. Though she couldn't possibly know him.

Rapunzel listened in rapt attention, glad the duke's son had not married the haughty Rainhilda. Perhaps the woman should marry Sir Gerek. But even Sir Gerek didn't deserve someone as unkind as Rainhilda. Rapunzel's cheeks were still stinging from the insults.

Mother could always find out the gossip of a new village within the first few days after arriving.

Mother walked a bit faster. "We are near the Marktplatz, so be looking out for pregnant women."

Fortunately, Mother didn't force Rapunzel to assist with the births she attended, as Mother's grandmother had forced her to do when she was a child. Sometimes Rapunzel did come along, if Mother thought it was to be a long labor, and she would bathe the laboring mother's face or run and fetch things. But being at the birth of a baby made her weak in the knees and light-headed. The smells and the moans made her want to run far away. Sometimes she would take the older children and play with them outside, to distract them—and herself—from the suffering. But mostly Mother allowed Rapunzel to stay home when she went to conduct her midwife duties.

Soon Mother, with her keen eyesight, saw not one but two women great with child, and she approached them and began speaking with them about their babies. Was this their first child? How had the births of the previous children gone? Were they looking for a midwife? Mother would allow them to pay with whatever they had if they would allow her to help birth their babies and tell their friends about her.

The conversation was a long one, as women seemed to love telling the details of their previous labors. So Rapunzel continued to look around at all the different styles of clothing.

There were almost as many styles of headdress as there were women, and the men's clothing was just as varied. No one wore the plain browns and grays that everyone wore in the villages. How plain Rapunzel must have looked to Sir Gerek, in her brown and green and gray kirtles, he who was accustomed to seeing beautiful clothing on the young maidens of Hagenheim.

How would Rapunzel manage to get these kinds of beautiful, colorful clothes? She was working at the monastery, but they were not paying her. What could she do to earn money? Perhaps she could find some other kind of job in Hagenheim.

Who might want to hire her? There were shops all around. Some sold candles, some sold cloth and other goods, some sold meat, and who knew what else. She doubted she could get hired in a shop wearing the rustic woolen kirtles she owned. Perhaps she could get a job cleaning.

When Mother was finished talking with the two pregnant women, they moved on to the Marktplatz. Today was a market day, so the open space, which was paved with cobblestones, was crowded with sellers and buyers and goods of all kinds. But what caught Rapunzel's eye was the magnificent castle just beyond.

Five towers, four of them round and the middle one square, loomed over the three-, four-, and five-story buildings surrounding the Marktplatz. The gray stone of Hagenheim Castle, which her mother had told her of, seemed to gleam in the morning sunlight, with a spot of color in the window of what must have been the stained glass in the castle chapel. What wonders lay inside those magnificent stone walls?

Perhaps she could get a job cleaning the castle. She could be a maidservant! Surely they would not mind her rustic clothing and would allow her to clean or fetch or start fires in the many rooms.

"What is the matter with you?" Mother said. "I walked away and lost you. You look moonstruck." Mother looked over her shoulder at what Rapunzel had been gazing at. "Enchanted by your first glimpse of a castle? Humph. It's only stone and mortar. Don't be so impressed. Those who live in castles are no better than anyone else, no matter what they think."

Rapunzel tore her eyes away from the castle and stayed close to Mother as she wove in and out among all the people. Of all the goods that the vendors were selling, the things she most longed for were the bolts of colored fabric. What would it be like to dress every day in red or pink or blue or purple? How would it feel to be unafraid to wear her hair free and flowing over her shoulders?

Mother found some more women to talk to about childbearing, and Rapunzel stood nearby, absentmindedly rubbing the scar on her palm with her thumb.

Standing at the east end of the Marktplatz, few people traveled in and out of the castle gate. As she watched a guard speaking to someone, she felt a prickling at the back of her neck, as if someone was watching her. She glanced to her right and immediately saw the man who had attacked her and her mother, the one with the strange smile. He stood staring at her.

A rush of air stuck in her throat.

Rapunzel turned and grabbed Mother's arm. "Mother, it's him! That man!"

Mother seemed reluctant to be interrupted, but turned and frowned at Rapunzel. "What? What is it?"

"It's the man who nearly killed Sir Gerek and tried to rob us! The smiling one. He was over by the fountain in the middle of the Marktplatz." She turned her head one way, then another, but didn't see him. Would he try to follow them home? Would he come and kill them tonight in their beds? A shudder went across her shoulders.

But Mother had already turned back to resume her conversation with the women. Rapunzel searched the crowd for him, but he seemed to have vanished.

What could she do? Who could she tell? Sir Gerek would certainly be interested. Perhaps he could send word to someone who could help them find the man and imprison him in Duke Wilhelm's dungeon.

When Mother finally finished her conversation, she said, "Do you see him now?"

Rapunzel shook her head. How could her mother be so calm? She was so much braver than Rapunzel. They continued walking among the vendors in the Marktplatz, her mother talking with women she saw along the way. Rapunzel became enamored again with looking at all the pretty things and forgot about her sighting of the brigand until they were leaving.

Rapunzel kept looking over her shoulder for the man. They

passed through the town gate and headed into the trees toward their own little house in the woods.

"Mother, do you think he is following us?"

"If he does, we will surprise him with another knife, and this time you might find his heart, hmm?"

Rapunzel stared at her mother. She appeared perfectly calm. "I-I don't want to stab him in the heart, Mother. I'd prefer he be caught and we not have to face him again."

"Of course, I would prefer the same, but if he does come looking for us, I know you have the skill to kill him this time, instead of just wounding him. Yes?"

"I suppose so." She didn't enjoy the thought, but yes, if the man came to their home, if he tried to hurt her or her mother, she supposed she could kill him. *But for pity's sake, O Father God in heaven, don't let it come to that.*

Chapter Eleven

It was late afternoon, and Gerek figured Rapunzel probably wasn't coming for her reading lesson. Not that he minded, but her presence did keep him from feeling as if the day was taking forever to end, and from wondering if he would be able to last five more weeks without going mad.

He had the time and the resources to study—Brother Andrew had brought him several books to read, some in French and Latin. But he wanted to be *doing* something. He was unused to lying in bed day after day. Brother Andrew had also brought him some things to copy, but they were dull letters and documents, and the work was tedious.

A knock sounded on the door. "Come in," he called, relieved to have someone to talk to.

The door opened and Rapunzel stood, breathing hard. She came inside but left the door open.

He scowled to mask how pleased he was to see her. "Were you running?"

She nodded, then swallowed, catching her breath. Some strands of hair had worked loose from the close-fitting head covering and lay haphazardly over her shoulders. Her golden-blond hair contrasted with her brown brows and lashes, bringing out the blue of her eyes. His heartbeat grew fast.

He must be addled from lying around too much. He shouldn't be noticing her hair color or how beautiful her eyes were.

"I saw the man, the one who attacked my mother and me."

He sat up straighter. "Where?"

"He was in the Marktplatz in Hagenheim. He was standing by the fountain, and he saw me too."

He pushed himself up to stand, then hit his fist against the bed. If only he did not have this broken leg! He would go after the man at this very moment. He would scour Hagenheim until he found him.

"I sent a message to my fellow knights in Hagenheim to be watching for him, but I shall send them another note to say he is in Hagenheim." Little good that would do since those men did not know what he looked like. Gerek growled.

"What should I do if I see him again?"

"Stay away from him, but go and find one of the guards. Here, I will write a note for you to give them. When they see my signature, they will know you are telling the truth." He reached for a piece of paper from the stack he was using to copy documents, carefully tore off a smaller piece, and wrote the missive.

"Do you think they would not believe me without your authorization?"

Another growl made its way into his throat, but he pushed it down.

"They would probably believe you, but this will give you extra credibility. With this, they will take him straight to the dungeon without question."

She nodded and placed the piece of paper in her skirt pocket. "I must go now."

"You will not stay for a reading lesson?"

"No, I only came to tell you about seeing . . . him. I will try to come back tomorrow."

He nodded, trying to look disinterested. She turned to leave.

"Wait." He reached into his leather money pouch, which he still kept attached to his belt. "Take this money. Go to the market in Hagenheim and buy yourself a new knife."

"I do not want your money." Rapunzel shook her head, her brows lowered in a troubled expression.

"It is to replace the knife you threw at the man when he was about to attack me. I do not want you to be without a knife. You need it to defend yourself."

Her gaze flicked from the money in his hand to his face. She shook her head again. "I have already replaced my knife." She lifted the flap on the leather purse attached to her belt. She slipped out a short dagger, then pushed it back in and closed the flap over the handle. "I found it in the cart our attackers abandoned."

"You lost your other one defending me. It is only right that I replace it." He thrust the money at her again.

Still, she shook her head. "I thank you, but I do not need it. Good day, Sir Gerek."

As soon as she was gone, he sighed. He placed his hands over his face and rubbed—rubbed his eyes, his cheeks, his growing beard. If only he could get on his horse, ride to Hagenheim Castle, and forget the last few days had ever happened.

Rapunzel carried her pottery water jar to the stream that was a short distance through the trees behind their house. Her hair flowed down her back, the air tugging it and tossing the shorter strands into her face. Her stomach clenched at the thought of someone seeing her—at what her mother would say if she saw her wandering around outside like this, reveling in the freedom of having her hair flowing and uncovered. How many times had her mother told her it was shameful to leave her hair exposed? How she hissed at

Rapunzel when her head covering shifted and exposed an inch of her hair.

She walked down the bank to the bend in the stream where a small pool of water had collected, left behind by the swifter current. Rapunzel set her bucket down and stretched out on her stomach, lying with her head hanging over the edge, careful to hold her hair back so it didn't get wet. She gazed down at her reflection.

In the still water, her hair formed a halo around her head and face. Was this how she looked when her hair hung loose? She turned her head one way, then the other. She smiled at her own foolishness, looking at herself so long. Mother would scold her and say she was vain.

She looked different without her hair severely drawn back from her face and covered. She looked . . . pretty.

If she were to walk around Hagenheim like this, would young men take a second look at her? Would they approach her and flatter her? Would people think she was pretty? Worthy? Important?

Rapunzel drew in a breath. Was that why Mother never wanted anyone to see her hair? Not because it was shameful or immodest, but because Mother was afraid men would notice her and desire her?

Being cautious of men, avoiding them, seemed like a good thing mothers should teach their daughters. But . . . were all men bad? Or had Mother instilled an unhealthy fear in Rapunzel?

She tried to think of a man she had known in the villages where they had lived who had seemed good. She remembered a few kind-hearted priests and friars. Brother Andrew at the monastery had seemed gentle and good. And even though Sir Gerek was arrogant, she had never seen any licentiousness in his eyes, nor any malice.

Thinking critical thoughts of Mother made her stomach clench. But she had always known she was not like other mothers. She loved Rapunzel, and Rapunzel loved her in return, but more and more, she felt a restlessness inside her to be free of her mother's control. After all, Rapunzel was nineteen years old or possibly even older. Most women her age were married and had one or two children.

She pressed her hand to her cheek as she gazed into the water. Would Mother be able to see the disloyal thoughts in Rapunzel's face?

But if Rapunzel were married, wouldn't she only be exchanging her mother's control for her husband's? If she were free from her mother, she would have to support herself and take care of herself—protect herself.

If she had some sort of job, she could do it. If she were to become a maidservant at Hagenheim Castle, she would have food, the protection of the castle, and perhaps a little money to buy clothing for herself. She was learning to read, which might make her more valuable as a servant.

She must make Sir Gerek teach her Latin, too, and to write in both languages. She hated feeling ignorant and poor and awkward even more now that she had seen the beautiful city of Hagenheim and its people, with their confident expressions and their colorful clothing.

She looked at herself in the still pool one more time before standing up and running her fingers through her ankle-length hair. She played with it, tossed it, wound it around her hand, and finally tied it in a loose knot at the base of her neck.

Picking up her water bucket, she fetched water from the stream and carried it toward home.

There was more cheer and good spirits on the streets of Hagenheim than in any village she had ever lived. She wanted that same confidence and joy. And as long as she lived with Mother, she didn't think she would ever have it.

After two weeks of Rapunzel coming for her reading lesson almost every day, Gerek could almost anticipate her knock. Today he kept glancing at the door. She had not come the day before, so he was sure she would today.

He closed his eyes and shook his head. In a few more weeks he could again fill his mind—and his time—with jousting practice and strategizing over which wealthy heiress he might marry.

The knock came.

"Come in," he called to her familiar tapping.

"How are you feeling today, Sir Gerek?"

He frowned instead of answering her question.

"I'm sorry to hear that. But I'm sure you will be much more cheerful when your leg is healed and you do not have to lay in bed all day."

Her smile inexplicably reminded him of Lady Rose. With so much time to think, his thoughts had drifted back to how Lady Rose had taken care of him when he had broken his arm as a young squire. In spite of the fact that her own little girl had drowned around that same time, she had taken an interest in him. She insisted he stay, not with the other squires, but in a tiny room off her son's chamber so she and the castle healer, Frau Geruscha, could keep a closer eye on him. That was when he and Valten had become close friends.

They had grown up together, trained together, and Gerek had appreciated Lady Rose's gentleness, along with Duke Wilhelm's uprightness and sense of justice and fairness. Valten would never know how fortunate he was to have such good and honorable parents.

"You look very thoughtful today," she said after taking off her patched and mended cloak and sitting down on the stool beside him. "What are you thinking about?"

"Nothing."

She lifted her brows and twisted her mouth.

"I was thinking of the last time I broke my arm. I was probably about eight or nine years old."

She nodded. "Did you have someone then who could splint it for you?"

"Yes." He vividly remembered how terrified he was of the old healer. "I was a squire at Hagenheim Castle. Lady Rose took care of me as if she were my own mother."

"She must be very kind."

"Ja, she is. Her oldest son, Valten, is only one year older than I. She made sure no one mistreated me while I was recuperating. Before I came to Hagenheim, I had been a page at a castle to the west of here, for the Earl of Keiterhafen. The pages and squires were not treated nearly so well there."

"I am very glad you came to Hagenheim, then." There was a soft, sweet look about her eyes and around her mouth that sent his mind back to the night he had listened to her singing and had felt a sweet ache in his chest. He had the same ache now as he looked at her.

"Why do you keep your hair covered?" He asked the question before he had time to think better of it.

Her cheeks turned pink and she stared down at her lap. "It is strange, isn't it? My mother, she insists I not show my hair."

"But why? Is it green or purple or some other strange color?" That seemed to amuse her and she smiled at him. "Are you a fairy changeling with pointed ears?"

She rewarded him with a laugh. "No, nothing like that." After she stopped shaking her head, she said, "My mother has strange ideas, I suppose."

"Like what?"

"She doesn't . . . she doesn't want anyone to see my hair. And she doesn't like or trust men. She gets upset when I even talk to a man or when a man talks to me. I think it has to do with something that happened to her a long time ago."

"I take it she would be very upset if she found out about you coming to me for reading and Latin lessons, then."

She nodded and sighed.

"And how old are you?"

"Nineteen." She tilted her head to one side. "Or thereabout."

"If you are nineteen, then why . . . ?" He thought better of finishing that question.

"Why do I let my mother tell me what to do with my hair? Why am I not married, with two or three children by now?" She shook her head, a slight movement. "My mother has never encouraged anyone's attention. I think she never will."

"So, how long will you let her force you to cover your hair?"

"I never said she *forced* me to cover my hair."

"Then take off your wimple. It's warm enough in here. You don't need it." He wasn't sure why he was pushing this.

"I don't want to have to put it back on when I leave." She sat up straight, half closing her eyes, and she almost looked like a noble lady delivering an insult to a lesser noble.

"Very well."

"Let us hurry and begin. I cannot stay forever, you know." She laid aside the woolen fabric she had wrapped around her hands on this colder than usual late-winter day.

"Why do you want to learn to read so badly?" He wasn't sure what made him ask again, but he wanted to know what she was thinking. "Most young maidens of . . . the villages never think of learning to read." He had almost said, *Most young maidens of your peasant class*. She would have accused him of being arrogant again.

She raised her eyebrows again. "I have always wanted to learn to read. Once, when I was eight years old, I found out that the daughter of the lord of our village knew how to read. She was only a little older than I was, and so I asked her if she would please teach me. She looked down her nose at me, as if I were a toad, and said, 'You? You are probably too stupid to learn. You're only a peasant.'"

Rapunzel's voice sounded haughty and airy as she mimicked the other child.

"It made me so angry, and she made me feel so lowly that I vowed someday I would learn to read. And in the meantime, I learned everything anyone would teach me. I learned to make paint from berries and clay and hulls from nuts. I taught myself to paint flowers and vines and birds. I learned all kinds of stitching and sewing and weaving, even though I don't like to sew. And I learned how to snare a hare and skin it."

"And how to throw a knife."

"I learned everything except midwifery. Mother is a midwife. But I don't like blood and pain and . . . midwifery." She shuddered.

"I am sorry that girl said that to you. No one should ever try to make another person feel unworthy." Memories flooded Gerek's mind, of his brother standing over him, and his father standing over his mother.

"Surely no one ever made you feel unworthy. You are noble born, are you not?"

"My father was the Earl of Rimmel. But that does not mean I was never made to feel unworthy. After all, I was a younger son." He didn't exactly want to tell her of his dark family history, the terrible thing his father had done, and how he wondered if his temperament was irreparably tainted by being the blood son of someone so . . . heartless.

"How did we start talking of this?" Gerek grabbed the book from the floor beside him and opened it, quickly turning to the page where they had left off.

Chapter Twelve

Sir Gerek was in his usual bad mood after talking about his past and his family, but Rapunzel was curious now. He cringed when he spoke of his father being an earl, and his tone was bitter when he mentioned his brother.

"Just because you are a younger son? Of an earl?" Rapunzel half smiled and shook her head. "That is nothing compared to being a peasant, and not only a peasant, but someone who was abandoned by their natural parents and left with a stranger."

"I can see how that would make you feel bad. But I'm glad you don't know what it is like to be hated. You were not blamed by your own brother for something unspeakable that your father did." He rubbed his hand over his mouth, as if his words left a bad taste.

Her heart squeezed in her chest at the pain etched on his face. What unspeakable thing had his father done?

"You don't want to talk about these things. You want to learn to read, and we were working on Latin." He rearranged the book on his lap. The message he was sending was clear, but her thoughts were spinning with wanting to know more. If Sir Gerek had bad things in his past, things that were painful to him, then perhaps he was just as human as all the fellow peasants she had known.

"How could your brother blame you for something your father did?"

He rubbed his big, sunbrowned hand over the short beard that covered his chin, then cleared his throat. He didn't speak.

"It's not as if I have anyone to tell." She spoke quietly, hoping he might trust her enough to confide in her.

"I may have to teach you to read, but I don't have to tell you my family's darkest secrets."

"Arrogant as ever," Rapunzel mumbled to herself.

"What did you say?"

"Nothing, nothing."

She allowed him to direct her thoughts to his copy of King Solomon's Proverbs, written in Latin. But learning Latin was much more difficult than learning to read in German. Still, she was interested in finding out what was contained in the Bible. Reading the letter to Timotheus had whetted her appetite to read the entire Holy Writ. She would not be satisfied until she had done so. But that would require learning Latin, so she applied herself to the lesson.

Sir Gerek frowned at her as much as usual when she made mistakes and said she asked too many questions, but he was not quite as gruff as usual. As she bundled herself up against the cold spell they were having, she said, "Your beard is coming in nicely. It doesn't look as terrible as most men's beards."

"Doesn't look as terrible? What kind of flattery is that?"

She shrugged. "It makes you look old and . . . lazy."

"That's the gratitude I get for teaching a maiden to read."

"Gratitude is not the same as giving false compliments. And flattery is spoken of as evil in the Bible, or so said a friar I once knew."

He glared at her. "Don't you need to get home before your mother—?"

"Fare well, Sir Gerek." She sauntered out the door and laughed softly on the other side.

Was she a bad person because she so enjoyed teasing this knight? Bad or not, she did enjoy it.

"Rapunzel, you have barely painted anything on the house. By now you should have covered this entire wall at least with flowers and vines and leaves and butterflies and whatever else you fancy. What have you been doing?"

Mother came home from her usual trip to Hagenheim carrying bread, sugar, and a basket cage with a live chicken in it, which she strapped to her back.

"Chicken? Mother, did you get a job?"

"Believe it or not, I assisted in a birth today."

"Mother, truly?" Rapunzel clapped her hands. "That is wonderful. The first one is always the most difficult to get, but they will spread word about you and—"

"Before you get too excited, listen to the story."

Rapunzel hoped Mother would forget to press further about what she had been doing and why she had not painted much.

"I was walking toward the Marktplatz when I heard yelling and groaning coming from a house. Someone appeared in the doorway and said, 'Aren't you that midwife? The new one?' And so they asked me to come in, and in the middle of the floor, there was a dog in great distress, trying to birth some puppies."

"A dog?"

"But it was the owner who was groaning. He said she was the best hunting dog he had ever had and he would pay me well if I could save her, and even more if I could save the puppies. So I did. The dog delivered seven healthy puppies, and I have money enough for this chicken and many more."

"He must have been very wealthy."

"Oh yes, and now two women on his street are already asking me to be their midwife when their time comes. Word of my skill spreads fast."

"Even though it was puppies you delivered?"

"Puppies are babies. It's all very similar." Mother waved her hand as she unloaded her things and placed them on the table, except for the chicken. "Can you go kill the chicken, my love, while I make a pie? Looks like we already have some water boiling for the scalding."

"Of course, Mother." Rapunzel took the basket and carried it outside. Taking a deep breath, she opened the top of the basket and pulled the chicken out by its neck. Careful not to look at the chicken's head, she held it as far away from her body as possible, then squeezed as hard as she could and slung the chicken's body around and around by its neck while counting to ten, breaking the neck and strangling it at the same time.

Taking another deep breath, she ignored the way the chicken was still twitching and flopping around. She lifted the small hatchet off its iron nail on the back door. With one hand, she laid the chicken's neck across a sawed-off stump, then chopped off its head with one hard whack. Grabbing it by its feet, she held it upside down and let the blood drip out.

She kept her head turned, humming a song to drown out the sound of the blood dripping onto the ground. After one entire song of seven full verses, she carried the chicken in the house and dropped it in the boiling pot of water on the fire. After a good scalding, she used a wooden paddle to fish it out again and started plucking off the feathers.

Mother took the pot outside to dump the water. She brought it back, refilled with water, and set it on the andirons over the fire.

"I noticed you are not covering your hair when you're at home." Mother glanced at her from the corner of her eye.

Rapunzel kept plucking and piling the feathers on the floor. When they dried, she would add them to the pillow she had been stuffing for the last year. Just a few more chickens or geese and it would be done.

"I like the way it feels when it's not covered."

Mother, whose own hair was untouched by the rays of the sun—she kept it wrapped tightly, then covered with a wimple—said nothing.

"Besides, I washed it and was letting it dry."

"I hope you aren't getting any ideas about going into town with it uncovered, just because you saw that Rainhilda with her hair hardly covered at all with that flimsy veil."

"Rainhilda wasn't the only young woman I saw with uncovered hair, Mother. I don't understand why—"

"It's indecent. I've told you this before. If you go around letting men see your head uncovered, your hair on display, you will see what it will get you. A broken heart and an illegitimate child."

"Mother! I hardly see how uncovered hair will cause me to have an illegitimate child."

"Men think they can get whatever they want from you. They pretend they love you, but they don't. If the men of Hagenheim were to see your beautiful blond hair, they would pursue you. They would tell you how beautiful you are, and then . . . and then they would tell you they loved you, and you would believe it."

Mother stared at the wall, that familiar, far away look in her eyes.

"Very well, Mother. Do not upset yourself. I am not planning to go through the streets of Hagenheim with my head uncovered and my hair streaming out around me. Look at me. I'm in our little house in the woods. No one can see me here except you."

Mother's chest rose and fell as she stared down at the pie she had been making and seemed to have forgotten. "You don't know what men are capable of, Rapunzel. You have never experienced their treachery. They know exactly what you want them to say and they will say it . . . to get what they want. You are so innocent. You don't know."

"Mother, please stop worrying about something that is never going to happen."

"How do you know it won't happen?" Mother slammed her fist on the table. "You don't know it won't happen. Just promise me you will stay away from men, Rapunzel. If you don't . . ."

Tears welled up at the crazed desperation in Mother's wide eyes.

"Mother, what happened to you? Tell me why you are so afraid of men."

"I am not afraid of men." Mother chopped viciously at the dried fruit between her knife and the thick wooden tabletop. "There isn't a man alive whose throat I wouldn't slash in a moment if he came near you." She raised the knife higher than was necessary and brought it down with a quick, hard slice.

Rapunzel's stomach turned at seeing her mother like this. Her face seemed to go dark when she was in one of these moods. But if she could get her mother to tell her what had so turned her against men, then perhaps she could convince her that at least some of her fears were unfounded.

"Mother, did a man attack you when you were young?"

"No." Her mother's voice was a hiss. "I was never attacked. You don't have to be attacked to be destroyed."

Mother's face was tight, her lips pursed, her eyes strange and dark.

"What happened?" Rapunzel asked softly.

Mother continued to chop. Finally, she stopped and looked at Rapunzel. "Men will tell you they love you, then they will leave you." She pointed her knife at Rapunzel. "You must not trust them."

"Yes, Mother," she whispered. She plucked, plucked, plucked the feathers while the bald spot of chicken skin grew larger. "Did someone tell you they loved you and then leave you?"

Mother got out their tiny pouch of spices and used her fingers to take out several pinches of the pungent brown powder and throw them into the pile of walnuts and dried fruit on the table in front of her. "You don't need to know that."

"Mother, you know I love you. I would love you no matter what you did in the past."

Neither spoke again while Rapunzel finished plucking the chicken and Mother finished preparing the pie, putting the top crust over it, and placing it in the edge of the hot ashes of the fire, while Rapunzel carefully dropped the plucked chicken into the boiling water.

"I wish you wouldn't keep secrets from me." Rapunzel kept her voice quiet, hoping not to anger her. As soon as she spoke, she remembered the very big secret she herself was keeping. She was being hypocritical. But she had long suspected Mother was keeping other secrets from her since she had told Rapunzel more than one version of how Rapunzel had come to be left with her.

Mother was slicing the bread she had brought home. She stopped and her shoulders stiffened. "Very well. Since you want to know so badly . . . When I was your age, I was just like you, Rapunzel. I wanted to get married."

Rapunzel had not said she wanted to get married. But she did not interrupt Mother.

"I met a young man. I fell in love with him, and he told me he loved me. He said when he was able to make a little money and have a house, he would marry me." Mother kept her back to Rapunzel, but she had stopped working and was standing still with her hands on the table, arms straight. "I was young. I believed he loved me. But it was all a lie. He got me with child, and then I never saw him again. He left me and went to England." She spat the word like a bitter, unripe walnut. "He left me alone with my grandmother and never came back for me."

Was he the person she had come back to Hagenheim to see?

Mother's voice was breathy and hard-edged at the same time. "When I discovered I was with child, I sent him word, but he only said he could not come, that he was going to England to make his fortune with Lord Claybrook. He abandoned me." Mother's face contorted and she bent forward.

"Mother, I'm so sorry. He never should have done that to you." Tears welled in her eyes, her insides twisting at the pain in Mother's face. She held her breath as she waited for what Mother would say next.

"The baby was born too early. A girl. She died after a few hours. And then God gave me you." Her voice broke and Mother's body shook in a back and forth motion, as if she were laughing, as she made a wheezing sound. "God felt sorry for me, that I lost my baby and the man I loved. You were always meant to be my daughter, don't you know that? You were mine, and I knew it from the moment I saw you." She drew in an audible breath and stared at Rapunzel.

Rapunzel's heart beat faster. Was Mother unwell? Perhaps she had let the moonlight fall on her face when she was sleeping last night. Hadn't there been a full moon? Everyone knew that caused madness.

"Of course, Mother. Of course I was meant to be your daughter. And I am so sorry for what that man did to you. He should not have dealt with you so falsely." This was why her poor mother had warned her over and over about men. She was still in pain from her broken heart. But it seemed as if there must be more to the story.

"Don't you see?" Mother finally turned and looked at Rapunzel over her shoulder for a moment before turning her back on her again. "How foolish I was . . . foolish for falling in love with him, for believing that he cared for me."

"You mustn't be so hard on yourself." Should Rapunzel go to her mother and put her arm around her? In the past she had learned that when Mother was angry, it was best not to get too close. "You could not have known that he would not honor his promise to you."

Mother spun around, still holding the knife in her hand. "That is where you are wrong. I should have known. I never should have let him touch me. You must never let them touch you, Rapunzel."

Mother's eyes were wide and strangely dark. Was she only imagining that Mother's face was darker and somehow different?

"Of course, Mother. Do not upset yourself. I will not let anyone touch me." Rapunzel's stomach churned.

"But I am not the only woman who was lied to and abandoned. My own mother warned me. She warned me that men are not capable of love. She told me, but I didn't listen. It happened to her too. She told me they lie to get what they want, and then they cast you aside. They have no real tenderness. You must not let them fool you."

"No, Mother, I won't."

"And now I have the chance to set things right," she went on. She shook the knife to emphasize her words. "To make him pay for what he did, for breaking his word. Not only him, but the son of the man who dealt so treacherously with my mother. I shall have my revenge on them both."

The knife in her hand shook.

"Mother, please." Rapunzel's breath was so shallow she could barely speak. She willed herself to breathe more evenly. "You are upset. You cannot mean that you would harm anyone." By the look on her mother's face, her words were having little impact. "Mother, listen to me. If you harm that man, Duke Wilhelm will put you in the dungeon."

She suddenly laughed, a harsh bark of a laugh. "Duke Wilhelm. He thinks he is so mighty and perfect." Her face twisted in a hard look. "I have my reasons for hating him too."

The look on Mother's face sent a cold shiver down Rapunzel's back. She had to take her mother's mind off these torturous thoughts.

"I'm sorry I asked you about it. I didn't mean to upset you. Please forgive me. We don't have to talk about it anymore."

Mother turned around again, her back to Rapunzel. "Never you mind about it. I-I never should have told you." Her voice sounded almost normal again. "Perhaps we shouldn't have come back here. Perhaps we should go."

She couldn't leave, not now that she was learning so much and was actually reading German and studying Latin. Surely her mother wouldn't actually take revenge on anyone.

"But, Mother, it is good that we came back here. You are already gaining a name for yourself as a skilled midwife. You were paid handsomely today for a job well done, and you have two more pregnant women wanting your services. This is a good place for us, for you, for your business. We will prosper here. Don't you see that, Mother?" She held her breath, waiting for her mother to respond.

"Perhaps."

Mother hardly spoke while they finished cooking. Even their feast of chicken and pie was not enough to change her morose expression.

That night, when they lay down to sleep on their straw mattress, Rapunzel sang to her mother a slow, soothing song. When she could hear her mother's even breathing, Rapunzel closed her eyes and tried to remember some of the scriptures she had been reading from Sir Gerek's Bible books. The lines, "Rejoice always, pray continually, give thanks in all circumstances, for this is God's will for you in Christ Jesus," came to mind.

Father God, I am rejoicing that you have given me my wish, to be able to read. I want to pray continually, which I thought only nuns and monks were able to do, but I will try to do as well. And I will give thanks in all circumstances, and so I thank you even now, when I am worried about Mother. Thank you, God, for allowing Mother to safely deliver the puppies today, for the two women who wish for her to help them with their births, and I thank you that we have a house and food and a warm fire.

She felt a bit less worried when she finished her prayer. Then she added, *And thank you that Mother will not do anything violent to that man, whoever he is.*

Chapter Thirteen

Rapunzel sat reading with Sir Gerek beside the river. The sun was shining and glinting off the ripples of water. Sir Gerek looked behind them. Rapunzel turned to see what he was staring at.

Mother came running at them, a knife upraised in her hand.

Rapunzel stood to get out of her mother's way. Sir Gerek stood, too, in spite of his splinted leg, and Mother raced toward him, screaming, "Don't touch my daughter!"

Sir Gerek knocked the knife out of her hand, but Mother began clawing at his eyes—clawing them out and blinding him. Rapunzel lunged at her mother to stop her, but when Mother side-stepped, Rapunzel fell headfirst into the river.

Water closed over her mouth, her nose, her eyes. She struggled, pushing with her arms to free herself from the water.

Rapunzel opened her eyes; she was in her bed, pushing her-self up onto all fours.

She collapsed, breathing deep draughts of air. It was only a dream.

A memory suddenly came to her. She was little. Blond curls hung about her face, falling in front of her eyes. She was in the trees. A boy, older than her—she had a feeling he was her brother—played nearby. She saw a pretty butterfly and followed it until she came quite close to the bank of a river.

Someone grabbed her leg and pushed her. She fell headfirst into the river. Just like in her dream, the water rushed over her. Then someone lifted her out. Rapunzel was so startled. She didn't cry, but she looked to see who was holding her and saw Mother.

That was all she could remember. At least, it seemed like a memory, and not quite like the dream she had been having.

Mother stirred beside her, then began talking in her sleep. The only words she could understand were, "Not yours. Not yours. Get away. No."

Perhaps there was a bad wind blowing outside, getting in the cracks of their drafty home and bringing them bad dreams. Or perhaps there was an evil spirit near them, causing these nightmares.

Rapunzel whispered, "Jesus." Her heart seemed to slow as she said the name. She said it again. "Jesus." She heard no sound from her mother. Rapunzel reached out to rub her back. Mother went back to breathing evenly.

Rapunzel drifted back to sleep.

The next morning, as they were breaking their fast with bread and cold chicken, Rapunzel silently practiced the Latin poetry Sir Gerek had made her memorize. When they were finished eating, she mended an old underdress while Mother put on her best dress. All the while, Rapunzel repeated the verses to herself, then another passage from the Bible that she had memorized in German. As soon as Mother left to go to Hagenheim, Rapunzel could run to the monastery for her lesson.

Rapunzel suddenly remembered her mother's words from the day before. "Mother, you are not going to search for that man in Hagenheim today, are you? Please tell me you won't harm him."

Mother did not meet Rapunzel's gaze as she folded some clothes that had been drying by the fire. Finally, she said, "I think you should go with me to town today."

Rapunzel looked up from where she sat on the floor with her mending in her lap. "To town? Today?"

"It is very strange to me that you don't want to go to town with me." Mother narrowed her eyes. "I thought you liked it the one time you went. You've always wanted to go to Hagenheim, ever since you decided you wanted to read."

"And I still want to read." Even though she had learned to read German, she did still want to learn to read in Latin. "Being around all those people made me a little uncomfortable. I felt as though I might get run down by a horse or a cart."

"You mustn't be so fearful. As long as you're with me, you're safe. Will you work on your painting while I'm gone?" She still looked at her with suspicion.

"Probably." Rapunzel would have to come back early from her lesson in order to get some painting done to tamp down Mother's suspicions.

Finally, Mother left for Hagenheim, and Rapunzel wrapped her hair up and set out for the monastery.

As she approached Sir Gerek's door, she heard a whistle. Glancing to her right, she saw Brother Andrew coming her way.

Her mind went instantly to what her mother had told her the day before, about what that man had done to her, how a man had betrayed her mother as well, that women were foolish for trusting them. Was Brother Andrew such a man? He was a monk, but was he trustworthy? Would he attack her to get what he wanted, the way those two men on the road had attacked her and her mother?

Her stomach twisted into a knot as Brother Andrew came toward her. She had the sudden urge to turn and flee. She placed her hand on her knife, her heart pounding in her throat.

He was smiling as he drew near. "Sir Gerek is waiting for you. I've just set him up in the sheep meadow so he can get a bit of sun. Come. I'll take you there."

Brother Andrew turned to lead her around the side of the monastery dormitory. Would he do something bad to her once they were on the other side of the building where no one could see them? She could hardly breathe as she followed him, her feet moving slower than his as she fell farther behind.

Were all of her mother's dire prophecies about what men would do to her finally coming true? Would this be her punishment for deceiving her mother by coming to the monastery, amongst all these men?

As they turned the corner of the building, Sir Gerek was sitting in the middle of the open meadow, his leg propped on a stool with a blanket underneath as he sat in the sun.

Brother Andrew stopped and glanced back at her. "I will leave you to your lesson." He turned back toward the monastery. He passed right by her with only a nod and a smile.

"Thank you," Rapunzel said, breathing a sigh and pressing her hand against her chest to tell her heart to stop pounding so hard.

Her knees were weak and she tried to calm her breathing before facing Sir Gerek. How very foolish she had been for thinking such things about Brother Andrew. Of course he would not harm her. But all of Mother's warnings had bombarded her at once. All of her dire predictions had filled her with fear.

Perhaps she and Mother were both mad.

As she continued to walk toward Sir Gerek, her mind flashed back to her dream. Sir Gerek was sitting just as he had been in her dream. Had she prophesied this? Would her mother come running and screaming toward them with a knife?

Rapunzel turned and looked behind her. No one was there. She looked back at Sir Gerek. Now that she thought about it, there was no river rushing beside Sir Gerek, and his clothes were not the same as in her dream. He also still wore his beard, whereas in the dream he had been clean-shaven.

Perhaps Rapunzel had slept with moonlight on *her* face last night. She would move their bed farther from the window when she got home. She passed a shaking hand over her forehead and cheek.

As she walked the rest of the way to Sir Gerek, she reminded herself that she could run away if he tried to attack her since he was injured.

Besides, she had been alone with Sir Gerek many times, although with his door open. His gruffness and arrogance had actually put her at ease. If he had been friendly and kind, she might have suspected him of wanting to trick or manipulate her in some way.

As she approached him, he looked up from the book on this lap. "Very pleasant weather, is it not?"

"It is, although still a bit cold."

He stared at her and finally said, "You aren't smiling today. You're usually smiling."

"I am smiling, see?"

"Is your mother well? She did not find out you are coming here for lessons, did she?"

"No, she did not find out." If she had, Rapunzel would not be here. She sat down.

"Shall we begin, then?" Sir Gerek opened the book and passed it to her. "This is where we stopped reading yesterday."

She began. After a few moments, she stopped. "I don't understand anything I'm reading. Perhaps I am too daft to learn Latin."

She pinched her nose and closed her eyes. She shouldn't be here. If Mother found out, she would be so upset, there was no foretelling what she might do. She should just go back home and stop trying so hard. What did it matter if she learned to read in Latin? Peasants had no use for Latin or reading or writing, especially peasants who were still living at home with their mothers who wanted to shelter them from the world forever. Besides, she was so suspicious of everyone because of Mother's warnings, she could not go out among people without cringing in fear, as evidenced by how she had just behaved.

"You are not daft."

Sir Gerek's words startled her into looking up.

"You are very clever. I've never seen anyone learn to read as quickly as you did."

He had never complimented her before. "You think I'm clever?" She stared at him openmouthed. But perhaps he was only flattering her for some sinister reason.

"I know you are. Now let's get back to our lesson before you have to run off."

Rapunzel concentrated harder than ever and learned many more Latin words by the time she realized she needed to go. When she left, she wished Sir Gerek a good day. He only grunted and nodded.

Good. He wasn't turning kind and friendly. She didn't have to like him or be too grateful to him—or fear she was falling prey to him as her mother feared—as long as he was grumpy.

Chapter Fourteen

Over the next two weeks, Rapunzel read more and more of the Holy Writ. A pattern seemed to be forming in the passages she read: God was like a loving father. She'd never had a father, and she'd never thought of God like this. All her life she had heard God described in many terms—holy, almighty, righteous, even vengeful.

He was a righteous Savior when he saved the Israelite nation from slavery in Egypt, and he was a righteous Savior in the form of Jesus, the crucified Lamb of God in the Gospels. She knew those things already, but she had never truly thought of him as loving.

Her heart ached to tell Mother what she was learning. Eventually, she would have to tell her, when her mother discovered that Rapunzel could actually read.

As she walked to the monastery through the forest, thick with ferns and beech trees that had not yet started growing their spring leaves, she caught a glimpse of someone not far away, walking in the same direction. Perhaps she should hide. But it was too late.

"I see you there!" the other young woman called, raising her hand in greeting. The maiden came toward her, walking at a slow, steady pace.

"Good morning. My name is Cristobel. Are you also on your way to the monastery?"

"Yes." Rapunzel couldn't help but smile back at the girl's

friendly face. She also couldn't help but notice that she wore absolutely nothing to cover her long dark hair, and it wasn't even braided.

"My brother is at the monastery. He has not yet taken his vows. I go to visit him sometimes."

Rapunzel nodded as the girl fell in beside her and they continued walking.

"What is your name?"

"Rapunzel." She must seem very rustic to the talkative girl.

"I like that name. I've never heard it before—as a name, that is. But it has a very pleasant sound."

"Thank you. I like yours . . . Cristobel."

"Thank you. My father wanted me to be a boy and wanted me to be named Cristof. So my little brother is Cristof and I am Cristobel. Are you going to visit someone at the monastery?"

Rapunzel hesitated. It went against her instincts to tell the girl exactly why she was going to the monastery. Mother certainly never told anyone anything when they asked. But Mother was not here.

"I am going for a reading lesson."

"A reading lesson?"

"Actually, a lesson in Latin."

"You are learning to read Latin?"

"Yes."

"My brother knows how to read. He told me I should go to the town school and learn, but Mother said I was better off staying home and learning to cook and sew and help her with the little ones. And now I am a maid at Hagenheim Castle." By the look on her face, she thought Rapunzel would be impressed.

"Do you like working there? I long to know what the castle looks like inside."

"It is hard work, but they treat me well and pay me with real coins every month."

Rapunzel made sure to look impressed. "Is it difficult to get a job working at the castle?"

"Ja, I should say so. You have to know someone who works there, someone who will say that you are honest and trustworthy."

"Oh." Who would do that for Rapunzel? She had been here such a short time and no one knew her. Not that Mother would allow her to work there anyway.

"We are almost to the monastery. My brother is usually in the garden or the vineyard working."

They came out of the forest and into the clearing where most of the monastery buildings were visible.

"Which building are you going to?"

"That one over there." Rapunzel pointed to the dormitory.

"I shall see you later. Shall I walk home with you?"

Suddenly, Rapunzel wanted that very much. "Yes. I will either be at that door there, or just behind the building, in the sheep pasture."

"I shall see you in an hour or two. Fare well!" Cristobel waved and hurried toward the vegetable garden.

Rapunzel knocked on the door, but when she didn't hear Sir Gerek's familiar call to enter, she walked around the building and found him where he had been sitting the last time, in the sun with his leg propped up.

"How much longer before you get the splints off?" She sat down beside him without waiting to be invited.

"Two weeks," he said, glancing up at her.

"Will you shave your beard then?"

"Perhaps not." He stroked the lengthening hair on his cheeks and chin. "It makes me look more ferocious, don't you think?"

"Frightening, as I told you before. But I thought you wanted to marry a wealthy lady. You aren't likely to attract any with that weasel fur on your face."

He scowled and mumbled, "Weasel fur," then humphed.

"Will you leave the monastery when your leg and arm are healed?"

"Of course. I'll go back to Hagenheim Castle and to my duties."

He would no longer be able to teach her Latin. Why hadn't she thought of this before?

He raised his brows at her. "I'm sure there will be a monk who will be willing to teach you when I'm gone," he said, as if reading her mind. "Only be careful. Not all monks are as safe and righteous as Brother Andrew."

Rapunzel wasn't sure she would trust anyone as much as she had trusted Sir Gerek. And it was only because of his injuries that she had trusted him; she could run away and he couldn't chase her down.

They began their Latin lesson, and later, when Rapunzel was staring hard at the page in front of them, sitting quite close by Sir Gerek's side, Cristobel's voice rang out.

"There you are! Are you done with your reading lesson yet?"

Rapunzel looked up at the girl. "Almost."

"There are some wildflowers in the next meadow I want to pick. I shall return in a little while."

"Who is that?" Sir Gerek asked as soon as she had walked away.

"A girl I met today. She came to visit her brother who lives here."

"She isn't wearing anything on her head." Sir Gerek was looking askance at her.

"Mother says it's not decent for a woman to go around bare-headed. And she doesn't wish for me to show my hair."

"That's ridiculous."

"What did you say?" She already knew, but she wanted him to elaborate. Perhaps she could use his argument with Mother.

"Your mother . . . ," he said with a thoughtful squint. He paused. "Is your mother unkind to you? Does she beat you?"

Rapunzel drew back. "Whatever made you think that?"

"I am only asking. She doesn't seem to realize that you are a grown woman, it seems to me, and not a child of ten. She doesn't want you to talk to men, doesn't want you to learn to read, and has you frightened to even show your hair. Does that not seem a bit strange to you?"

Was he right? Was Rapunzel addled to allow her mother to control her so much? But she had no choice. She and Mother had been taking care of each other all of Rapunzel's life. What would she do without Mother? What would Mother do without her?

"Does she beat you?" he asked again.

"No, she doesn't beat me."

"Then why do you not uncover your hair?"

"It feels . . . immodest."

"Do you think Cristobel looks immodest?"

"No." So if it was acceptable for others, why not for her? But still, she was not about to take off her wimple.

"A man might marry you if he could see a bit of your hair."

"And of course, all I could possibly want is to marry." Mother would have thought of something much more biting to say.

"Well, do you not want to marry? What else would you do?"

"Why would I want to marry a man who would probably tell me reading was foolishness? How would I ever read the rest of the Bible if I were married? Besides, I could work in a shop, or even work at Hagenheim Castle, instead of getting married."

"Would you prefer working for money to being married and having children?"

"Perhaps I would. Yes, I certainly would." She stared defiantly at him, daring him to argue with her.

He shrugged. "If you wish to work in Hagenheim Castle, you would have to wear a certain type of dress and wear your hair partially uncovered. All the maids must dress the same."

She did not know that. But . . . "I could do that. It would not be a problem." She smiled at him and lifted her chin.

"Perhaps we shall see each other there, then."

"You are in and out of the castle very often?"

"Yes. The knights often eat in the Great Hall with the family." His familiar arrogance showed in the tilt of his head and the informal tone of his voice.

Cristobel was walking toward them.

"I should go. Thank you for the lesson today."

He nodded.

Once the girls reconvened, Cristobel linked her arm through Rapunzel's. "Who is that man?"

"Sir Gerek. He's teaching me Latin."

"Are you and he . . ."

Rapunzel's cheeks heated. "No, no. He is one of Duke Wilhelm's knights and very virtuous." Or so she hoped. "He is only teaching me to read because the monks are forcing him to while he waits for his broken leg and broken arm to heal."

Cristobel tilted her head and scrunched her brows. Then she shook her head and smiled. "Whatever the reason, I envy you. He is very handsome."

"How can you tell with all that hair covering his face?"

"He is a knight, isn't he? Besides, I can see he is well-looking. If I were being tutored by a handsome young knight, I would uncover my hair and wear a more revealing dress." She looked pointedly at Rapunzel's chest, which was covered nearly to her chin in her modest kirtle and underdress.

"It is too cold to wear something revealing."

"*Pfft.*" Cristobel expelled air through her teeth and rolled her eyes.

"Besides, he doesn't want to marry me. He means to marry a wealthy heiress, a lady of noble birth."

Cristobel laughed. "He doesn't have to marry you. If you have his baby and he claims it, you could get money out of him, or a nice house, or a position in the church for your child, if it turns out to be a son."

Rapunzel's face was burning. "I don't wish to . . . have children." Not in *that* way, at least. "I was thinking I want to work, like you."

"Ach, but yes, it is much better to work for coin than to have babies. My sister has two babies and is married to a farmer, and every time I go to visit her, she is crying. But I told her she should not marry a farmer who has so little land." Cristobel shook her head. "I plan to save my coin and marry a burgher—a butcher or blacksmith or tailor. Then I can live in Hagenheim and buy my bread every day instead of making it, and be rich enough to hire a nurse and a cook and other servants."

That did sound like a good plan.

"Perhaps I can help you get a position at the castle. And with Sir Gerek to put in a good word for you, I'm sure you will get hired."

"Truly?" But Mother would be so furious . . . and hurt.

Rapunzel parted from her new friend at the door of her house, with a promise from Cristobel to come for a visit.

As she quickly got out her paints and a brush, she pondered all that her new friend had told her. Could she defy Mother, leave her, and get a job at the castle? It was hard to imagine. But was she foolish, as Sir Gerek seemed to think she was, for allowing Mother to make her believe she should always cover her hair?

Rapunzel sighed. Her simple life suddenly seemed complicated.

Chapter Fifteen

The next day, Mother set out for Hagenheim to check up on her pregnant women.

Rapunzel also set out, in the opposite direction, after watching her mother disappear into the forest.

The smell of spring infused the tiny breeze that brushed her face, and spring was in the songs of the twittering birds around her. It was good to hear birds again after the long winter.

She pictured the words Sir Gerek had taught her the day before, the new Latin words. She was saying them to herself when she thought she heard something behind her. She glanced over her shoulder but didn't see anything. A few minutes later, she was sure she heard someone walking, with the crackling of twigs and leaves not far away. She stopped and listened, but all she heard was the birds.

She kept walking, her heart beating faster, but when she heard the sound again, she called, "Cristobel, is that you?" Her heart was beating in her throat as she tried to hold her breath to listen.

Then she saw a tiny movement, a flash of gray cloth. "Who is there?"

A figure emerged from the bushes, but it was not Cristobel. It was the man who had attacked her and her mother on the road.

His smile sent a bolt of lightning through her stomach. She turned and ran toward the monastery.

He crashed through the undergrowth behind her, running after her.

O God, help me. Jesus. A sob caught in her throat as she ran as fast as her legs would go. Would she make it to the monastery before he reached her?

She could see the clearing ahead, but it seemed so far. If she could reach the open pasture and get someone's attention, she might be saved.

Her lungs burned as she forced herself to run faster. He was getting closer. She heard him laugh—he was so close! Suddenly, her wimple was wrenched off her head. She kept running as her hair was loosed down her back.

The clearing was just ahead. She could see the monastery dormitory. "Gerek!" she screamed. The man grabbed her hair and jerked so hard, her feet left the ground and she landed on her back.

She screamed until he clamped his hand over her mouth. Then he sat on her stomach.

He leaned over her, still smiling. "Now you will be sorry for throwing that knife at me." He struggled to get something off his hip, then held up a knife—her knife. "Remember this?"

Rapunzel could barely breathe with him sitting on her stomach and his hand over her mouth. She clawed and slapped at his hand. He removed it, but when she took a breath to scream, he placed the knife to her throat.

"If you scream, I'll slit your throat from one side to the other."

With every breath, the cold blade of the knife pressed against her throat. She gulped the air anyway, until her vision became less fuzzy. He was still talking.

"I shall cut you and watch you bleed. Now tell me how sorry you are."

She must be dreaming. It looked as if Sir Gerek was standing just behind him with his sword. Was it the angel of the Lord?

"You rancid piece of dog meat," he said.

The smiling man pulled the knife away from Rapunzel's throat and started to turn his head to see who was behind him.

Sir Gerek slammed the butt of his sword into the man's temple and he fell over. The knife fell from his loosened grip and Rapunzel grabbed it. She scrambled to pull her legs out from under the dead weight of her attacker and stood to her feet, still clutching the knife.

Sir Gerek's face was a dark mask as he stared down at the man. But when he turned and looked at her, the mask disappeared and his entire face went slack.

"Are you hurt?"

She shook her head. Then her arms and legs began to tremble. She took another step away from her attacker, whose eyes were still closed. Glancing at Sir Gerek, she mumbled, "You shouldn't be walking. You will injure your leg."

He stood up straight in spite of the splint. He held his sword in his right hand, his splinted arm by his side. "Can you go get someone to tie him up? I'll guard him while you're gone."

Her knees threatened to collapse behind her, but she nodded and hurried away, stumbling but righting herself.

She came upon a group of three monks hoeing in the garden. "Can you come? Sir Gerek has caught a criminal at the edge of the forest and needs someone to help tie him up."

All three men hurried back with her, no doubt curious to see the sight.

By the time they reached them, her attacker was waking up and groaning. While Sir Gerek held his sword to the smiling man's chest, the monks tied his ankles and his hands behind his back. Sir Gerek gave instructions for someone to go to Hagenheim

Castle and summon a group of guards to take possession of the prisoner. Meanwhile, they dragged the man, who was rather small, by his feet and locked him inside one of the guest rooms in a small shed.

It was all over. She was safe. The smiley man couldn't get out, and Duke Wilhelm's men would come soon and take him to the dungeon. So why was she still shaking? And blinking back tears?

Sir Gerek was standing at the edge of the clearing, still looking at her.

"You must get off your leg," she told him.

He slapped a hand on the bulky splint. "Doesn't even hurt anymore. I think it's healed. Come." He held out his hand to her. "You need to sit down."

But instead of taking his hand or walking toward the dormitory, she started sobbing.

She must look a fool, but she couldn't stop. She covered her face with her hands.

Remembering her terror, and how the man had held the knife to her throat, she sobbed harder, her shoulders shaking. She had run as hard as she could. She had cried out to Jesus. But the man had caught up to her anyway. He had pinned her and threatened to slit her throat. And he might have, if Sir Gerek had not come with his sword.

She cried so hard she thought her heart would burst—until Sir Gerek put his arms around her.

Gerek watched in horror as she started to cry, her whole body shaking as she sobbed into her hands. Was she injured? Was she in pain? He should have killed that evil beast for attacking her again. He might yet go and beat his face in.

His heart knotted inside him at the sound of her sobbing. He'd not been around a lot of women in his lifetime, except for Lady Rose and the duke's daughters, and only from a distance. The few times he had seen one of the duke's daughters upset, Lady Rose had put her arms around them.

So Gerek stepped toward her, laid his sword on the ground, put his arms around her, and patted her shoulder with one hand.

It seemed to work because Rapunzel's sobbing lessened and soon stopped altogether. She stiffened in his arms and stood unmoving. Her arms were pressed against his chest, and he wished she would put her head against him, so much his chest ached.

She stood sniffing and wiping her eyes with her hands, and he continued patting her shoulder, putting his hands in contact with her thick hair. The golden-blond color was as beautiful as it was unusual, and it felt like silk against his fingers.

She pulled away from him and he let her go, the ache intensifying in his chest. She turned away from him, still wiping at her face.

"Are you sure you aren't hurt?"

"I am sorry for crying. I am well." Her voice was still shaky as she continued to wipe her face with her hands. "You must get back to the dormitory before your bones grow back crooked."

Before he knew what she was doing, she bent and picked up his sword and handed it to him.

"Can you walk?" she asked.

"Of course I can walk. I ran—or an approximation of running with this heavy splint—all the way to the edge of the forest when I heard you scream."

She crossed her arms and stared up at him, opening her mouth to say something. But then she closed it and gave her head a slight shake. "Thank you."

They walked slowly, side by side, back to the dormitory. At least he had been able to get to her before that madman hurt her.

Had it been wrong to hold her? No, he did not believe so, but why had she stiffened? Why had she turned away from him? His stomach sank, but he clenched his teeth and shook his head. She still did not trust him.

Once they were back in the dormitory and sitting down, Rapunzel couldn't stop thinking about what had happened, about the man grabbing her, throwing her down on the ground, and holding the knife to her throat. Tears kept coming into her eyes. She did her best to hide them from Sir Gerek. Thankfully, he seemed oblivious. He opened a book and started talking about Latin. She tried to pay attention, but her thoughts kept wandering.

He held the book out to her, asking her to read. When she reached for it, her hand was shaking.

Instead of giving her the book, he laid it down and grasped her hand. "You are not well." He held her hand firmly in his much bigger, calloused one, then reached and took her other hand.

Her back instantly straightened. She wanted to pull her hands away, but he could prevent her. After all, he was much stronger than she was. Her heart trembled at the truth: He was only being kind. He did not want to take advantage of her. So why was fear welling up inside her?

She could not look him in the eye. The tears streamed down her face. The warmth of his gentle grip was unbearably sweet, and it made her heart swell. She kept her head bowed so he couldn't see her tears. How shameful she was. She had no right to ask for his kindness. He was a knight.

"I shall get you some wine." He let go of her hands and stood up, shuffling to the other side of the room.

Meanwhile, she struggled to get her tears under control, wiping her face with her sleeves. She pressed her hands to her cheeks. Their warmth—warmed by his touch—made her stomach flip.

He came back and touched the back of her hand with a small cloth, and she used it to finish drying her eyes and her nose. When she dared to peek up at him, he was holding a cup out to her. "This will make you feel better."

She took it, and the sharp scent of the red wine filled her nose. She took a sip. She and her mother never drank wine, as it was too expensive. The taste lingered on her tongue and wasn't as pleasant as she thought it would be—it was rather like drinking vinegar. She took another sip to be polite and then handed it back to him.

He pushed the cup back toward her. "It isn't enough to make you drunk, if that's what you're worried about. Drink it. You'll feel better."

"No. I don't like it." If he thought he could push her around, just because he had saved her life again, and just because she had shown weakness by crying, he was mistaken. He was being too kind to her, paying her too much attention. She kept an eye on the door. She could run away. With his splint, he could not catch her.

He took it and frowned. "Hardheaded, you are." He drank it himself in one gulp.

"Better to be hardheaded than always grumpy."

"Is that right?"

"Yes." He was back to his grumpy self. Good.

Chapter Sixteen

Gerek sat back on the bed and propped his leg up again. He rather liked it when she stood up to him.

At least she wasn't crying anymore. He couldn't bear to see her cry, and hearing her sob had made his stomach hurt. And now that she was no longer crying, and her hair was completely uncovered, he let himself look at her.

He had always thought her beautiful—for a peasant girl. But with that golden hair falling around her, it made her face and eyes glow like some kind of enchantment.

He was thinking like an addle-headed knave.

"Will you help me get a position at Hagenheim Castle?"

Her question startled him out of his thoughts. "What sort of position?"

"As a maidservant. I can cook or do any sort of cleaning."

Lady Rose would like her very much. "Is that what you wish?"

She nodded.

"I shall write Lady Rose a letter, listing your virtues and skills." He reached down and drew up a piece of real paper—much crisper than parchment—and found a reed pen. "Let's see, what shall I say? You are hardheaded . . ."

"Don't you dare." But this brought a smile to her face that she was obviously trying to suppress.

"And terrified of letting anyone see your hair . . ." He found his ink and writing board.

"You wouldn't say that!" She self-consciously twisted her long hair and then flung it over her shoulder. It was like molten gold, flowing over her shoulders, reaching all the way to the floor. The silky texture of it shimmered and floated with her every movement . . . Mesmerizing. No wonder her mother made her cover it.

He wrenched his gaze from her hair, dipped his pen in the inkwell, and started writing. "You have very strong ideas about propriety."

She huffed. "If you will not write a proper letter to help me get the position, then I pray you not write her at all."

"I shall write to my lady and tell her that you will make a hardworking, honest, clever maidservant."

"Thank you."

Rapunzel read the German Bible while he wrote the letter. When he finished, he fanned it in the air to dry the ink, then folded it. Rapunzel held his wax stick close to the flame of the fire in the grate, and then he sealed the letter with the wax and imprinted it with the seal on a ring he wore.

While the hot wax was cooling, she asked, "What sort of person is Lady Rose? I believe you said she was kind."

"She is very kind."

"Even to maidservants?"

"Of course. Lady Rose is not like other noble-born ladies I have met. She is kind and thoughtful to everyone, from visiting dukes and duchesses, to her own children, to the pages and squires, to the lowliest maids in the kitchen. She is a virtuous lady who believes in every word of the Holy Writ. There is no other lady like her, I would avow."

She was gazing at him with raised brows. "You do think very highly of her."

He felt his cheeks flush. He didn't want anyone, even Rapunzel, to know just how highly he had thought of her, when he had been a mere boy, missing his mother. It could even be said that he had been a little in love with her.

"Everyone thinks very highly of Lady Rose."

"What must I do to make her approve of me?"

"Only be yourself. She will approve of you."

She looked suspicious of his compliment.

"As long as Lady Rose sees you treating others kindly and performing your duties, she will approve of you."

She nodded. "I suppose I should go."

He handed her the letter. She took it, then said, "Do all knights marry noble-born ladies?"

Why was she asking him that? Perhaps because she was having tender feelings for him after he had saved her a second time from that brigand.

"Not all knights marry noble-born ladies, though most do. The reason I wish to marry a noble lady is because my father did something terrible when I was a boy, and my older brother blamed me for it. He has hated me since I was very young and refuses to allow me any inheritance. And since I cannot allow my idiot brother to best me—he has inherited the family estates, which includes a large castle and much land—I plan to marry an heiress with great property."

"That hardly seems like a good reason. No, I would not say that you *must* marry an heiress or a noble-born lady, just because you want to best your brother."

Heat bubbled up from his chest into his forehead. "You don't understand what my brother said to me, how he believes that God has made him superior to me because he is older. If I marry a noblewoman, and if I gain lands and wealth, it will prove that God is favoring me at least as much as him." When he said it aloud, it didn't sound as strong an argument as it did in his head. "It doesn't matter if you understand. That is the way it must be. I will marry an heiress or I shall not marry at all."

She frowned slightly but said nothing. What was she thinking? And why in creation did he care?

"Besides that, I can't marry someone who is expecting me to love them, and noblewomen usually marry for political reasons, not for love."

"What? You don't want to love your wife?" Her eyes were wide.

"That's not what I meant. But my father . . . if you knew what he did, you would understand."

"What did he do?"

He had never told anyone, except Lady Rose, when he was just a boy and still grieving what had happened. "My father . . ." He wasn't sure why he was telling her. "My father killed my mother. And then . . . he killed himself by leaping from a tower window."

Her eyes went wide and her lips formed an O as she stared at him, finally clamping her hand over her mouth. "How?" she whispered.

"He hit her, then pushed her down the stairs. She was dead, her neck broken, by the time she reached the bottom." He tore his eyes away from the compassion in her expression. He spoke quickly, to finish the story. "They had been arguing about whether to send for me and bring me home for Christmas. My father wanted to leave me at Keiterhafen, where I was a page, but my mother wanted to bring me home."

That old familiar pain weighed down his heart—shame, guilt, sorrow. It overshadowed him like a dark cloud. He shouldn't have told her.

"That is very sad. You must have been . . . devastated."

He shrugged. It could not hurt him anymore, surely. He was a grown man now. "My brother blamed me, which hurt me very much since I was but a boy and looked up to him as my older brother." An invisible fist seemed to squeeze his throat. "I don't want to talk about it anymore."

"I still don't understand how that keeps you from marrying someone who expects you to love them."

Wasn't it obvious? "He was my father. He had a terrible temper. When he was angry, he would hit anyone who got in his way. He killed his favorite hunting dog just because the dog let a fox get away. He beat me, he beat the servants, he beat his wife. And I am his son."

She still didn't look as if this was explanation enough, so he said, "I have his blood in my veins. If he would beat his wife and children, the people he loved, then I would do it too."

She shook her head. "I know that is what people think. If a man is a thief, his child will also be a thief. If a woman lies with other men besides her husband, her daughters will do the same. If a man beats his wife, his sons will beat their wives. But don't you think that has more to do with what their children grow up seeing their parents do?" She tilted her head to one side and put her hands on her hips. "How old were you when you left home?"

He growled and shrugged.

"No, this is important. Tell me how old you were."

"I was seven years old, the same as most boys who are sent away to be pages and to train to be knights."

"Yes. You were a child of seven who went to live at Hagenheim Castle, who saw how kind Lady Rose was. You spent more time with Duke Wilhelm and his sons than you did with your own father. Now, I've given this a lot of thought." She wrinkled her brow slightly as she stared down at her hands. "My mother abandoned me when I was very small, but I would never do such a thing to my child. The only mother I have ever known would also never abandon her child. She has loved me, and I will love my own child—if I should ever have a child.

"And you, you will not be like your father. You will remember what he did and you will strive to not be like him. You will remember the good example you saw in Duke Wilhelm, and you will choose to be a kind husband, not a cruel one. We all have a choice, after all, to be our own person, to be the person we wish to be."

His heart swelled in his chest just as it had the first night he had listened to her sing. He had never heard this reasoning before. What if she was right? They stared at each other. His mind was churning.

"But the fact remains that I must marry an heiress. Otherwise I will have nothing, which is exactly what my brother told me. He hated me and wished me to perish. I think he might have killed me if a servant had not sent me off to Hagenheim in the middle of the night." He wasn't sure why he even remembered that. He hadn't thought of it in years, and he'd never told anyone.

"I am so sorry that happened to you." Her eyes began to shimmer. Was she about to cry again?

"It was a long time ago, and I have lived a very good and interesting life. I have fought in tournaments with the greatest champion of all time, Valten Gerstenberg, the Earl of Hamlin, and I have had the time and resources to be as much of a scholar as I wanted to be, studying the Holy Writ and learning languages. I will not have you pitying me."

She only stared, her eyes still misty.

"Now, if you do not go back home, I am afraid your mother will never let you leave the house again. And you without your head covering."

"Oh, yes, my wimple. I must go find it." She stood up but seemed unable to move.

"What is it?"

"Nothing."

She just stood there, her mouth open as she stared at the doorway.

She had just been attacked by a madman. Was she afraid to walk back through the woods alone?

"I'll send for my horse and take you back. It will be faster."

"Oh, I cannot—"

"I insist."

"But your leg."

"It is well as long as I have this splint. Come." He walked to the door and stepped out. "You, there!" he called to a postulant who was walking nearby. "Fetch my horse."

Rapunzel walked to the edge of the forest to retrieve her head covering. He watched her pick it up and begin twisting her long hair and stuffing it inside the wimple. What a pity to see the golden locks disappearing inside the piece of fabric.

He managed to mount his horse—it wasn't as difficult as mounting with full armor—and walked Donner to where Rapunzel was standing.

"Put your foot in the stirrup and I'll pull you the rest of the way. You can sit in front." He moved back in the saddle to show her that there was room.

She only stared at him, one side of her mouth twisting.

"You can sit sidesaddle."

Still she hesitated. Finally, she put her foot into the stirrup. He took her by the arm and hauled her up in front. She sat sideways, her skirts covering her legs and feet.

"What if I feel like I'm falling?"

"You'll have to grab either me or the horse." That should have been obvious. He nudged Donner forward.

They moved rather slowly through the trees, and she held on to the pommel of the saddle. As Rapunzel told him which direction to go to her home, he thought about what she had said. It made sense. He could decide not to be like his father, could choose to be a kind and loving father and husband. After all, he hardly even remembered his father, and Duke Wilhelm had been a good example to him. He'd never known a better man than Duke Wilhelm. It seemed so simple and true. How had he never thought of it? He'd had to have it pointed out to him by Rapunzel.

Beautiful, clever, hardheaded Rapunzel, who had broken down and cried, whose hair was as beautiful as a sunset.

But it was immoral to think of her that way, to think of her beauty and her many appealing qualities, since she was only a peasant and he could never marry her.

He could go back to Hagenheim Castle now. He was able to sit a horse, he had no more pain in his leg or his arm, and if there was a need, Frau Lena could make new splints for him.

But he would not be able to teach Rapunzel to read anymore. Did this bother him so much that he would consider staying at the monastery instead of going back?

"Since my leg is so much better, I'll be going back to Hagenheim tomorrow."

He might very well never see her again, and that thought sent a pain through him.

Rapunzel's heart lurched. The lessons with Sir Gerek were over. She hadn't realized his announcing the end of them would make her heart sink to the pit of her stomach. "That is good. You will be glad to see your friends again."

He didn't answer. Then finally he said, "Yes, I will. I've been away for a while, as I escorted Lord Gabehart and Lady Sophie back to Hohendorf after a visit, and I was on my way back to Hagenheim when . . . when I saved you from that thief, the first time he attacked you."

"And I saved you when he was about to kill you." She couldn't help adding that.

"Yes."

She glanced back at him, but instead of looking annoyed, there was a smile on his lips.

"You have now saved me twice, and so it is my turn again."

He grunted rather than answering.

"If you cross this little stream, you can follow it the rest of the way."

His wrist brushed her arm as he used the reins to guide the horse, sending a rush of warmth through her, much like when he had held her trembling hands. Was this how it felt to have a friend, a true friend she could trust? Someone she was not afraid would attack her and mistreat her? To feel warm inside, safe, and accepted?

When they came in sight of her home, she saw it through Sir Gerek's eyes. The entire structure leaned to one side, and the thatched roof was obviously housing a lot of small animals. If he got any closer, he might see the cracks in the walls.

"Please let me down here." Rapunzel slid off the saddle before he could get the horse stopped. "Thank you for the lessons and for helping me today." She turned and hurried away, not waiting for him to reply.

She entered the house. Mother was standing there, her lips thin and bloodless.

Chapter Seventeen

What did you do?" Mother's voice was like the hiss of a boiling kettle. She stepped toward her and grabbed Rapunzel's shoulders. "Where have you been with that man? What did he do to you?" Her voice escalated higher and louder with each word.

"He didn't do anything—"

"If he has got you with child, I will go to Duke Wilhelm. I will force him to make the man pay for what he did to you."

"Mother, he hasn't done anything to me!"

"Don't lie to me. I know what men are about. Did I not tell you? But I'll take care of this."

"Mother, nothing happened!"

"Why were you with him? Why?" Mother started to wail and suddenly put her face in her hands. "I'm losing you, I'm losing you." She was sobbing and wailing, a high-pitched sound that made Rapunzel's stomach roil and twist.

"Mother, what are you saying? I will tell you everything if you will only be calm and stop crying so."

Mother suddenly ceased her weeping and looked up. "You tell me now. Tell me now what you have been doing while I was away the last few weeks. You will not lie to me. You will not deceive me." Again her voice began to climb until she was fairly screeching.

"Mother, I have been going to the monastery for reading lessons." Her stomach was still twisting, and she was wringing her hands at Mother's wild eyes and horrified expression. "I asked one of the monks to teach me, and he asked Sir Gerek to teach me."

"Aha! Sir Gerek." Her lips twisted as if his name itself were poison. "I knew he wanted you. I could see it in his eyes when he looked at you. He's lecherous and deceitful. Teaching you to read was only a ploy to make you fall in love with him."

"No, Mother, no. He didn't even want to teach me. He was very honest with me, and he never even tried to make me fall in love with him. Nothing happened between us at all."

"He did not touch you? I don't believe he did not try—"

"No, Mother. He never tried to touch me." Not in the way she meant.

"Then why were you riding with him on his horse, sharing his saddle?"

"That smiley man who attacked us and then tried to kill Sir Gerek followed me when I left home today, and Sir Gerek saved me from him. He was taking me home because I was nervous." The memory of it caused tears to form in her eyes again. "But you don't have to worry because he's leaving the monastery tomorrow and I won't be taking lessons from him anymore. So please, don't be upset. Nothing happened."

"How can I trust you? Why should I believe you?" That dark look was on her face again, her eyes narrowing and her lips twisting. "You lied to me. You said you were painting and making up new songs, but you were sneaking away to go see that knight. I knew he was trouble. O God, where did I go wrong?" She clenched her fists as she bent over double, as if she'd been punched in the stomach.

"Mother, please stop. Please listen to me. You will make yourself sick."

"No, you listen to me." Her voice was gravelly, and she stuck her finger in Rapunzel's face. "You are never to leave this house again without me. Never." She turned and started looking all around the room. "We will pack tonight and leave in the morning. That way he can never find you again. For I know he will never leave you alone. He is determined to have his way with you and then discard you, like an old rag. We must leave here." She grabbed an old blanket and laid it on the floor and started throwing things into the middle of it.

"Mother, stop! Please!" Had her mother lost her mind? What could Rapunzel say to calm her? "We have only just come here. We can't leave." She desperately searched her mind for reasons why they should stay, something that would convince Mother. "You have those two pregnant women who are counting on you delivering their babies. You were doing well. Hagenheim is good for you." She decided not to mention the man she had come here to seek revenge on.

"But it is bad for you." Mother was shaking her head. "Didn't you say that man attacked you again? He found you. He must have heard me say where people could find me, in the cottage in the woods." She suddenly turned around. "Did he hurt you?"

"No, Mother. He tried to hurt me, but Sir Gerek came in time to save me. I am well, but I am worried about you. You look frantic and not well. We cannot leave, and you are—"

"Frantic? Unwell?" Mother let out a loud cackle, so loud and so long that it made the hair on her arms stand up and her skin tingle. "I come home and find you gone. I don't know where you are. Then I see you riding up in the very saddle with that knight. Of course I am frantic and unwell!" Mother had filled the blanket with their belongings and was lifting the corners and tying them together.

"Mother, please." Rapunzel tugged on her arm, but Mother shook her off. "Mother, stop. Please stop." But she didn't stop; she only hurried to fetch more things. "I promise I will go with you every day to Hagenheim. I promise. I will not see Sir Gerek anymore. He'll be gone to Hagenheim Castle to resume his duties there tomorrow.

I don't want to go to another place. Cannot we stay here a few more days at least?"

"Why? So you can run away with Sir Gerek?"

"No, Mother, of course not. I know you are hurt because I was not truthful with you, but I was just so desperate to learn to read, and I knew you would not like it if you knew I was being taught by a man. But I do know how to read now. I can read German. It is so wonderful, and I can teach you if you wish. Only, please do not leave here so hastily. I have not fallen in love with anyone, and no one is in love with me. Please, cannot we stay?" She wasn't even sure why she wanted to stay so badly. But she felt her future was here. She did not want to go to some tiny, obscure village again.

"Men will hurt you, Rapunzel. You must not trust them. How could you have trusted him?" Her face scrunched up, her open-mouthed stare imploring. Would she start wailing again?

"Yes, Mother, I know. But he is gone now, and he did not hurt me." Rapunzel reached out and rubbed her mother's shoulder, trying to soothe her.

Mother spun away from her. "I do not know what to think. You deceived me." She shook her head, her back to her.

"I know. I am sorry. Please forgive me."

Mother simply shook her head. "It is very hard when a mother cannot trust her own child."

Rapunzel resisted the urge to huff out a sigh. Yes, she felt guilty for deceiving Mother, but wasn't she overreacting? "I did not intend to hurt you. I only wanted to get reading lessons. I am truly sorry. Let us have some pottage and I will sing to you and braid your hair. I will make the soup. You sit and rest your eyes."

But Mother ignored her and continued to pack up their things.

Rapunzel put the pea and oat pottage they had had for breakfast that morning back over the fire pit. She stirred the ashes underneath, but there wasn't an ember left. She moved the pot back out of the way and set about relighting the fire while Mother kept gathering things and packing them into blankets.

Her heart beat anxiously as she struck her flints together, creating a spark that ignited the dry beech tree bark. She added some more fuel to the fire—bark, straw, and sticks—until it was burning strong enough to burn the larger pieces of wood. The smoke stung her eyes, but she ignored it and put the pottage back over the fire.

Mother planned to leave in the morning. Rapunzel had to make a decision. Would she go with her?

She touched the pocket inside the lining of her skirt where she had tucked Sir Gerek's letter recommending her for a maidservant position at Hagenheim Castle. For once, Rapunzel had a choice. She did not have to go with Mother.

Rapunzel's heart continued to pound and skip. What would Mother do if Rapunzel refused to go with her? What if she sneaked away early in the morning and went to Hagenheim Castle? No, that would be cruel. Mother wouldn't know where she was. She would have to tell her mother what she planned to do.

Her breath seemed to leave her at the thought of defying Mother.

She finished reheating the cold pottage. Mother was still throwing things together into cloths, bags, and baskets and muttering to herself. Truly, it was times like this that she wondered if Mother was sane. Other mothers pushed their daughters to marry as soon as possible. Rapunzel had always been grateful her mother was not like that, but at the moment, she didn't feel grateful, she only felt . . . smothered. Trapped. Desperate.

She simply could not face leaving again, going to a new town, a new village, being the outsider, the strange midwife's daughter. She was tired, weary to the bone of moving over and over again and never feeling like she belonged. She knew how to read, and now she wanted to read and learn and see and do and be a part of something.

"Mother, I don't wish to leave with you tomorrow." Dishing up a bowl of pottage, she sat cross-legged on the floor with her wooden spoon and glanced across the room at Mother. "I want to stay in Hagenheim."

Mother went still, then turned her head in Rapunzel's direction. "What did you say?"

"I don't want to move, Mother. I want to stay here. And I want to go with you tomorrow to Hagenheim."

Mother didn't say anything. She also did not eat the bowl of pottage that Rapunzel tried to give her. Instead, she sat quietly crying, not bothering to wipe the tears.

When they were getting their bed ready that night, Mother still had not spoken. Then she turned and looked at Rapunzel. Mother's eyes were red rimmed and wild. "If you see that man, Sir Gerek, again, I will give you a sleeping potion and take you far away from here, where no one can find you."

Rapunzel's insides felt hollow and a cold sweat chilled her temples.

Rapunzel did not answer her. They lay down on the bed and Mother turned her back to her.

Her mind went back to the man who had attacked her and how he had seemed eager to hurt her and take revenge on her for throwing the knife into his arm. She shivered and lay facing Mother's back, reliving the terror as she had tried to outrun him, as she screamed Sir Gerek's name, as the man threw her on the ground and sat on her. She wrapped her arms around herself, curling into a ball, and squeezed her eyes shut. Then she remembered the bone-deep relief of Sir Gerek appearing with his drawn sword.

She had expected that her mother, when she heard what had happened, would put her arms around Rapunzel and comfort her. But instead, her mother had screamed at her and ranted and cried for hours.

She had to face the truth that it was no longer safe to stay with her mother.

Sir Gerek. She had always thought him arrogant and irritable, but he had been more compassionate than her mother. He'd even put his arms around her and patted her shoulder. She had thought she disliked him. But whatever it was she felt about him now, it was not dislike. Would she never see him again?

Rapunzel awoke from a dream about a squirrel hitting her on the head with a bunch of nuts. With barely a hint of light coming through the cracks in the shutters, she still heard the tapping sound. Someone was knocking on their door.

Mother got up and yelled, "Who is there?"

"Is this the home of Gothel the midwife?"

Mother opened the door. "I am Gothel the midwife."

"Please come. My mistress has been having pains since last evening."

Mother turned and reached for her birthing bag. "Rapunzel, get up. You're coming with me."

"Yes, Mother." She was dressed in her underdress, but hurried to pull her brown kirtle over her head, the one she had worn the day before with Sir Gerek's letter still in the pocket.

Rapunzel followed her mother out the door and into the dark gray of predawn.

Chapter Eighteen

Rapunzel always felt like she was in hell at a birth, with all the moans and groans and occasional rantings and screams, and this was no exception. She huddled in a corner while the laboring woman's husband and servants obeyed Mother's instructions.

One of the older servants, the cook, came into the room and pointed at Rapunzel. "Can you go to the market for me?"

The woman started moaning and crying as Mother called out, "I can see the head. Keep pushing." Mother didn't even glance up.

Rapunzel hurried out of the room with the cook, who asked her to get some calamus to help the new mother sleep once the baby came, as well as pears, because pears would help her produce more milk.

Rapunzel stepped out onto the street, thankful they were not far from the market, but her heart was pounding; this was her chance to escape.

She glanced around at all the people. It was strange and exciting and frightening all at the same time. She kept her head down as she went in the direction of the Marktplatz. No one seemed to be paying any attention to her.

When she reached the market, she found a woman selling pears and bought six. "Can you direct me to someone selling calamus?"

"The herb sellers should have some. Check in the center, near the fountain."

"Thank you." Rapunzel threaded her way through the people

and the lines of sellers and their booths. Finally, she found the sellers with their bunches of green and dried herbs laid out in small piles. Having picked herbs with her mother many times, she recognized the calamus, stepped up, and asked for a small bunch.

She walked quickly through the streets back to the house. She went in the kitchen door and gave the cook the items and turned and left without a word.

She hurried back to the town square, her blood pulsing in her ears. The five towers of Hagenheim Castle rose behind the buildings of the square, and Rapunzel made her way toward them.

Approaching the castle gatehouse, her knees went weak as she stared at the guard. He barely glanced at her as she was passing through, but Rapunzel shifted directions and walked toward him instead. "I want to work in the castle. Would you tell me where I should go?"

The guard studied her with a hard expression. "You want to be a maidservant?"

"Yes."

"Go in the back there"—he pointed to the right side of the castle—"through the kitchen door, and ask for the mistress of the maidservants, Frau Adelheit."

"Thank you."

He nodded and she kept walking.

A path had been worn toward the back of the castle, so she followed it to a stone building that was connected to the castle by a covered walkway. The door was open.

No one looked her way, so she stepped in and tried to find someone to ask. A large pig was roasting over a fire in a giant oven recessed into the wall, where the smoke all seemed to be disappearing instead of going into the room. Even though it was huge, this place for the fire, with its escape hole for the smoke, seemed to work even better than Sir Gerek's in his monastery room.

A woman stood stirring a pot at the edge of the fire, then swung an iron arm that held the pot's handle with a hook so that the pot was back over the fire. Younger women sat chopping and peeling vegetables and fruits at a long wooden table. They were all wearing the same blue cotehardie and the same white head covering, which was more like a kerchief. It pulled their hair away from their faces and tied underneath in the back, but left uncovered the hair that flowed down their backs.

Rapunzel stepped toward them. "Can you tell me how to find Frau Adelheit?"

One young woman stood up. "I can help you find her."

"I thank you." She followed the young woman out of the hot little building and across to a huge wooden door. Within the large one was a small door just tall enough and wide enough for them to pass through. They opened it and entered a dark corridor.

"Are you inquiring about the servant position?" the young woman asked.

"Ja."

"You will need to know someone who works here. Do you know anyone?" They came to a door.

"I know Cristobel."

The young woman knocked on the door.

"You may enter," a voice said on the other side.

The woman opened the door and said, "Someone is here about the servant position, Frau Adelheit." She held the door open and Rapunzel walked through. The young woman closed the door and Rapunzel was alone with a woman who appeared to be about forty years old.

Frau Adelheit sat at a small table holding a pen in her hand. She put down the pen and stared at her, but not unkindly. "What is your name?"

"Rapunzel."

"And I am Frau Adelheit, the mistress of servants at Hagenheim

Castle. What makes you think you should work at this castle for the duke and his lady?"

"I-I am willing to work hard and do whatever is required of me, Frau Adelheit."

"And why do you want to work hard and do whatever is required of you?"

"Because I-I have no family except for a mother, and I wish to work and live independently."

"That is a lofty goal for a peasant girl." But she tempered the words with a small smile.

"Lofty? I'd say it's more desperate." Rapunzel expelled a breath that was half laugh, half sigh.

Frau Adelheit raised an eyebrow.

"But I am a good worker, and I am very discreet and loyal."

The woman continued to study her. "Who would recommend you for this position? Do you know anyone who works here?"

"I know Cristobel." She suddenly realized she didn't know Cristobel's last name or exactly what her duties were at the castle.

"Cristobel?"

"Ja, Frau Adelheit." She held her breath, but when Frau Adelheit said nothing more, she stuck her hand inside her pocket. "And I have this letter from one of Duke Wilhelm's knights, Sir Gerek."

Now both her brows went up in an expression Rapunzel hoped meant she was impressed. She reached out and took the letter from Rapunzel's hand.

While Frau Adelheit read the letter, Rapunzel glanced about the room and saw large trunks and folded linens lining the shelves and two large baskets of linens—obviously a linen storage room.

Frau Adelheit looked up from the letter. "Will you want to sleep in the maids' quarters with the other live-in maids?"

Rapunzel only hesitated a moment. "Yes."

"When would you like to start?"

"As soon as possible." Rapunzel's breath caught in her throat. Was she giving her the job?

"You may begin folding these linens in the baskets and placing them in that trunk there. I shall see if Lady Rose wishes to meet you now or later. She is very particular about wanting to meet all the new servants."

"Yes, Frau Adelheit."

Rapunzel moved toward the first basket as the older woman left the room.

She picked up a wide linen sheet from the top of the pile. Her hands trembled, but she forced her fingers to glide along the edge of the fabric and find the corners, then bring them together in a fold.

What will Mother do? No doubt she will be furious. She had said she would give Rapunzel a sleeping potion and take her away from here and lock her up where she'd never defy her again. Tears pricked her eyelids. But she couldn't cry now. She might be face-to-face with the lady of the castle at any moment.

How terrifying to think of sleeping with strangers tonight. But more terrifying was what her mother might do when she discovered Rapunzel had gone to the castle. She didn't want to hurt her mother. She loved her. She was the only person in the world she belonged to or who cared for her. And sneaking away to the monastery to be taught reading by a young handsome knight . . . of course Mother had been upset when she found out. But Mother knew she wanted to learn to read and might never have found a way for her to learn. Rapunzel had to make her own way.

She could not think about Mother's anger or pain or her own guilt just now. She would think of Frau Adelheit and how best to please her, of what Cristobel would say when she saw her here, working in the castle, and of Sir Gerek. Had he already returned to the castle? It was still early in the morning. Rapunzel finished folding all the linens in the first basket and was starting the second basket when Frau Adelheit returned.

"Lady Rose will speak with you as soon as you change your clothes. Come with me."

Rapunzel followed the woman to a small room where Frau Adelheit handed her the same white chemise and blue cotehardie that the other maidservants were wearing. When she had changed and taken her braided hair out of the wimple, Frau Adelheit pinned the small, white head covering over the top of Rapunzel's hair. It did not even begin to cover all her hair.

What would Mother say? Her hair was exposed for anyone to see. She couldn't help asking, past the lump in her throat, "Are you sure my hair is covered enough?"

"Covered enough?"

"Yes. I don't want to appear indecent."

"Because your hair is so thick and long? It looks very well. Do not worry."

Frau Adelheit led her through a series of corridors and up some stairs before pausing in an open doorway.

"Come in, Frau Adelheit."

Frau Adelheit motioned for her to follow her inside. But Rapunzel hesitated when she saw Sir Gerek.

He knelt in the middle of the floor wearing a new splint that allowed him to bend his knee and only covered the lower half of his leg. He was bowing before a lady sitting in a cushioned chair that was the most luxurious piece of furniture Rapunzel had ever seen. She was also beautiful, though around the same age as Frau Adelheit.

"Please rise, Sir Gerek." Lady Rose—for that great lady could be no one else but the duke's wife—smiled at Sir Gerek. "Thank you for bringing those letters to me from my children, Gabe and Sophie. I am overjoyed to receive them. And I am so sorry about your leg and arm. Frau Lena says they are healing well?"

"Yes, my lady. Thank you."

Frau Adelheit and Rapunzel hung back against the wall, but now Lady Rose raised her gaze to them and motioned them forward.

"Good morning. Who is this beautiful maiden?"

Rapunzel walked forward. Was she allowed to speak? She wished it were permissible to fall to her knees like Sir Gerek, but she was afraid the proper response was to curtsy. She did her best to put one foot behind the other and dip her body. She hoped it was not too wobbly.

"My lady, this maiden is Rapunzel," Sir Gerek interjected. "She and her mother are the two women I told you about, that I found being attacked on the south road to Hagenheim. And this is the maiden who saved me from that attacker the next day by throwing a knife into his arm."

Rapunzel lifted her head. Lady Rose was smiling at her.

"That is very impressive, Rapunzel. I like your name. Where are you from?"

"My mother and I are from Hagenheim, but we moved away many years ago. We came here from Ottelfelt." She had run out of air after speaking so many words and paused to breathe. Lady Rose probably thought Rapunzel awkward.

"Rapunzel also knows how to read and is learning Latin."

"Oh, very good." Lady Rose turned her attention on Rapunzel again. "What made you want to learn Latin?"

"I-I suppose I wanted to be able to read the Bible."

"Oh, I have a Bible that is written entirely in German. I will let you read it sometime. But it is also very good to know Latin." Lady Rose looked to Frau Adelheit. "Perhaps Rapunzel could take Britta's place as my personal maid on Sundays and whenever she cannot be here."

"Of course, my lady." Frau Adelheit bowed her head respectfully.

"But Frau Lena, our healer, also needs another apprentice to help her in the sick chamber. Perhaps you would enjoy that, Rapunzel."

"I-I am not very much help around people who are bleeding and in pain. My mother is a midwife."

Lady Rose smiled. "I understand. We will not force you to be around people who are bleeding and in pain. But I shall see you soon and certainly on Sunday." She glanced at the mistress of the maidservants. "Thank you, Frau Adelheit. Sir Gerek. Rapunzel. You all may go."

Soon the three of them were walking back down the stairs and Rapunzel's thoughts were spinning. Should she talk to Sir Gerek? He looked very well in the colors of the rest of Duke Wilhelm's guards—green, black, and gold. His face was freshly shaved and his dark hair clean and freshly cut. How well his shoulders filled out his uniform. She was certain there could be no more handsome knight than Sir Gerek. He glanced at her once or twice.

When they reached the bottom of the steps, Frau Adelheit said, "Wait here. I'll be back in a moment to take you to the kitchen."

When she was gone, Sir Gerek turned to her. "What did your mother say about you working at the castle?"

"Nothing. I left without telling her."

He raised his brows and nodded slowly.

"Did you return this morning?" she asked.

"I came back last night with the knights who came to fetch the prisoner. And it is good you are here because Duke Wilhelm will want you to tell him what happened."

Would she have to talk to the duke as well as Lady Rose? It was all so overwhelming. But she simply nodded. "I am glad you are walking now," she said, looking at the new shorter splint on his leg.

He let out a breath. "Not as glad as I am. And in three or four weeks, I can take this off, Frau Lena said."

They stood looking at each other. Finally, he said, "If you need anything, I'm sure Frau Adelheit will take care of you. But I will try to look in on you from time to time."

"Thank you." The idea that Sir Gerek the Irritable was being kind to her made her stomach do a strange flip.

He turned and started to walk away, but then said over his shoulder, "Your hair looks pretty."

Again, her stomach did the flip, and she watched him stride down the corridor, one hand on his sword to keep it still. How soon would he end up marrying that noble-born, wealthy heiress he was hoping for? Probably very soon, and she should keep that in mind.

Chapter Nineteen

Two days later, Rapunzel was helping knead the bread dough when Sir Gerek came into the kitchen. He looked straight at Rapunzel.

"Duke Wilhelm needs to see Rapunzel in the Great Hall."

Such a summons did not require Cook's permission to obey, so Rapunzel wiped her hands on a cloth and took off her apron. The other maidservants' eyes were on her as she followed Sir Gerek out.

Sir Gerek waited for her to catch up, then said in a low voice, "Duke Wilhelm wants you to tell what happened with that man, how he attacked you, and wants you to identify him."

Rapunzel swallowed, her breath leaving her. "I will have to see him, then?"

"I am afraid so, but he will be chained and I will be there. He cannot hurt you now."

It was very kind of him to reassure her. But Sir Gerek wasn't supposed to be kind. He was supposed to be slightly arrogant and very irritable, forcing her to be rude back to him. She liked it much better that way. Didn't she?

They reached the Great Hall. Duke Wilhelm sat on the raised dais, but the trestle table that was normally set up during mealtimes was absent. Behind him on the wall hung the massive shields and battle-axes his ancestors had used in battle, tournaments, and pageantry.

Sir Gerek walked her straight up to the duke and Rapunzel curtsied, trying to force herself to breathe normally.

"State your name, if you please," Duke Wilhelm said.

"Rapunzel Scheinberg, your grace." A guard was standing near Duke Wilhelm, and a clerk sat writing at a table next to the duke's chair. Sir Gerek stood beside her, but no one else seemed to be in the room.

"Sir Gerek has told me what he knows about the man who claims his name is Balthasar. And now I would like to hear you tell what happened concerning the man who attacked you."

Rapunzel began to tell him what had happened but as briefly as possible. Her voice was breathy and halting, but she felt encouraged by Sir Gerek's presence and was soon speaking normally. She finished the rather long narrative by saying, "Sir Gerek knocked him senseless and had him tied up. I have not seen the man since then."

Duke Wilhelm gave her a quick nod. "I know you probably do not wish to see him, but if you are willing, I need you to look at him one more time, to ensure we have the right man."

"Yes, your grace. I will."

He nodded to the guard beside him, who left the room.

Duke Wilhelm said something quietly to the clerk, who handed the duke the piece of parchment he had been writing on. The duke stared down at it until the guard returned with two more guards who were leading a man with chains on his wrists and ankles.

Her stomach twisted and her face tingled. It was the smiling man—Balthasar.

"Is this the man who attacked you?"

"Yes, this is the man."

Duke Wilhelm waved his hand at the guards and they pulled on the man's arms, trying to turn him around. He snarled and resisted them for a moment, curling his top lip in an even more sinister version of a smile, looking directly at Rapunzel.

It was hard to breathe as they led the man away with the clanking of his arm and leg chains.

Duke Wilhelm was speaking. "I shall keep him in the dungeon for a while and then make sure he is banished from Hagenheim forever. Would you like to be present when I pronounce his sentence?"

She thought for a moment. "No, your grace." She never wanted to see the man's face again. Ever.

"I am very sorry that such a frightening thing happened to you," Duke Wilhelm said.

"I thank you, your grace. You are very kind." Which was why she was having trouble blinking back tears. If everyone would cease being so kind to her . . .

Sir Gerek walked with her out of the Great Hall while she concentrated on breathing evenly and remaining composed.

Sir Gerek said nothing as they made their way toward the kitchen door. Just before she reached it, she glanced at him, then away, remembering how he had comforted her after this Balthasar had attacked her the last time. "I must get back to work." She hurried into the kitchen before he had time to respond.

After almost a week of working in the kitchen, being surrounded by people every moment of the day and night, Rapunzel was given permission to leave the kitchen early.

She put away her apron and hurried outside. The sun was just setting and the sky was streaked with deep pink and orange. She glanced around for some place where she might sit and be alone with her thoughts. She drew near the maidservants' quarters and pushed the door open a bit and listened. Voices. Someone, at least two people, were inside talking and laughing. Rapunzel turned and hurried away.

She walked behind the servants' quarters. Beyond was the huge stable, and beyond that were the buildings where the knights and male servants slept. She would have to go out the town gate in order to get beyond those buildings.

One enormous tree stood between the kitchen and the stable. It was so large and its limbs so low to the ground, her feet hurried toward it. Once she was on the other side of its giant trunk, she sat down and gazed at the bright sunset through its spidery branches, leaning back against the wrinkled bark.

Rapunzel sighed. It had been so long since she had been alone. She didn't want to think about her guilt at hurting Mother and leaving without saying where she was going. She pushed back against the pain of her mother's madness and the cruel things she had said, of her not believing in Rapunzel's innocence and threatening to give her a sleeping potion and carry her away against her will. She also didn't want to dwell on the fact that she thought entirely too much about Sir Gerek. She just wanted to breathe in the fresh air, drink in the beauty of the sky, and listen to the breeze and the—

Shouts came from near the stable and the men's sleeping quarters, followed by a laugh and more voices. But at least they were not talking to her. She could still pretend to be alone and unseen.

She also didn't want to think about how every night she went to the maidservants' quarters and was surrounded by a half dozen other young women. Instead of wanting to sleep or sit quietly with their own thoughts, they all wanted to talk. They talked and talked, and Rapunzel tried to pretend to be asleep, mostly hoping they would not talk to her. She was tired, she was lonely, and the guilt over leaving her mother was almost overpowering. The last thing she wanted to do was make conversation with strangers.

Cristobel had made sure Rapunzel's bed was next to hers. Rapunzel was so thankful for her new friend who helped her know what to do in the kitchen when Rapunzel was unsure. Thankfully, when Frau Adelheit asked for helpers to do some sewing and mending, others had volunteered, sparing Rapunzel from her least favorite chore, which she was not very good at. The other girls seemed so comfortable with each other, and Cristobel was friends with every other girl who worked at the castle, and she wanted Rapunzel to know them all as well. But Rapunzel listened, smiled, nodded, and answered their questions with as few words as possible.

They talked of things Rapunzel knew nothing about. They seemed eager to finish their work so they could talk, and they laughed—so loudly! Talking and laughing, they looked like they were so full of joy and were completely at ease. Was there something wrong with Rapunzel because she did not want to join in? Would she always be the strange girl?

The sky had lost most of its color and was growing dark. All around her the sounds of voices were low and muted, far away, as people finished their work and headed to wherever they needed to go. But Rapunzel had nowhere to go, and no one to go to. Mother . . . what was she doing now? Did she hate Rapunzel? Would Rapunzel break her mother's heart with worry? Truly, she must be the worst daughter ever. But the truth was, she was afraid of Mother. Still, she should get word to her. She should tell her where she had gone. And she would. Soon.

The next morning, while Rapunzel was working in the kitchen, Sir Gerek came in to get some food. He said he'd missed breakfast because he was helping a sick friend get to the healer's chamber.

While the cook was fetching him something, he started walking toward Rapunzel.

"How are you liking the work?" He stared at her with those intense brown eyes.

"I like it very well." Rapunzel kept chopping, aware that all the other kitchen maids were now staring at her and Sir Gerek.

He picked up an apple and bit into it. Then the cook gave him the food wrapped in a small cloth. He took it and nodded to everyone around the room. "Thank you, fair maidens. Keep up the good work." He gave them a jaunty smile and left.

"Rapunzel has a sweetheart," one of the maids called out in a singsong voice. "Rapunzel, why did you not tell us? A secret like that?"

Her heart thudded against her breastbone. She shook her head. "He is not my sweetheart." But her words were drowned out by the exclamations of the other servants.

"Leave her alone. They're only friends," Cristobel defended. The girls protested, so Cristobel went on. "You are all so crude and wouldn't understand. Can she help it if he had to save her from robbers on the road?"

"Oo, I wish Sir Gerek could save me from robbers!" someone exclaimed. Cristobel's defense had only made things worse.

Later Cristobel whispered in her ear, "Is something between you two, something more than friendship?"

Rapunzel shook her head. "Of course not."

Then Frau Adelheit summoned her outside the kitchen door and handed her a small book. "Sir Gerek asked me to give you this. He said you didn't have anything to read and would need to practice your skills."

Frau Adelheit's face was unreadable as Rapunzel took the book from her. She hid it in her skirt pocket and went back to work.

That night all the maidservants were together again, and she dreaded a return to the subject. All she wanted to do was run away, find a secluded place—perhaps the apple orchard behind the castle—and be alone with her thoughts. She also could feel the book heavy in her pocket. What book was it? But she did not dare take it out and let the others see it and make more insinuations about her and Sir Gerek.

Tomorrow she would finally have a few hours to herself, as she had the morning off before taking over Britta's duties with Lady Rose and her daughters. Perhaps she would go to find Mother and let her know that she was well.

The other maidservants were talking amongst themselves, and Rapunzel lay down on her bed and faced away from them. If she was fortunate, they would forget about her tonight. She patted her pocket, feeling the book inside, and marveled at Sir Gerek bringing it for her.

Of course she knew, as the other servants did not, that he was not the least interested in her. He was too honorable to take advantage of her, or at least, she hoped so. He intended to marry a wealthy heiress, and Rapunzel was the furthest thing from it.

Even if the other maidservants did think untrue things about her and Sir Gerek, she was still thankful for a friend—especially now that she cried herself to sleep every night thinking about Mother and about how angry and lonely and hurt she must feel. *O Father God, please forgive me.*

Rapunzel walked out of the town gate toward the meadow on the hill overlooking Hagenheim. The cool air caressed her cheeks while the sun warmed her head. Under her feet, green grass was beginning to peek through the brown leaves.

Part of her wanted to keep going, all the way to the little hovel in the woods, and explain to Mother where she was, that she was safe and working, but she simply did not have the courage. Yet.

She sat on the ground with her back against the trunk of the lone tree at the top of the hill and pulled out the book Sir Gerek had given her. The title was *Parzival*, an epic poem by Wolfram von Eschenbach. She had heard of this story. Parzival was a knight in the service of King Arthur who searched for the Holy Grail. She began reading the story-poem and found herself quickly turning the pages to find out what would happen next.

The faint sounds of a horse's hoofbeats drew her mind and her eyes away from her book.

"I thought that was you sitting here." Sir Gerek stopped his big black horse a few feet from her.

She drew her knees up and made sure her ankles were covered. She had almost gotten used to having her hair showing. Almost. She touched the thick braid that lay across her shoulder as she gazed up at him.

"You're not wearing your splints anymore."

He dismounted. "No. Frau Lena said the bones were probably healed now. What do you think of the book?"

"I like it very well." She couldn't hide her smile as joy welled up inside her. She was reading a book. She was reading.

"I found that illuminated copy of *Parzival* when I was competing in a tourney in Koln with Valten—Lord Hamlin. The illustrations are very colorful, don't you think?"

"Yes, they are quite wonderful. But the story is my favorite part."

He fiddled with his horse's reins.

"I shall return it to you when I finish."

"No hurry. I know where to find you if I want it back. How do you find working at the castle? Is it to your liking?"

"It is interesting, but a little overwhelming. Sometimes I think I will scream, being around people constantly. I am not used to that. I rather enjoy being alone, walking through the trees and listening to birds singing and the rustle of the wind." Alone, except for Mother. And she did miss her.

"There is none of that alone time at Hagenheim Castle." One side of his mouth went up.

"I do not wish to complain. Everyone is kind, and the work is not too hard for me."

He nodded. "It is difficult when you are never quiet with your own thoughts. I shall leave you, then, so you can enjoy some time alone."

She opened her mouth to tell him she didn't want him to leave, but instead she said, "Thank you so much for the book. I am enjoying it."

"When you finish, I can loan you others."

"I would like that very much."

He turned his horse and rode away, the horse's hooves quickly eating up the ground, throwing small clods of dirt up behind each footfall.

Why was Sir Gerek so kind to her? He hadn't grunted or growled at her once since she came to the castle. Would he expect something in return? Mother would say so. Mother never would have allowed her to accept the book, or allowed him to teach her to read. Mother . . . what was she doing at this moment? Was she looking for Rapunzel? Would she do something terrible to her if she found her? Or was she only worried and sad?

She glanced around the wide-open space. No one was near. The springtime sun was warm but the air was still cold, and she pulled her hood over her head.

She tried to go back to reading, but her thoughts kept pulling back to Mother. Sometimes she could hardly believe she'd had the courage to leave and ask for a job at the castle. Guilt still pricked her. But it had been the right thing to do. Still, she would eventually have to face her.

Chapter Twenty

That afternoon Rapunzel went with Frau Adelheit to the family's chambers and to Lady Rose so she could start working with her, taking Britta's place on Sundays and occasional times when Britta was away. As they approached the solar, Rapunzel wiped her palms on her skirt and took a deep breath. Lady Rose was the wife of a duke. Would she think Rapunzel too awkward to work with her? Would Rapunzel know what to do? She had never been very good at fixing hair or mending or all the other things a lady's servant should know about. Perhaps Lady Rose would realize she had made a mistake asking Rapunzel to be her new maidservant.

When they reached the top of the stairs and stood in the doorway to the solar, Lady Rose was reading to a small girl about five years old. Two older boys were playing a game with carved wooden figures, and a young pregnant woman was sewing in a corner.

Lady Rose finished reading and looked up. "Here is our new helper," she said to the little girl. "Her name is Rapunzel." She stood and reached out and quickly squeezed Rapunzel's hand. "I'll show her around, Frau Adelheit. Thank you."

Frau Adelheit curtsied and left. The little girl said, "Take me with you, Mama." So Lady Rose took her hand.

"Come with me, Rapunzel. I'll show you where the girls sleep, and you can help us with our hair tonight and any other little things we need."

"Yes, my lady," Rapunzel said as Frau Adelheit had instructed her.

She followed Lady Rose down the corridor. Lady Rose knocked on a door.

"This is where Lady Margaretha and Lady Kirstyn sleep." She opened the door and inside were two beds, some trunks, two chairs, and on the wall a large looking glass. "You can help them with their hair in a few hours—brush it and braid it—and then come and help me with mine. These pitchers need to be filled with fresh water every night and these towels replaced with fresh linens from the linen room."

Rapunzel nodded to show she knew where it was. Then she became aware of someone standing just outside the door in the corridor.

"Mama, can I go play with Margret?"

"Yes, liebling."

The little girl ran to the young woman standing nearby, who caught the girl in her arms and lifted her up high in the air, making the girl squeal.

"That little feisty bundle of liveliness is my daughter Adela and the young maiden is her nursemaid, Margret."

Rapunzel nodded.

"So tell me more about yourself, Rapunzel. Do you have brothers and sisters?"

"No, my lady. I was left with my mother, who is a midwife, when I was a baby. My mother never married or had children. Only me."

"And you did not want to be a midwife. I remember. What do you like to do?"

"I like to sing and make up songs. I also paint a little."

"A songwriter? I would love to hear one of your songs. Do you know how to play any instruments?"

"No, but I have always wanted to learn. Is there anyone here who would teach me?"

"Perhaps you can learn with Kirstyn. She is just learning to play the lute."

"That would be wonderful," Rapunzel said in a breathy tone, awed at the prospect.

"You said you like to paint. What do you paint?"

"I paint flowers and birds and vines. I paint them on our houses since I never like the plain white plaster. Mother likes that I paint our houses . . . or she used to."

"She used to? She doesn't like it anymore?"

Should Rapunzel be afraid to tell Lady Rose that she had run away from home to work at the castle? Would she force her to go back? Rapunzel was nineteen now, so surely she would not.

"I . . . my mother is angry with me just now. She did not want me to come here to work."

Lady Rose put a hand on the back of Rapunzel's shoulder. "I am sorry she made you feel like she didn't approve. Did she want you to get married instead?"

"Oh, no. She does not want me to ever get married at all. Does that seem strange?"

Lady Rose seemed to consider that question carefully as she stared past Rapunzel. "I think it is very difficult for mothers—and fathers—to let go of their daughters. It will be difficult for me to see mine marry and go away to their own homes. But I have sons who have brought me daughters-in-law whom I love as my own children. It must be much harder for your mother since she has only you."

Rapunzel's heart sank a little.

"Still, if your mother loves you, she should understand that you must make your own life. We mothers have to let go of our children and let them become adults. It is difficult, perhaps, but necessary and a healthy part of life."

She couldn't imagine Mother ever being able to accept Rapunzel being an adult, or being able to see that loving Rapunzel meant letting her make choices. Truly, it was a rather strange concept. Daughters were married off by their parents to the man who would make the best match for them, whether wealthy or poor. As a grown daughter, being able to make her own choices in life was something that appealed to Rapunzel very much.

But it would not please Mother.

"Perhaps she will realize you need to have your own life."

Rapunzel wanted to agree. "Perhaps."

How strange—and wonderful—that Lady Rose would want to have such a conversation with her maidservant.

Rapunzel had been at Hagenheim Castle for two weeks when Duke Wilhelm decided to give a banquet.

"What is the banquet for?" Rapunzel asked Cook as she prepared apples and plums for the sauce.

"Not *what* but *who*," Cook said. "It's for Lord Claybrook, a new suitor for Margaretha, the duke's oldest daughter."

"I hear he is from England and that he's very handsome," Cristobel said.

Claybrook. That was the name Mother had mentioned. The man who had deserted her—she said he had gone to England with a Lord Claybrook.

"Cook, may I help serve the first course?" Cristobel asked.

"No, that's the job of the pages and squires."

Cristobel's face fell, as did the other maidservants'.

"But I suppose, during the main course, if the pages need help, you can help serve."

Smiles broke out on every face.

The reason her mother wanted to come to Hagenheim was to seek revenge on the man who had wronged her, the man who had just come back from England. What would Mother do now that he was back? Did the man still care for Mother?

The pace of the preparations grew more feverish as the night went on. Rapunzel and her fellow servants continued to work for hours, and always there was more to do, more dishes that Cook wanted them to prepare, more meat, more sauces, more frumenty, more diced-meat-and-fruit pies.

Finally, it was time to start taking the food out to the Great Hall and to the grand feast. The squires and pages lined up to accept the dishes and carry them out. One by one Rapunzel watched them carry the large, full platters. The food never ran out, but neither did the squires. The other maidservants were beginning to frown and grumble to each other. Still, Cook barked orders and they all continued to work.

Suddenly, Rapunzel looked up but did not see Cook. The other servants were whispering excitedly. Cristobel came and leaned over her shoulder. "We're going to go peek into the Great Hall. Want to come?"

Rapunzel dropped the knife she was using to chop walnuts and followed Cristobel and the other servants. They ran across the walkway to the door that led to the Great Hall. They giggled and whispered. When they reached the door, someone opened it only a crack. "I can't see!" "Move out of the way!" "Open the door."

The door was forced open wide, and Rapunzel was pushed from behind until she was standing in the doorway with the others.

She stared, trying to make out the different people sitting at the banqueting tables. Duke Wilhelm and Lady Rose sat on the dais, of course, with the rest of their family members. Duchess Kathryn, Duke Wilhelm's mother, was not present, as she was very old and sickly and rarely left her chamber anymore. But seated across from Lady Margaretha was someone Rapunzel had not seen before.

"Is that Lord Claybrook? He is handsome." They all gave their opinions of the new suitor from England.

Lord Claybrook was wearing the most elaborate hat Rapunzel had ever seen. At the moment, he was smirking, his shoulders thrown back, his brows lifted in a most haughty fashion. Compared to Sir Gerek, he didn't seem very handsome.

Unimpressed with Lady Margaretha's suitor, Rapunzel searched the lower tables for Sir Gerek.

There he was, sitting with other knights on one side of the table, with a row of ladies seated opposite. And seated directly opposite Sir Gerek was the maiden Rapunzel had bumped into in town, the one who had called her an ignorant peasant and belittled her clothes. Rainhilda. She was wearing a similar veil to the one she'd worn in town, secured to her head with a circlet of ribbons. Sir Gerek and Rainhilda were smiling at each other.

"Look at Rainhilda flirting with Sir Gerek," Cristobel whispered, making a gagging sound. "She thinks she's so pretty."

And she was quite pretty in her pink silk cotehardie. Rainhilda was smiling and tilting her head, making her blond ringlets bounce, and paying no attention at all to the poor squire standing by her shoulder, trying to ask if she wanted some pheasant from his platter. But Sir Gerek was not discouraging her. He leaned his head forward and laughed.

Rapunzel was no one. Rainhilda was a beauty and an heiress, the daughter of a wealthy landed knight. Rapunzel was the daughter of . . . she didn't even know who.

And the only mother she had ever known probably hated her now.

But why was she reacting this way? She didn't even like Sir Gerek. He was arrogant and grouchy and did not wish to marry for love, due to his strange idea that if he loved his wife, he would mistreat her the way his father had done.

Her heart still squeezed in compassion at the thought of him as a little boy, learning that his father had killed his mother in a rage over an argument about him. And thinking of him marrying Rainhilda made her feel sick. Rainhilda was not the sort of wife Rapunzel would wish for him.

Cristobel whispered, "I've heard Sir Gerek is planning to marry a wealthy widow."

"Is the widow here?" Rapunzel whispered back.

"I don't think so."

"What are you girls doing?" Frau Adelheit's voice scattered the group of maidservants and sent them running back to the kitchen.

She tried to remember Sir Gerek as he had been when she and her mother had first come across him, slightly rude and arrogant, and how he had not wanted to teach her to read, but had only agreed because the monks were taking care of him and asked him to. If only he hadn't started being so kind to her, speaking in a friendly way to her at the castle, and even loaning her a book to read. Then she wouldn't feel this ache in her chest.

Sir Gerek and his fellow knights went into the Great Hall for their midday meal. Lord Claybrook was there, speaking with his captain, Sir Reginald, near the doorway.

"Is she trustworthy?" he heard Lord Claybrook ask in his native English.

"She will do whatever I tell her to," Sir Reginald answered.

Lord Claybrook smiled and nodded, and they both made their way toward the trestle tables where Duke Wilhelm was already seated.

Gerek couldn't help wondering who they were talking about. Something about this Claybrook fellow, his captain, Sir Reginald, and all the knights and guards he had brought with him seemed suspicious. Claybrook lived in England, so why was he seeking a bride in the German regions of the Holy Roman Empire? Yes, his uncle controlled Keiterhafen, which was nearby, but that made his presence here even more suspicious. Hagenheim had been so peaceful for so long, perhaps Duke Wilhelm was not on his guard against possible attack as he should be.

Claybrook complimented Duke Wilhelm on his defenses, on the obvious strength of the wall around the town and of the castle. "Indeed," Claybrook said, "I have not seen a better fortified town anywhere, not even my uncle's town of Keiterhafen."

When Duke Wilhelm turned to speak to someone else, Claybrook looked at Sir Reginald out of the corner of his eye and smiled.

One of Gerek's friends drew his attention away to ask if he was going with Duke Wilhelm, Valten, Claybrook, and several other knights to search for the robbers who had been plaguing the north road. Several rumors circulated about the number of robbers, as well as their identities.

"No, I have other business I must attend to," Gerek told him.

He had not seen Rapunzel for a few days. Was she still working at the castle, or had she gone back to her mother? She had said she was tired of being around people all the time and wished for some time alone. Listening to the conversations around him, he was feeling the same way. Perhaps he would take a ride today.

His companions stood and he stood too. He turned and caught sight of a maidservant coming toward him. It was Rapunzel.

She had something hidden in the folds of her skirt as she approached him. Thankfully, no one was paying attention to them as she said, "I finished your book. Thank you so much for allowing me to borrow it." She surreptitiously held it out to him.

"Did you enjoy it?"

She smiled. Saints above, but she was pretty, with her thick blond braid hanging down her back and peeking out of her small head covering. She had the most perfectly sweet features.

He tore his gaze from her face and cleared his throat.

"I very much enjoyed reading about Parzival. It was good, but I was wondering—"

"Would you like to borrow another book?"

She smiled and nodded.

"Of course. I'll go get one now."

"No, you don't have to go out of your way to do it now."

"It's no trouble. Where will you be?"

"I can wait for you somewhere. I was going to the meadow."

"I'll meet you there and bring the book." His step was light and quick as he strode toward the door.

He had practically leapt at the chance to give her another book. But was it wise? Perhaps he should go back to treating her like a peasant and not paying attention to how pretty she was, but he couldn't resist the smile that lit up her face when he gave her new reading material. Besides, what harm could it bring? She disliked him, and with any good fortune, he would be married soon.

In no time he had fetched three small books and his horse and rode toward the tree at the top of the hill in the meadow overlooking the castle. Rapunzel was already there, standing and looking up through the branches at the sky.

When she heard him coming, she looked in his direction, shading her eyes with her hand. She wore a woolen shawl around her shoulders to guard against the chilly spring air.

He reined Donner in and dismounted, taking three books out of his saddlebag. "Here is the gospel of Saint John, the letter to the Romans, and I brought *The Poem of the Cid*."

"Thank you." She accepted the books, and their fingers brushed. Her cheeks were pink, but he couldn't tell if the color was from the crisp air or if she was blushing.

"You didn't have to bring three."

He shrugged. "They are all short. I found this copy of the gospel of John in a little shop in Heidelberg."

"Thank you. I enjoyed the story of Parzival, but the Holy Writ is more . . . comforting."

The way she caressed the books, holding them close to her, made his heart miss a beat. He cleared his throat.

"Are you practicing your war maneuvers today?"

"No, today Duke Wilhelm is taking Lord Claybrook on a tour of the town. I am taking Donner for a ride."

"Donner?"

"That's my horse."

She nodded. "I suppose it is rather inconvenient having Lord Claybrook's men here."

"I'm not sure why he had to bring so many guards. But he's from England. Maybe that's how all their noblemen travel."

"I caught a glimpse of him. The other servants and I were looking through the door at the feast on the day he arrived." She paused. "I saw Rainhilda flirting with you."

"You saw that?" He ran a hand through his hair.

"She is very beautiful. Will you marry her? I have heard she has a very large inheritance and dowry."

"Perhaps. But I think it more likely I'll marry the widow of Lord Lankouwen. She has no heirs, and she is looking for someone who can defend her castle."

"That sounds like a very good situation for you. And she's probably less . . . immature than Rainhilda."

He grimaced. “I must seem very greedy and grasping to you.”

“I understand that you want to do well for yourself. I would not presume to judge you.”

Well, she shouldn’t judge him. But he did wish she could admire him. *Foolish, foolish thought.*

“You should marry Lady Kirstyn, Duke Wilhelm’s second daughter. She is a very sweet girl.”

“Duke Wilhelm would never let one of his daughters marry me. I am only a landless knight. No, I could not hope to marry a duke’s daughter.”

Rapunzel stared down at the books in her hands.

“I should let you be alone. Fare well.” He swiftly remounted his horse.

“Thank you for the books. I shall return them.”

He gave her a quick nod and steered Donner toward the woods. He skirted the edge of the forest, letting Donner go as fast as he wished, letting the cold air sting his face, hoping it would distract his thoughts from the beautiful peasant girl with the golden braid and blue eyes.

Chapter Twenty-One

That night Rapunzel was brushing Lady Rose's hair and thinking of how Mother used to brush her hair every night. Rapunzel would sing while Mother braided her hair. But she did not sing to Lady Rose. Instead, she listened while Lady Rose talked to her.

"Sir Gerek has been with us for a long time."

"Yes, he told me." She should not have admitted to knowing that intimate bit of knowledge. "That is, I know that knights are sent as young boys to live with the noble family where they will train as knights."

"He told me how you saved him from that brigand by throwing a knife and striking his arm. Where did you learn to throw like that?"

"Some village boys were throwing knives and I wanted to know how to do it too. I asked them to teach me and they did."

"Did you know the knife would strike him in the arm?"

"That is what I was aiming for. My aim is good since I used to practice a lot." She could see Lady Rose smiling in the mirror.

"Did you know I had another daughter besides Margaretha, Kirstyn, and Adela?"

"You *had* another?"

"Yes, and she had hair as blond as yours." Lady Rose stared at Rapunzel's yellow-blond braid in the mirror, which lay across her shoulder.

"What happened to her?" Rapunzel asked softly.

Lady Rose sighed. "When she was three years old, she fell in the river. We never found her body." Tears glistened in her eyes.

"I'm so sorry that happened."

"Thank you, my dear. It was a horrible time, but God comforted me. Margaretha was a baby, and I had to be strong for my two older boys, Valten and Gabehart. But it still feels like there's a hole in my heart. Have you ever felt that way?"

Rapunzel thought for a moment. "If I let myself think about it, I sometimes feel that way about my parents. I'll never know who they were, I suppose, and it does leave an emptiness inside me."

Lady Rose nodded. "I think it is very understandable that you would feel that way." She turned around and clasped Rapunzel's hand and smiled. "I'm so glad you're here with us, Rapunzel."

Tears pricked her eyes. She missed her mother, but she also wished her mother was as kind and loving and nurturing as Lady Rose. If only she could throw her arms around her and feel comforted.

"If you don't need me anymore, I'll go and take care of Lady Margaretha and Lady Kirstyn."

"That will be very good. Thank you, my dear."

She let go of Rapunzel's hand, and Rapunzel rushed out of the room before any tears could spill.

"Rapunzel." Frau Adelheit motioned her forward with her hand. "I need some help with the linens." She looked at Cook. "That is, if you can spare her."

Cook turned her hand back and forth in the air. "We are not busy. Take her."

Rapunzel followed Frau Adelheit out of the room. She only hoped she would not have to sew.

Duke Wilhelm, Lord Hamlin, Sir Gerek, and Lord Claybrook had all been away for the last week, so Rapunzel and the other kitchen maids' work had been much lighter.

She was not exactly sure where they'd all gone—something about capturing brigands on the roads north of Hagenheim. But gossip said that Sir Gerek had gone to arrange a marriage with Lady Lankouwen. And if a few tears leaked onto Rapunzel's pillow the last couple of nights as she thought of him marrying, she would not admit it to anyone. Sir Gerek had been her friend, and she had always known he would marry an heiress. It was as she had expected and as it should be.

Frau Adelheit led her to the laundry storage room and pointed to a large basket filled with linens. "I need you to fold these."

Rapunzel immediately set to work, and Frau Adelheit began counting sheets, making notes on a piece of parchment on her little desk, and then started folding from another large basket.

Rapunzel glanced around. There were no less than six large baskets full of linens just like the one Rapunzel was folding from. They would be here a long time.

Frau Adelheit suddenly broke the silence. "I heard about what happened to you, getting attacked on the road and Sir Gerek saving you." She snapped the sheet she was holding before folding it in a perfect square. "Has he behaved in a suitable manner toward you?"

"Very much so." She ran her thumb over the scar on the palm of her right hand and reached for another sheet. "He lets me borrow his books." There had never been anything improper between them, though no one seemed to believe it.

Frau Adelheit asked her more questions, and she even told Rapunzel about her own childhood. They had to pass the time, and since they had to work in the same room together, talking to Frau Adelheit was less awkward than remaining silent.

Frau Adelheit's parents had both worked at Hagenheim Castle but were now dead, and so was her husband—and Rapunzel told her how she had run away from her mother to work at the castle. She learned about Frau Adelheit's three grown children, and Rapunzel told her about the strange things her mother had said when she saw Rapunzel with Sir Gerek.

"I think you did the right thing by getting away from her," Frau Adelheit said. "But perhaps she will change now that she sees the consequences of her words."

"Yes, perhaps."

When had she ever talked to anyone like this? She had not even told Cristobel all these things. Mother had made her feel as if she could not trust anyone, and she realized now that was not normal. Other people were not so closemouthed. Other people were not afraid that all men were unscrupulous. Mother's influence had caused Rapunzel to think in a way that was not healthy or conducive to having relationships with people. People had faults and were not perfect, but they weren't all out to hurt her, as her mother had tried to convince her.

They only had one more basket of linens to fold, and they both started on it.

"For a long time," Rapunzel said, "I've wondered if my mother lied to me about where I came from."

"What makes you think she may have lied to you?" Frau Adelheit asked.

"She used to tell me that she found me as a baby in the rapunzel patch behind our house. Then she changed the story and said I was abandoned at her front door when I was about three years old. I always got the feeling that there was more to the story than she was telling me, but she would become angry if I questioned her about it.

"And I have this scar on my hand." Rapunzel held out her right hand so the candlelight was shining on it for Frau Adelheit to see. "I asked Mother about it once, but she said she didn't know how I got it. I thought that was strange, if the second story was true. After all, if I was a baby when someone left me in her garden, then I must have gotten the scar after I came to live with her. How could she not know how I got it? Although if the other story was true and I was three when she found me, then— What's wrong?"

Frau Adelheit had taken hold of Rapunzel's hand and was staring at it with her mouth open. "O holy angels in heaven," she rasped. "It cannot be." Tears glistened as she turned her body to face Rapunzel and stared at her—not into her eyes, but at her face, as though searching her features.

"What is it? Tell me."

"I think . . . I think . . . Oh, heavenly saints." She made the sign of the cross over her chest as a tear dripped from her eye.

"Tell me!" Rapunzel's heart was in her throat. "Do you know who my parents were?"

"You have the exact same scar that—" Her breath hitched. She pressed her hand over her mouth, then said, "The same scar that Duke Wilhelm and Lady Rose's oldest daughter, Elsebeth, had."

Rapunzel's face tingled. "Duke Wilhelm and Lady Rose? That is not possible. They would never abandon their child." A realization was washing over her. She tried to grasp it.

"No, of course not. But when Elsebeth was three, she fell into the river. I knew the nursemaid. She was watching Elsebeth and Gabehart, and she tried to get to the little girl, but she was carried downriver. They never found her body, but we all assumed she had drowned." Her eyes were wide and tears puddled under her bottom eyelid. "But . . . but she could have lived."

Frau Adelheit found a small cloth and wiped her cheeks. Her

voice shook. "When little Elsebeth had just turned three, she was running and fell. There happened to be a piece of pottery, a shard from a broken pitcher, on the ground, and it cut her right hand very badly. I was nearby and ran to get a cloth to wrap around her hand, and they carried her to Frau Lena. It made quite a scar—a curved scar just like the one on your hand, in just the same place. Rapunzel, I think . . . I know . . . you are Elsebeth."

Rapunzel was numb all over, her thoughts spinning. "I-I don't understand. Why would Mother lie about where she found me? Could she have known who I was?" She covered her own mouth as her lips and chin began to tremble. Was it possible? Could she be the daughter of Lady Rose and Duke Wilhelm?

"But I-I look nothing like Duke Wilhelm or Lady Rose."

"There is a resemblance. Kirstyn and Adela both have blond hair, though not quite as golden as yours, and though your eyes are as blue as Duke Wilhelm's, they have the same look as Lady Rose's. I have heard that the duchess, Duke Wilhelm's mother, had golden-blond hair like yours. Oh yes, you definitely have the family resemblance." She nodded over and over as she stared at her.

Rapunzel examined the scar on her hand, her heart thumping erratically. "Are you sure? Are you sure it's the same scar?" Could she truly be the lost daughter of Lady Rose and Duke Wilhelm? It made sense, but it also seemed the most far-fetched thing imaginable.

Frau Adelheit took her hand and turned it toward the light again. "It's exactly the way I remember it. And you look to be the correct age—three years younger than Gabe and two years older than Margaretha."

"What . . . what should I do?"

"You have to tell Lady Rose."

"I'm afraid to tell her. What if we're wrong? Perhaps I should talk to Mother first."

Frau Adelheit looked thoughtful. “I suppose it cannot hurt to wait. But as soon as you show Lady Rose that scar, she will know you are her Elsebeth.”

Mother must have found Rapunzel . . . Elsebeth . . . in the river and didn’t know who she was. “I have to find Mother and ask her.” But what if she had deliberately stolen Rapunzel away from her rightful parents? No, surely she could not have done anything so horrendous.

“I will first speak to Mother about this. I must find out what she knows, what she did . . . how this happened.”

“But didn’t she threaten to give you a sleeping potion and take you away from here and lock you up? I do not think you should confront her, not alone. If she did take you, knowing you were the duke’s daughter, then she may do something terrible. You don’t know what she might do. Promise me you will not leave the castle.”

“Very well. I promise.” A heaviness settled inside as she thought about how her mother—the only mother she could remember, the mother who needed her to brush her hair and sing to her at night or she couldn’t fall asleep—must have known whose child she was and took her as her own anyway. How could she be so cruel? The breath squeezed painfully out of her chest, her mind going blank with the horror of it.

Gerek was back at Hagenheim Castle. He had been gone for several days, as he had gone to visit Lady Lankouwen to arrange a marriage with her. He had found her quite willing. Although nothing was settled and they were not betrothed, Lady Lankouwen wished to send a letter to the king and await his approval. Then they could publish the banns and marry.

He should feel joyful about the prospect of securing his own future, a sturdy castle, and fertile lands. The arrangement was wise and profitable, and Lady Lankouwen seemed pleased. She had even kissed him on the cheek when he left, and he had kissed her hand. Perhaps it would even be an affectionate marriage.

In his absence, Duke Wilhelm and Valten had gone and would not be back for several more days. So when he saw three of Claybrook's guards huddled together, he wondered why they and Lord Claybrook were not with the duke.

One of them looked up and saw Gerek, and they stopped talking and took a step away from each other.

"Good morning," Gerek said.

"Good morning," they mumbled.

He walked past them, but when he looked over his shoulder, they were leaning in to continue whatever conversation he had interrupted.

Were they scheming something? Gerek stopped just out of sight of them and listened, but he couldn't make out what they were saying. Not wanting them to discover him eavesdropping, he continued on down the corridor.

Perhaps Gerek could find out something from listening in to some of the other guards' conversations.

He strode out of the castle and toward the gatehouse, trying to look like all the other people milling around the castle bailey who were either servants or skilled craftsmen, like the castle blacksmith and the saddle maker. Having just come back from Lady Lankouwen's estate, Gerek wasn't wearing his usual Hagenheim colors, and he hoped to blend in.

As he stood looking in at the blacksmith's open work area, he glanced at the gatehouse and noticed the same three guards he'd seen talking in the corridor now walking toward the gatehouse. Only one of Duke Wilhelm's guards was inside, and he stepped outside to greet them. The three of Claybrook's men moved toward him in a rush, then pushed him inside.

Gerek started forward, reaching for his sword at his hip, but then remembered he'd left it in the barracks. He glanced around, but no one else noticed what they'd done.

He watched two of the men drag the guard's limp body to a nearby shed. They soon emerged and walked back to the gatehouse to join the one who had stayed, as if he belonged there.

With a sick feeling, he realized Lord Claybrook and his men were starting to take over Hagenheim.

None of Duke Wilhelm's guards were in sight. He needed armed men loyal to Duke Wilhelm. He needed to warn all of the guards and knights at the castle, and someone needed to inform Duke Wilhelm.

He worked his way to the other side of the shed, where Claybrook's guards couldn't see him, and slipped inside.

An open window let in enough light for Gerek to see the poor man slumped on the floor, his head and shoulders propped against the wall. He placed his fingers on the side of the man's neck, feeling for the sign of a beating heart. He felt the blood flowing. A bleeding bump on his head seemed to be his only injury.

Gerek hurried out of the shed and back toward Hagenheim Castle. He went around to the barracks to retrieve his sword. No one was there, so he went inside. Many of the knights and guards had gone with Duke Wilhelm, including Valten. Were there enough men loyal to the duke to fight off the foreign guards?

He strode into the corridor and, upon approaching the Great Hall, he heard Claybrook's voice. He stepped cautiously forward until he saw one of Claybrook's men guarding the door.

Gerek went back toward the kitchen, but everywhere he looked, he saw only Claybrook's guards. Duke Wilhelm's guards were nowhere in sight.

He entered the kitchen. The only people inside were the servants.

Rapunzel, along with the others, was chopping vegetables. He went toward her and bent to speak near her ear.

"Have you seen any of Duke Wilhelm's guards this morning?"

"No." She stared hard at him. "What is wrong?"

The other servants were talking as they worked and were far enough away not to hear if he spoke softly. "I think Lord Claybrook is trying to take over Hagenheim Castle. You should leave while you're still able to get away."

"What makes you think that?" Rapunzel's blue eyes grew rounder.

"I saw them knock the guard at the gatehouse unconscious and hide his body in the shed. They're probably taking them out one by one to give themselves a greater advantage."

Rapunzel set her jaw and narrowed her eyes. "We must warn Lady Rose."

"You warn Lady Rose. I'll try to warn the duke's other guards, then I'll come back for you."

"Shouldn't you go find Duke Wilhelm and bring him back here?"

"It will take two days or more to get to him, but yes, I will. But I had to warn you. I want you to be safe." His heart squeezed at the truth of his admission.

"I can take care of myself, but I'm not leaving here without Lady Rose and her family. They mean a lot to me, more than I can explain at the moment." She paused. "I'll stay here and do what I can to protect them, or help them escape."

Was there ever a more courageous maiden? He wanted to at least squeeze her hand, but the other servants were starting to send furtive looks their way.

"Go on. We'll defend ourselves very well."

There was nothing else to do but nod and leave.

Rapunzel ignored the questions of her fellow maidservants and hurried out of the Great Hall. But before she could get more than two steps into the corridor, she heard Lady Rose's strident voice. "This is outrageous. You may tell Lord Claybrook that I am angry and disappointed that he would dare to stop me from going on a picnic with my family."

Rapunzel placed her hand over her knife, which was tucked in her pocket, as she crept forward. Four of Lord Claybrook's guards were leading Lady Rose and her children up the stairs toward the solar.

Rapunzel turned around—and came face-to-face with Gothel.

Chapter Twenty-Two

Mother had the same dark look on her face that she'd had the night before Rapunzel left home.

"So you left your mother to become a maidservant." Her face twisted as she said the word *maidservant*. "Did you think Sir Gerek would love you more than I did? He will never marry you."

She stepped toward Rapunzel, and Rapunzel took a step back. They were in the castle corridor, halfway between the Great Hall and the door that led outside to the kitchen. No one was around.

"You threatened me," Rapunzel said, her voice strangely calm in spite of the way she was feeling. "I was afraid of you, after the things you said and the way—"

"You broke your mother's heart. I didn't know where you were. After all that I have done for you, you rejected me. What a daughter you have turned out to be." Her jaw was set, her eyes black and cold as stone.

"Have you come to give me your potion and drag me away? Why are you here, Mother?" She cringed at calling her that.

"I am here . . ." She smiled. It sent a shiver across Rapunzel's shoulders. "I am here because I am helping Lord Claybrook in his take-over of Hagenheim." She crossed her arms and lifted her chin. "Duke Wilhelm will finally get his comeuppance, and I will be a part of it."

"Why would you do that? Did you know all along that they were going to take over the castle?" She kept her voice low and glanced around to make sure Claybrook's guards weren't close enough to hear.

"Sir Reginald told me." The look on her face was like that of a child who had just accomplished an impossible task. "When he left me, he became the captain of Lord Claybrook's guard. He still loves me and always hoped to come back and marry me. At first I didn't believe him, but after all these years, he wants to marry me after he and Lord Claybrook seize Hagenheim."

Rapunzel stared at her. After all the things she had said about trusting men who said they loved her . . . "How could you?"

Mother suddenly grabbed her arm and pulled her into the nearest open door—the linen storage room. "Sir Reginald was a knight in the service of the Earl of Keiterhafen. He left with Lord Claybrook and promised to return for me someday, and now he has. He and Lord Claybrook will defeat Duke Wilhelm, and the Gerstenberg family will finally fall. The Earl of Keiterhafen is just arriving with the rest of his guards and knights. And if you try to help Duke Wilhelm's family, you will not be spared."

Rapunzel stared at the woman before her. "But why? Why do you hate Duke Wilhelm and his family?"

Gothel exhaled a long breath, her lips twisting, her eyes dark. "Because I was the illegitimate child of Duke Wilhelm's father."

"What?"

"Yes, that's right." Gothel sneered. "Duke Nicholas was my father, and Duke Wilhelm is my half brother."

Rapunzel's mind reeled. "If Duke Nicholas was your father . . ."

"My mother was his lover. But when she got pregnant with me, he cast her off. She is the one who first taught me to distrust any man who said he loved me.

"Duke Wilhelm does not want to believe his father had a baby with my mother, but his mother knew it was true. Everyone knew. But it's just like Duke Wilhelm to believe that his father could not have done such a thing." She wiped her mouth with a hard swipe of the back of her hand. "My mother gave me to my grandmother to raise, and she never let me forget that no one wanted us in Hagenheim. But I got them back. I hurt them just like they hurt me."

"Yes, you hurt the Gerstenberg family. Duke Wilhelm and Lady Rose. My parents. Isn't that right, *Mother*?"

Gothel's face went slack, but she said nothing.

She shoved all that Mother had just told her to the back of her mind so she could ask the question that had been burning inside her. "Tell me the truth about where I came from. Where did you find me? The truth this time."

Mother narrowed her eyes. "What is it you think you know?"

"Frau Adelheit saw the scar on my hand—the same scar that the duke's third child, Elsebeth, had on her hand. Where did you find me, Mother?"

"You." She sneered. "You think one little scar proves anything?" Mother tried to laugh, but the sound was more of a wheeze.

"Tell me. Did you steal me away, knowing who I was? Stealing me was your revenge, wasn't it?"

Her expression went hard again. "I watched you and your brother playing next to the river. I'd lost my baby a month before, and my grandmother met with her unfortunate accident a week later. She sneered at me one too many times for being just like my mother, for having an illegitimate child. She didn't approve of me taking you—she never approved of me—and I was afraid she would tell them. She made it so easy when she stepped to the edge of that overhang."

A chill went down Rapunzel's back. She practically held her breath as she listened to Gothel.

"But I had no one. My family—even *Oma*—did not love me. The duke—my half brother—had two more children besides you and your brother, and it wasn't fair. Why should I lose my baby and yet they had so many?" Her eyes were wide and vacant, unfocused.

"I was thinking about taking you. I wanted you. You were so pretty and so innocent. I was your aunt, after all, and I would take very good care of you, not leave you with a careless nursemaid. So I distracted the lack-witted nursemaid by sending a little boy over to ask her a question. I told him to stand behind her so she would turn away from the water. I was hidden on the side of the riverbank where she couldn't see me. Then I grabbed your foot and pulled you in.

"I dove in and swam under the water until we were out of sight of anyone, then I pulled you out, ran, then hid. They never found you because I had you. I took you and went far away to a little village, and they never knew. All this time, no one knew except me." She smiled such a cold, dark smile that it reminded her of Balthasar, her attacker.

Rapunzel's stomach sank to her toes. "Did you not have any compassion for the poor man and woman who thought their child had drowned, the parents who mourned and grieved over their three-year-old girl? You are heartless."

"Do I deserve nothing? Is that what you think? Do I not deserve a bit of joy and love? Do I deserve loneliness and hatred because no one wanted me? Because the man I loved did not marry me? Because I was the illegitimate child of the duke? But I got my first bit of revenge on all of them when I left and took you with me."

Rapunzel's heart clenched in pity, then hardened at the woman's reasoning. She had hurt innocent people, not Duke Nicholas, her father and the one who had actually hurt Gothel and her mother. "That wasn't revenge. That was simply vengefulness and spite."

"And you will make the same mistakes my mother and I made . . . you and your Sir Gerek." Her jaw twitched.

"No, I won't. Sir Gerek is not the same kind of person as . . ." Why was she even engaging in this mad argument? It would be better to learn what information she could to try to help Lady Rose and her children escape. "So now you plan to help your former lover defeat Duke Wilhelm, just because he never acknowledged you as his sister?"

"His mother knew about me and no doubt told him to reject me. But now Sir Reginald has returned, and I will have revenge upon them."

"But what do you mean, Duke Wilhelm rejected you? What did he say? What do you and this Sir Reginald plan to do? Hurt more innocent people?"

"Duke Wilhelm had plenty of opportunities to make right what his father had done. Seventeen years ago I even sent him a note, hoping he would help me, give me a dowry, so Sir Reginald would marry me. But he ignored me."

"Still, it was not right for you to steal his child."

"What do you know about what is right?" She put her face so close to Rapunzel's that Rapunzel could see the red veins spidering over the whites of her eyes. "You left me to be a *maidservant*, to be with Sir Gerek." She shook her head. "Perhaps I will not cast you off when Sir Reginald is ruling beside Lord Claybrook and I am his wife. I shall even ask Sir Reginald to watch over you and to not let any evil befall you, should a battle ensue. You know I am your true mother. You were meant to be mine. Rapunzel?"

Rapunzel turned away from her, practically running out of the room. The mad, cruel woman. Rapunzel must refocus. She had to help Sir Gerek. And Lady Rose—her true mother! Lady Rose . . . she had only known her for a few days, and already she felt she was the only loving woman Rapunzel had ever known.

But Rapunzel could not dwell on that now, did not have time to deal with Gothel's madness. She had to do something to help defeat Claybrook and Sir Reginald—to save her true family.

Rapunzel hurried back to the kitchen. One of Claybrook's guards stood at each door—the one that faced the castle as well as the back door. The guard did not speak as she approached, but opened the door for her as she passed inside.

The half dozen other maidservants turned to see who was entering the kitchen. Their faces were pale and their eyes wide. Cook was stirring a pot and wiping under her eyes with a corner of her apron.

Cristobel walked toward her and seized her hand. "Lord Claybrook is taking over Hagenheim Castle! What will happen to Lady Rose and the rest of the duke's family? Claybrook's men may slaughter us all."

If the maidservants already knew, Claybrook's guards would never allow Gerek to leave to retrieve Duke Wilhelm. Had they captured Sir Gerek already?

The other maidservants gathered around her, asking questions. "Did you see anyone?"

"What is happening?"

"Has Duke Wilhelm come back?"

Rapunzel held up her hands. "I don't think so. All I know is that Sir Gerek saw Claybrook's men knock the guard in the gatehouse unconscious and now Claybrook's men are guarding the entrance and are keeping Lady Rose and the rest of the family in the solar."

Cook started weeping aloud, and several others gasped and called on God and the saints for help.

"What happened here?" Rapunzel asked.

"Claybrook's guards told us we couldn't leave the kitchen." Cristobel placed her hands on her face, her eyes almost bulging from her head. "He's going to kill us."

"No, I don't think so." Truthfully, she had no idea what Claybrook might do, but it would not help to panic.

She patted the knife in her pocket.

"Cook," Rapunzel said, "give us some water and pasties to take up to Lady Rose."

"I don't think they will be hungry at a time like this," Cook said in quivering voice.

"But doesn't she usually have something sent up about this time? I need a reason to get back into the castle."

"You aren't trying to escape and leave us here, are you?" She put her hand on her hip.

"I need to find out if Sir Gerek was able to escape. If he did, he will find Duke Wilhelm and tell him what is happening here. We need to help in whatever way we can."

"What makes you think you would be able to help?" one of the maidservants said.

Rapunzel gave her a cold stare.

Cook sniffed and said, "I will get the pasties ready. Two of you—Rapunzel and Cristobel—can take them up to her if the guards will allow it. Does anyone know what's happened to Britta?"

No one seemed to know. Rapunzel would keep an eye out for her as well.

Rapunzel took the bucket to fetch some water. She opened the kitchen door and was immediately confronted by the large man guarding the door.

"I need to get some fresh water from the well."

He stared at her with expressionless eyes. "Come back quickly."

Rapunzel nodded and hurried toward the well at the center of the castle yard. All the while she was searching the courtyard.

Three of Claybrook's men were guarding the castle gate and gatehouse. She didn't see any of Duke Wilhelm's men. She looked toward the stable and saw no activity. While standing at the well, slowly pulling the rope on the windlass, a man stumbled out of the stable. He was not wearing any outer clothing, only hose. His chest and head were bare, and a trickle of blood was moving down the side of his face from his hairline.

One of Claybrook's men, who stood near the gatehouse, suddenly trotted toward him. Rapunzel strained to hear what they were saying to each other.

"... Gerek ... Hit with something ... Horse is gone."

Gerek must have taken the guard's tunic in order to look like one of Claybrook's men. *O Father God, please let it be so. Please let him escape and find Duke Wilhelm.*

The two men were joined by two more, and they ran into the stable, no doubt to fetch their own horses and ride after Sir Gerek.

Rapunzel made her way back to the kitchen. Cook got the food prepared, and the servants readied a pitcher of water. Then she and Cristobel carried trays bearing the pasties and water out of the kitchen.

The guard at the door glared at them. "Where are you going?"

"It is time for Lady Rose's morning repast. We have water and pasties. Would you like to try one?" Rapunzel smiled sweetly. If there was one thing she had learned since coming to work at the castle, it was that men found her ... appealing. The guard's glare softened.

She slipped her hand under the cloth covering the tray of food that Cristobel was carrying and held it out to him. He took it from her hand and took a bite. "What's in the pitcher?" he asked without bothering to chew and swallow his bite of food first.

"Water. Would you like some?"

He scrunched his face. "Move on, then. But don't go anywhere except the solar." He grunted. "The guards may not let you in."

Rapunzel and her friend made their way to the castle door. The guard followed and opened the door, then shut it behind them.

When they reached the bottom of the stairs leading to the solar, Rapunzel saw one of Claybrook's guards farther down the corridor. He started moving toward them.

"What do you have there?" he called.

Rapunzel slipped another pasty off the tray and handed it to the guard. He took it and sniffed it. "Where are you going?"

"To the solar, to take Lady Rose her morning repast."

He lifted the cloth on the tray.

"Is Lord Claybrook in charge of Hagenheim Castle now? Is that why you are questioning the maidservants? Or do you suspect the maidservants of wrongdoing?"

The guard glared down at Rapunzel. "You may go."

Rapunzel led the way up the stairs. When she reached the top, four guards were standing outside. Heat rose inside her at the invasion of this room, which was Lady Rose's favorite place to spend time with her children.

Rapunzel walked straight up to them. "We have Lady Rose's morning repast. If you will step aside."

One guard lifted the cloth over the pasties and took one of them as Rapunzel brushed past them with her full pitcher of water.

Lady Rose watched them as they brought in the tray of food and the pitcher of water and set them down on a table by the window. The guards stayed just outside the door, so when Lady Rose walked over to them, Rapunzel whispered, "Sir Gerek has gone to find Duke Wilhelm and tell him what is happening here."

"Thank you," she whispered back. "Stay safe, my dear."

In a normal voice, meant for the guards to hear, she said, "Is there anything else we can do for you, my lady?"

"No, thank you. You may go."

As they made their way down the stairs, Rapunzel urged Cristobel to move slowly. Once in the corridor, they stood still, listening. No one was around. But someone was coming. Footsteps were shuffling toward them.

"Let's get out of here," Cristobel whispered, nudging Rapunzel in the back.

"Wait a moment." Finally, three men came into view from the direction of the castle courtyard. Two were Claybrook's guards and the other one, walking between them, was one of Duke Wilhelm's guards. His face was bloody, he shuffled his feet, and his head lolled on his shoulders.

Rapunzel's stomach felt queasy. The man could have been Gerek, except for the red-blond hair. *O Father God, please keep Sir Gerek safe.*

Rapunzel moved forward as the guards noticed them. She guessed they were taking the badly beaten soldier to the dungeon, and she kept her eyes focused straight ahead as she and Cristobel headed back to the kitchen.

Silently she prayed for God to deliver her and her true mother and sisters from Lord Claybrook, Sir Reginald, and Gothel.

Gerek managed to escape from Hagenheim with his horse, only having to knock one of Claybrook's guards unconscious. He would not have minded killing him, if it had come to that, but the man did not appear to be terribly skilled at battle.

Gerek rode hard. But every time he thought about leaving Rapunzel and the other men and women at Hagenheim, including Lady Rose and all of the duke's family, his chest tightened with guilt. Had he done the right thing?

If he had stayed, he could have helped his fellow knights and guards to fight Claybrook's men. But if they were defeated, Duke Wilhelm would come home to an ambush.

What would happen to poor Lady Margaretha? Claybrook would undoubtedly force the duke's oldest daughter to marry him in an attempt to make a stronger claim for Hagenheim. The poor girl.

And what about Rapunzel and the rest of the maidservants? Would Claybrook allow his guards to take advantage of them, as usually happened in these situations?

He urged his horse to go faster.

Chapter Twenty-Three

Rapunzel." Cristobel caught Rapunzel's wrist as they prepared to serve the midday meal to Claybrook and his men. "I just heard that Claybrook's guards released all Duke Wilhelm's prisoners from the dungeon."

For a moment, Rapunzel just stared at Cristobel. "What? Why?" If all the prisoners were released from the dungeon . . .

"Claybrook said he would release them if they would fight with him against Duke Wilhelm's men."

"That means . . ." The man who had attacked her, Balthasar, was free and possibly roaming Hagenheim Castle as a guard.

"Don't worry, Rapunzel. We won't let that man hurt you."

"Thank you." Her knees were trembling as she helped carry the food into the Great Hall.

Claybrook's men filled the tables. They were loud and unruly until Lord Claybrook stood and yelled, "My men will behave as noble knights, not as ruffians and cutthroats. I cannot hear myself think." Lord Claybrook looked almost pouty as he plucked at his sleeves and plopped back down—in Duke Wilhelm's chair.

The men did grow quieter, she was thankful to see. As she set the platter of pork and stewed fruit on the table, she glanced at the next table and saw Balthasar grinning at her.

Her heart stuttered as she gave him stare for stare, then turned with a lift of her head and strode back to the kitchen.

"Was he there?" Cristobel asked her.

"Yes. He saw me too." She wanted to pretend she was not frightened, but when she pushed a stray lock of hair behind her ear, her fingers were shaking.

"Oh, my dear. Sit down on the stool. You can put the last touches on the sweet cakes while we serve the rest of the food."

Rapunzel started to sit down, but then straightened. "No. I will not let that"—what had Sir Gerek called him?—"that piece of rancid dog meat make me afraid." She took the platter out of Cristobel's hands, turned on her heel, and marched back to the Great Hall.

She glared until she caught Balthasar's eye, then did her best to snarl, actually curling her lip, while mentally calling him *cur*, *swine*, *lout*, and *evil knavish imp*, and vowing silently, *I've got a new knife, and this time I won't be aiming for your arm.*

Balthasar's evil smile faltered. He stopped chewing and his mouth went slack.

Rapunzel laid the platter on the table and stalked out.

Thanks be to God, Lady Margaretha had managed to escape the castle the first day of Lord Claybrook's treachery. That night Rapunzel slept in the tiny room between Lady Rose's chamber and her older daughters' room. Lady Rose and Lady Kirstyn, who was only two years younger than Margaretha, were anxious for Margaretha's safety, even though they were grateful she was not there, at Claybrook's mercy.

After Gothel's shocking revelations, Rapunzel managed to speak to Frau Adelheit and tell her everything Gothel had said about how she had taken Rapunzel—Elsebeth—when she was three. With all the turmoil, Rapunzel decided it was not the right time to tell Lady Rose, and she and Frau Adelheit agreed that she was safer if she went on with her servant duties for now.

Lord Claybrook allowed everything to go on as usual—except that he didn't always allow Lady Rose and the family to leave the solar to eat their meals in the Great Hall. Rapunzel was still allowed to attend Lady Rose and her daughters two evenings per week.

She had cared for Lady Rose and her daughters that evening. She cherished every moment, holding the knowledge of her identity close to her heart as she brushed their hair and helped them undress.

As she lay in bed, purposely pushing away all thoughts of Gothel, her mind went to Sir Gerek and whether he could truly be content to marry the widow, Lady Lankouwen. Instead of thinking about that, she should be praying for his safety and his success in finding Duke Wilhelm.

She felt for the books Sir Gerek had loaned her. Perhaps tomorrow night she would ask Lady Rose if she could have a candle. She held them to her heart and closed her eyes, conjuring the image of Sir Gerek when he gave them to her. But she had to stop thinking about him since he would soon be married.

How strange it was that Hagenheim had seemed like the safest, kindest place on earth only a week ago, and now, with Claybrook having taken over, it seemed the most precarious.

She did her best to close her mind to all thoughts of fear and danger and concentrate instead on her prayers. After her more formal prayers, she asked God to take care of everyone she cared about—her precious mother, Lady Rose, Sir Gerek, Cristobel, the rest of the maidservants, and all of Duke Wilhelm's—her—family. She even prayed for Gothel, asking God to change her heart. *And thank you for keeping me safe from Balthasar. You have kept me safe before, and I believe you will keep me safe again.* As she finished her prayer, she closed her eyes, feeling more peaceful than she had in a week, and fell asleep.

A week had passed since Lord Claybrook took over the castle. The maidservants never saw any of Duke Wilhelm's knights or guards. They must all have been killed or locked in the dungeon—besides Sir Gerek and the ones who had gone with Duke Wilhelm.

Rapunzel rarely went anywhere, even the privy, without another maidservant with her. But as Rapunzel was leaving the Great Hall, heading back to the kitchen after serving some food, Gothel came around the corner and grabbed her arm. "So, where is your Sir Gerek?" she asked. "He has deserted you, hasn't he?"

Rapunzel bit back the retort that bubbled to her lips. "I have to get to the kitchen." She tried to dodge Gothel, but at that same moment, Sir Reginald came out of the Great Hall and came to stand beside Gothel. He put his arm around her shoulders and looked down at Rapunzel.

"Is this her? Is this Rapunzel?" he asked. He stared at her, even turning her slightly so she faced the torch on the wall, as if to get a better look at her. He pierced her with bold brown eyes. His face was dark and his hair streaked with gray. This was the man to whom Gothel had given her heart and her loyalty.

"This is my Rapunzel, the daughter I told you about."

Sir Reginald may have been a handsome man in his youth, but the sun and age had turned his skin to brown leather. There was also a hardness in his eyes. What had Gothel told him? Had she admitted that Rapunzel was a Gerstenberg? Or had she told him the same lie she had told Rapunzel, that Rapunzel had been abandoned on her doorstep, or the other story, that she'd found her in her garden in the rapunzel patch?

He studied her face, and Rapunzel suddenly wondered if he suspected Rapunzel might be his own daughter.

He finally spoke. "Gothel has brought us the weapons we needed from the wagon Balthasar was bringing to us. She is as valuable as any soldier in the fight against the Gerstenbergs."

Sir Reginald smiled down at Gothel, and Rapunzel's stomach felt sick.

"She has also been helping us by going into Hagenheim and finding out what the townspeople know and if they would help Duke Wilhelm if he were to be attacked."

"May I go now?" Rapunzel clenched her teeth to keep from saying anything.

"If your mother has nothing more to say, then you may." Sir Reginald bowed, sweeping his hand behind him.

"This woman is not my mother," Rapunzel said and strode past them, praying for God to intervene and save Hagenheim from the evil likes of Gothel and Sir Reginald.

After three and a half days of hard riding, Gerek found Duke Wilhelm, who was on a quest to capture the brigands who had been terrorizing the north road to Hagenheim. Valten and a few of his knights and trained soldiers were with him.

When Gerek told the duke and Valten what was happening in Hagenheim, they did not delay, but turned their horses toward home.

At night, they stopped to get a few hours of sleep and to let the horses rest. Duke Wilhelm said, "We'll likely be outnumbered. No doubt Claybrook will have enlisted his uncle's help, the Earl of Keiterhafen, who will have sent all his knights and soldiers to join with Claybrook's men. We will have to raise an army from the people of Hagenheim." Duke Wilhelm made the statement as if it were as easy as building a fire or saddling a horse.

The people of the Hagenheim region were loyal to Duke Wilhelm, but they were not fighting men. If Claybrook had been able to close the town gates and keep people from leaving, Duke Wilhelm would have only farmers, woodcutters, and the few knights and soldiers he had brought with him when he attacked Lord Claybrook's highly trained soldiers. Still, they'd be fighting for Duke Wilhelm and for their own lives, and that should be enough to embolden and motivate them.

Gerek only had a few hours to sleep before they would be off again at sunrise. He stretched out by the fire, turning his back to the flickering flames, but kept his eyes open while he prayed. There seemed to be so much to pray for, so much danger ahead of him, and yet he found himself praying first and last for Rapunzel's safety.

Word went through the kitchen late the next evening that Lady Margaretha had been caught. She'd been brought back to Hagenheim by Lord Claybrook's men.

Rapunzel's heart sank. "When did she return?"

"Just an hour ago, the stable boy said."

What would happen to her now? Would Claybrook force Margaretha to say vows and then force himself on her? If he wanted to hurt Duke Wilhelm, that would be a good way to do it.

"Keep your eyes and ears open," Rapunzel said to her fellow maidservants, "for ways we might be able to help Lady Margaretha escape again."

They nodded, but doubt clouded their faces.

It was not Rapunzel's day to help Lady Rose, but since Britta had never returned after Claybrook took over, she asked Cook if she could be excused from her kitchen duties to see if she would be allowed to wait on her.

She slipped an extra knife in the leather sheath at her belt, hoping for an opportunity to sneak it to Lady Margaretha. She seemed a feisty enough person to be able to put a knife to good use.

Walking quickly through the corridor, her hand rested on her thigh where her two knives were concealed. She looked from left to right and back again, but did not see Balthasar. Hurrying up the stairs, she encountered a guard at the top.

"Where are you going?"

"I'm Lady Rose's maid. She needs me to help her—"

"Not tonight."

"But the maidservants are supposed to go about their regular duties."

"Not tonight. Captain Reginald's orders. No one is supposed to visit the family."

"I'm not visiting. I'm serving."

"What's the difficulty here?" Sir Reginald appeared on the stairs behind Rapunzel.

"Sir Reginald, I simply want to do my usual service for Lady Rose." She purposely didn't add, "and her daughters," knowing Margaretha's presence must be what was causing their extra caution.

"No one, not even servants, are allowed with them tonight. And you can tell the cook they'll be taking their evening meal in the solar."

Not seeing any point in arguing with the man, Rapunzel turned to go. Perhaps she could find a way to slip the knife to Lady Rose when they brought them their food.

She was almost to the bottom of the steps when she noticed someone blocking the corridor. In the flickering light of the wall torch, at the bottom of the steps, stood the man with the strange smile, Balthasar.

Chapter Twenty-Four

Rapunzel froze, only four steps away from him. His eyes shone black. His smile bespoke evil pleasure at finding her alone.

She took a step backward, up to the next step, two steps. Then she turned around and ran back up. "Sir Reginald!"

When she turned to look over her shoulder, she ran into something solid.

Sir Reginald grabbed her by the arms. His dark brows were low, and there was a deep crease between his eyes. He shook her, making her head fall back and then sling forward. "I don't have time for—"

"That man at the bottom of the stairs. He's waiting to do me harm."

Sir Reginald suddenly took hold of her wrist and, without a word, started down the stairs, pulling her behind. Balthasar was still standing at the bottom.

"Get away from there," Sir Reginald barked.

Balthasar's smile turned angry. He hesitated a few moments, then skulked down the corridor.

Sir Reginald pulled Rapunzel the rest of the way down the stairs and glared down at her. "Get back to the kitchen and don't be roaming around the castle, or something bad will happen to you. And it will be your own fault."

Rapunzel's breath came fast and she clenched her fists. She wanted to tell him she was not responsible for that man's evil, and she was not to blame for Claybrook's despicable choice to release wicked men from the dungeon to terrorize good people. Instead, she glared up at him and said, "You disgust me." Then she spun on her heel and walked back to the kitchen.

When she reached the kitchen door, she flung it open.

"Did you see Lady Rose? Were you able to give her the knife?" Cristobel asked softly. All the maidservants were looking at her.

Rapunzel was still breathing hard, her knees trembling. "I was not even allowed to see Lady Rose."

Their shoulders slumped as they went back to their work.

The next day Lady Rose and even Lady Margaretha and Lady Kirstyn were seated on the dais in the Great Hall for the midday meal. Claybrook sat at the head of the table in Duke Wilhelm's place like a puffed up bullfrog. Claybrook had let the squires and pages out of the knights' quarters where he had been keeping them. They were serving now, so Rapunzel and the other maidservants stayed in the kitchen, supplying the boys with platters of food.

The gossip was that Claybrook would force Margaretha to marry him tonight at vespers. The duke's oldest daughter—Rapunzel's own sister—would be married to that evil man by nightfall, and he was demanding a big feast for after the wedding.

As Rapunzel added the cherry sauce to the roast pheasant, she suddenly had an idea.

Rapunzel whispered her idea to Cristobel, who nodded with an excited glint in her eye. "Let us do it."

Rapunzel dribbled the dark red cherry sauce across her fingers and onto a cloth, soaking it through. Then she whispered her plan to Cook, who gave them permission to abandon their work.

She and Cristobel left the kitchen. As soon as she saw the guard outside the door, Rapunzel cried out, then moaned, tensing her face as if she were in great pain. She held her left hand with her right, with the cherry-stained towel wrapped around it.

The guard's brow rose high as Cristobel cried, "She just chopped her fingers! I think she may have chopped one of them off. Oh, please let me take her to see Frau Lena at the healer's chamber."

Rapunzel kept up a constant moaning and gasping.

The guard looked a bit pale and waved his arm. "Go on, then. Go."

Cristobel took Rapunzel by the elbow and walked quickly around the side of the castle toward the southwest tower where they would find Frau Lena in her chamber.

Rapunzel kept up the moaning and crying out as they passed another guard until they reached Frau Lena's door and went inside and closed the door behind them.

The chamber looked empty. "Frau Lena, are you here?"

The red-haired healer emerged from the storage room at the other end of the chamber. She came quickly toward them, her eyes riveted on the bright-red cloth around Rapunzel's hand.

"Is anyone else here?" Rapunzel asked.

"No, I am alone."

Rapunzel unwrapped the cloth around her hand. "I feigned an injury. Can we ask your help?"

"Of course." Frau Lena stepped closer.

"We came to ask if you have any poisonous berries or leaves. I have an idea to sicken Lord Claybrook tonight so that he cannot harm Lady Margaretha and so that she can possibly escape again."

"Oh, ja. That is a good idea." Frau Lena's face lit up and she held a hand to her chin, her eyes gazing up at the ceiling. "Something that would sicken Lord Claybrook . . . I know!" She raised her finger as a smile broke out on her face. "Holly berries would make him vomit and feel very sick, and I happen to still have some left over from Christmas." She turned toward the wall.

Christmas decorations of holly branches, complete with the bright-red berries, lay on a shelf attached to the wall and around the window. She grabbed a branch and began picking the berries and putting them into a small pouch.

"The berries don't taste very good, but you could probably crush them and put them in his wine and he would never know."

"That is what I was thinking," Rapunzel said. "Perhaps we could wait until he was half drunk and then poison his wine, when he won't be as likely to notice the taste."

Cristobel and Rapunzel helped her pick all the berries off the holly branches decorating the healer's chamber.

"I wish I had enough to poison his entire guard, but still, it should be enough to make Lord Claybrook and several of his knights extremely sick." When they were done picking the berries and putting them into the pouch, Frau Lena handed the pouch to Rapunzel.

"Do you think it's enough to kill him?"

Frau Lena shrugged. "Probably not, which is a great pity." She looked hard at Rapunzel's hand. "Now, let's get you bandaged up so you can serve tonight."

Frau Lena wrapped her uninjured hand until it was more than double its normal size. Then she talked to them for a while longer about various plants and berries and the effect they have. Finally, they thanked Frau Lena and Rapunzel tucked the pouch of holly berries in her skirt pocket and did her best to look weak and tired as they made their way back to the kitchen.

"Is she well?" the guard asked.

"We had feared she would lose her finger," Cristobel said, "but

Frau Lena sewed it back on. I hope she will be well enough to help with the feast preparations."

"Don't worry. I can work with only one hand," Rapunzel said. "Frau Lena wrapped it up so I won't get blood in the food." She gave the guard a weak smile as they entered the kitchen and then shut the door.

The other servants were already hard at work on the night's feast—Claybrook and Margaretha's wedding feast. Frau Lena had made Rapunzel's bandage loose enough that she could slip it off and work just as hard and help prepare the feast. She simply had to make sure she didn't forget to put it back on before she left the kitchen.

Hour after hour they obeyed Cook's frenzied orders as she worked to make a feast fit for the wedding of their beloved Lady Margaretha—even though it was a forced wedding to that fiend, Lord Claybrook. Nearly every minute Rapunzel was thinking about the holly berries in her pocket. She made silent pleas to God as she worked, for success, and also that those little berries could somehow help save her own sister from a terrible fate.

Gerek's body was weary after riding hard for days. But he was buoyed not only by the fact that they were now very close to Hagenheim and preparing to fight, but that they had been joined by Lady Rose's nephew, the Duke of Marienberg, and all his knights and soldiers. Even though they would not need to recruit the local men to help them fight, many of them were coming voluntarily.

Darkness was falling, but Duke Wilhelm and his men would not sleep tonight. The plan was to attack Claybrook and his men at dawn and take back the castle and the town.

An Englishman named Colin le Wyse was there, along with his father, an English earl, and his men. Colin had also been at the castle the day Lord Claybrook had begun his take-over, and he and Margaretha had escaped together, intent on reaching Marienberg to bring the duke and his men back. But Margaretha had been captured and taken back to Hagenheim by Claybrook's men, while Colin had gone on to Marienberg to secure the help of their allies. His courage and success in bringing the Marienberg forces would be perhaps the most important key to their victory over Claybrook.

Since Gerek was the only one who spoke English very well among Duke Wilhelm's men, he and Colin had talked a lot over the course of the last twenty-four hours.

"I need your help to speak to Duke Wilhelm," Colin had said as they rode side by side.

"Of course."

"I want to ask him to allow me to marry his daughter, Margaretha."

Gerek was speechless for a moment. The expression on Colin's face—somewhere between desperation and determination—made him feel a little sorry for him.

Gerek had always hoped never to feel that way about anyone. The way he felt about Lady Lankouwen was much preferable—dispassionate, cool, practical.

"It will be my pleasure to translate for you."

Colin must have fallen in love with Lady Margaretha when they had been traveling to Marienberg. He must be suffering a great deal at this moment, wondering if Lady Margaretha was in danger, wondering if she had already been forced to wed Lord Claybrook, and if Duke Wilhelm would agree to his suit to marry her.

Gerek thought about Rapunzel, hoping she was well and had not been molested or harmed in any way. But that was only because . . . well, she was a good girl, having suffered an odd upbringing at the hands of a mother who was quite possibly insane, and now Rapunzel had no one to care about her. It didn't mean he was in love with her, simply because he thought about her and prayed for her safety.

Duke Theodemar of Marienberg came forward to introduce Colin to Duke Wilhelm and then moved away, allowing Colin to speak to Duke Wilhelm while Gerek translated.

"Your Grace," Colin said. "I came to the Holy Roman Empire with the intention of capturing Claybrook and taking him back to England to face the consequences of a murder he had committed there. I was attacked and left for dead by his men and was brought to your healer at Hagenheim Castle."

Colin held himself erect, doing well at disguising his nervousness. "Before I could recover enough to come to you with my story, you had left Hagenheim. I explained to Lady Margaretha about Claybrook's true character, and she eavesdropped on Claybrook and discovered what he was about to do in Hagenheim. We were both captured by him, but we escaped and tried to make our way to Marienberg. We traveled for several days—"

"You traveled with my daughter? Who accompanied you?" Duke Wilhelm's eyes were intense as they stared at Colin.

"Sir, we were alone most of the time." He continued quickly, and Gerek translated as fast as he could. "But I assure you, your daughter is as virtuous as pure snowflakes, and I wish to ask your blessing and permission to marry her, if she is willing, for I have fallen in love with her."

Duke Wilhelm studied him with narrowed eyes. "And how does my daughter feel? Is she in love with you?"

"I don't know, sir. I would like to discover that myself, as soon as I see her again."

"And where is my daughter now?"

Gerek could feel the tension as he translated their words. Indeed,

Duke Wilhelm already had been told by his scouts that Claybrook's men had brought her back to Hagenheim Castle.

"I do not know for certain. She was taken by Claybrook's men. I believe she should have arrived back at Hagenheim one or two days ago."

Duke Wilhelm said nothing, but stared at Colin from beneath those lordly brows of his. To his credit, Colin gave him stare for stare, without flinching.

Colin went on to explain that he would inherit his father's title of Earl of Glynval upon his father's death. He also said, "You have my word that I would cherish your daughter and treat her well, for I fear God and know that I shall answer for how I treat a godly woman like Margaretha."

Surely this was the kind of man a father would want his daughter to marry, someone who would truly love her, not someone like Gerek who only wished to marry for land and property.

It was a sobering thought, but he didn't have time to dwell on it as he continued to translate the two men's words.

"I believe you are an honorable man," Duke Wilhelm said. "If Margaretha wishes it, and if her mother approves of you, you have my blessing to wed."

Colin seemed relieved and grateful. Now they just had to save Margaretha and the rest of Hagenheim before it was too late.

Chapter Twenty-Five

Cristobel returned from the privy. "Margaretha and Claybrook have just been wed."

Everyone paused in their work to stare. "Lady Rose was disguised as Lady Margaretha."

The servants gasped. Rapunzel's mouth went dry.

"But Claybrook discovered it before the ceremony was over and forced them to change places. Margaretha refused to give her consent, but the priest pronounced them man and wife even so."

The servants shook their heads, frowned, and went back to work.

Rapunzel pulled out the pouch of holly berries and a stone pestle and mortar and started grinding the first small handful of berries.

One of the maidservants came running into the kitchen. "Sir Reginald is coming! He wants to inspect the food—"

Rapunzel shoved the berries and the mortar and pestle under the counter, covering them with an upturned pottery bowl. Then she grabbed her bandage and was slipping it back on when Sir Reginald entered the room.

Everyone was quiet, pretending to work and ignoring the tall man as he walked slowly around the kitchen. Rapunzel had no work in front of her, so she grabbed a head of cabbage and started cutting it.

When Reginald came to Cook, who was stirring a stewpot over the fire, he said, "What is for dessert?"

Cook raised her head and shoulders proudly and said, "Fried fruit pastries, sweet custard with cherry sauce, and almond cream and ricotta in puff pastry shells."

Sir Reginald raised his brows but said nothing. He continued walking. Rapunzel kept chopping as he paused behind her. The back of her neck prickled as she chopped awkwardly with her right hand, not using her "injured" left hand.

Surely he couldn't see what was hidden under the counter. She didn't dare turn and look at him or pause in her work.

"What is the cabbage for?" Sir Reginald asked.

Cook spoke up. "I am putting it in the pottage, for the servants."

Finally, Sir Reginald moved on.

Rapunzel's heartbeat didn't steady until after Sir Reginald left. She breathed a sigh, took the holly berries out of their hiding place, and started pounding and grinding them again.

Meanwhile, the pages and squires and some of the menservants were taking the platters of food out to the Great Hall.

"Lady Margaretha looks quite defiant," one of them reported.

"She'll escape again," someone else said. "The rumor is that she knows of a secret passageway somewhere in the castle."

Good. Putting the holly berries in Lord Claybrook's wine would give her that chance.

"Are those berries ready yet?" Cook asked.

Cristobel appeared at her side. "I'm ready to give that Claybrook a good dose of them."

"We should wait until the end so that he doesn't start vomiting during the feast. Let him get sick at the end so the guards will not realize what we did and Lady Margaretha will have time to escape before they find out."

But it was hard to wait. Rapunzel's fingers trembled slightly whenever she reached for more berries to crush. Finally, she began transferring the berry paste into a flask of wine and swirling it around. She and Cook decided to put the berries into two flasks and made sure to instruct the servers that those two were only for Lord Claybrook and his knights.

They might all get hanged for poisoning Lord Claybrook, but no one seemed to be thinking of that. They shot furtive glances at each other and smiled as the serving boys carried out the two special flasks of wine.

Rapunzel inhaled a shaky breath. It was certainly worth the risk.

After hours of work, and the strain of trying to poison Lord Claybrook, Rapunzel and the other servants were moving slowly as they cleaned the kitchen and began to go off to their sleeping quarters. But she couldn't help wondering if her holly berry poisoning plan had worked. Were enough of the knights sick too? Was this a good time to help Lady Rose and the family escape?

She simply didn't want to go to bed now. She wanted to do something.

"Are you ready?" Cristobel asked, suppressing a yawn. "I'm so tired, I may sleep until noon if Frau Adelheit doesn't come and drag me out of bed."

"I'll be there soon. I just want to see if I can find out what is happening in the castle."

"Be careful."

"Don't worry. I have two knives in my pocket." Rapunzel smiled and slipped out the door.

No guards were in sight, so she scurried across the way to the castle and went inside.

It was dark, as some of the torches on the wall had burned out. Rapunzel moved cautiously along the wall toward the stairs that led up to the solar and also led to the second-floor corridors where the family's bedchambers were located.

Rapunzel put one foot on the bottom step when a shadow moved to her left. It was Balthasar, emerging from the library.

She backed away, her throat suddenly dry. He advanced toward her. She put one foot behind her, then the other.

"I have you now," he said quietly. His teeth shone in the dim light.

"Stay back or I'll scream."

"Scream all you want. Nobody will help you. They're all drunk." He kept walking toward her.

Rapunzel slipped her hand inside her pocket and closed her fist around the handle of her knife. "Stay back."

He lunged at her and closed his hands around her throat.

Rapunzel raised the knife and sliced across both his forearms.

He cried out, like the snarl of a wild animal. He squeezed her throat hard, then let go. She couldn't breathe, but she turned around and ran.

Seeing the door of the linen room ajar, Rapunzel ran inside and closed the door behind her, slamming the crossbar down to lock it. The man crashed into the door, shaking it and making a loud boom, but the crossbar held and the door stayed closed.

Rapunzel sucked air in, gasping and coughing past the pain in her throat.

"Who is there? What is that sound?"

Rapunzel turned to see Frau Adelheit, her face illuminated by several candles.

"Rapunzel. Who is that beating on the door?"

"It's the man who attacked me."

"What does he want? Why is he beating on the door?"

Rapunzel was still clutching the knife in her hand. She took several steps back. "It's Balthasar. He wants revenge against me for throwing a knife and hitting him in the arm."

Frau Adelheit's lips thinned into a firm line. "I don't think he can open the door, and we shall pray that someone will come to our aid. It will be dawn in a few hours."

The man was still pounding on the door every few seconds and growling. Rapunzel took off her fake bandage and rubbed her hands together.

"You must be very tired," Frau Adelheit said. "We may as well use these linens to make something of a bed for ourselves."

"But these are clean. We'll get them dirty."

"We cannot worry about a little thing like that, not when that monster, Lord Claybrook, has wed our sweet Lady Margaretha." Frau Adelheit's lower lip quivered and she bit it.

"We poisoned him," Rapunzel said.

"What?" Frau Adelheit furrowed her brow.

"We, the other servants and I, poisoned Lord Claybrook's wine with some holly berries we got from Frau Lena. I would be surprised if Lady Margaretha does not escape him tonight."

"Oh. That is . . . marvelous." Frau Adelheit expelled a quick laugh.

Since there was little else in the room besides linens, it did not take them long to lay some sheets on the stone floor and lie down. While the man continued to beat periodically on the door, Rapunzel and Frau Adelheit lay still, waiting.

They talked of various plans to try to escape, but since the room had no windows, there seemed to be no real options.

It had been quiet for a while. "Perhaps he has left." Rapunzel forced herself to stand and walk to the door. She put her ear up to it.

"Be careful," Frau Adelheit whispered. "He may be waiting quietly on the other side so that you'll think he's gone."

She listened again and heard nothing. So she knocked quietly, then louder. Still nothing. Finally, she pounded on the door and shouted, "Can anyone hear me?"

"I hear you!" It was Balthasar. He let out a wild laugh that sent shivers over her arms and down her back. "Come on out. I have something for you." He laughed again.

Rapunzel went back and sat down. "I'm so sorry you got trapped in here with me."

Frau Adelheit shook her head. "I'm not sorry to be able to keep our dear Elsebeth company at such a time as this." A tear slipped down the older woman's cheek.

And they might remain the only two people, besides Gothel, to know that she was Elsebeth. Eventually Balthasar would be able to convince someone to bring a mace or an ax and break down the door. Or he might go and get one himself and return before they knew he was gone.

"We may as well sleep," Rapunzel said and lay down. She closed her eyes, but her mind was wide-awake. Almost immediately, Balthasar started pounding on the door again and shouting, making sure she never forgot he was there, waiting for her.

Chapter Twenty-Six

Wake up! He's breaking through the door!"

Rapunzel must have fallen asleep because she opened her eyes to Frau Adelheit leaning over her.

Rapunzel sat up and scrambled to her feet. She found both knives in her pocket and handed one to Frau Adelheit and clutched the other one in her own hand as a hole appeared in the door. Balthasar peered in, his leering grin partially visible as well. "You're mine now." His laugh was hoarse.

Frau Adelheit screamed. He slammed the mace into the door, widening the hole. Frau Adelheit screamed again. He hit the door and she screamed. Over and over.

Rapunzel looked around for something else, anything she might use as a weapon, but there was nothing big or heavy enough. The knives would have to do.

He finally reached into the hole in the door, scrabbling at the small but thick iron bolt. She drew back her knife to thrust it into his hand but decided to wait. Stabbing his hand would not stop him.

He lifted the bolt, flung open the door, and stepped inside.

He did not even glance at the older woman but walked toward Rapunzel. She aimed for his shoulder and threw the knife, but it slipped off her fingers and went flying past his ear.

Fear slammed into her like a lightning bolt and she stumbled backward. Frau Adelheit was screaming so loud, she was drowning out Balthasar's laughter.

"You missed me." His hair was sticking out in every direction and his eyes were red rimmed and bloodshot. He didn't seem in any hurry to reach her, though.

If only Frau Adelheit would think to toss her the other knife or to fetch the one she threw past him.

During a brief break in her screams, Rapunzel said, "Go get help." Perhaps the calmness of her voice would bring Frau Adelheit back to her senses.

Frau Adelheit ran toward the door. Balthasar did not make any move to stop her.

Now Rapunzel was alone with him and without a weapon.

"What will you do?" she said, her voice steady. "Claybrook's guards will be here soon and will stop you from harming me."

"They won't stop me." He shook his head, still smiling. "I've already gotten Sir Reginald's permission to get my revenge on you, as a reward for my loyalty to him. He said I could do anything I want to you, as long as I don't kill you."

Rapunzel heard noises in the background. From the pale light behind him, she could see it was dawn. Muffled shouts came to her, as if from far away, and the clang of metal on metal. Someone was fighting.

Balthasar took another step toward her. "You are sorry for stabbing my arm, are you not? Perhaps you would like to know what it feels like."

Rapunzel forced herself not to step backward so she wouldn't be pinned against the wall. Instead, she took a step to the right. Balthasar followed her, his hands up, as if ready to lunge.

Something was lying on the floor a little farther to the right. She forced herself not to look directly at it. If it was the knife she had given Frau Adelheit, perhaps she could—

He lurched toward her, but she threw herself on the ground and closed her hand over the object, which was indeed the other knife. She brought the blade up as she twisted her body around to face him—just as he threw his body on top of hers.

Gerek was the first of Duke Wilhelm's men to reach the castle gate. Two of Claybrook's guards were in the gatehouse. Only one drew his sword. But instead of charging Gerek, they both backed away. They must have seen they were outnumbered.

Gerek plowed forward, leaving the two so Duke Wilhelm's men could take them as prisoners.

The castle courtyard was strangely empty. Three guards rushed to the door of the castle. Gerek roared his battle cry and ran at them. He struck the first one with all of his strength, bringing his sword down and knocking the man's sword to the ground.

He slammed his sword into the shoulder of the second one while sidestepping a swing from the sword of the third. They, too, must have seen Duke Wilhelm's men behind him because they laid down their swords and surrendered.

Duke Wilhelm's men surrounded them, and Gerek pushed through the door and into the castle. The first thing he heard was the repeated screams of a woman. He ran past the Great Hall, which was empty, and continued down the corridor.

One of Claybrook's guards came running at him with his sword drawn.

Gerek slashed at the guard, who blocked the blow with his blade. They fought for a few moments before Gerek beat him back and pinned him against the wall. Behind him, Duke Wilhelm's men were making their way through the corridor. Gerek once again turned his opponent over to them, and he rushed to see who was screaming.

"Over here!" Frau Adelheit was motioning him forward. "In the linen room."

Another scream came from the linen room, but this time he recognized the voice. Rapunzel. Strength rushed through his limbs. He raced toward the open door of the linen room, which lay on the floor in splinters.

Another of Claybrook's guards came at him, stepping into the corridor from the outside door, his sword drawn. With both hands, Gerek swung his sword and knocked the man to the ground.

Gerek yelled as he charged through the doorway. Rapunzel was lying on the floor, pushing her way out from under a man's body. Gerek kicked the man off of her and onto his back. A knife was sticking out of his chest, over his heart. His eyes were staring up and blood was trickling out of his mouth. Balthasar.

Gerek placed his hands under Rapunzel's arms and lifted her to her feet. She looked into his eyes for a moment, then threw her arms around him.

He pulled her close with one arm, still holding his sword in his other hand. "Shh. All is well . . . All is well." Her golden hair was falling around her shoulders in disarray. How his heart swelled with joy at seeing her safe, her arms around him, the way it felt to touch her and hold her . . . which he should not be doing. But the way she was clinging to him felt so good he could barely breathe.

She suddenly pulled away and looked up at him, her face quite pale.

He glanced past her at the body lying on the floor. He was definitely dead.

"Are you hurt? Did he hurt you?" He held her at arm's length and looked her over.

"No. He fell on my knife. I turned and he fell . . ." Her voice shook and she shuddered. "I was only trying to protect myself. Do you think God will forgive me?"

"Of course. He deserved it. And if he hadn't fallen on the knife, I would have killed him myself." He had such a strong urge to pull her to him that he wrenched his gaze away.

"Are you hurt? There's blood on your face." She reached out and touched his cheek.

"It's not mine."

Her mouth suddenly broke into a smile. "Good."

Even with dark circles under her eyes, she was beautiful. So beautiful.

"I should get back to the fight."

A cheer resounded inside the castle, and another cheer echoed from outside. He let go of Rapunzel's arms and went into the corridor. Through the window he saw Duke Wilhelm's men were rounding up Claybrook's guards and confiscating their weapons. It was strange that they had prevailed so easily. Where were all of Claybrook's men? The ones they were leading out of the barracks looked as if they were either drunk or sick.

When he turned around, Frau Adelheit was embracing Rapunzel in the corridor behind him.

"Oh, thank God, thank God," she said. "You are safe and unharmed. You are so brave. Such a brave girl."

She was brave, but she looked exhausted. He strode over to her. "Duke Wilhelm has defeated Lord Claybrook. Hagenheim is safe again."

"Thank you. We are so grateful," Frau Adelheit said.

He had been too late to help Rapunzel. A stab went through Gerek's chest at what might have happened to her. "Are you sure he did not hurt you? What was that man doing, running around loose in the castle?"

"The first thing Lord Claybrook did was set all the dungeon prisoners free. He's been trying to get me, and he finally almost did." She let out a shaky breath. "Frau Adelheit and I were locked in the linen room for the last few hours, with him pounding on the door. Then this morning he started beating a hole in the door."

No wonder she looked so tired.

A maidservant came running toward Rapunzel. "You are safe!" She threw her arms around her. "We were afraid something terrible had happened to you. Is that blood?" She gasped, staring at the bloodstain on the front of Rapunzel's clothing.

"It's not mine." The edges of Rapunzel's lips lifted as her eyes met Gerek's. She took her friend's arm and led her to the door of the linen room. She showed her Balthasar with the knife in his chest.

"Is he . . . dead?"

"Yes."

The two of them stood talking for several minutes while droves of Duke Wilhelm's men came in through the outside door to the Great Hall. They spilled into the corridor, and Duke Wilhelm and several more of his men came down the stairs from the solar. They began to swap stories about the guards they had defeated. Apparently Colin le Wyse, the Englishman, had disarmed Claybrook himself. Not a very difficult feat since he'd been poisoned the night before—or so they were saying.

Duke Wilhelm broke away and approached Frau Adelheit. Gerek heard him ask her, "Do you think Cook could have some food prepared for my men?"

"Of course, your grace."

Rapunzel and her friend followed Frau Adelheit. Rapunzel hesitated and looked over her shoulder. Her eyes locked on his for a moment.

She was his friend, a maiden he had taught to read, to whom he had loaned some books, whose life he had saved twice and who had saved his once. But that was all. And if he thought about her a lot, it was only because she was his friend, and he was hers.

Soon he would be married and no longer living at Hagenheim Castle. He would forget her, and she would forget him. But if the pain in his chest was any indication, it might be a painful process.

He looked out the window. The men were clapping each other on the back, trying to be heard as they all told their tales of bravery and battle prowess. A woman caught his eye. She very much resembled Rapunzel's mother. He stared, trying to make sure, but she was hidden from view as she slunk off behind the kitchen, as if trying to avoid being seen.

If it was Rapunzel's mother, surely she wouldn't try to harm Rapunzel or force her to leave, as she had once threatened. There were too many people around. But it was strange that she was here, especially now, while the castle was being freed from Claybrook's clutches. Could Rapunzel's mother have had anything to do with the capture?

Lord Glynval, Colin's father, suddenly appeared and clapped him on the shoulder. He asked Gerek about his battles, and they moved toward the Great Hall where the rest of the knights and Duke Wilhelm's men were congregating.

He didn't want to worry Rapunzel, but perhaps later he should warn her that he thought he had seen her mother.

Rapunzel's mind was still whirling as she went to the servants' quarters and changed her kirtle, which was soiled with Balthasar's blood. She braided her hair with trembling hands, replaced the head covering that she'd lost, and walked back toward the kitchen.

She pressed her hands over her cheeks. She had killed a man

this morning, albeit in self-defense and rather accidentally. It still made her feel sick when she remembered it. But, truth be told, she had been willing to kill him, and had even intended to kill him if she had to. Besides, Sir Gerek would have killed him if she had not.

She closed her eyes for a moment, remembering how it had felt to see Sir Gerek appear, reaching down and pulling her up. She sighed deeply. His arms were so strong and comforting around her, holding her tight against his broad chest. She drew in a hiccupped breath, a cross between a laugh and a sob.

Oh, Sir Gerek . . . was it just as Mother had said? That she was in love and would do anything he wanted her to, no matter how wrong or foolish?

But she could *not* be in love with him, and she would *not* do anything Sir Gerek asked her to do. She would no longer allow Gothel to poison her mind and make her believe that all men were evil. Sir Gerek wouldn't ask her to do anything foolish or wrong, not only because he was honorable, but also because he didn't even want her.

He wanted his wealthy widow.

But she didn't want to think about that. She would think about how her breath had stuck in her throat when he had looked into her eyes. How fierce and protective he had been. How rugged and masculine he had looked with several days of stubble on his cheeks and chin.

Why should she be so affected by Sir Gerek? He was only a man who had saved her life and had taught her to read. He was a knight in Duke Wilhelm's service, so of course he saved her. He would save anyone who was in need of help.

But it was more than that. He liked her. She knew he did. He cared about her and considered her a friend. At this moment she had his books inside her kirtle pocket, where she kept them so she could reread them when she had a free moment. She should give them back to him, now that he had returned and all was once again back as it should be, with Duke Wilhelm in his rightful place.

Lingering outside the kitchen, she said a prayer for Lady Rose, her mother, that she and Rapunzel's brothers and sisters were well now. She should be helping the others in the kitchen, preparing a feast for Duke Wilhelm and his men, who had freed them from Lord Claybrook.

She took a step and a shadow fell across her path.

"Here you are." Gothel stood, her hands folded in front of her.

"You startled me." Her skin prickled. Somehow Gothel had eluded capture by Duke Wilhelm's men. Or perhaps no one realized that she had been helping Claybrook and Sir Reginald. She'd been their spy, bringing them news of what the people in Hagenheim knew about Duke Wilhelm's whereabouts and who knew what else.

"Are you pleased with your decision to come to Hagenheim Castle to be a kitchen servant?" Gothel's face twisted into a sneer. "Why have you not told Duke Wilhelm and his precious Rose that you are their daughter? Are you afraid they won't believe you?"

"I was waiting until things settled down." She need not defend herself or feel pressure to tell Gothel anything.

But this was the woman who'd raised her, the woman who took care of her when she was sick, who braided her hair every night and told her she was the most talented and lovable person in the world. To think that she was cruel enough to steal her away from her loving parents suddenly hit Rapunzel's heart like a battle-ax.

"Where is Sir Reginald? Will you not try to rescue the man you love from Duke Wilhelm? Perhaps you can steal him away just as you stole me."

Gothel's face was nearly blank, her eyes strangely vacant as she stared down at the ground. "Sir Reginald . . . is dead."

"Dead? Oh, Mother, I'm so sorry." She had promised herself never to call her that again. But in her sympathy, it slipped out.

"He deserved to die. He would have betrayed me—again. He was only using me. He had already been granted permission from Lord Claybrook to marry Duke Wilhelm's niece, Anne."

Rapunzel took a step back.

Gothel stepped toward her. "I was still not good enough for him. And I was right. All those years that I told you never to trust a man, that men only wanted one thing from you, that a man would not marry you if he would gain nothing in the bargain . . . I was right. But I did not listen to my own words of wisdom. It was your fault." She pierced Rapunzel with a look.

"My fault? How?"

Gothel's breath seemed to come faster, even though she was standing still. "If you had not deserted me, if I had not been alone and weighed down with sorrow, I would not have been duped by him again. I would have realized he was not sincere, that he was using me and making a fool of me again." She stepped closer to Rapunzel. "I would not have listened to his lies about marrying me. But things can go back to the way they were before . . . before I listened to him . . . before you abandoned me."

Suddenly, Gothel grabbed Rapunzel by the nose and by her hair, stuffed something inside her mouth, and held her head back so far she became disoriented. She lashed out with her hands but was only beating the air. When she tried to kick, she nearly fell on her back. She tried to spit the substance out, but she couldn't breathe and was forced to swallow whatever it was.

She clawed at Gothel's hand, but by the time she was able to pry her loose, Rapunzel's vision was fading. And she was falling.

Chapter Twenty-Seven

Gerek ate heartily while listening to the story of Lord Claybrook's capture. Colin's face turned pink while he and Lady Margaretha explained what happened. Apparently Colin had been distracted by Lady Margaretha, and Claybrook had come up behind him with a raised sword. But Colin defeated him in a brief sword fight, shortened by the fact that Claybrook had been poisoned the night before by the maidservants. In fact, many of Claybrook's knights had been poisoned by the kitchen servants and were too sick to fight well.

That was one story he was anxious to ask Rapunzel about. She no doubt had a hand in that brave act.

Someone tapped him on the shoulder. He turned to see Frau Adelheit standing just behind him.

"Sir Gerek, I am sorry to interrupt your meal, but Rapunzel is missing. None of us have seen her since she went to change her clothing, and that was before the preparation of the meal."

Gerek stood and stepped over the bench where he was sitting at the raised dais with the family. "Perhaps she went for a walk. She likes to sit under the tree in the south meadow."

"No, I sent someone there to look for her. I am afraid something has happened to her." Her eyes were round, and she was clutching her hands.

It seemed strange that Frau Adelheit was so anxious about a maidservant. But Rapunzel was special—strong, kind, and reliable.

"What makes you think something has happened to her?"

She hesitated. She knew something that she didn't want to tell him. "I have reason to think that her mother—Gothel—may be planning to do something terrible to her."

Gerek felt the blood start to pump through his veins, as if he was preparing for battle. "I saw her mother. She was in the castle yard by the kitchen."

Frau Adelheit's lips turned white. "Oh no. She must have taken her. You must go after her."

"Surely her mother wouldn't hurt her."

"She would. I believe she would! Please, you must find her and bring her back. She will give Rapunzel a sleeping potion. I believe she would do anything to get her away from Hagenheim."

"I shall find her."

Without pausing to tell anyone where he was going, Gerek hurried out to the stables, saddled his horse, and started out to the small house where Rapunzel and her mother had lived.

He arrived at the house in the woods without seeing them. He dismounted and knocked on the front door, which creaked open at the first knock.

"Rapunzel? Are you here?" He stepped inside. There were no live coals in the fire pit, and their belongings had been removed. He walked around the entire one-room house, which took only a few moments. He stepped out the back door, but there were no animals. She had undoubtedly taken the donkey, the ox, and the cart with her—and she must have stopped by the castle to get Rapunzel as well.

Where had they gone? What had she done to Rapunzel? How would he ever find them?

His heart sank a little more with each question. But he had no time for despair. He had to make haste and find her, find their trail.

As he mounted his horse and rode back toward Hagenheim, he urged Donner into a gallop. He had to see if he could pick up some kind of trail from the location where her mother must have taken her.

He arrived several minutes later at the castle. He walked behind the kitchen, where he could see the maidservants' sleeping quarters—a small wooden building several feet from the kitchen. Between the two buildings he noticed the dirt path was slightly churned up. Was this where Rapunzel had encountered her mother?

He looked carefully at the new spring grass. The ground was soft from recent rain. He followed the two lines her feet had made until they ended beside some cart tracks.

During the confusion just after the battle, Gothel must have brought her donkey and cart into the castle yard and waited for Rapunzel to come out. She intercepted her just outside the servants' sleeping quarters, and must have either knocked Rapunzel unconscious or given her some kind of potion to make her lose her strength.

Rapunzel didn't deserve to be mistreated. Inexplicably, the memory of his mother floated in front of his eyes. His mother had not deserved to be abused and thrown down the stairs just because she had wanted her son home for the Christmas holy day. And Rapunzel didn't deserve to be taken against her will by an insane woman bent on only-God-knew-what.

"God," he whispered into the air, "make me her champion. Give me the strength and ability to find her. Show me where to look, where to go, how to find her."

He heard someone approaching and turned to see Frau Adelheit. "You didn't find her?"

"I went to her house, but her mother has taken everything and left. I think she brought her donkey and cart here and took her. I'll follow this trail as far as I can and hopefully overtake them, but they have at least a two-hour head start."

"Should you take someone with you?"

"No time." He mounted his horse. "Tell some of the men to follow me." Although he didn't truly think she would be able to convince Duke Wilhelm's men to go after a maidservant.

He followed the cart wheel tracks in the dirt, but they did not stay on the road. He dismounted, frantically searching the ground for any sign of them.

Several of Duke Wilhelm's guards stopped on the road where he had left Donner.

"I need a tracker over here," Gerek yelled.

He recognized the first two men who reached him. "I lost the trail here. I'm tracking two women, a cart, a donkey, and possibly an ox. One woman is probably on the cart."

The men went to work, touching the ground, sniffing bits of leaves and dirt. One called the other over and they consulted, then called out, "We found the trail."

Gerek could just make out the cart wheel tracks in the grass. It looked as though they were following the road, but out of sight of it, in the edge of the trees. Gerek and the other men remounted their horses and followed the two trackers. They kept going for an hour or more before they lost the trail again. This time even the best trackers could not pick up any signs.

"Let's split up," Gerek said. "Two men in every direction."

Gerek took the best tracker with him, but eventually it was clear that they had completely lost the trail. The tracker held out little hope of finding it again. But they pressed on, hoping and praying to miraculously intercept their trail again or to even find the two women themselves.

They stopped midafternoon to rest their horses.

"Shouldn't we turn back?" the tracker asked. "We've been searching for hours and haven't found them."

"Of course we shouldn't turn back! Turn back? For what?" Gerek took a slow, deep breath and fought to rid the anger from his tone. "Let us keep looking. We could find them at any moment." But it was less and less likely as time wore on, and he knew it.

They finally found a road and a man with an ox and cart, carrying a load of thatch. Gerek asked the man if he had seen two women and a donkey cart.

"No, I haven't seen anyone like that, no women at all."

Gerek was too disappointed to say another word. He could no longer convince his tracker to stay, so the man headed back to Hagenheim.

Gerek continued searching alone. He soon came to a small village and asked several people if they had seen two women with a donkey and a cart traveling that day. No one had seen them.

He went back the way he had come and tried to think at which point it was most likely that they had gone off a different way.

It was impossible. There was no way to know which direction Gothel had taken her. Along the way were fields and roads and woods, but where they had gone was a complete mystery.

He couldn't let despair overtake him. He had bought some food at the village and he stopped now to eat it, water his horse, and rest.

He couldn't stop thinking about her fighting off her attacker at the castle. Even though she had wanted to make it clear that Balthasar had attacked her, had fallen on her knife, she didn't collapse in hysterical crying or screaming at realizing the man was dead, as he might have expected a young woman to do. She had no one in her life except a mother who had threatened to do terrible things to her, but she was not overcome by her circumstances, not grasping and desperate to marry the first man she could cling to.

And yet . . . she was thoroughly feminine and beautiful and sweet.

He wouldn't even let himself think he might be in love with her. He was nearly betrothed to Lady Lankouwen, but she had said she would marry him if he was willing. Lady Lankouwen was the best thing for him—sedate, wealthy, and in need of a protector. He would be helping her, and with her money and her estate, which was as grand as the castle where he had been born, she would be helping him show his brother that even though Gerek was the younger son, he was just as worthy.

But what would happen to Rapunzel? If her mother was able to force her to take a sleeping potion and seize her, bearing her away against her will, what else might she do to her? The woman was obviously mad.

He stood and put away the food and interrupted Donner's grazing. They would search until nightfall, sleep in the woods, then search some more tomorrow. For as long as it took.

Rapunzel's head felt weighed down. She opened her eyes, but everything was moving and she couldn't focus. A dry, herbal taste clung to her tongue, and her throat burned. The smell of animal dung assaulted her nose, and she was lying on something that was moving and rocking. By the gentle breeze, she knew she was outdoors. When she opened her eyes again she could see, blurred above her, blue sky and white clouds.

Gradually she started to remember the last few days, how Lord Claybrook's men had captured Hagenheim Castle, and all that had followed. Then she suddenly remembered her mother admitting that she had stolen Rapunzel away from her rightful parents. Her mind quickly jumped to Sir Gerek's muscular arms holding her tight against his chest after helping her up off the floor.

To think, what a grouch he used to be. She had disliked him and thought him arrogant and unkind. Then Mother—Gothel—had grabbed her and put something down her throat and forced her to swallow it. She had indeed made good on her threat to poison Rapunzel and drag her away from Sir Gerek and Hagenheim.

Her body seemed too heavy and limp to move. Was she paralyzed? Had Gothel given her something that would keep her from being able to walk again? But no, she moved them slightly, not wanting to draw Gothel's attention. She had been given a powerful sleeping potion, so powerful her body was still having trouble waking up.

She had to think of a plan. Gothel undoubtedly intended to take Rapunzel away from Hagenheim forever. Could Gothel truly make her a prisoner?

Even knowing of Gothel's cruelty, it was still difficult to stop thinking of her as her mother, this woman who had raised her. She had suspected she was mad, had worried that she was becoming more and more irrational, but she never imagined she was wicked enough to steal someone else's child.

Why had she stolen a child?

She had been all alone after the man she loved had left her pregnant, then her baby had been born too early and died. She was so suspicious and bitter toward people. She must have thought the only thing for her to do was to steal a child for herself, a child to replace the one she had lost, a child who would not question her suspicion and bitterness.

Rapunzel not only had been wrong about Sir Gerek, but she had been even more wrong about Gothel.

O Lord God, I don't ever want to be like her. She may have raised me, but make me like someone else, like Sir Gerek or Lady Rose or Frau Adelheit, but not like this woman.

Her body still felt weak and unwieldy. She only wished she could have some water. But first she had to think of a plan to escape.

It was starting to get dark, and waves of sleepiness were washing over her again. Could she even hope to escape when she was barely able to stay awake, barely able to move?

Chapter Twenty-Eight

*Gerek awoke to the old familiar anger, the overpower-*ing kind that had plagued him off and on since he was a boy. He had not felt it in a long time. It had inexplicably disappeared when he was traveling with Valten for two years over the Continent, entering jousting tournaments and fighting the best knights in the world. He had thought he had learned to channel the anger, to control it, and to use it to defeat his opponents without any real malice toward them. So why was it back now, that out-of-control feeling? Was it a reminder that he was his father's son after all? If someone was in front of him right now, would he take his anger out on them? Would he strike Rapunzel's mother if he found her now, whether it was necessary or not? Was he capable of doing what his father had done?

No. Whatever he felt for Rapunzel, he could never imagine striking her or even the woman who had harmed her, unless it was absolutely necessary. The thought of striking a woman made him physically sick. It was against everything he had pledged to be as a knight. All of Duke Wilhelm's knights had to swear an oath to protect and defend women, and Gerek had embraced that oath—as a defiant act against his father, but also because he saw it as his Christian duty. Jesus had given his life for others, and a knight must do the same, and nothing was nobler than saving a young woman. A young woman like his mother.

But this was about more than being chivalrous and noble. This was about Rapunzel. An overwhelming desire rose inside him to save her. If anything happened to her . . . Pain tore through him, making him gasp at the sharp suddenness of it, as if the pain of his mother's death were fresh and new instead of nearly twenty years old.

He got back on his horse and started searching again for Rapunzel's trail. He traveled on the dusty, rutted road for a while, questioning every person he saw, but no one had seen them. So he went back the way he had come and tried a different direction, going south instead of east from the point where he had lost their trail.

He felt a renewed sense of hope. Perhaps this was the way they had gone. It made sense because they had come to Hagenheim from the south. Maybe Rapunzel's mother was taking her back to the last place they had lived.

He made his way to the south road and rode hard, stopping to question people he encountered along the way. No one had seen them. But by now, they had a whole day's head start.

He would eventually find them if they had come this way. He simply had to keep going, keep looking, and keep asking.

Rapunzel awoke to darkness and a small fire not far away. Her throat was burning worse than ever and she was desperate for water.

She tried to sit up and realized she was still lying on the cart, which was loaded with bundles all around her. She managed to roll to her left side, but couldn't seem to move her left arm. When she tugged at it, metal clanked against metal. Something was holding her fast.

Her wrist was tied with a piece of rope to the side of the cart, and their metal cooking utensils were tied to the rope.

Still, she managed to sit up and look around.

Mother was walking cautiously toward her with a cup in her hand.

Without speaking, Rapunzel reached for the cup. She was so thirsty that she didn't pause until she had drunk it all.

Some bits of something solid slid down her throat. Her stomach sank and her head pounded with an awful foreboding.

"What was in that water? What did you just give me?" The breath went out of her as fear gripped her. "Do you feel the need to poison me and tie me up? To treat me like an animal? You must hate me."

Mother's face was hard and dark, just as it had been when she'd seen Sir Gerek bringing her home on his horse. "I could not let you tell anyone who you were, could I?"

Pain streaked through Rapunzel, but she pretended to feel nothing. "I have to visit the privy." Although she knew there was no privy. They were in the middle of the woods.

Mother untied the rope, and Rapunzel walked away to find a thick bush to squat behind. But when she finished and stood up, she became so dizzy, she stumbled several steps, then fell on her side on the ground. Her eyelids were too heavy to open.

Traveling the south road for two days had yielded nothing. No one had seen the two women or their donkey and cart. Gerek asked at every village, asked every traveler. What could he do now except go back and try another direction?

But perhaps someone had found them and brought them back to Hagenheim. After all, the other men had gone in all directions. It was not too far-fetched to believe that they may have found them.

With this heartening thought, Gerek turned back toward Hagenheim.

How many days had passed since Gothel had taken Rapunzel away from Hagenheim? She spent them either asleep or in a daze. Did Sir Gerek realize what had happened to her? Was he worried about her? He would surely search for her when he found out she was missing, even if he didn't know what had happened to her. Surely he would guess what Gothel had done to her.

It was nearly nighttime. Rapunzel slipped her hand into her pocket and pulled out a book, *The Poem of the Cid*, and she quietly tore off a piece of a page. Then she dropped it over the side of the cart.

Would Sir Gerek be angry with her for ruining his book? She hoped, if he was looking for her, he would say it was worth it if it helped him find her. And if he never found her . . . it wouldn't matter.

Had Frau Adelheit told Lady Rose that she suspected Rapunzel was Elsebeth? No, she wouldn't want to upset Lady Rose. She wouldn't want her to be devastated at losing her again, for Rapunzel was truly lost unless she could escape from Gothel and make her way back to Hagenheim. And that was exactly what she had to do. She had to stay alive so she could get back to Hagenheim, back to her true mother.

Every night Gothel gave her a cup of water, and every night Rapunzel drank it because she was so thirsty and there was no other way to get water. Gothel kept her tied to the side of the cart, and she'd had no opportunity to untie it, being so weak from whatever was in her water, and Gothel was never far from the cart for long. She had even stopped untying the rope to let Rapunzel relieve herself. She simply did her relieving beside the cart.

Rapunzel wasn't sure how many days she'd been away from Hagenheim. She kept ripping off pieces of paper as quietly as possible and dropping them onto the ground, praying Gothel would not notice.

A few hours later, Gothel gave her a bit of food. She had eaten very little for the last however many days they had been traveling, and she was ravenous. She ate the morsel of bread and cheese, wishing she could throw it in Gothel's face, but knowing she needed the strength to escape. She could barely swallow it, not having drunk anything all day. Finally came the cup of water. She took a sip. Gothel was looking away, staring at the fire, so Rapunzel poured the water out onto a cloth bag beside her, swirling it in the cup to make sure she got rid of the bits of herbs or crushed root or whatever it was in the bottom of the cup.

When Gothel turned back to her, Rapunzel made sure the cup was at her lips, as if she were just drinking the last bit. Gothel came toward her and Rapunzel held out the cup. "May I have some more water?"

Gothel stared hard at her. Finally, she took the cup and poured some water into it.

Rapunzel drank it, so glad to finally have something to drink that she knew wasn't poisoned. But a few minutes later, she pretended to be overcome with sleepiness and lay down and closed her eyes.

Rapunzel kept peeking at Gothel, waiting for her to go to sleep. It seemed forever before she finally kicked some dirt over the fire. But instead of lying down on the ground to sleep, she climbed on the cart beside Rapunzel.

Now how would she get away? She waited until Gothel's breathing was loud and steady, and then she started trying to slip the small noose off her wrist. The skin on her wrist was worn off and bleeding, but she eventually worked the rope off her hand.

She inched her way down the cart on her stomach, wriggling slowly, painfully down the bundles. Gothel didn't move, but Rapunzel kept her eyes on her, listening for any noise or movement. She kept wriggling, inching, scooting, trying not to rock the rickety cart. Her feet were hanging off the end. Finally, her feet touched the ground. Now it was easier to slip the rest of the way down and stand up.

The cart shook a bit. She could no longer hear Gothel breathing, but she hadn't moved. Rapunzel took one step backward, then another, then turned and ran. But her legs were weak and it was dark. Tree limbs slapped her face and she stumbled. She pushed her weak knees to hold her up and her feet to keep running. Suddenly, a root caught her toe and she fell on her face.

She pushed herself up with her hands. She was shaking all over, but she managed to get to her knees, then to her feet. Taking a trembling step forward, she heard someone behind her. Pain suddenly crashed through the back of her head as something hit her. Then everything went black.

Gerek reached Hagenheim after a day and a half of hard riding. He found Frau Adelheit, who looked frantic when she turned and saw him there. "Did you find her?"

"No." The breath went out of him. So she had not made it back to Hagenheim. He rubbed his hand over his short beard. "Is anyone still out looking for her?"

"There are a few guards looking for her, but Duke Wilhelm is becoming suspicious about why so many of his men are searching for a maidservant. But go. Get a bath and a good night's sleep and you can look for her again tomorrow."

What had she meant, that Duke Wilhelm was becoming suspicious? And why *were* so many men willing to look for a maidservant? Gerek was looking for her because . . . because she . . . she was his friend and he cared about her. What had Frau Adelheit told the other men to convince them to go after her?

Whatever the reason, he was grateful. He certainly needed a bath and some supplies before going out again, but he would not spend the night at the castle. A man didn't pause to shave and he did not sleep in a bed when he was on a quest. He was a knight, not a prince, and in an hour he was ready to go again, after a brief conversation with another knight who told him where he thought the other men were still looking.

This time Gerek took the north road, veering toward the northeast. He would go all the way to Thornbeck if he had to.

He traveled for only a few hours before it became too dark to see. Sleeping on the ground did not bother him, but lying awake, wondering what was happening to Rapunzel, feeling frustrated and helpless, was becoming the worst part of every day. But tomorrow he might find her, so he should not ruminate on evil imaginings.

The next morning was rainy and misty, and he found very few people along the road to ask if they had seen Rapunzel and her mother. He finally came to a village, but no one had seen anything.

By nightfall, he had been wet all day, cold, and nearly despairing. How would he ever find them? And if Rapunzel had not escaped from her mother by now, what did that mean? Had her mother harmed her? Was she unable to walk? To scream? To get help?

It was maddening, not knowing what was happening to her, and not even knowing where to look for her.

The truth was, the Holy Roman Empire was a vast, open part of the Continent. He had no idea where she was. He could search for months and even years, and it would be a miracle if he ever found her.

But he would never stop searching. And when he found her, he would never let anyone harm her again.

Chapter Twenty-Nine

Rapunzel could feel something under her arms, pulling her. Her feet were being dragged along something hard and uneven, across hard edges, like stone steps. Her head throbbed, her throat burned, her face was hot, but the rest of her body felt cold. Wherever she was, it was dark and smelled of mold. She was too tired to even hold her eyes open.

When she was awake again, she was lying flat on her back. She still wore her maidservant's clothing—blue cotehardie and white underdress—though now it bore rips and streaks of dirt. Above her was a gray stone ceiling, high and arching. A sharp pain at the back of her head reminded her of getting hit when she had tried to run away.

She slowly sat up and propped herself on her elbow. The room was a strange shape—round, but with squared walls connecting at wide angles. There were eight walls in all and two windows. It was rainy and misty outside, and tree limbs crowded the open windows. The walls around her were made of gray stone and mortar that were crumbling and old.

Beside her was a bucket of water. She pushed herself up onto her knees, dipped her hand in, and brought the water to her lips. She didn't know if it was poisoned water or not, but she was too desperately thirsty to care. She splashed a little on her heated face and shivered, then drank some more.

With the cool water hitting her empty stomach, it growled. She looked around but didn't see anything that could be food. There was no furniture in the room, but she did find a stack of her own clothing and some blankets.

She picked up a blanket and wiped her face on a corner of it, then wrapped it around her shoulders. Her feet were bare, so she found some woolen footed hose and put them on. She looked all around the room but . . . where was the door? How had she come to be in this round room without a door?

She walked to the window and leaned out, then quickly drew herself back in, her head spinning. She was in a tower, very high. There must have been at least three levels beneath the one she was on, so there must be stairs leading up. Perhaps there was a secret door.

Feeling for loose stones, she found many of them, as the mortar between many was crumbling, but none of them led to a door. Finally, on the opposite wall from the window, she found a place where the stones didn't match very well, where there were no windows, and where the mortar between them was damp. Had someone put up a wall where the doorway had been?

The thought sent her scrambling for something hard or sharp. But there was nothing metal to be found. She picked up a stick—the largest one she could find was still very small—and started digging away at the damp mortar.

"Rapunzel? Can you hear me?"

She startled at the sound of Gothel's voice. It was coming from outside, below the window.

"Rapunzel? Are you awake? I have some food for you."

Rapunzel's hands trembled.

She hid the stick underneath the pile of clothing on the floor and walked over to the window, hardening herself against the emotions threatening to overwhelm her.

Looking down, she noticed for the first time that there was a bucket tied to a very long rope, which ran along a pulley wheel attached to the wall next to the window. Gothel was putting something into the bucket. Then she took hold of the rope and began to pull, hand over hand, and the bucket began to rise.

When the bucket reached the window, Rapunzel took it and set it on the window ledge. She took out the cloth bundle and unwrapped it.

It was a warm bun stuffed with something. She bit into it, so ravenous it was as if she had brought it to her mouth by instinct instead of choice. The filling was minced pork and cabbage. Delicious.

If Gothel had bought a stuffed bun and it was still warm, there must be a village nearby. Hope ignited in her chest. Perhaps if she shouted loud enough, someone would hear her.

She went to the bucket of water and drank some water, then ate the rest of the bun. If only there had been more! Her mind wanted more, but her stomach felt full.

She heard the pulley squealing and knew Gothel was using the rope to bring the bucket back down to the ground.

"Rapunzel? I'm going to get in the bucket and I want you to pull me up."

Rapunzel didn't answer.

"Rapunzel, if you pull me up, I'll give you more food. I have your favorite—fried apple pasties."

Her mouth watered at the thought. But it wasn't worth it. Besides, she wasn't sure she had the strength, even though Gothel was a very small person. Gothel would stop her from tearing through the moist mortar and getting out of her tower prison. Instead of answering her, Rapunzel found her stick and started scraping at the mortar again.

"Rapunzel?"

She ignored her and continued digging. It took awhile, but she finally dug through one line of mortar, about four inches long, but instead of being able to poke her stick all the way through, there was something hard at the other side.

She dug through some mortar farther over and found the same problem. Had someone put up two walls of mortar and stone, purposely staggering the rocks and mortar, to keep her from escaping?

Of course she had. Gothel may be lacking in sanity, but she was clever. And now the mortar was beginning to harden. She kept scraping at it anyway, getting as much of the mortar out as she could. Finally, she was able to work her fingertips around the edges of one stone and remove it. The stone was about one foot wide, one foot deep, and six inches high. But just as she suspected, there was another stone wall behind it. Fortunately, the mortar between those stones was also still damp. She started digging at it with her stick. After another long while, she broke through.

She tried to see through the crack she had made, but there was less light on the other side. She saw nothing but darkness.

The mortar was almost set, so she dug faster. Finally, she was able to take out a second stone approximately the same size as the first one. She stuck her arm through and pushed and pulled at the stones beside the hole, but they wouldn't budge. She pulled and pushed at the stones on her side as well, but the mortar was hard. It was too late. Her window of time had closed.

She leaned her back against the wall and put her head in her hands, trying to catch her breath and calm her racing heart. "I'm trapped," she whispered. But there must be another way out. Perhaps she could climb out the window somehow. She just had to wait until Gothel was gone.

Thinking of Gothel . . . Perhaps she had left. She had not heard her calling her name for a while.

She crept toward the window on her hands and knees. But after being thirsty for so long, she couldn't pass the bucket of water without stopping for a drink, especially now that she knew it was not laden with sleeping potion. She paused to clean off her hand before dipping it into the water. Her fingertips were bloody from scraping them on the stones of the wall.

No matter. She tipped it up and drank directly from the bucket.

She continued the rest of the way to the window and peeked out. It was beginning to get dark. The bare tree limbs moved slightly in the breeze. Rapunzel got closer and stuck her head over the ledge. Gothel lay on the ground below, curled up with a blanket.

There lay the woman she had believed loved her, the woman who taught her to sew and cook and pick good herbs and nonpoisonous berries. Her heart longed for the mother who had braided her hair and told her how talented she was . . . then the memories of her cruelty overwhelmed her. She sat back and closed her eyes. "I won't think about it. I won't," she whispered. "I will only think about how to escape. How to get back to Hagenheim and my true friends. People who will not mistreat me. People in Hagenheim who will love me. Where I will be safe. I must escape from here. I will escape. O God in heaven, help me escape."

She let the tears squeeze free and run down her cheeks. She would allow herself to cry, to hurt and mourn, but only for a few minutes. Then she would be strong, and she would escape.

Rapunzel awoke just as dawn was sending light into the air around her. It hurt to move. She was sore all over, but at least she didn't feel feverish anymore. She sat up on her blanket—her only bedding—and looked around.

This tower must have been abandoned long ago. Acorns and leaves and sticks littered the stone floor. Why was it here? To whom did it belong? If only the owners would come back and free her.

She moved to the window. Gothel was no longer lying on the ground below. Rapunzel realized this was her chance. She called out, "Help me! Someone, please! Can you hear me? Help me! I'm trapped in a tower." She yelled as loud as she could, and even screamed, hoping that sound would carry farther. Perhaps Sir Gerek was nearby, having followed her trail of pages from his book. She was not sure how many days she had traveled before she started leaving them.

But she could not wait for Sir Gerek to come and rescue her. And Gothel might have given up on Rapunzel ever speaking to her again. She may have abandoned her to die.

The bucket was still attached to the rope and was near the ground. It looked sadly empty. She was so hungry, her stomach had stopped growling. There was only a constant ache in the hollowness.

Rapunzel had already thought about trying to ride down the rope to the ground, but with the pulley wheel, she would fall straight down and break her legs, or worse. She could possibly step into the bucket while holding on to the rope on the opposing side of the pulley, but she did not think she had the strength to bear her own weight, or the dexterity required to climb out of the window and hold the rope simultaneously.

The tree limb near the window was close enough to reach, but it looked much too spindly to hold her weight.

The ruins of a castle stood next to the tower. Apparently the rest of the castle had mostly been made of wood and had collapsed, and the stone tower was all that was left of it. Beyond the piles of wood and the stone foundation was a lake that glistened in the cool spring sunlight.

Perhaps she could climb down the side of the tower.

She hung her head out the window. Were there enough grooves for her toes and fingers? The wall looked quite smooth. But since the mortar was crumbling . . . it might be possible. But the more she stared down from that height and thought about trying to climb the wall, the dizzier she got. No. It just was not possible.

But she wouldn't give up yet. She would keep thinking.

"Rapunzel," Gothel's voice called.

Gothel was standing at the bottom of the tower.

"I have your favorite fried apple pasties, and also some plum pudding cakes and some fresh water. But I need you to help pull me up in the bucket."

Rapunzel clenched her teeth. It was on the tip of her tongue to tell her to take her fried apple pasties and her plum pudding cakes and choke on them. She would be completely justified in making all manner of condemning reprimands to this woman who had called herself her mother for the past sixteen years. But she needed to concentrate on escaping. And she couldn't escape if she lost her strength. Besides, she suspected her fever from the day before was caused by not drinking enough water. She did not have much choice. She needed Gothel to survive.

"You may come up," Rapunzel said.

She watched as Gothel stepped into the bucket and held on to the rope. Gothel was lighter and smaller than Rapunzel. They both pulled on the rope, and she started to rise. If Rapunzel let go, Gothel would go plunging back to the ground. Even though she was furious with her, she had no desire to kill her. Vengeance belonged to the Lord, as she had once heard a priest say.

When she had pulled the bucket level with the window ledge, Gothel took hold of the window casing and stepped onto the window. Rapunzel let go of the rope and helped her inside.

Gothel untied the cloth bag from her belt and gave Rapunzel the food. Again, it was still warm.

"There is a village nearby." Rapunzel said it as a statement, not a question.

"It is not very near," Gothel said slowly. "There is a woman I found who cooks very good pasties and bread. She lives outside the village."

Rapunzel nodded.

"So you are not angry with me anymore?" Gothel said.

"I am as angry with you as I would be with my own birth mother if she had given me poison, forced me from my duties and my friends, forced me to lie in a state of unconsciousness, dragged me into an old tower, locked me away inside, starved me, denied me clean water—"

"Enough!" The black center of Gothel's eyes dilated. "You betrayed me with that knight, Sir Gerek, then sneaked away in defiance so that you could do something great? No! So you could be a maidservant."

"I betrayed you? In what way did I betray you?"

"You deceived me."

"So that I could learn to read. You knew I wanted to learn, you led me to believe that you would help me find lessons, and yet you never did."

"After all I have done for you, would you dare—"

"Yes, after all you did for me, stealing me away from my rightful parents, from my rightful place, from people who loved me and could give me everything."

Gothel said nothing. Rapunzel tried to slow her breathing and control her thoughts. Becoming angry was not the way to concentrate on making a plan of escape. It was foolish to defend herself to this woman.

"How is your apple pasty? Is it the way you like it?"

Rapunzel refused to answer. She ate slowly.

"I think I can tie our straw mattress to the rope and we can haul it up."

"Hmm."

How strange to have a conversation with this woman, as if the woman had not robbed her of her own human dignity. But she had to pretend to be calm so she could keep her mind clear.

After they ate, Gothel walked around the tower room making plans about how to furnish it and make it more comfortable.

"So you expect me to stay trapped in this room, never leaving, because you wish it?" Rapunzel couldn't stop herself, couldn't stop the breathless, disbelieving tone.

"You left me no choice, Rapunzel." Gothel's voice was hard. "I didn't want to do this, but you forced me."

Rapunzel wanted to scream. But she concentrated on breathing slowly.

Rapunzel asked her questions, discovering that Gothel had hired a man from the nearby village to lay the stones and mortar to close up the doorway to the high tower room.

"Did this man see me lying on the floor?" Rapunzel asked, making her voice unemotional and matter-of-fact.

"No, I covered you up. He did not know you were in the room."

"Weren't you taking a chance that I would die up here? You could not get up here to help me unless I woke up and was strong enough to eat and drink by myself."

Gothel did not answer. Apparently she had been willing to take the risk. Finally, she said, "Do not think Sir Gerek will come and rescue you. As long as he thinks you are only a peasant girl, only a maidservant, he will not come searching for you."

Heat rose into Rapunzel's cheeks. She was breathing hard when she said, "I will never listen to anything you say ever again."

"He does not love you. I am the one who loves you."

Rapunzel turned and lay down on the hard stone floor, staring out the window at the trees and the sky beyond them.

Later that afternoon Gothel finally said she needed to leave to fetch their mattress. Rapunzel helped lower Gothel down and watched her walk away.

She blinked back angry tears. *O God, help me find a way of escape.*

Chapter Thirty

Gerek had not found anyone on the north road who had seen Rapunzel and her mother, so he struck out to the west, traveling, wandering around for days, which turned into weeks, talking to people, searching the woods, the villages, and the roads.

By the time he returned to Hagenheim, he had been searching for six weeks. His beard was quite long now. He couldn't even bring himself to go to Frau Adelheit and tell her he had failed to find any sign of where Rapunzel might be.

Feeling like a defeated challenger, rather than the champion he had prayed to be for Rapunzel, he went to sleep in his own bed in the knights' barracks. He slept all night and part of the next day. He bathed and went into the chapel.

The stone chapel was lit with candles and the sunlight streamed through the stained-glass windows. He thanked God that it was empty.

Kneeling before the large crucifix, he prayed, "See my suffering, Sovereign Lord. See my affliction. Though it is not as great as your own when you went to the cross, please have mercy and show me the way. My quest is noble. I seek an innocent girl who has been taken against her will. Merciful God, do not forsake me. Do not forsake Rapunzel. Forgive me for being unkind to her at times. Forgive me for not recognizing what an exceptional woman she is."

He felt a great weight on his shoulders and chest. "O Sovereign

Lord, I wanted to marry Lady Lankouwen. I wanted her for her castle. I wanted to be her defender, but not out of love for her. O God, you know the motives of my heart. I wanted to prove that I was better than my brother. I wanted to be greater and wealthier than he." It hurt to admit it, but the heaviness on his shoulders lifted a bit.

A verse from the Proverbs came into his mind. *Trust in the LORD with all your heart and lean not on your own understanding; in all your ways submit to him, and he will make your paths straight.*

Gerek had thought his plans were wise. He had thought he understood success and what he wanted. But he had been leaning on his own understanding. He had not trusted in the Lord with all his heart or submitted his ways to God. He'd been wise in his own eyes, thinking he knew what was best.

Rapunzel. She was one hundred times nobler than he had been, and he loved her.

"Forgive me for wanting riches and status more than to give love to a woman who deserves it. I promise, if it is your will, I shall marry Rapunzel and give her everything I am, everything you provide, and I shall begin by giving her my love."

He meditated on the Savior's love, on how great was the Father's love for his children, for himself, for Rapunzel, and even for Lady Lankouwen, since God surely had another man for her. How much greater was God's love than man's love! How much greater, more perfect, more holy. But God knew man, that he was but dust, that man's love would fail, to various degrees and in various ways.

So selfish was Rapunzel's mother's love for her child. She had forbidden Rapunzel to speak to a man and had made her mistrustful of all men. And when she could not bear to see Rapunzel free and living away from her, she had seized her and fled far away. Gothel must have done something truly atrocious to keep Rapunzel from being able to escape and come back to Hagenheim.

As the day turned into evening, Gerek continued to fast and pray. Eventually, his mind turned to his own father and mother.

What must his mother have felt, being yelled at and beaten by her husband?

He had not cried over his mother's death since he was a little boy, but now, as he continued to kneel before the altar and crucifix, he wept for his mother, and he wept for himself and the guilt, shame, and pain of what had happened to her, of what his father had done, killing her in a drunken rage. He wept for the older brother who had been his hero but who had taken his grief out in anger on Gerek. And he wept for Rapunzel, the courageous young woman who had saved his life, who had gracefully endured his ingratitude and irritability when he had been forced to teach her to read. She was clever and beautiful, and she had no one to protect her from the one person who should love her the most.

Just like his mother.

When Gerek looked up, the crucifix was glowing.

Take the north road toward Thornbeck and listen for my instruction.

The words just seemed to appear in his mind. When no other words came, he fell prostrate on his face. "Thank you, Sovereign God. Worthy are you, O Lord. I thank you with all my heart."

He stood up, the weight gone from his shoulders.

He went to the Great Hall and found all his friends gathering for the evening meal. They clapped him on the back, asking, "Did you find the girl, Rapunzel?"

If he had expected them to tease him for still looking for a maidservant, he was surprised to see that they seemed genuinely concerned for her.

"After what Frau Adelheit said, we all looked, but there was no sign of her. It was as if she vanished."

But Gerek had guidance now. He knew where to look, or at least where to start—the road to Thornbeck. He believed he would get further instruction when he needed it.

He had also decided on a new course that filled him with joy—he would ask Rapunzel to be his wife.

Rapunzel gazed out the window. She still shouted for help sometimes, even though her shouts had never brought anyone. It seemed worth the effort anyway, and Gothel was usually gone all day and only came back at night to bring food and water and to sleep.

Every night Gothel still asked her, "Won't you sing to me tonight, Rapunzel, one of your songs?"

She had not sung a single note or thought of a single verse of song since Gothel had taken her away from Hagenheim.

Rapunzel always answered, "I will sing when you set me free."

Today Gothel smiled as she was preparing to leave for the day. "I will have another child soon."

"What do you mean?"

"I am attending a young maiden who is with child. She doesn't want it and says she will give it to me."

Rapunzel tried to think of something to say. Gothel would do this to another person, the same thing she had done to Rapunzel—poison her against men—and poison her literally if she ever defied her and tried to get away.

"Then you will not need me anymore," Rapunzel said. "You can set me free."

Gothel simply shook her head, averting her gaze. "I cannot do that, of course."

When she was gone, Rapunzel stared out the window. Leaves had started growing on the trees, particularly the tree that was nearest

Rapunzel's window. The air was warmer, the sun stayed out a little longer, and the birds tweeted and sang from early morning to night. The squirrels and chipmunks were hard at work, scurrying around, gathering food. And Rapunzel was still trapped.

Where was Sir Gerek today? She couldn't stop hoping that he was searching for her and would find her someday. It was too painful to think otherwise. It occupied so many of her thoughts, especially when she lay awake at night. The pain of being trapped, the injustice of what Gothel had done, was so heavy in her chest, she couldn't even cry. Oftentimes she just felt numb.

Her comfort was the three books that Sir Gerek had loaned her and she read them every day. She supposed she was getting lazy because she hadn't even tried to memorize them. It was the consequence of being able to read and to actually have the books in her possession.

Today she opened to where she had left off in the letter to the Romans. She read, "Be joyful in hope, patient in affliction, faithful in prayer." That was certainly a passage she could easily commit to memory. She read on. When she reached chapter fifteen, there seemed to be a lot of verses about hope. Rapunzel's hungry heart latched onto them.

"May the God of hope fill you with all joy and peace as you trust in him, so that you may overflow with hope by the power of the Holy Spirit."

She could easily let anger close her off from hope. And fear of disappointment would cause hope to wither. She had to believe Sir Gerek would find her. Besides, Frau Adelheit knew she was the daughter of Duke Wilhelm and Lady Rose. She would keep sending knights out to look for her. But what if Frau Adelheit didn't want to hurt Lady Rose again? She would not want them to know that their long-lost daughter, whom they had mourned for many years, might still be alive, if there was any possibility they might never find her. Frau Adelheit wouldn't want them to go through unnecessary pain.

Perhaps she had not told anyone. Perhaps no one was looking for her.

But Sir Gerek would look for her. He might not want to marry her, but he was still her friend. He would certainly try to find her and save her. He would surely realize that Gothel had done something to her. He knew of her threats.

She had been through all these thoughts many times before. They ran through her mind like a pack of dogs chasing their tails. At night, when she couldn't sleep, she wondered if there was anyone anywhere in the world who thought of her, cared about her, loved her.

No. She would not think like that. "'Be joyful in hope, patient in affliction, faithful in prayer,'" she said aloud.

Tears stung her eyes. It was painful to hope, but it was better than despair. She could not, would not despair.

But the eyes of the LORD are on those who fear him, on those whose hope is in his unfailing love.

The words seemed to leap into her mind. She sat staring up at the sky. *Thank you, God. Thank you. My hope is in your unfailing love.*

Instantly, a song rose inside her and she began to sing. She sang new words, a new song to God, in praise of his hope and his unfailing love. When she had sung for several minutes, she stopped and whispered, "I will never sing for Mother again, but I will sing to you, God, as long as I have hope."

Gerek followed the north road toward Thornbeck. When he had been traveling for three days, he saw a small piece of paper on the ground about five or six feet off the road.

He dismounted, walked over, and picked it up. The paper had obviously gotten wet and then dried, as the writing on one side was faded from the sun and rain. The other side also had writing. It had been torn and only had a few words on each side, but the words were familiar. Suddenly, he realized it was from *The Poem of the Cid*.

Rapunzel had his book. Could she have had it with her, in her pocket, when Gothel snatched her?

He quickly grabbed Donner's reins and pulled the horse off the road, searching the ground. There, up ahead, was another piece of paper.

He ran and seized it and read the words. The first letter on the page had a familiar style, flowery and decorated with purple and gold paint. Yes, it was his book. He was sure of it. Praise to God in heaven, now he would find her!

He hurried forward, finding a faint trail, which paralleled the road. As he went, he found another piece of paper, then another. Then, away from the road, he found evidence of a fire, as if someone had spent the night there. He searched around the abandoned fire but he saw no more pieces of paper.

God, what now? Where should I go? He closed his eyes, forcing back the panic and frustration and concentrating on listening.

Keep going. He was supposed to keep going, of course, but where? *In the same direction.*

Gerek went back to the road, which was nearby, and kept going in the same general direction Rapunzel's trail had gone. Within half an hour, he arrived at a village. It was around midday and he paused to look around.

Several men were sitting outside the bakery, so he headed that direction.

"That's a beauty of a horse," one man said, moving the straw in his mouth so he could spit.

"He's strong, but he's skittish of loud noises." Gerek and the man talked for a few minutes about horses and other animals. Finally,

Gerek asked, "Have you seen two women around here, strangers, one very young and fair, and the other about middle age with a mole just here on her cheek?" He pointed to his own face. "They were probably traveling with one or two donkeys and a cart."

The man twisted his mouth to the side, as if trying to remember. "No, not two women. But there has been a woman with a mole as you describe. She's small and slight?"

"Yes, that's her."

"She's been buying food from my wife every day. She won't say who she is or what she's doing here. She only just came about . . ."

"Six or seven weeks ago?"

He cocked his head to one side. "Ja, about."

Gerek's heart thumped against his chest.

"She comes to my house in the forest, not too far from here, every morning and every evening. She pays money. I told my wife not to keep selling her our food. What do we need of money? It's food we need, not coin."

He would have to lie in wait outside the man's house and follow Gothel back to wherever she went, or force her to tell him where she was hiding Rapunzel. He refused to believe she was not still alive.

"I heard a woman ghost." A boy skipped toward them. He looked about ten or eleven years old.

"A woman ghost?" Gerek asked him.

"I heard her singing, in the tower of the old castle. All I could see was long blond hair in the window, and everybody knows that the tower is abandoned. That's how I knew it was a ghost."

His heart went from pounding fast to stopping and stuttering. "Did you call out to her? Did she know you were there?"

He shook his head. "My Oma taught me to run away from spirits, should I ever see one."

"Will you take me to the tower? I'll give you anything you want."

"Will you give me my own knife?"

Gerek opened his saddlebag and pulled out his extra knife. "Do you like this one?"

His eyebrows shot up and he nodded.

"Let's go."

Gerek led Donner by his reins and followed the boy through the village and into the woods. He wished the boy would go faster. They were following a trail through the woods, with bushes and brambles and beech trees on either side.

Finally, the boy said, "It's just ahead. But I don't want to get too close. I don't want the ghost to get me."

"As soon as we see the tower, I'll give you the knife and you can go."

The boy nodded and kept walking. In another minute, he pointed. "It's there."

A gray stone tower was just visible through the trees in a clearing ahead.

Gerek gave him the knife, and the little boy smiled and ran back the way they had come. Gerek strode forward, his eyes on the tower window, his heart pounding. When he was almost to the clearing, he tied Donner to a tree. As he did, he heard Rapunzel singing.

The breath rushed out of him. The song was different from the one he had heard Rapunzel singing before, but the voice was the same.

Gerek's heart leapt. He left Donner and ran toward the tower, unsheathing his sword as he went, in case Gothel was nearby.

Just as he entered the clearing, he saw long blond hair flowing out of the highest window of the tower.

"Rapunzel."

Her face appeared in the window. "Gerek!" She covered her mouth with her hand.

He stopped at the foot of the tower, looking all around for a way up to her. "Is there a door?"

"The only way up or down is with the rope." She pointed to the rope and pulley wheel. "I prayed and prayed to escape. But I knew you would come and find me. I knew you would." Her voice cracked on the last word, and she bit her lip, as though to hold back tears.

He sheathed his sword, took hold of the rope, and quickly raised the bucket up to her window. "Rapunzel, come down. I will catch you if you fall."

She disappeared from the window. Was her mother up there? Was she trying to hurt her?

"Where are you?"

"I'm here." She was smiling, her face radiant as she held a bundle under one arm.

He held tight to the rope—and held his breath—while she stepped out of the window, putting one foot in the bucket and holding on to the rope, then she put her other foot in. She kept her eyes on him the whole time as he slowly lowered her with the rope.

His heart pounded faster the closer she got to him.

When she was still a few feet from the ground, she let go of the rope and reached for his shoulders. He caught her in his arms, and she buried her face in his neck.

"I have you," he whispered, letting his lips brush her temple. "I have you."

Her feet dangled above the ground, and she laughed. Her whole body shook in his arms. Gradually, her laughter sounded more like sobbing.

"What did she do to you?" he murmured against her hair, holding her tight. She was so thin, he could feel her ribs.

He lowered her bare feet to the ground and she loosened her hold enough that he was able to look at her face. Tears trembled on her eyelashes. She pressed her lips together and shook her head.

"I wish you could take me away from here before she comes back.

But . . . she is planning to take another baby and raise her up in this madness. We have to stop her."

The pain in her eyes was almost unbearable. "Your safety is more important than anything else."

She shook her head. "I am well, but I cannot be at peace until Gothel is stopped. She stole me away from my parents, and I can't bear to think of her doing the same to someone else."

His heart swelled at her bravery. This was the lady he wanted by his side—and in his arms—for the rest of his life.

"Very well. I shall find her and bring her back to Hagenheim."

Rapunzel's heart soared at the protective look on Sir Gerek's face. He had come for her! It would be so much easier to cling to him and let him take her away as fast as possible and not look back. But how could she rest if Gothel was running around free and able to hurt someone else? No, she should not get distracted by how noble he looked, or how compassionate his deep voice sounded when he'd said her safety was more important.

Even with a few days of stubble on his jaw and chin, he was still the most handsome man she had ever seen. And she was so grateful she had changed into her best dress, a pink silk bliaud with purple trim, this morning after Gothel had brought enough water for her to bathe.

"She always goes in this direction." She started to walk toward the west, but Sir Gerek did not move. He was staring down at her face. She met his eye and he did not look away. What was he thinking? Had he missed her?

"I'm so glad I found you." He put his arms around her again, and she buried her face in his chest.

"Thank you. Thank you for finding me." How comfortable and good it felt to be close to him, to feel his arms around her. But she had no right to cling to him this way. He was marrying Lady Lankouwen.

She pulled away and turned toward Gothel's trail through the woods.

"Wait. Let us go get my horse."

She turned to follow Sir Gerek, but he stayed close by her side as they made their way to the horse.

A slight rustling sound came from behind them.

Rapunzel turned, clutching Sir Gerek's arm.

Gothel stood several feet behind them.

"So you found her, did you?" Gothel narrowed her eyes at Sir Gerek.

Rapunzel's heart raced as she clung to him.

Gerek said, "Give yourself up to me, Gothel. I am taking you back to Hagenheim."

"I do not think so." Gothel sneered. "If you try to take me, I will kill her." She flicked her gaze at Rapunzel.

Gerek placed his body between Rapunzel and Gothel and drew his sword. "I will never let you harm her again."

"Come and get me then." Gothel cackled a laugh that sent a chill up his spine as she headed back into the forest.

Gerek went after her, and Rapunzel followed.

They ran through the trees, and in a few moments, Gerek had nearly caught up with Gothel. Then he stopped, holding his arm out to stop Rapunzel as well.

"It's a trap," he whispered.

Gothel spun around and held up a dagger. "Come and get me."

Gerek didn't move. "I see the rope snare you set for me. You might as well give yourself up. All I have to do is walk around it." Then he proceeded to skirt around the snare that was all but hidden in the leaves, but Rapunzel saw the rope running up the tree beside it.

"Get back." Gothel lunged at him with the long knife blade.

Gerek swung his sword. His blade connected with hers and knocked her knife to the ground. He stomped his foot down on it, then grabbed Gothel by the arms and pulled her hands behind her back. Gothel screamed, a sound of rage.

Sir Gerek held her by her wrists while she screamed out threats and insults. He pulled her back through the woods toward the tower, and Rapunzel bent and snatched up Gothel's dagger and slipped it into her own pocket.

Once they reached the clearing, with Gothel still heaping abuse on both Sir Gerek and Rapunzel, Sir Gerek walked around to the back side of the tower. There was the donkey Gothel had used to pull the cart.

Sir Gerek nodded toward the donkey, keeping his hold on Gothel. Rapunzel quickly untied the animal, then they all walked back to Sir Gerek's horse, just as Gothel seemed to be running out of breath.

"You'll be sorry you did this," Gothel threatened. "I'll kill you both in your sleep. I stabbed Reginald through the heart, and I'll do the same to you."

Rapunzel gasped. How could Gothel kill the man she had once loved? But she had said Sir Reginald had rejected her again, that he was planning to marry someone else. Perhaps her hatred was stronger because she had loved him once. But the thought of her stabbing and killing the man made the bile rise in her throat, so she pushed it away and concentrated on Sir Gerek's movements.

"Get my rope out of my saddlebag," he said.

She hurried to open the leather bag attached to his saddle and pulled out a length of rope.

Sir Gerek tied Gothel's wrists together in front of her, then tied her wrists to the donkey's halter, which was still around its neck. Next he tied the donkey's halter to his horse's saddle.

"I am going to put you on the donkey now," Sir Gerek said to

Gothel in an even voice. "You can either stay on the donkey"—he lifted her up and put her on the donkey's back—"or you can be dragged by its side."

Rapunzel held her breath. Gothel simply stared straight ahead and remained on the animal's back, unmoving.

Gerek turned to Rapunzel. He took her hand in his and led her the few steps to his horse. "We'll have to ride together," he said near her ear, then placed her hands on the pommel, took hold of her leg, and boosted her into the saddle. Then he propelled himself behind her, wrapped an arm around her, and allowed Donner to move at a fast walk, pulling on the rope that connected them to the donkey.

They skirted around the village until he reached the road back to Hagenheim.

Rapunzel held on to Sir Gerek as she sat sidesaddle, but she turned so she could press her face against his chest. He was so warm and solid and strong.

Perhaps it had not been wise to capture Gothel and take her with them. What if, while they were traveling on the road, Gothel somehow got the upper hand, the way Balthasar had? What if she slipped a sleeping potion into their water or killed Sir Gerek in his sleep? She shuddered, pressing her face harder against his chest.

Sir Gerek said softly, "You're safe now," and he caressed her hair with his hand.

She was almost afraid to breathe, not wanting to ruin the moment. If he made a jest or said something flippant or gruff or grouchy like he used to, she didn't think she could bear it. So she kept silent, holding on to him, pretending he loved her as much as she loved him.

What would he do when he found out she was Duke Wilhelm's daughter? She was too terrified to tell him. After all, look at what had happened when she told Moth—Gothel. She had nearly destroyed Rapunzel, turning her life into an unholy nightmare.

But surely nothing bad would happen if she told Sir Gerek. In fact, once she told him, perhaps he would want to marry her.

What would Duke Wilhelm and Lady Rose say? Would they believe she was truly their daughter? They might not think the scar was enough proof.

She wouldn't think about that now. It was enough that she was free and safe and that Sir Gerek had come looking for her. She sighed and felt herself smiling against his chest. He had come for her.

Chapter Thirty-One

When Gerek had steered his horse onto the road, Rapunzel put both arms around him and lay her cheek against his chest. The feeling she created inside him, tucked against him, her arms around his back, was better than winning a tournament, better than a hot bath after a long journey, better than anything. He wanted this feeling to last forever . . . at least the rest of his life.

After almost two months of looking for her, the warmth of her in his arms was all he could have hoped for. She was safe.

But her look of fear when she'd seen her mother again worried him. What had Gothel done to her? He knew she had dragged her away from Hagenheim, taken her on a long journey against her will, and locked her in the tower. She had obviously gone to great lengths to make sure Rapunzel never escaped from the tower prison. And she would have had to physically harm Rapunzel in order to do all that.

The woman was truly mad.

Rapunzel was sure they had been traveling for at least two hours when Sir Gerek said, "Do you want to stop and rest for a few minutes? I need to water my horse and the donkey, and I have some food for us."

"I brought some food too."

Sir Gerek took out both of their bundles. He helped Gothel off the donkey and managed to dodge her foot when she tried to kick him. He set her down beside the donkey, her hands still tied. When she demanded to be untied so she could go to the woods to relieve herself, he told her, "No, not yet." But he did eventually allow her a little privacy, and Gothel did not try to run away.

Rapunzel shared her mince pie and fried apple pasties and Sir Gerek shared his cheese and bread, apples, walnuts, and raisins. Her fingers touched his when she gave him a portion of the pie. His hand brushed hers as he passed her the bread, but it didn't feel awkward. It felt . . . good.

They still had not said much to each other as she sat cross-legged on the grass and Sir Gerek lay on his side, propped on one elbow.

Rapunzel studied his face. "How long did you search for me?"

"Since the day you were taken. I realized what had happened when Frau Adelheit came and said you had disappeared. I actually saw your mother in the castle yard during all the confusion after we took the castle back from Claybrook and his men." There was an intense look in his brown eyes. "What did she do to you? Did she hurt you? How did she make you go with her?"

"She forced some kind of sleeping potion down my throat." Rapunzel described some of what had happened those first few days.

He sat up and shook his head slowly. "I wish I could have saved you from all of that."

His compassionate words made her heart stutter. *Thank you, Sir Gerek. May God bless you for caring about me.*

They packed up the rest of their food. There were so many little touches—when he took the food bundles from her, when he helped her into the saddle, when his arm brushed hers as he took the reins. How strange it was to be so near to Sir Gerek, letting him touch her, with Gothel watching them the entire time. And yet neither of them could exactly help it, since they were sharing the same horse. And this was Sir Gerek. She trusted him.

As they rode along the north road to Hagenheim, Rapunzel said, "I still have your books."

"Perhaps you can read from them later," he said.

"It's good they are in German, because you never finished teaching me Latin."

"We'll have to get back to it, then, won't we?"

"Yes." Would he really want to continue teaching her? She glanced up at him and he was looking down at her. His hair was so dark and thick. What would it feel like to touch it? He seemed to be staring at her lips. Was he imagining what it would feel like to kiss? Because she was.

Would Rapunzel do what Gothel had done, which was to give in to whatever the man she loved asked her to do?

She shuddered. Even though she was silent, it was as if Gothel was still controlling her thoughts. Didn't Rapunzel know Sir Gerek well enough to know he wouldn't hurt her, and certainly wouldn't desert her? But how could she know that? How did a person ever know another person well enough to trust them, to absolutely trust that that person wouldn't hurt them?

"You can relax," he said. "I don't mind."

"Are you sure?" Her lower back was beginning to hurt from holding herself upright in the saddle.

"Of course." He put one arm around her as before, his hand clasping her upper arm.

She leaned her shoulder against his chest. "How far are we from Hagenheim?"

"We can make it in three days."

She almost said, "There's no hurry, is there?" but then he might realize how much she was enjoying being with him.

When the sun went down, Sir Gerek said, "I may not be able to find shelter for us every night, but I know of a castle not far from here where we can sleep tonight. It might keep us from getting our throats cut by your mo—by Gothel."

"That is good. Whose castle is it?"

"My brother's."

Gerek felt a weight pressing on his chest as they came into view of his family's ancient seat of power, Castle Rimmel. The van Hollans had controlled this region for over a hundred years, and now his brother, Mennek, controlled it. He had not seen it in nearly twenty years.

The castle seemed smaller than it had when he was a boy, and the region was rather small as well, especially compared to Hagenheim. Would his brother also be different? He shouldn't count on it.

The light from the sun was quickly disappearing altogether as he walked the horse and donkey closer to the castle gatehouse.

The guard approached them. As soon as Gerek told him that he was a knight in Duke Wilhelm's service and that he was escorting a prisoner back to Hagenheim, the guard let him in and sent a younger guard to walk them the rest of the way.

He would not allow his brother to stir his anger. He couldn't afford to since he did not want any harm to come to Rapunzel, or even Gothel, for that matter. Perhaps he would not have to tell his name and his brother would never know. After all, they had not seen each other since they were both children.

A stable boy took their horse and donkey, and Gerek led Gothel by her rope as she grumbled under her breath. A guard met them at the enormous wooden door.

The guard who had accompanied them told the other one that the bound woman was a prisoner being taken back to Hagenheim, and he agreed to take her to the dungeon and feed her.

"Be very careful of that one," Gerek told him. "She is much more dangerous than she looks. But treat her well or Duke Wilhelm will not be pleased."

The guard grunted, but nodded and took her away.

He might have breathed a small sigh of relief if he didn't know he had to face his brother. "Is Lord Rimmel here?"

The guard nodded. "They are having supper in the Great Hall. I shall take you there now. Knights are always welcome at his table."

At least Mennek had that much courtesy.

They followed the guard through the dark corridor the short distance to the Great Hall. Rapunzel kept close by his side.

The guard walked in ahead of them and stopped, facing the table on the raised dais. The man at the head of the table looked down at them, then nodded at the guard.

"Lord Rimmel, this is a knight in the service of Duke Wilhelm, who is traveling with this woman and another woman who is his prisoner, now in the dungeon." The guard bowed.

He stared at Gerek. Mennek's hair was a bit darker and his face had grown quite plump, nearly unrecognizable from the skinny boy of fifteen who had yelled at Gerek, "It is your fault she's dead!" He had then picked up a large pottery pitcher next to him and threw it at Gerek. The pitcher had just missed his head and crashed into pieces on the floor. Had it been in this very room?

"And what might the name be of this knight in Duke Wilhelm's service?" Did Mennek suspect he was his brother?

"I am known as Sir Gerek of Hagenheim."

Mennek's eyes seemed to draw together. "Gerek?" He continued to stare, then slowly rose from his chair. "Gerek? Not my brother Gerek?"

Gerek bowed slightly. "The same." Gerek no longer felt small in his brother's eyes. His brother had grown soft and paunchy while Gerek was battle-ready, muscular, and well trained. Mennek might have a title, but Gerek was strong. He would not feel inferior.

Mennek continued to stand, and now the Great Hall had grown hushed. "What brings you here?"

"I am seeking shelter for the night for my prisoner and this lady." He said the word smoothly, not wanting Mennek to know she was but a maidservant.

Mennek nodded. "You are very welcome here. Please, come up to my table." He snapped his fingers at a passing page. "Bring these two guests a trencher and goblet. Quickly."

Gerek held out his arm to Rapunzel, who took it and walked beside him up the step to join Mennek.

His other guests made a place next to Mennek. Gerek found himself sitting opposite an older couple who looked vaguely familiar.

"Gerek, you may not remember your aunt and uncle, Hinrich and Ursel."

Gerek nodded politely to them. Ursel smiled and said, "You were such a handsome little boy, and you are still quite handsome."

His uncle Hinrich said, "You have grown into a fine knight, as we all have heard of your tournament exploits with Lord Hamlin."

Gerek bowed his head respectfully. He could not remember, but he was fairly certain these were his mother's sister and her husband.

"This is Rapunzel Scheinberg," he said as formally as possible. He turned to Rapunzel. "And this is my brother, Mennek van Hollan, the Earl of Rimmel."

Rapunzel inclined her head in the most natural way, as if she had been greeting earls all her life. "Very pleased, Lord Rimmel."

They had been traveling all day, but Rapunzel still looked beautiful. She wore a very becoming pink gown. Her thick, golden braid lay over her shoulder, as she had nothing to cover it with.

Hinrich and Ursel chatted with them in a most friendly way, with Mennek chiming in occasionally while they ate. But Gerek was very aware of his brother sitting, nearly silent, beside him. Did he still hold a grudge against Gerek?

The food might have tasted good, but he didn't notice. His uncle asked him questions about his life and about Duke Wilhelm and Valten, who would one day be the ruler of Hagenheim. Rapunzel, meanwhile, seemed to make a good impression on his aunt, as Ursel laughed at each of Rapunzel's jests, no matter how slight, and called her "a delightful girl."

When it was finally time to retire for the night, Mennek said, "I shall show you two to your room."

Had he said "room" or "rooms"? Gerek wasn't sure, but if his brother dared insult Rapunzel or make lewd insinuations, he would not let him get away with it.

Hinrich and Ursel wanted to walk with them, so they all tramped through the Great Hall and the corridor to the stairs.

"I hope you will not be leaving too early in the morning," Ursel said. "Perhaps you could even stay a few days."

Gerek opened his mouth to answer her, but Rapunzel beat him to it.

"I'm afraid we must leave very early. I must get back to Hagenheim. But if you are ever traveling to Hagenheim, I will hope to see you there."

"Would you like an escort?" Mennek asked. "I can send two of my guards—"

"No, I thank you. But I would ask if you would do something else for me."

Mennek stopped and stared at him. Strange that Gerek was now taller than him.

"If you could keep my prisoner here until I can get Rapunzel back to Hagenheim, Duke Wilhelm will send guards to fetch her." Gerek stared him in the eye, challenging him to say no.

"I can do that. For Duke Wihelm, and for my brother, of course."

"Will you ask your guards not to mistreat her?" Rapunzel said in a quiet voice.

Mennek seemed a bit startled by her request. "Ach, but of course."

"She is very devious," Rapunzel said, "so you mustn't let her escape. But I do not want the guards molesting her in any way." Rapunzel smiled at him.

Mennek smiled back, obviously charmed. "My dear, I shall see to it."

Mennek slowed at one door. "Here is your chamber." He looked at Rapunzel. *"Gute nacht."*

"Gute nacht."

"I shall show her around and make sure she is comfortable," Ursel said and followed her into the room.

Hinrich clasped arms with Gerek. "You are an honorable man, Sir Gerek, and have brought honor to your family name."

His words actually made Gerek's eyes sting. He didn't trust himself to speak, so he simply nodded.

"I hope I see you again someday. Fare well, Sir Gerek."

"Thank you. Fare well."

Hinrich continued down the corridor.

Mennek had stopped at the door nearest to Rapunzel's. "Here is your room. I thought you might like the one adjoining the lady's."

"What is that supposed to mean?" Gerek looked him in the eye.

"I don't mean any disrespect, but the way you both looked at each other, I simply thought . . . You are human, are you not?"

"Whatever you think being human is, she is a virtuous maiden. But I thank you for putting me near enough to her that I can protect her should anyone in your household impose on her. I shall have her bolt her door just in case."

Mennek glared back at him. "No one in my household is allowed to do such things. But that is probably wise, no matter whose household you are in."

The tension gradually left his face and he said in a milder tone, "Gerek, I don't know if you remember, but I said some things to you, after what Father did . . . after Mother died. I hope you do not begrudge me my foolish accusations. You were only a child and what I said was . . . unjust."

Whatever Gerek had expected him to say, it was not that. Gerek cleared his throat.

"And if you ever need anything, you can depend upon me. You are always welcome here, and I hope you will visit often, whenever you are able."

Gerek thought of all the pain he had carried around because of what his brother had said to him. What Mennek had said *was* unjust. Truly unjust. But Gerek didn't want to hold that against him anymore. Besides, Jesus commanded forgiveness.

"I forgive you, Mennek, and I shall try to come more often." He wouldn't promise him Christmas, however.

"I have a child now," Mennek said. "He is almost one year old. Would you like to see him?"

Gerek actually took a step back. "I didn't know you were married."

"I am not. The child's mother . . . I did not marry her. She was a girl from the village. When she was dying, I promised her the child would be my heir." Mennek shrugged. "I don't think I will ever marry, especially now."

Gerek stared at his brother a moment, then said, "I would like to see the child."

Mennek smiled, the first time he had smiled all evening. "He's probably asleep, but you can see him."

Gerek followed him down the corridor and up another flight of stairs. He halted in front of a door, then opened it. Inside a candle burned beside a baby bed, and a woman slept on a cot next to it. The woman awakened and sat up as they walked inside.

Mennek ignored her and went straight to the side of the baby's bed. He whispered, "What do you think? Does he look like me?"

The child was sleeping on his back, his curled hands by the side of his chubby cheek. Delicate wisps of brown hair covered his head. "I think there might be some resemblance in the cheeks," Gerek answered.

Mennek elbowed Gerek but kept smiling.

Once they were back out in the corridor, Gerek said, "He is a fine boy, Mennek. I'm glad you're taking good care of him." But what his brother had said about not ever getting married . . . Mennek had witnessed more of their parents' fights, more of his father's anger and violence. For the first time, Gerek realized *he* was the fortunate one. He'd resented Mennek for being the oldest, for spending more time with their mother, for inheriting the castle and the title, for not being sent away to train as a knight. And yet Gerek was the one who had escaped some of the violence, had missed the horrible night when his mother was killed and his father jumped from the upper window. Gerek had grown up with Valten, a good and kind man, seeing the example of Duke Wilhelm, a truly noble man, and Lady Rose, a wonderful lady who had mothered him and shown him kindness.

Gerek had much to be grateful for.

They were both silent as they neared Gerek's bedchamber door. Finally, Mennek said, "Hinrich and Ursel have been very good to me, like parents, especially when I was younger. I hope you also had someone like them, Gerek."

"I did."

Mennek nodded, clapped Gerek on the shoulder. Mennek turned to leave and Gerek went into his bedchamber.

He barely glanced at the bed, but went to the door that adjoined his room to Rapunzel's. He knocked on the door, then opened it a crack. "Rapunzel?"

"Yes, I am here."

"I am here too," Ursel called. "You can come in, if you like."

"I only wanted to make sure Rapunzel was safe." Gerek closed the door, then waited, listening for Ursel to leave. A minute or two later, he heard their muffled voices, then the sound of the door closing. He knocked again. When he opened it, Rapunzel was directly on the other side.

"I like your aunt. She made me feel so . . . lovable." She was smiling, as if amused at herself.

Lovable? Oh yes. She was lovable.

"Do you need anything?"

"No, Ursel is sending a servant to bring me some things."

"As soon as the servant leaves, will you knock on the door?"

She gave him a quizzical frown but nodded.

A few minutes later the door opened, then moments later, shut. Then came the gentle knock on the door between them.

He opened the door. "Did you put down the crossbar on your door?"

"Yes." She stared up at him, her feet bare, and her hair was just as bare and hung around her shoulders like a curtain of gold in the dim light.

"Please leave this door unbarred in case something happens, so I can come in and help you."

"Very well."

"If you need me, just scream."

"I will." She gave him an amused smile.

"So you trust me, then?"

She looked him in the eye, her face only a foot away from his. "I do."

"You trust me not to do all those things your mother said—"

"Not my mother. She is Gothel."

"You trust me not to do all those things Gothel warned you about?"

"I do. I trust you."

Was he the only person in the world who knew how precious her trust was, who knew how difficult it was for her to give it? "Thank you." He yearned to caress her cheek, to enfold her in his arms. But that could chase away her trust.

"Gute nacht, Sir Gerek."

"Gute nacht, Rapunzel."

Rapunzel gathered sticks while Sir Gerek started the fire.

They had traveled all day after leaving Castle Rimmel early that morning, and Rapunzel felt pleasantly drowsy. She wasn't sure when she'd felt so safe and relaxed, even though they would be forced to sleep on the ground tonight.

Sir Gerek toasted some of the bread over the fire and also fried some meat that his brother had provided. How wonderful that they were able to leave Gothel at his brother's castle. Now she would not be constantly worried that Gothel would escape and slit their throats.

They talked companionably until it was time to go to sleep.

He handed her a gray wool blanket, then lay down next to the fire.

"Don't you have a blanket?"

"I forgot to get one when we were at the castle, but I don't need one. It's warm enough now."

"The nights are still quite cool. Here, you take the blanket and I will put on the rest of my clothes. It's the perfect solution."

"No, thank you. I don't need it."

She let out an exasperated sigh. "Why are you being so kind to me? When I first met you, you couldn't say a kind word to me. You disdained me because I was a peasant."

"I never disdained you."

Then it occurred to her. "Did Frau Adelheit tell you something about me?"

"What do you mean?"

"I mean, did she tell you who my parents are?" But even as she said the words, a lump formed in her throat.

"What do you mean?" He sat up. "Did you find out who left you with Gothel? Who your parents are?"

Apparently he didn't know, and she wasn't ready to tell him just yet. "I am only wondering why you became so kind to me. I'm trying to remember when it started." She sat down near him, still holding the blanket, still determined to give it to him. "Did you start being kind to me when I began working at Hagenheim Castle? Or was it before that?"

He had an anxious look in his eyes, his brow furrowed. "I was always kind to you. I saved your life, more than once."

"Oh no, you cannot claim to have always been kind to me." She laughed. "You did save my life, but when I tried to help you, when you had the broken leg and the broken arm, you told me to leave you alone and stop trying to kill you, just because I was trying to help you off with your wet clothes. Remember that? And there was the time you told me you would never marry a peasant girl so I would stop talking to you."

Now he looked miserable, his sad brown eyes boring into hers. "I'm sorry I said that. I was insufferable and arrogant."

"That is exactly how I would have described you."

"Even now, you still think I'm so?" He leaned toward her, his face only inches from hers.

"Why . . . no." His tender tone and the suddenness of him moving toward her caused her to scoot back.

"I know your mother—Gothel—taught you never to trust anyone," he said, "but I'm not one of those men who takes a maiden's love and then tosses her aside. I would never do that . . . to you or to anyone."

Her throat suddenly went dry.

He stared at her a long moment, then said, "Good night, Rapunzel." He turned over and lay with his back to her.

She got up and put another underdress and kirtle on over the clothes she was already wearing. Since she was thinner now, they all managed to fit.

Sir Gerek was lying down near the fire, his eyes closed. Rapunzel moved as quietly as she could toward his still form, then carefully laid the blanket over him.

She lay down with her head near his and closed her eyes.

Her eyes popped open. Something was touching her legs and was very gradually being laid over the rest of her body. She suspected it was the gray woolen blanket she had laid on Sir Gerek. When he finished, he walked back over to where he had been sleeping and lay down again.

Gerek awoke with the blanket laying over him. How had she managed to cover him without him waking up? He sat up. She lay asleep on her side, her thick braid touching her cheek. The sun was casting a soft glow over her and making her look even more otherworldly.

He found himself smiling as he draped the blanket over her while she slept.

When she awoke, he already had Donner saddled and breakfast ready.

"When did you do this?" She held out the blanket. With the scolding half frown and lowered brows, she took his breath away.

What would she do if he put his hands on either side of her face and kissed her lips? Probably slap him.

He truly needed to get her back to Hagenheim as soon as possible. Because once he told her he wanted to marry her, the temptation to kiss her would be even stronger.

He shrugged. "You looked cold."

She eyed him, shook her head, then folded the blanket.

The morning started out sunny and slightly warm, but now that it was midday, storm clouds began to roll in.

"Rain is coming," he told her. "We can either go back to the village we passed more than two hours ago and ask someone for shelter, or we can go on and try to find shelter ahead of us somewhere."

Rapunzel looked up at the sky. "Perhaps it will not rain. The clouds may pass us with barely a sprinkling. It happens that way sometimes."

"Perhaps."

They kept moving and the clouds did seem to break. The wind grew quite strong in the afternoon and the air much cooler. Rapunzel had started to huddle against his chest with her arms tucked into him instead of around him.

Just when he thought it wasn't going to rain after all, the late-afternoon clouds began to darken again. He didn't think there were any villages nearby, so as the rain began to fall in large drops, there was nowhere to take shelter except the trees just off the road. But even in the trees, they were still getting wet. Rapunzel shivered against his chest.

He had to find them shelter, so they pressed on. This part of the country was hilly and rocky, as they passed along the northern edge of the Harz Mountains, but on this particular stretch of road, he saw no rock outcroppings.

He followed the road while staying in the trees, finally spotting something, a small hill amongst the spruce and beech trees, so he headed toward it.

When he reached the small hill, he dismounted. He moved some branches aside and discovered a dark hole in the side of the hill. He squatted beside it. It was only tall enough for him to enter on his knees.

"I found a cave," he told Rapunzel as he dug inside his saddlebag. He pulled out a tarp-covered torch and hovered over it to keep it dry while he lighted it. When he finally got it burning, he approached the open hole of the cave. Rapunzel was right behind him.

"Stay back." He put his arm out to keep her behind him. "Anything could be inside—a wild boar, a bear, or even a wolf."

He got down on his knees, holding the torch out in front of him as he proceeded into the dark little cave.

Chapter Thirty-Two

Rapunzel shivered inside the large rock chamber of the cave. Her teeth chattered uncontrollably as she hugged herself with one hand and held the torch with the other.

Sir Gerek came back and picked up the bag he had brought with him. "You have to get out of those wet clothes. I'll go back into the small corridor while you change."

"You have to change too." Her speech sounded funny as she tried to talk through her rigid jaw and chattering teeth. And even though he was just as wet as she was, he wasn't shivering. He still looked as masculine and handsome as ever—maybe more so—while she probably looked as bedraggled as a drowned weasel.

They each found their extra clothing, which was mostly dry, and Gerek propped her torch in a crack in the wall, then disappeared around a bend in the cave corridor.

Rapunzel stripped off her wet clothes as quickly as she could. Her extra underdress and kirtle were both safely in place when Sir Gerek called through the echoing chamber, "Are you dressed?"

"I am."

He came in and snuffed out his torch on the floor of the cave. "No need to waste it," he said. "We might need it later."

He pulled out the woolen blanket that they had taken turns covering each other with the night before. While at Castle Rimmel his brother had offered him food and whatever supplies he might need, but he had not thought to get an extra blanket.

Rapunzel sat on the cool stone floor of the cave and started trying to unbraid her wet hair with stiff, cold fingers. She was still shivering, but the chattering of her teeth had lessened.

"You have to get warm," Sir Gerek said.

She wouldn't argue with that. She only wondered how he proposed for her to do it. "I'm unbraiding my hair so it will dry faster," she said, her mouth still not working properly so her words sounded stilted. "And so I can squeeze the water out."

"Come here." He motioned to her with his hand as he went to stand by the wall.

She came and they sat down. He leaned against the wall, pulled her back against his chest, and wrapped the blanket around her.

He seemed very businesslike, even as he took her braid and squeezed the water from it. He had it unbraided in only a few moments.

She put her hands inside the blanket and under her arms. He wrapped his arms around her over the blanket, making her feel like a caterpillar in a cocoon.

"You can lean your head back," he said.

"My hair will get you wet."

"It's all right." He touched her forehead and gently pulled her head back to rest on his shoulder.

She suddenly felt cozy and comfortable. He was delightfully warm. Her feet were like ice, even though Ursel had given her some leather slippers since she had no shoes. But her feet had gotten wet, and now she tucked them underneath her to try to get them warm. But with the wool blanket and his arms around her, and with the surprising heat emanating from his chest warming her back, she soon stopped shivering.

Their closeness should have felt awkward. One of them should speak and break the silence.

"Rapunzel." Finally, he spoke, his deep voice rumbling beside her ear. "Why did Frau Adelheit want me to find you so badly? She even convinced the rest of the knights to go out searching for you."

Her stomach lurched at the thought of telling him, even though she believed he would want to marry her as soon as he found out. Something held her back.

"Are the other knights still looking for me? How interesting that you were the one to find me."

"No, they had returned to Hagenheim after a month or so."

"But you continued to look?" She held her breath as she waited for his answer.

"Of course."

He was resting his jaw against her temple. She could feel his prickly facial hair against her skin. Her breathing became shallow, and she didn't move.

"I fasted and prayed," he said softly, his chin brushing against her temple with every word, "and God told me which way to go."

Her breath came faster now. Finally, she whispered, "Thank you."

"Were you surprised when you saw me?"

"I was a little surprised since I had not seen anyone except Gothel for such a long time. But I was also not surprised. I believed you would come for me." She closed her eyes and thought back to that moment when she heard his voice and saw his face. "I was overjoyed to see you, to see a familiar face, someone who could help me escape from my mother."

For a moment he was very still. Then he squeezed her arm and said, "I should go see if it's still raining." He stood up, relighted his torch, and left.

He returned. "Still raining. We should probably sleep here. It's almost night anyway." He brought out their food, and they ate.

They talked a bit about various priests they had known throughout their lives. And those stories led to stories about their childhoods. Sir Gerek's stories were mostly adventures involving Valten and Gabehart, and she couldn't help but realize she was hearing about her own two older brothers as she learned more about Sir Gerek.

Suddenly, she had an idea. "Were you there when Elsebeth, Valten and Gabehart's sister, fell and cut her hand when she was three?"

He raised his brows. "I was not there, but I heard about it. I had not been at Hagenheim very long and was a new page. But little Elsebeth showed her hand to me a few days later, when she saw me in the Great Hall. How did you know about that?"

"Frau Adelheit told me."

"I remember thinking what a pretty little girl she was." He stared at the wall, not really seeing it. "I was so sorry for Lady Rose when the little girl died. Her heart was broken over losing her. It was terribly sad." He suddenly turned toward her. "I think I was rather in love with Lady Rose when I was a boy."

"With Lady Rose?"

He nodded and smiled. "I was so young, and she was so kind to me when I arrived in Hagenheim. She knew about my mother being killed. I know she gave me preferential treatment, and she let me sleep in Valten and Gabe's chamber. She asked about me often and took care of me herself when I was sick."

"I can see why you would love her."

"It was a boyish infatuation. You know how all the minstrels sing of courtly love and chivalry. I suppose I saw myself as her champion. But at some point, I realized Duke Wilhelm would not be tolerant of my infatuation, and I got over it."

Rapunzel smiled. "Did you never have a sweetheart your own age?"

"There was a maidservant who very much wanted me to marry her when I was eighteen, but I told her many times that it was not possible. And then I went with Valten to fight in the tournaments, and she married a cobbler's son."

"Ah, yes. Because you wanted to make your fortune by marrying an heiress."

"You make me sound very mercenary, and I was. But I've changed." A mysterious look came over his face.

"You have changed?"

He nodded.

"How?"

"I will tell you . . . on the last day of our journey."

"Very well. And when you tell me your secret on the last day of our journey, I shall tell you mine." She resisted the urge to look at the scar on her hand. Instead, she raised her brows at him and gave him her own mysterious smile.

Rapunzel ran as fast as she could. Gothel was chasing her with a handful of holly berries. Rapunzel fell, her face landing hard in the dirt. She was just pushing herself up when she opened her eyes. It was a dream. She heard her own raspy breathing as she laid her head back down, but even though her eyes were open, she could see nothing but darkness. Why could she not see?

Then she remembered—she was in a cave with Sir Gerek, and he had extinguished the torches when they lay down to sleep.

She shivered as the dream came back to her. Gothel's eyes had been so vivid, so dark and sinister. Rapunzel's heart beat hard against her chest. She had been so afraid. And Sir Gerek had not been there. She'd wanted him to come and save her, but he was not there.

She reached out. Her hand touched something solid. She had

insisted that Gerek sleep next to her under the blanket, too afraid of the dark cave and the thought of some wild animal coming in and attacking them in their sleep. But once he had extinguished the torch, she had fallen asleep quickly.

"Rapunzel?" The vicinity of Gerek's voice let her know it was probably his arm she was touching. He rolled over and she felt his breath on her hand. "Are you well?"

"I-I had a bad dream . . . about Moth—about Gothel. But I am well."

He put his arm around her and pulled her close. She buried her face in his chest. *O Lord God, please let this be love.*

They lay perfectly still for a few moments before Gerek said, "Will you feel better when I get this torch lighted again?"

"I feel better now." Her voice was muffled against his tunic.

She felt something briefly touch the top of her head. Had he just kissed her?

After a few more moments, she asked, "Do you think it's morning?"

"I'll go and find out. Stay here."

He stood and she heard him moving toward the entrance. A few minutes later, he came back carrying the lighted torch.

"It's just after dawn."

Rapunzel stood. Once outside again, Rapunzel was grateful to see it wasn't raining. The sun was up and casting a yellow light over everything.

Sir Gerek seemed eager to be off, so they ate quickly and left the little cave. Rapunzel was not so eager to make it back to Hagenheim, after Sir Gerek had said he would tell her his secret on the last day of their journey.

She was terrified to hope that he wanted to marry her, but couldn't seem to stop herself.

Chapter Thirty-Three

Gerek was glad the day had passed uneventfully. They had only entered one village, where they had bought food and an extra blanket. He was too afraid of the temptation of sharing a blanket for another night.

Could she tell he was nervous, thinking about what he would say to her tomorrow? He was never more sure about anything than he was about asking her to marry him. And she would surely say yes. So why was he so nervous?

That night he lay awake long after she was asleep. But all he could do was pray that God would make him a good husband, someone completely different from his own father.

The next morning he knew it was the last day of their journey, but did Rapunzel know?

While they rode, Rapunzel read aloud from the letter to the Romans. Her voice was so sweet and lilting, his heart seemed near bursting inside him, and he broke out in a cold sweat; he was just as in love with her as Colin had been with Lady Margaretha.

What if he couldn't love her like he should, the way Colin would love Margaretha, with integrity and gentleness and patience and sacrifice? What if he hurt Rapunzel? What if he yelled at her and made her cry and disappointed her?

If Valten knew what Gerek was thinking, he would probably tell him he was being a coward and ask him where his courage was. Lady Rose would assure him of what a good man he was and what a good husband he would be. Besides, Rapunzel needed him. He could take care of her and protect her from harm. Who else did she have? She had no one, not a single family member to take care of her.

When they halted to let Donner have a rest and eat a midday meal, Gerek noticed for the hundredth time that day how beautiful Rapunzel looked. She sat gazing up at him. He reached out and lifted a lock of her golden hair, which lay next to him, and let the hair sift through his fingers.

"I'm glad you're not afraid anymore to let your hair down."

Her smile faded. "I am too. And I don't want to wait anymore to tell you what I have to tell you." She looked so serious, her eyes big as she glanced away from him, fidgeting with her hands.

"I am listening." They were sitting in a grassy spot next to a small, clear stream. The sun was lighting her hair, like a halo around her head. When she met his eye, she opened her mouth, then hesitated.

Finally, she said, "I asked you if you remembered when Elsebeth fell and cut her hand."

He nodded. The back of his neck started to prickle.

"And I told you that Gothel was not my birth mother. She told me that I was left with her. Once she said at the front door and another time in the garden. But when I was folding linens one day with Frau Adelheit, she saw the scar on my hand. She told me . . ." Rapunzel bit her lip. She had been staring down at the ground, and now she lifted her eyes to his as she lifted her hand, palm up.

"What is it?"

"Look at my hand."

On her hand was the same scar that Elsebeth had on her little three-year-old hand.

"But how?" Gerek took her hand in his and stared down at it. "Do you remember this?"

"I have a vague memory of falling and someone picking me up, and of someone sewing up my hand. I also have a memory of falling into some water and going under. These are my earliest memories."

"So . . . Elsebeth didn't drown?" *Could it be?* A tremor streaked through his stomach.

"They never found her body, because Gothel stole me." Her lip and chin trembled. "She confessed it all. She pulled me into the river and then took me out downstream."

"Dear Lord God." Gerek crossed himself. "She is truly evil. What will Lady Rose say? She'll be . . . She will be overjoyed. To get her daughter back." But if Rapunzel was Duke Wilhelm's daughter . . . He would never be allowed to marry a duke's daughter. He was only a knight, the second son of an earl, with no inheritance and nothing to offer.

His heart sank all the way to his toes. He stared back at her.

Her cheeks lost their pink color. "What is it? What?"

"Rapunzel, I-I wanted . . ." No, he shouldn't tell her.

"What? You wanted what?"

"Nothing."

"You said you had something to tell me, that you had changed."

"I wanted to tell you . . ." His throat was as dry as a shock of hay. "I changed my mind. I don't want to marry Lady Lankouwen anymore."

She seemed to be waiting for what he would say next.

He shrugged. "That is all."

She looked askance. "There is something you aren't telling me."

"I-I was . . ." But she would never believe him now. She would think, *Of course he wants to marry me. I'm the duke's daughter. But he never would have married me when I was a peasant.* Why should she believe that he had decided days ago that he would ask her to marry him?

He suddenly realized he was still holding her hand, the one with the scar. If only she was not Elsebeth. If only she had not told him. If only she did not have that scar. But his fate was sealed.

And now he could not marry Lady Lankouwen or Rainhilda or this beautiful maiden in front of him. Because he was in love . . . desperately, hopelessly, painfully in love . . . with the duke's daughter.

Rapunzel couldn't understand Sir Gerek's reaction, and yet she had been afraid to tell him all along. He should have been pleased. He should have wanted to marry her, knowing she was Duke Wilhelm's daughter. What had happened? He said he didn't want to marry the wealthy widow. Why did he look so stricken by the fact that she was Duke Wilhelm's daughter?

"Are you upset with me?"

"No, of course not. Let us be off. Donner should be rested by now."

Her heart twisted. Perhaps she was imagining that he was upset. Perhaps he was only surprised. Why was he not pleased?

They mounted up and rode down the road toward Hagenheim. Sir Gerek kept both hands on the reins and seemed to try not to let his arms brush against hers. She sat up straight, refusing to allow herself to touch him either.

Finally, her breaths coming faster, she said, "Are you not glad I discovered what happened to me, that I have a loving family after years of thinking that my parents didn't care about me? Are you not pleased that Lady Rose is about to find the daughter she thought was dead?"

"Yes, of course." But there was a guarded look on his face.

"Then why do you behave as if you cannot be friends with me anymore? I will always be your friend. Why would I not be? Valten is your friend, and he's the duke's oldest son."

"Of course we will always be friends. I know that. And I am very pleased for you. You deserve wonderful parents like Lady Rose and Duke Wilhelm. I am only sorry . . ." She saw his throat bob as he swallowed. ". . . sorry that you did not experience their love all these years, that your rightful childhood was stolen from you. It is very cruel."

That seemed more reasonable. But still, he seemed stiff and . . . strange. Tears stung her eyes. He did not want to marry her. Even though Duke Wilhelm could possibly give her a large dowry.

By the end of the day, a heavy boulder was sitting inside her chest. His formality, his awkwardness . . . What was wrong with him? He had been so warm, even loving, that morning when he had held her in his arms because of her bad dream. The night before he had dried her hair and held her against his chest because she was cold. Now he couldn't bear to touch her. Was he afraid of Duke Wilhelm? It didn't make sense, but how could she ask him?

She wanted to hit him. Perhaps she would.

Gerek's heart was a hard knot inside his chest. He wanted to tell Rapunzel that he loved her, but how could he? She was the daughter of a duke. She should marry a wealthy nobleman who could give her all the things she had been denied. She wouldn't want a knight who owned no home or property, whose own father had abused him, murdered his mother, then killed himself.

There was no reason to tell her he loved her. She would not believe him now, would think he was still being mercenary, as he had been when he'd plotted to marry Lady Lankouwen.

"We are only about an hour from Hagenheim now," he told her.

Even though she seemed angry with him, she must have become too exhausted to stay upright because she had laid her head against his chest.

His tunic felt damp. Was she crying? His knotted heart twisted inside him.

She suddenly sat up and leaned away, glaring at him. "Why do you not wish to marry Lady Lankouwen?" She hurled the words at him. "I thought she was what you wanted."

"It no longer matters."

She crossed her arms, her face angled away from him. She was sitting rather precariously, so he said, "If Donner gets startled by something in the dark, you will fall. You need to hold on."

Instead of putting an arm around his waist, she held on to the saddle pommel.

He had sacrificed for two months, riding in all kinds of weather, riding halfway across the Holy Roman Empire searching for her. If not for him, she would still be locked in that ancient tower.

Not that he minded. It was worth it to know that he had rescued her, even if she wasn't grateful. But she was grateful. Or she had been. Everything had changed when she told him she was Duke Wilhelm and Lady Rose's daughter. She must have expected him to react differently. But how could he tell her that she had shattered his plans with those words, making it impossible for him to make her his wife?

Let her be angry with him. Knowing she hated him would make it easier when Duke Wilhelm married her off to a duke or margrave or earl.

It was just before curfew by the time they arrived, so dark Gerek could barely make out the town wall.

"I want you to know that I am very pleased that you will have a family now, Rapunzel. I am truly glad for you. It is wonderful news." His chest ached, even though he meant what he said. "Will you tell the news to Lady Rose and Duke Wilhelm right away?"

"I don't know."

"Lady Margaretha is getting married to Lord Colin. I heard it when I came through here a week or so ago. The wedding should be very soon."

"I shall wait until after the wedding, then. I don't want to take away from Lady Margaretha's joyous day."

Her words sounded reasonable, but the way she said them proved that she was still angry.

"You should go to the wedding."

"I won't be invited."

"Then you should go with me." He said the words before he had time to think about them. But it would be a shame if she didn't go, since she was Margaretha's sister.

Finally, she looked back at him. "Are you sure you want me to go with you?"

"Yes, I am sure. I shall escort you."

They were entering the castle gate, and when the two guards spotted them, they cheered. Other guards and knights saw them as they moved toward the castle and also cheered, running forward to praise Gerek and to welcome Rapunzel back.

Lady Margaretha's wedding was to be in three days. Rapunzel would only have to keep her secret a little longer. She had discussed with Frau Adelheit her plan not to tell Duke Wilhelm and Lady Rose until after Margaretha's wedding, and she approved. In order to get the knights to go search for Rapunzel, Frau Adelheit had actually told some of them that Rapunzel was from a noble family and not a maidservant at all, and if they were to find her, Duke Wilhelm would reward them. They probably were still wondering if the story was true.

Rapunzel and the rest of the servants at Hagenheim Castle were caught up in the excitement and all the work required for

Lady Margaretha's wedding and the ensuing feast and celebration. So Rapunzel was surprised when Lady Rose summoned her to her chamber the morning before the wedding.

Lady Rose was sitting in a chair by the window, reading. When Rapunzel came in, she stood and held out her hands to her.

Her heart leapt. Had someone told her?

"You poor dear girl," Lady Rose said, embracing her. "I am overjoyed to have you back and so sorry your mother kidnapped you! How wonderful that Sir Gerek found you."

Rapunzel smiled back at her.

"Are you well? Are you unhurt?"

"I am well. My mother"—she had to swallow the lump in her throat to go on—"did not hurt me, beyond forcing me to drink a sleeping potion. She knows a lot about herbs and berries."

"She may not have hurt you physically," Lady Rose said softly, "but what she did to you must have hurt you a great deal." She held Rapunzel's hand.

Rapunzel took a deep breath. "I know that the way she treated me is not normal, and it's not the way a mother should treat her child." She didn't look Lady Rose in the eye. The compassion in her face made Rapunzel's throat ache with holding back the tears.

"No, it is not. I'm so sorry she did that to you." Lady Rose hugged her again, and this time Rapunzel put her head on the woman's shoulder, as she was slightly taller than Lady Rose, and tried not to think.

"If you want to talk about it, you can talk to me."

"I am very well." Rapunzel lifted her head and pulled away slightly. "I know you have your daughter's wedding tomorrow. You should not be thinking about me now."

"Oh, do not worry about the wedding." She smiled. "Margaretha is spending nearly every minute with Colin. I have plenty of time to talk with you. Come, sit down."

They sat on the bench by the window, and Lady Rose kept hold of her hand.

"Tell me what happened."

Rapunzel took a deep breath. "My mother locked me in an abandoned tower. When Sir Gerek found me, Gothel was away, so he helped me down."

"Were you overjoyed to see Sir Gerek?"

"Oh yes, of course. I was glad. Very glad." Her throat ached again at the thought of Sir Gerek's strange behavior the last day of their journey. Had she truly expected him to want to marry her? How foolish she was.

"Duke Wilhelm is planning to reward him in some way for saving you."

"That is very good." Sir Gerek had been so kind and friendly, even loving, when he found her. Remembering that made the tears come, and this time she could not hold them back.

"What is wrong, my dear?"

"Nothing." She wiped at the tears, but they just kept coming.

Lady Rose handed her a cloth. "There, there. You can tell me about it. It will make you feel better."

She buried her face in the cloth. Her heart ached as if it would burst. She had to relieve it somehow. "I love him."

"You love Sir Gerek?"

"Yes. So horribly."

"Love is not horrible."

"But he doesn't love me. I thought perhaps he did, but . . . he doesn't want me. And I don't know how to live if he doesn't love me back."

Lady Rose gathered her in her arms and she sobbed on Lady Rose's shoulder. She couldn't seem to stop herself. She should not have told Lady Rose all of this. How foolish and weak to love him when he didn't love her! Had she fulfilled Gothel's prophecy about her by falling in love with a man who ultimately didn't want her? Was she just like Gothel? And now she was wetting Lady Rose's shoulder with her tears.

When her sobs subsided and she was able to wipe her face with the cloth, Lady Rose let her pull away, and she looked her in the eye. "Listen to me. You deserve to be loved. And someday I pray that you will get married and your husband will love you. But in the meantime, your heavenly Father loves you more than any man on earth could love you. Do you believe that?"

"Yes, but . . . God can't put his arms around me and . . . and tell me he loves me."

"God is putting his arms around you at this very moment." Lady Rose's arms held Rapunzel tight. "He is telling you he loves you now."

What did she mean? Rapunzel sighed.

"Let me tell you a story." Lady Rose pulled away and allowed Rapunzel to sit back against the chair beside hers. "When I was very young, I wanted to get married to someone who would cherish me and make me feel loved. When I married Duke Wilhelm, my dream had come true. He loved me and he cherished me. But deep in my heart, I still did not feel satisfied. And when my husband had to go on journeys, to do the things that a ruling duke must do for the sake of his people and his region, I would feel sad and lonely and disappointed. I would have that same desperate feeling I had when I was a girl, longing for someone who would love me.

"And then, when my little girl Elsebeth died, I thought my heart was broken and would never mend. But I realized that my husband was also devastated and heartbroken. Only God could heal our pain. And if I loved my husband as I said I did, then I needed to comfort him. That is when I began to understand that he was only a man—a very good man who loved me, but a man nevertheless. He was not God. So I stopped trying to make him the god of my life, expecting him to bring me healing, and started expecting perfect love and satisfaction from God alone.

"So, you see, a man can love you, but only imperfectly. It is God alone who can be God."

Rapunzel nodded, even though she didn't understand how God could give her healing from Gerek not loving her.

"Can you tell me exactly what happened between you and Sir Gerek?"

Rapunzel inhaled a shaky breath and began from the beginning, telling what had passed between her and Sir Gerek from the first day they had met. When she came to the part about being alone with him for the journey back to Hagenheim, she said, "But on the final day, his manner toward me changed. I still don't understand it." It must have had something to do with her secret, but she wasn't ready to tell Lady Rose about that.

"He did not take advantage of you in any way when you were alone, did he?"

"No, no. He never even kissed me." The tears started to come back again, but she blinked them away. "He just doesn't want me."

Lady Rose was quiet for a few moments. Then she said, "I have known Sir Gerek since he was a boy. You might not realize it at first, but he is very thoughtful. He thinks a long time before he makes a decision. Because of the way his father was, he has a fear of being impulsive and of falling in love."

She paused, placing her hand on Rapunzel's shoulder, then said, "Here is my old Psalter. I want you to have it." She reached into a box by her chair and handed her a leather-bound book. "I want you to read it, and every place that speaks of God's love, I want you to believe that it is talking about you. In Psalm 18, when David writes, 'He reached down from on high and took hold of me; he drew me out of deep waters,' I want you to know that this is about you. God saved you from that tower prison because he loved you. Just like the psalmist, I want you to say, 'I trust in His unfailing love.'"

Rapunzel nodded, holding the book lovingly between her palms.

Lady Rose embraced her again. "I am very glad you talked with me today. I shall want to hear how you are feeling in a day or two."

"Yes." Rapunzel embraced her mother. "In a day or two, I shall tell you how I am feeling." And much more.

Chapter Thirty-Four

The wedding day arrived, and Lady Rose sent Rapunzel a dress—a red silk cotehardie—to wear to the wedding. It was bright and shimmery and the most beautiful thing she had ever worn. And when Sir Gerek sent a maidservant to tell her he was ready to escort her to the wedding, she took a deep breath and thanked God she could face Sir Gerek wearing something beautiful.

He had that pained look on his face again. She remembered what Lady Rose had said. If Rapunzel truly loved Sir Gerek, then she should realize he was a man and think about what he might be feeling.

He offered her his arm, and she placed her hand on it. "Thank you for escorting me to the wedding. It is very kind of you."

He looked surprised. "I think it is important for you to be here. I hope you will tell Lady Rose your news very soon after the wedding."

"I will."

They made their way to the front of the castle to wait for the joyful couple to emerge and lead the way to the Hagenheim *Dom.* The Hagenheim Cathedral had been the site for Valten's wedding almost two years before, as the other servants had explained to her, but Gabe had married his wife, Sophie, in Hohendorf three years before. He, his wife, and his two children had arrived a week ago for his sister Margaretha's wedding.

How odd it was to know that Valten and Gabe were her brothers, and to see her sisters, Margaretha, Kirstyn, and Adela, as well as her other brothers, Stefan and Wolfgang, and the little Toby, whom Lady Rose and Duke Wilhelm had recently adopted into their family. None of them had any idea that she, Rapunzel, was their lost sister, Elsebeth.

Finally, the beautiful bride and her handsome English husband, both smiling—mostly at each other—led the way to the cathedral. They acknowledged their vows in front of the church door and the priest. Afterward, they all went inside for the wedding mass.

On the way back to the castle, Rapunzel's heart felt heavy. Would she ever be as overjoyed as Lady Margaretha, or feel loved the way she wished to? But she reminded herself of what Lady Rose had told her: a man could only love her imperfectly, but God could give her the perfect love she desired. Lady Rose had learned to comfort her husband in his pain instead of expecting him to heal her own.

She glanced up at Sir Gerek. He seemed almost afraid to look at her or speak to her. The corners of his mouth drooped and his brows were drawn together to form a crease between his eyes. Truly, she did not know why he seemed so despondent, but her anger left her and she suddenly wished she could comfort him.

As they walked with the rest of the crowd, who were all talking among themselves, she leaned closer to Sir Gerek.

"I am sorry I was so cross with you on the night we arrived back in Hagenheim."

His eyes eagerly met hers, but then he quickly lowered his gaze.

"I am so grateful to you for saving me from that tower. If you had not persevered and kept searching for me, I don't know how long I would have remained there. So I want to thank you."

His throat bobbed as he swallowed. "I am grateful that God led me to you." If the intense look in his brown eyes was any proof, he meant it.

When they returned to the castle, Rapunzel said, "It was a beautiful wedding. Thank you for escorting me. Now I have to go help in the kitchen—after I change clothes, of course."

He opened his mouth but didn't say anything. So she turned and started walking toward the servants' quarters.

"Wait." His hand wrapped around her arm.

He came around in front of her. "Rapunzel." He ran his hand through his hair and blew out a loud breath of air. "I . . ." He glanced around. People were walking by, turning their heads to look at them. "I need to talk to you. Please."

"Very well."

Her heart beat fast as he took her hand and led her around the side of the castle. He passed the kitchen and walked toward the giant beech tree that stood between the kitchen and the stable.

No one was around, and no one could see them from the castle courtyard.

He brought her to the other side of the enormous tree trunk, then turned her around and faced her. He leaned his hands against the trunk on either side of her head. She tried to step back, but her foot hit the tree and her back pressed against the trunk. Her breath seemed stuck in her throat. It was the way he was looking at her, so intent and anxious.

"I have to ask you something." He scrunched his brow, opened his mouth, then closed it. For a long moment, he said nothing, his expression growing even more anxious.

"Then ask me. If you have something to say, don't be a coward. Say it."

He leaned closer. "I want to know how you feel about me."

"You want to know how I feel about you? After I rode with my head on your chest, hugging you for hours? After I cried on your shirt? How many men do you think I've ever embraced in my life? How many men's shoulders do you think I've cried on?"

He leaned closer, and his intense brown eyes locked on hers. "Please. Just answer the question."

She crossed her arms in front of herself, hiding behind her anger and defiance. Still, something made her answer truthfully, "I love you."

His chest rose and fell quickly, his eyes boring into hers. "You are a duke's daughter. You deserve to marry a duke, or someone else wealthy and powerful."

"Do I look like I want to marry a duke? Have I ever seemed as if I wanted to be wealthy or powerful?" She wanted to yell at him, to beat his chest with her fists and accuse him of being addled and stubborn and blind.

"I said things." He narrowed his eyes. "I did things. When I thought you were poor, I said I wanted to marry a wealthy heiress. I was rude to you. How can you not hate me?"

"What were you going to tell me the last day of our journey? You were going to tell me something about why you no longer wanted to marry Lady Lankouwen. What was it?" She leaned closer to his face.

He looked away.

She jabbed his chest with her finger. "Tell me."

The pained look was back in his eyes. "I was going to ask you to marry me."

"When you thought I was only a maidservant?"

"You don't believe me. I knew you wouldn't."

"I want to."

"Then believe me."

He reached out and touched her face, his fingertips caressing her cheek. Her breath came fast and shallow as she gazed into his eyes.

"I realized it would be wrong not to marry you." His intense stare dipped from her eyes to her lips. "Would be wrong to marry Lady Lankouwen when I loved you, Rapunzel." His thumb brushed her chin. He leaned down and hovered, his breath on her temple. Then he pressed his lips to her cheek.

Her heart stuttered and her breath froze in her chest. He kissed her other cheek. She lifted her face to look up at him. He cupped her face with one hand and pulled her closer with the other. He kissed the corner of her mouth, then gazed into her eyes.

She slid her hand behind his head and closed her eyes. He kissed her full on the lips.

Her knees went weak, and he lifted her feet off the ground, reminding her of their embrace when he had rescued her from the tower.

He suddenly broke off the kiss and put her down. "I shouldn't have done that." He was breathing hard as he pressed his forehead to hers.

"Why not?"

"Because I love you, and your father will not like it."

"Duke Wilhelm will be pleased. That we fell in love."

"I will ask him, then." He brushed his lips over hers. "If I can marry you."

Her heart soared. She stood on tiptoe and kissed him. "He will say yes. Lady Rose will tell him to."

He held her face between his hands. "Duke Wilhelm will think I only want to marry you because you're his daughter. I would dare to defy Duke Wilhelm to marry you, Rapunzel. But are you sure you want me? Are you sure you wouldn't regret marrying me, a man who has nothing to give you except his heart?"

"Your heart is what I want. I want your love. I want . . . I want you. Just say you'll love me forever." She clung to his shoulders.

"I promise. Forever."

"And never hurt me."

"I will never, ever hurt you the way your mother hurt you, or the way my father hurt my mother."

"I know." She never imagined trusting someone could fill her with so much joy.

He kissed her again, in the shade of the giant beech tree, between the kitchen and the stable.

The next day, as Colin and Lady Margaretha left on their journey to England, Rapunzel prepared to return her dress to Lady Rose—and to reveal her news.

She climbed the steps to the solar. Lady Rose appeared to be alone and called to Rapunzel to come in.

"Oh, my dear, you didn't have to bring back the dress so soon."

"I also had something I wanted to talk to you about. It is very important." Rapunzel's stomach did a somersault inside her.

"Come and sit beside me." Lady Rose patted the long bench. She smiled. "My girls have deserted me. Gisela is taking care of her baby in her bedchamber, and Kirstyn is moping about because she misses Margaretha. Adela and the boys—including little Toby—are on an outing with some of the servants, playing a game of blind man's buff in the sheep pasture, and so it is only me here today. Not that I mind, but Toby has been my constant shadow these last few weeks, and Duke Wilhelm thought I needed some time alone." She smiled and sighed contentedly. "But I am glad to see you. Tell me what it is you wanted to talk about."

"I-I want to tell you something that I learned from Frau Adelheit."

Lady Rose tilted her head to the side with a look of curiosity.

"Just before I was given a sleeping potion and taken away by Gothel, Frau Adelheit told me how your daughter, Elsebeth, fell and cut her hand when she was little." Her heart stuttered in her chest. Could she truly go on and claim to be Lady Rose's daughter?

"Yes?" Pain and confusion shone behind Lady Rose's eyes. Rapunzel had to explain.

"For as long as I can remember, I have had this scar on my hand." Rapunzel lifted her hand, palm up. "Frau Adelheit says it is identical to the scar—"

Lady Rose grabbed her hand and gasped, staring hard. "Oh! What does this mean? Could it be?"

"Gothel, the woman who raised me, confessed everything. She said she pulled me into the river, then rescued me downstream. She knew I was your daughter and she . . ."

Lady Rose was weeping now, tears streaming down her cheeks as she reached out to touch her face. "How did I not know it was you? How did I not know as soon as I saw you? Oh, my baby. My Elsebeth." She pulled Rapunzel close, clutching her shoulders.

Rapunzel hugged her, tears wetting her own cheeks, her heart swelling inside her. "I love you, Lady Rose."

"You should never have to call me Lady Rose." She half laughed, half choked on her tears. "I am your mother." Her voice broke on the word *mother* and she pulled away. "I just want to look at you. You're so beautiful. I can hardly bear this joy, to have you back again." She pulled her close and began weeping again.

Rapunzel was overjoyed and held on to her, crying just as much as Lady Rose. She knew she should be full of joy at being reunited with her mother . . . such a loving mother . . . but she couldn't help crying over the lost years, the lost love she could have had, and the pain and suffering her own good-hearted mother had gone through. And yet here they were.

She suddenly did not want to waste one more moment on pain or sadness or anger. "Please don't cry, Mother," Rapunzel said, forcing back her own tears. "I don't want you to feel sad."

"I am not sad!" Lady Rose—Mother—laughed through her tears. "I am overjoyed. I have you back."

When Rapunzel went to talk to Lady Rose, Gerek headed to see Duke Wilhelm.

Duke Wilhelm was in the library, sitting in the back corner at his desk. "Sir Gerek." He stood as he greeted him. "I want to congratulate you on saving the maidservant, Rapunzel. Lady Rose is very fond of her."

"You are not annoyed with me for spending two months away from my duties?"

"Of course not. It was a noble quest. I am always in favor of noble quests." He came around the desk and the two stood side by side, staring out the library window at the hill in the distance.

"Thank you, your grace."

"And now that my oldest daughter is married, I suppose I'll be having to search for a husband for Kirstyn. Although, I hope she will find her own, as Margaretha did. It seems to have worked out better than when I was trying to find her one."

"Yes, your grace." Gerek was glad Duke Wilhelm was in a talkative mood, as it gave him time to gather his courage.

"Why do you not get married, Gerek? I think Sir Edgar's daughter would say yes if you asked her, although—"

"I am not interested in marrying Rainhilda, your grace."

"Then I won't have to warn you about what she did to my daughter-in-law. I heard you were also thinking of marrying Lankouwen's widow. Is that what you're here to talk to me about?"

"Not exactly. I do want to marry, but not Lady Lankouwen."

Duke Wilhelm gave him a hard stare in reply.

"I am in love . . . with Rapunzel."

"The maidservant? The one you rescued?"

"Yes, your grace."

He smiled and clapped him on the back. "Then I shall have to reward you with a house."

"I would be very grateful, your grace, since you know I have no inheritance or fortune."

"You are a good man, Sir Gerek, a man of integrity. You will do well in life."

"Thank you, your grace. I also wanted to speak to you about sending for Rapunzel's mother, Gothel, whom we left at Castle Rimmel."

Duke Wilhelm raised his brows at him. "Why did you not let me know before? I did not know you had been able to apprehend her."

"I had a reason for not telling you sooner."

"I shall send some guards for her today. But what is the reason you waited—what?—four days to tell me?"

"It is a bit complicated. You see, Gothel was not Rapunzel's mother. She had stolen her away from her rightful parents when Rapunzel was a small child. She confessed everything, but there is a reason, which I will reveal in a moment, why I did not want you to confront and judge her just yet." He took a breath and plunged ahead. "Duke Wilhelm, what would you say if I said I wished to marry one of your daughters? Would you be angry?"

Again, Duke Wilhelm gave him a hard stare. "I don't know how to answer such a question. You wish to marry Rapunzel, not Kirstyn, correct?"

"Yes, your grace. I was just wondering what your reaction would be if a knight fell in love with one of your daughters."

"Is one of my knights planning to ask for Kirstyn?" His brows lowered, his mouth open. His expression was the same as it had been when he had led his men into battle when they took back Hagenheim Castle from Claybrook. Not a look he would want directed at him.

"No, your grace, not that I know of. I was only asking because . . . there is something important you should know, something Rapunzel is telling Lady Rose and will want to tell you. And they should be here any moment."

He thought he heard them in the corridor. Soon Lady Rose and Rapunzel entered the library, their arms around each other. Both women's eyes were wet, their faces blotchy and red.

"My dear," Lady Rose said, reaching out to Duke Wilhelm. Her voice was halting as she said, "Rapunzel has just told me something. It seems she was told all her life that she was left with the woman who raised her when she was a small child. But that woman, who took her away from here two months ago . . ." Tears started flowing down Lady Rose's face. "That woman, Gothel, confessed everything to Rapunzel after she stole her away. She said she took our Elsebeth from the river and ran away with her. This . . . is our Elsebeth, come back to us."

Lady Rose seemed to make an effort to not break down in sobs. She took Rapunzel's hand and held it out, palm up, to Duke Wilhelm.

It seemed wrong for Gerek to be a witness to such an intimate family moment, but Rapunzel had insisted that she'd wanted him to remain.

Duke Wilhelm took her hand and stared down at it. Then he looked at Rapunzel's face. "Can it be true?"

"I think it is," Rapunzel said.

He enveloped them both in his arms.

After several minutes, they seemed to realize Gerek was still in the room.

"Come here, Sir Gerek." Lady Rose motioned him forward with her hand as she dabbed at her eyes and nose with a cloth. "My dear," she said, speaking now to Duke Wilhelm, "Sir Gerek and Rapunzel are in love. They want to marry. You must give them permission."

"Why should I give you permission to marry my daughter?" Duke Wilhelm said, but at least he wasn't glaring. "I haven't seen her in seventeen years. I'm not ready for you to take her away."

"Your grace, I know I have no right to marry your daughter, but I fell in love with her before I knew she was your daughter. I know—"

"I'm not asking you to defend yourself, Gerek. But you will have to wait for her."

"Yes, your grace." His eyes met Rapunzel's. Her whole face seemed to emanate joy.

And even though he didn't want to wait, at least he had not forbidden him the request. Duke Wilhelm's answer was the best Gerek could have hoped for.

Rapunzel moved into the castle, into Kirstyn's chamber that she had shared with Margaretha, since Kirstyn said she missed having Margaretha in the room with her every night.

Rapunzel's days were full, spending time with Sir Gerek when he was not busy with his duties and getting to know her new family. She found she did not miss being alone. For the first time she had brothers and sisters and even a father who was tender and kind, though quieter than the other members of her new family. Still, there was a quality of strength and goodness about him that filled her with joy, knowing she was his own daughter and he loved her.

Sir Gerek was attentive and kind, so much so that one day when they were in the solar with the rest of the family, she whispered to him, "You know you cannot keep this up."

"Keep what up?"

"All this kindness and goodness and giving me my own way all the time."

He frowned, reminding her of his old self. "I can. You told me yourself that I'd changed."

She laughed. "I don't mind if you want to be grumpy sometimes. I rather like it. It reminds me of the old you."

His jaw twitched and he leaned down to growl in her ear, "I shall put up with your teasing because of my great fortitude and magnanimous heart."

She couldn't help laughing again.

"What are you two carrying on about?" her mother asked.

"Sir Gerek is just reminding me of his good qualities," Rapunzel answered.

He gave her a warning squeeze on her arm. "And she is reminding me of her sense of humor."

Duke Wilhelm—Father—entered the room just then, instantly taking down the noise level and calming the younger children. He greeted them all, letting Adela give him a kiss, and then sat down in front of Sir Gerek and Rapunzel.

"Gothel should be here within the hour. Elsebeth, would you like to confront her? It is your choice."

"I-I think I would, one last time, if I may."

Her father nodded, then sighed. "You know she is my sister, my father's daughter—did she tell you?"

"Yes."

"I did not respond to her as I ought to, when she first contacted me." He stared at the wall behind them, then down at his folded hands. "I did not want to believe my father could have done what my mother later confirmed was true. And then, when I tried to find Gothel, to make amends, she had left Hagenheim. I had my men search for her but we never found her. I now realize she had taken you"—he nodded at Rapunzel—"and had fled the region. Perhaps if I had acknowledged and accepted her—"

"No, Father, you must not think like that." Rapunzel reached out and squeezed his hand. He clasped it in his. "She was a woman with warped thoughts, full of madness and spite and vengefulness. You are not to blame. No one could have imagined what she would do."

They sat, none of them speaking, while the rest of the family was oblivious to them and carried on their own conversations. Finally, Rapunzel spoke up.

"I do want to speak to Gothel one last time. There is something I have decided I want to say to her."

As they made their way down the stairs to wait for the guards to bring Gothel, Rapunzel clutched Sir Gerek's hand, hoping to imbibe some strength from his firm grip.

Soon they heard a commotion in the castle yard. As they stood in the corridor, the door opened from the outside and two guards came dragging Gothel in, one on each side, while she kicked and spit at them, struggling against their hold.

"I will get free someday, and I shall kill you all in your beds!" Gothel's voice was so strained and her face so distorted, she was barely recognizable as the woman who used to braid Rapunzel's hair every night.

She suddenly saw Rapunzel standing a few feet away. "You." Her voice was laden with accusation.

Rapunzel felt a tremor go through her. Was she able to do this?

Yes. She was strong. She was no longer a little girl, helpless and afraid. She was loved, protected, and safe.

She looked Gothel in the eye. "For all the things you did to me, I realize you were only afraid of being alone. You told me you loved me, but it was fear. Fear made you do cruel things. And for those cruelties, I forgive you."

Gothel's mouth went slack and she stared back as if stunned.

The guards dragged her away, her body suddenly limp, and they half carried her toward the dungeon steps.

Once she was out of sight, Sir Gerek put his arm around her shoulders.

"What will happen to her?" she asked her father.

"She will probably stay in the dungeon." Duke Wilhelm sighed. "I don't think I can take the risk of ever letting her go free."

Rapunzel nodded. Some part of her still felt pity for the woman, but this was justice.

Every day Gerek managed to see Rapunzel, at least at mealtimes. She was no longer working in the kitchen, of course, and Gerek had other duties—more than the usual since the other knights were forcing him to make up for the time he was away. They loved teasing him about how he had been more diligent in searching for her than any of the others, and how he had snagged himself a duke's daughter in the process. He didn't even mind their teasing, much.

A few times Lady Rose had given him permission to take Rapunzel on a picnic, but never alone. She'd say, "Not until Duke Wilhelm sets a date for the wedding."

But they had still found ways to snatch a few minutes alone, usually by the shady beech tree behind the kitchen. Those stolen kisses and conversations were sweeter than any he had ever imagined, perhaps because he had waited for them and had never broken his vows.

Today Duke Wilhelm was taking him and a few other knights on a journey to see Keiterhafen Castle. After hearing what the Earl of Keiterhafen had done, along with his heir, Lord Claybrook, the king had ordered that Keiterhafen no longer be under the earl's control and his heirs would not inherit. The earl and his knights had been summoned to answer to the king for their crimes against Hagenheim, and the king had given charge of the castle and the region around it over to Duke Wilhelm.

Traveling west, it took them only one day to reach Keiterhafen Castle. It was in a bit of disarray, but there were still some guards there who had agreed to protect it from vandals and thieves until a new lord should arrive to take charge of it.

The gray stone castle brought back some vague memories of being sent here when he was a small boy. But he remembered little of it. This was where he had learned the news that his father had killed his mother, then killed himself. It had been the worst moment of his life, and he had returned to Castle Rimmel in great misery. His older brother had yelled at him—stricken with his own grief and misery, no doubt, so that he had been grateful to be sent to Hagenheim as a page.

He did his best to put those thoughts and memories from his mind.

All the guards showed deference to Duke Wilhelm when he arrived, recognizing him as the one in authority over them and over the castle. On the first evening, as they all sat down together in the Great Hall for a meal, Duke Wilhelm stood to give his speech.

"I want to thank the knights and soldiers who chose to stay with Keiterhafen Castle and defend it. And since the earl and his nephew Claybrook behaved with treachery, the king has placed me in charge. He has given me permission to grant this great castle and the lands belonging to Keiterhafen to the man I wish to give it, a man well able to defend it and its people against attack."

He paused for a long moment, looking out over the crowd. "I hereby bestow it upon one of my noble knights, a man of great integrity, strength, and ability, a man who has not only been a faithful knight in my service, but whose tenacity and perseverance have restored to me my stolen daughter, Elsebeth."

Gerek's mind went numb. Duke Wilhelm and the other knights were turning to smile at him.

"And not only did he save her life, but he won her heart. I wish to bestow this castle and its lands to Sir Gerek van Hollan, who is promised to marry my daughter, Elsebeth Gerstenberg. This castle shall belong to them and their heirs, from this day and forevermore, or as long as God gives them favor." He motioned for Gerek to come and join him at the head of the table.

As if in a fog, Gerek made his way to Duke Wilhelm and stood beside him.

"Your new lord, Sir Gerek van Hollan."

The men shouted and cheered.

Of course, it wouldn't be that easy. He would have to win the men over, but . . . was he truly the lord of the castle, of Keiterhafen? He would be able to give Rapunzel the kind of life she deserved. It seemed too good to be true.

The next night and day were a blur of activity and of men welcoming him and swearing allegiance to him.

On the third day, Gerek and Duke Wilhelm were touring the town near the castle, and they went inside the cathedral, which was rather large and ornate for a small town.

"I suppose this is where you and Rapunzel will marry, so that your men and the townspeople can attend their new lord's wedding. I have obtained the king's permission and will have the banns cried this Sunday."

"Thank you, your grace." Gerek's heart was full as he pictured Rapunzel in the church, with the colors of the stained-glass windows painting her and setting her golden hair on fire. "But are you sure you won't regret not saving Keiterhafen for one of your sons?"

Duke Wilhelm shook his head. "Valten will inherit Hagenheim, Gabe and Sophie have Hohendorf, Margaretha and Colin have land

and estates in England, and Keiterhafen can't wait for my younger sons. It needs a strong fighting man to defend it from any possible usurpers bent on taking it. No, you are the right man to rule Keiterhafen. And since you are marrying my daughter, and since you will not be too far, I thought it most appropriate."

"I am more grateful than I can say."

"Besides, you will be the kind of ally I can always rely on, since you will be married to my daughter, and we can come and see her and our grandchildren as often as Lady Rose wishes—or almost as often."

When they departed the cathedral after that conversation, there was nothing left for Gerek to possibly wish for, except to be with Rapunzel.

Four weeks later, their day had finally come. Though Rapunzel's family called her Elsebeth and she was getting used to that name and liking it quite well, she did not mind that Sir Gerek still called her Rapunzel. And the way he said her name when they were alone made her heart turn inside out. He was still occasionally the grouchy frowner he was when she first met him. But they had both changed, and she felt no doubts or hesitancy about becoming his wife.

Cristobel was with Rapunzel as she came down the stairs of Keiterhafen Castle in her wedding gown and veil. Gerek took the steps two at a time to meet her in the middle.

He took her hand. "You are so beautiful."

"I know you like my hair down," she whispered, for his ears only.

"I do." He leaned down to kiss her temple before they joined the rest of her family at the bottom.

After a few moments of checking to make sure everyone was there—Duke Wilhelm and Lady Rose, her brothers, Valten, Steffan,

Wolfgang, and Toby, and her sisters, Kirstyn and Adela, and Valten's wife, Gisela, and their baby girl—they departed the castle through the Great Hall.

Gerek held her hand as they walked. How her life had changed since she came to Hagenheim. The peasant girl who had longed to know how to read so she could write down her songs, who had always lived in small villages and felt like an outsider, who had believed her parents didn't want her, who had been completely controlled by the woman she called Mother and told she should never trust men or let them hear her sing . . . that girl was now a woman with a large, loving family, the daughter of a duke, and the soon-to-be wife of Sir Gerek, the new lord of Keiterhafen.

Rapunzel's fortunes had reversed, and so had Gerek's, for now he had her love—and an entire region, with men to command and a castle and town to protect.

She gazed up at him as they neared the church, and he winked at her. "Will you dance with me tonight at our wedding feast?"

"Of course."

"You aren't to dance with anyone else. I want you all to myself tonight."

"That should not be a problem."

They approached the door of the cathedral where the priest stood. As they began to agree with the priest, as he spoke to them of their duty to each other, she kept glancing at the reverent look on Gerek's face. Truly, he had become what she had initially thought him to be, that day on the road to Hagenheim when he had saved her from the two men attacking them—her knight and defender. And in spite of the evil that had been done to them, God had restored their hope, and their faith, in love.

Acknowledgments

First, I have to thank my wonderful editor, Becky Monds, for all her help in getting this book ready and in the best possible form. Becky is like a coach or personal trainer. Without her, you know you could not have achieved your full potential. Thanks, Becky, for asking the tough questions and making me do the hard work! You have a great mind for what would improve a story.

I also want to thank my line editor, Natalie Hanemann, for whipping and shaping and smoothing, and for all your input. The book is much better for it!

I want to thank Terry Bell for suggesting the idea for my Rapunzel heroine's identity. It had never occurred to me before she mentioned it on Facebook. At first I dismissed the idea, but it stuck in my mind and I quickly began to see the potential of it and how it would work into a Rapunzel retelling. I knew you had given me the perfect idea for a great heroine. Thanks, Terry! I'm so thankful for your friendship.

I want to thank those who pray for me and encourage me often, like Regina Carbulon and Linda Bailey and Sue Williams. Also, Karma Malone, Reta Broadwater, Ken and Dene Finley, Bonita Story, Dan and Katrina Doty, Debbie Lynne Costello, Mary Freeman, Kathy Bone, and any others I am missing or don't even know about. You are appreciated.

For the greatest cheerleaders an author ever had, Rachel Miller and Donna Mynatt, and the best website guru, Rachel. Thank you!

Also, my daughters who support me and even help me brainstorm—Grace Dickerson and Faith Dickerson. I love you.

I want to thank my critique partner and friend, Katie Clark, for whom I am so grateful, as well as Adriana Gwyn, who has been my go-to expert on all things German language. Thanks for helping me with the pronunciations!

I thank God for you all!

Discussion Questions

1. Do you think Rapunzel made good use of her time in all the small villages where she lived with her mother, learning various skills?
2. Can you imagine not being able to read and how it would feel to want to learn? Rapunzel cleaned rooms at the monastery in exchange for reading lessons. Would you be willing to do the same if it was your only chance to learn to read?
3. How was Sir Gerek different from the other men Rapunzel had known in the villages where she'd lived?
4. Why was Rapunzel so frightened and suspicious of men? Would you have felt the same way if you had had Gothel as a mother? Who or what has influenced your opinions and impressions of the opposite sex?
5. Why was Sir Gerek so opposed to teaching Rapunzel to read? Did you think he was arrogant? Or just grouchy?
6. Why did Sir Gerek not want to marry a peasant? Do you think he had a good reason for wanting to marry someone wealthy?
7. Why did Rapunzel want to get a job in town?
8. Why do you think Gothel told Rapunzel it was "indecent" to show her hair and forced her to cover it? Are there any parallels to "rules" people followed through history? Can you think of any parallels to certain "rules" of propriety some people follow today?

9. Do you think Rapunzel was justified in leaving Gothel without telling her she was leaving or where she was going? At what age should a young woman be able to make her own decisions and live on her own?
10. What happened when Balthasar broke through the door and threatened Rapunzel? Do you think God would forgive her for killing Balthasar? Why?
11. When Rapunzel was trapped in the tower, what did she say about who she would—and wouldn't—sing for, and why? How do you keep hope alive when you've prayed for something a long time but still have not received it?
12. Do you understand why Rapunzel forgave Gothel in the end? What did she say was her reason? Do you think Gerek forgave his brother Mennek for how he treated him when they were boys? Have you ever forgiven someone who hurt you very deeply?

From *New York Times* bestselling author Melanie Dickerson comes a reimagining of the Wild Swans—and the first book in a new series of fairy-tale retellings set in medieval England.

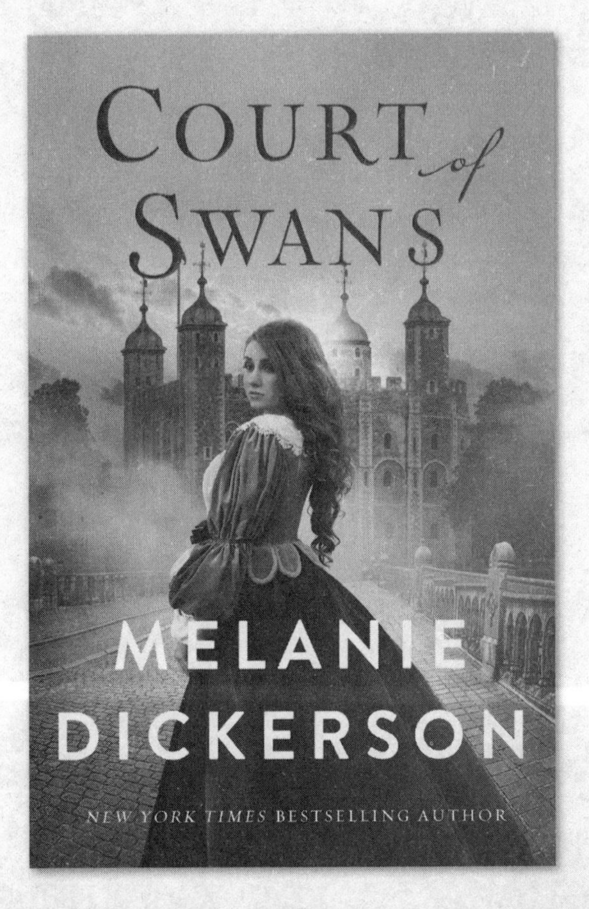

About the Author

Jodie Westfall Photography

Melanie Dickerson is a New York Times bestselling author and two-time Christy Award winner. Melanie spends her time daydreaming, researching the most fascinating historical time periods, and writing and editing her happily-ever-afters.

Visit her online at MelanieDickerson.com

Instagram: @MelanieDickerson123

Facebook: @MelanieDickersonBooks

Twitter: @MelanieAuthor